# WHAT IS GNOSTICISM?

# What Is Gnosticism?

## KAREN L. KING

THE BELKNAP PRESS OF

HARVARD UNIVERSITY PRESS

*Cambridge, Massachusetts*
*London, England*

*2003*

11/03

*Library of Congress Cataloging-in-Publication Data*
King, Karen L.
What is Gnosticism? / Karen L. King.
p. cm.
Includes bibliographical references (p. ) and index.
ISBN 0-674-01071-X (alk. paper)
1. Gnosticism.    I. Title.

BT1390.K55 2003
299'.932—dc21
2003041851

# Contents

Preface                                                         *vii*

Abbreviations                                                   *xi*

Introduction                                                    *1*

1   Why Is Gnosticism So Hard to Define?                        *5*

2   Gnosticism as Heresy                                        *20*

3   Adolf von Harnack and the Essence of Christianity           *55*

4   The History of Religions School                             *71*

5   Gnosticism Reconsidered                                     *110*

6   After Nag Hammadi I: Categories and Origins                 *149*

7   After Nag Hammadi II: Typology                              *191*

8   The End of Gnosticism?                                      *218*

Note on Methodology                                            *239*

Bibliography                                                   *249*

Notes                                                          *277*

Index                                                          *341*

# Preface

Historians are in the process of rewriting the history of earliest Christianity, partly on the basis of newly discovered papyrus manuscripts containing a wealth of previously unknown early Christian texts. Not only do we have new discoveries; but we also have new questions to address to those materials. Issues of pluralism, colonialism, difference, and marginality all appear in our scholarship with increasing frequency. Specialists are developing new methods and reconsidering past theoretical paradigms and frameworks. At this time we are only able to catch a glimpse of what new narratives of early Christian history will look like. But one point is assured by the new discoveries: early Christianity was much more diverse and pluriform than anyone could have suspected a century ago. Moreover, historians will have to write a story in which Christian triumph over pagan culture and Christian supersession of Judaism no longer have an unambiguous historical grounding, and in which women are an active presence.

The surviving literature from antiquity attests that Christians of the first centuries were deeply engaged in controversies over such basic issues as the meaning of Jesus' teaching, the significance of his death, the roles of women, sexuality, visions of ideal community, and much more. When disputes arose, however, there were no structures in place to decide who was right or wrong—no New Testament canon, no Nicene Creed, no fixed hierarchical male leadership, no Christian emperor. The history of early Christianity is therefore not only the story of those controversies but also the account of the invention of those structures.

My own interest, which lies primarily in early Christian identity formation and the critique of current scholarly categories of analysis, has been shaped largely through the study of Gnostic heresy. Supposedly emerging in the Greek and Roman colonial world of the ancient Mediterranean, Gnosticism has been defined both in antiquity and in contemporary discourse by difference and marginality. It has been called heretical, syncretistic, Oriental, radical, rebellious, and parasitic. This book does not provide a description of all the groups, texts, and ideas that have been attributed to Gnosticism; nor is it an exhaustive account of the study of Gnosticism in the twentieth century. Rather, it aims to contribute to the larger enterprise of rewriting the history of Christianity by examining how modern historiography came to invent a new religion, Gnosticism, largely out of early Christian polemics intersecting with post-Enlightenment historicism, colonialism, and existential phenomenology.

This book also aims to identify where certain assumptions that were formed in ancient battles against heresy continue to operate in the methods of contemporary historiography, especially regarding those constructions of purity, origins, and essence in which difference is figured as divisive, mixing as pollution, and change as deviance. I suggest not only that these assumptions are entangled in academic methodologies, but also that they continue to support particular notions of religious normativity and operations of identity politics in our own day. As a historian of the ancient world, I am also concerned that the current understanding of Gnosticism distorts our reading of the ancient texts, oversimplifies our account of early Christianity, and confounds the use of historical resources for theological reflection. Asking the question, "What is Gnosticism?" can help remedy these problems and open new vistas for investigating the terrain of ancient Christianity as well as the dynamics of contemporary identity politics.

This book has been in the making for at least twenty years. During that time, I have profited enormously from conversations with numerous colleagues, friends, and students, to whom I owe a great debt for their criticisms and encouragement. Unfortunately, it is not possible for me to name them all here, but I would like to acknowledge my appreciation. My sincerest thanks go as well to the individual colleagues and organizations who made it possible to present initial ideas and drafts on various occasions: at the Gaston Symposium, University of Oregon, Eugene; the

Annenberg Institute, Philadelphia; the Institute for Antiquity and Christianity, Claremont, California; the Women's Studies Seminar of the Huntington Library, Pasadena, California; Harvard Divinity School, Cambridge, Massachusetts; the Center for the Study of Religion in Public Life, Trinity College, Hartford, Connecticut; The 1999 Showers Lectures in the Christian Religion, University of Indianapolis, Indiana; Thomas L. King Lecture in Religious Studies, Washburn University, Topeka, Kansas; Remsen Bird Lecture, Occidental College, Los Angeles, California; Fifth International Congress of Coptic Studies, 1992, Catholic University of America, Washington, D.C.; Congress of the International Association of the History of Religions, Rome (1990) and Mexico City (1995); a plenary address for the North American Patristics Society, Chicago, Illinois; and various national meetings of the Society of Biblical Literature and the American Academy of Religion, a plenary address at the 1998 regional AAR meeting, and an invited lecture at the 1999 International SBL Meeting in Helsinki and Lahti, Finland.

Earlier versions of a few points of my argument appeared in the following articles: "Translating History: Reframing Gnosticism in Postmodernity," pp. 264–277 in *Tradition und Translation. Zum Problem der interkulturellen Übersetzbarkeit religiöser Phänomene. Festschrift für Carsten Colpe zum 65. Geburtstag*, ed. Christoph Elsas et al. (Berlin: Walter de Gruyter, 1994); "Mackinations on Myth and Origins," pp. 157–172 in *Reimagining Christian Origins: A Colloquium Honoring Burton L. Mack* (Harrisburg, Penn.: Trinity Press International, 1996); and "The Politics of Syncretism and the Problem of Defining Gnosticism," pp. 461–479 in *Historical Reflections/Réflexions Historiques* 27.3 (2001).

Warm thanks go to Tom Hall, who edited the entire manuscript *sans remboursement;* his wit, wisdom, and unforgiving attitude toward misuse of the English language saved me from many infelicities while providing many a chuckle. My thanks also to Margaretta Fulton, my editor at Harvard University Press, for her support, and to Christine Thorsteinsson for her editorial labor.

I would also like to offer special thanks to colleagues who at various points gave me invaluable feedback and encouragement: Virginia Burrus, Anne McGuire, Patricia Cox Miller, Laura Nasrallah, Karen Jo Torjesen, and Dale Wright. My deepest gratitude belongs to Daniel Boyarin, Elaine

Pagels, Elisabeth Schüssler Fiorenza, and Hal Taussig for their constant support, unfailingly helpful criticism, and generosity in giving precious time to reading full drafts of the manuscript. The book's remaining short-comings are my own, but many strengths came from their help at crucial moments. Most precious of all to me is the sweetness of this friendship among colleagues; for that there is warmest affection.

# Abbreviations

## Ancient Literary Works

| | |
|---|---|
| *ActsPeter12* | *The Acts of Peter and the Twelve Apostles* |
| *AgHer* | *Against Heresies* |
| *ApJames* | *The Apocryphon of James* |
| *ApJohn* | *The Apocryphon of John* |
| *A Plea* | *A Plea Regarding Christians* |
| *ApocAdam* | *The Apocalypse of Adam* |
| *I ApocJames* | *The First Apocalypse of James* |
| *II ApocJames* | *The Second Apocalypse of James* |
| *ApocPet* | *The Apocalypse of Peter* |
| *1 Apol* | *First Apology* |
| *AuthTeach* | *Authentic Teaching* |
| *BookThomas* | *The Book of Thomas* |
| *DialSav* | *The Dialogue of the Savior* |
| *DialTrypho* | *Dialogue with Trypho the Jew* |
| *EcclHist* | *The Ecclesiastical History* |
| *EpBarn* | *The Epistle of Barnabas* |
| *EpFlora* | *The Epistle to Flora* |
| *EpMag* | *The Epistle to the Magnesians* |
| *EpPhil* | *The Epistle to the Philadelphians* |
| *EpSmyr* | *The Epistle to the Smyrnaeans* |
| *Eugnostos* | *Eugnostos the Blessed* |
| *ExSoul* | *The Exegesis on the Soul* |
| *GosEgypt* | *The Gospel of the Egyptians* |
| *GosMary* | *The Gospel of Mary* |
| *GosPhil* | *The Gospel of Philip* |
| *GosSavior* | *The Gospel of the Savior* |
| *GosThom* | *The Gospel of Thomas* |

| | |
|---|---|
| *GosTruth* | *The Gospel of Truth* |
| *HypArch* | *The Hypostasis of the Archons* |
| *InterKnow* | *The Interpretation of Knowledge* |
| *LetPetPhil* | *The Letter of Peter to Philip* |
| *OrigWorld* | *On the Origin of the World* |
| *PrayerPaul* | *The Prayer of the Apostle Paul* |
| *PresHer* | *Prescription against Heretics* |
| *Ref* | *Refutation of All Heresies* |
| *SophJesChr* | *The Sophia of Jesus Christ* |
| *StelesSeth* | *The Three Steles of Seth* |
| *Strom* | *Stromateis* |
| *TestTruth* | *The Testimony of Truth* |
| *ThoughtNorea* | *The Thought of Norea* |
| *TreatRes* | *The Treatise on the Resurrection* |
| *TriTrac* | *The Tripartite Tractate* |
| *ValExp* | *A Valentinian Exposition* |
| *Zostr* | *Zostrianos* |

## Journals, Serials, and Periodicals

| | |
|---|---|
| AAR | American Academy of Religion |
| *ANRW* | *Aufsteig und Neidergang der römischen Welt* |
| BCNH.SÉ | Bibliothèque copte de Nag Hammadi. Section Études |
| BJS | Brown Judaic Studies |
| BZNW | Beiheft, *Zeitschrift für die neutestamentliche Wissenschaft* |
| CCL | California Classical Library |
| *HTR* | *Harvard Theological Review* |
| *JBL* | *Journal of Biblical Literature* |
| *JECS* | *Journal of Early Christian Studies* |
| *JTS* | *Journal of Theological Studies* |
| NHMS | Nag Hammadi and Manichaean Studies |
| NHS | Nag Hammadi Studies |
| *NovTest* | *Novum Testamentum* |
| SAC | Studies in Antiquity and Christianity |
| SBL | Society of Biblical Literature |
| SHR | Studies in the History of Religions (Supplements to *Numen*) |
| TU | Texte und Untersuchungen |
| *VC* | *Vigiliae Christianae* |
| *ZNW* | *Zeitschrift für die neutestamentliche Wissenschaft* |

# WHAT IS GNOSTICISM?

Men can do nothing without the make-believe of a beginning. Even Science, the strict measurer, is obliged to start with a make-believe unit, and must fix on a point in the stars' unceasing journey when his sidereal clock shall pretend that time is at Nought. His less accurate grandmother Poetry has always been understood to start in the middle; but on reflection it appears that her proceeding is not very different from his; since Science, too, reckons backwards as well as forwards, divides his unit into billions, and with his clock-finger at Nought really sets off *in media res*. No retrospect will take us to the true beginning; and whether our prologue be in heaven or on earth, it is but a fraction of that all-presupposing fact with which our story sets out.

George Eliot, *Daniel Deronda* (1876)

# Introduction

In 1945, an Egyptian farmer named Muhammad Ali went out into the hills near the town of Nag Hammadi to dig for fertilizer. By serendipity, he uncovered a clay jar. In it were fourth-century c.e. papyrus books, containing nearly forty-six different works, most of which had previously been unknown. There were new gospels, including the *Gospel of Thomas* and the *Gospel of Truth,* recounting unknown sayings of Jesus and interpreting his death and resurrection, not in terms of sin and atonement, but as enlightenment overcoming ignorance and suffering. There were grand myths telling of the creation of the world and humanity by the wicked God of Genesis, who sought only to dominate the divine spark in humanity and imprison it in mortal flesh. There were stories of Mary Magdalene as a spiritual disciple and leader, as well as feminine images of God. There were hymns and prayers, oracles and wisdom sayings, and much more.

Almost from the beginning, the find was characterized as a Gnostic library. But what is Gnosticism? Although scholars have expended considerable effort on determining the origin and development of Gnosticism, delimiting its background and sources and defining its essence, no consensus had been established on any of these issues. The situation has only been aggravated by the discovery of new texts, which are seriously challenging some of the most basic elements of a minimal definition of Gnosticism.[1] Specialists are recognizing more and more that previous definitions of Gnosticism are inadequate to interpret the new textual materials without seriously distorting them.

Why is it so hard to define Gnosticism? The problem, I argue, is that a rhetorical term has been confused with a historical entity. There was and is no such thing as Gnosticism, if we mean by that some kind of ancient religious entity with a single origin and a distinct set of characteristics. Gnosticism is, rather, a term invented in the early modern period to aid in defining the boundaries of normative Christianity. Yet it has mistakenly come to be thought of as a distinctive Christian heresy or even as a religion in its own right, and libraries are replete with books describing its central beliefs, discussing its origins, and considering its history.

But having said that no religion called Gnosticism existed in antiquity, we still have to account for all the ideas, writings, persons, and practices described by ancient polemicists, not to mention the texts found at Nag Hammadi and elsewhere. If they are not Gnostic, what are they? How are we to locate them historically and interpret them?

Some have responded to this challenge by turning away from definitional tasks altogether, at least for the time being. Gershom Scholem has summarized this general sentiment by pointing out that "research into the problems of gnosticism, which has entered a new phase in our generation, is still far removed from a state where valid generalizations can be established with any amount of confidence. This is largely due to the prevalence of hypotheses which rest on tenuous foundations. What is needed most, as it seems to me, is the analysis of details on which such general conclusions could be built."[2] Indeed, generalizations must be based on detailed and disciplined studies of the primary materials in order to guard against superficiality, arbitrariness, and partiality. Until these studies have progressed further, it might be prudent to suspend the use of the term, along with the definitions and categories associated with it, since at this point, generalizations about Gnosticism seem counterproductive

Scholars have not, however, found it possible to dispense with the term altogether. Although we have been working to point out the deficiencies in previous definitions of Gnosticism, few think that we can get along without the term.[3] The main reason is that it continues to do seemingly indispensable intellectual work. But what work is Gnosticism doing? What problem or interpretive framework requires it?

The initial insight is quite simple: the problem of defining Gnosticism has been primarily concerned with the normative identity of Christianity. Gnosticism has been constructed largely as the heretical other in relation to diverse and fluctuating understandings of orthodox Christianity. This means that modern historical constructions of Gnosticism reflect many of the characteristics and strategies used by early Christian polemicists like Irenaeus and Tertullian to construct heresy. Although the two constructions are by no means identical, the continuities between discourses of heresy and characterizations of Gnosticism are notable. This is true both for typological definitions of Gnosticism and for attempts to define Gnosticism historically by locating its origins and tracing its development.[4] Indeed, it is largely apologetic concerns to defend normative Christianity that make Gnosticism intelligible as a category at all.

As in comparable dualistic categories of self and other (such as citizen/foreigner, Greek/barbarian, Jew/Gentile, Christian/pagan), the other achieves its existence and identity only by contrast to the self. Such categories are totally inadequate when it comes to understanding the tremendous social and cultural diversity of those others because they were invented, not to do justice to the groups and materials they encompass, but to satisfy the needs of defining the self. In this way, the category of Gnosticism was produced through the Christian discourse of orthodoxy and heresy. The result is an artificial entity, reified by applying elements of heresiological discourse to the historical materials grouped under the rubric of Gnosticism. As such, Gnosticism has been classified as a marginal, sectarian, esoteric, mythical, syncretistic, parasitic, and Oriental religion, in contrast to mainstream, authentic, ethnic, historical, rational, or universal religions, such as orthodox Christianity. Such characterizations are more useful for the politics of religious polemic than for historical inquiry.

So long as the category of Gnosticism continues to serve as the heretical other of orthodox Christianity, it will be inadequate for interpretation of the primary materials and for historical reconstruction. Although I fully agree with the proposition that Gnosticism is an unhelpful artificial and rhetorical construction—and no less a construct than Judaism, Christianity, Oriental religion, paganism, or other terms of religious identity—I do not put the term in quotation marks, as is increasingly the habit of many other scholars. Indeed, the term "religion" itself is a construct serving a range of discursive and rhetorical purposes.[5] The same could certainly be said for a variety of other over-determined categories like orthodoxy and heresy. For any such terms, the interesting issue is not that they are artificial constructs but rather how they are constructed and to what ends.

In this book I analyze the twentieth-century study of Gnosticism in order to illustrate where and how it has been entangled in the ancient Christian discourse of orthodoxy and heresy, and then disentangle them. This enterprise involves rethinking the framework, methods, and categories, not only for Gnosticism, but also for the study of ancient Mediterranean religion more generally. (For more on the approach I use in this book, see the Note on Methodology.)

Throughout this book I contest the adequacy of current definitions of Gnosticism, and yet I continue to use the term. This practice may understandably occasion some difficulty for the reader. This difficulty can be eased somewhat by remembering that in this book I consider Gnosticism, not as an ancient religion or even a set of groups and materials from antiquity, but rather as a problematic term that must be reevaluated. For this limited purpose, I will define Gnosticism as it has been employed in twentieth-century historiography.

Historically, Gnosticism is a term that belongs to the discourses of normative Christian identity formation. It has been used to refer to the following:

1. all varieties of early Christianity that are characterized by these discourses as having too little or too negative an appropriation of Judaism;

2. an outside contamination of pure Christianity, either as the force that contaminated Christianity (as in theories of Gnosticism as an independent religion) or as a form of contaminated Christianity (where Gnosticism is understood to be a secondary deviation from the pure Gospel);

3. any of a number of traditions said to be closely related to this contaminated Christianity, whether or not they contain explicitly Christian elements, such as Hermeticism, Platonizing Sethianiam, Mandaeism, Manichaeism, the Albigensian heresy, or the tenets of the medieval Cathars.

It is these understandings of Gnosticism that I will explore in the following chapters.

# I

# Why Is Gnosticism So Hard to Define?

*gnosis:* esoteric knowledge of spiritual truth held by the ancient Gnostics to be essential to salvation

*gnostic:* an adherent of gnosticism

*gnosticism:* the thought and practice esp. of various cults of late pre-Christian and early Christian centuries distinguished by the conviction that matter is evil and that emancipation comes through gnosis

*Webster's New Collegiate Dictionary*

Despite the relative ease with which Webster's dictionary tackles the problem, defining the term "Gnosticism" is one of the greatest challenges in Gnostic studies. The term is used so widely and in so many different senses that its precise meaning in any given case is often hard to discern. Indeed, not only is Gnosticism used to refer to certain types of ancient Christian heresy, but it has come to have significant application in a variety of other areas, including philosophy, literary studies, politics, and psychology.[1] It has been connected with Buddhism, nihilism, and modern movements such as progressivism, positivism, Hegelianism, and Marxism.[2] Gnosticism was pivotal to Carl Jung's reflection on the collective unconscious and archetypes.[3] Gnostic themes have been detected in the novels of Herman Melville, Lawrence Durrell, and Walter Percy, among others.[4] The literary critic Harold Bloom even contrived a new Gnostic novel, *The Flight to Lucifer: A Gnostic Fantasy.*

Gnosticism can also claim contemporary churches and practitioners, most especially the Mandaeans, who have survived for at least sixteen centuries in the lands between the Tigris and Euphrates Rivers, but who now through persecution and emigration face the dire possibility of extinction as a distinctive religious tradition.[5] Moreover, Gnosticism is particularly well established among New Age groups.[6] A student in my Gnosticism seminar at Occidental College who had been raised in the Los Angeles Gnostic Church was in the class to learn more about his tradition, just as other students might wish to learn more about theirs. And all this is but the tip of the iceberg for contemporary Gnosticism.

Ubiquity, however, is not the only problem in defining Gnosticism clearly. Even if we were to agree to limit the discussion to the ancient Mediterranean world of the first to fifth centuries, the problem would not be resolved.[7] Indeed, no widely accepted consensus has resulted from the many recent attempts to define Gnosticism, to characterize its nature and essence, to list its essential characteristics, or to establish its origins and trace its development. Scholars of Mediterranean antiquity are deeply divided over basic issues. The problem has become so muddled and so contentious that some have even suggested abandoning the term altogether and starting over with a fresh category.[8] Simple as that solution may sound, until we resolve the fundamental issues, the debates over new terms and categories will doubtless be as problematic as the old debates, even if cloaked in new dress. It is crucial that we understand why Gnosticism is so difficult to define.

At one time it seemed that the problem was a matter of limited sources. Until recently, information about ancient Gnosticism came almost solely from the work of its detractors, primarily the Christian polemicists who wrote to promote their own theological views by refuting those of other Christians. Then came an influx of works stemming from both living and long-extinct groups categorized by modern scholars as Gnostics. Manuscripts were brought to Europe from lands as far flung as China, Egypt, Iran, and Iraq. The most significant discovery was the cache of papyrus books found in 1945 near Nag Hammadi. These fascinating new primary works might have been expected to solve the problem of definition, but in fact they only exacerbated it by multiplying further the already wide variety of phenomena categorized as Gnostic. Through circular reasoning, this huge amount of data seemed to provide irrefutable evidence of the actual existence of Gnosticism, masking its artificial nature as a scholarly invention.

How did such a variety of materials come to be classified under the single heading of Gnosticism?[9] Modern scholars have tended to group together a wide variety of ancient persons, ideas, and texts described in the writings of the ancient Christian polemicists. With a few significant exceptions, early Christian polemicists did not call such groups Gnostics; rather, they labeled them heretics.

Bentley Layton has argued that the term "Gnosticism" was first used by Henry More in 1669, in the context of Protestant anti-Catholic polemics. More characterized Catholicism as "a spice of the old abhorred Gnosticism," a kind of false prophecy that seduces true Christians to idolatry.[10] He probably coined the term from the title of a second-century C.E. work by Irenaeus of Lyon, *Exposé and Overthrow of What Is Falsely Called "Knowledge"* (commonly known as *Against the Heresies*). The term "knowledge" is translated from the Greek word *gnosis,* but in Gnosticism it has come to stand for false knowledge, in short, for heresy.

The early Christians understood Gnosticism to be a particular kind of heresy. Modern scholars have generally divided the earliest varieties of Christianity into three categories: Jewish Christianity, Gnosticism, and orthodoxy. The first appropriated too much Judaism and took too positive an attitude toward it; the second appropriated too little and took too negative an attitude.[11] Orthodoxy was just right, sailing between this Scylla and Charybdis, apparently safe from both dangers.

Gnosticism as a category served important intellectual aims, defining the boundaries of normative Christianity—especially with reference to Judaism—and aiding colonialism by contrasting Gnosticism as an Oriental heresy with authentic Western religion. Moreover, it offered a single category to refer to a vast range of ideas, literary works, individuals, and groups. Repetition of the term by people of repute reinforced a sense of realism, until its existence seemed unquestionable.

Once Gnosticism had been accepted as a discrete historical phenomenon, scholars sought to locate its origin and characterize the content of its teaching. The writings of the ancient Christian polemicists fostered the search for a single origin based on their claim that heresy had one author, Satan, even as truth had one author, God. Scholars accepted in principle that all the manifold expressions of Gnosticism could be traced to a single origin, but they searched for the source in more historical places, like heterodox Judaism or Iranian myth. Yet because they drew so heavily on the descriptions of the polemicists, they ended up characterizing Gnosticism

almost solely in the polemicists' terms: that the true God did not create
the world and humanity; that the world creator of Genesis was an ignorant and jealous pretender; that Christ never truly took on flesh and died,
but only appeared to do so in order to fool the lower God and his angels;
that one should love the spirit and hate the flesh, a view that could only
lead either to a false ascetic rejection of life or to a libertine flaunting of
traditional mores. Gnostics were variously characterized as alienated reb-
els, nihilistically opposed to the world-affirming values of their day, as immoral and impious perverters of divine Scripture, or as individualistic elit-
ists who thought they were spiritually superior to everyone else and hence
need not obey the priests and bishops. Such ideas were understood to
mark the presence of Gnosticism.

More recently some have applauded the Gnostics, seeing them, as Tom
Hall puts it,

> like the romantics in rebellion against the structure of classicism (or-
> thodoxy), they focused on the individual rather than the group; they
> were liberals rather than holy tories; the Quakers and Anabaptists of
> their day, not the Romans or High Anglicans. They were hippies,
> not corporate executives; spiritual people rather than attendees at di-
> vine services; they saw salvation in enlightenment, not ecclesiastical
> sanction; they were seekers after blessedness, not recipients of bless-
> ings; a priesthood of believers rather than believers in the priesthood.
> They were idealists, not church-builders; people who would cheer
> for Ivan Karamazov, not for the Grand Inquisitor in his poem.[12]

Yet this portrait of Gnostics is equally reliant on the attacks of the polemicists—only the appraisal differs. Whether such portraits provoke ad-
miration or condemnation, they both manage to present the polemicists'
views as objective history.

There are other problems with the category as well. Some supposedly
Gnostic ideas, such as cosmological dualism, can be found in a wide variety of non-Gnostic literature, while they may be absent from many of the
so-called Gnostic works. The literature defies attempts to force its theological diversity into snug categorical cubbyholes. It is a bit like the child's
game of putting the correct shape—a cylinder, cube, or pyramid—into

the correct hole. If you do not have blocks that match the holes, you can force them to fit by making the holes big enough to accommodate any of the shapes, or you can whittle away at the pieces until they have been re-shaped to fit. But you can never really get the different-shaped blocks to all fit into the same hole without some violence to the evidence.

Nor, despite considerable intellectual energy devoted to the topic, have scholars been able to establish clear links between the new literary works and the persons or groups classified by the polemicists as heretics. The complexity and diversity of the materials complicate all such attempts. So profound is the problem that the very existence of Gnostic groups has been called into question. Some have suggested that because the content of Gnostic texts is so varied, it is possible that no distinct group corre-sponds to this designation. Instead we might be dealing with an unknown number of groups so distinct from one another as to require separate treatment. Or perhaps the variety shows Gnostic thought to be so "indi-vidualistic" and "anti-authoritarian" as to preclude any group identity or organization. As Jonathan Z. Smith puts it, we might consider Gnosti-cism to be merely "a structural possibility within a number of religious traditions."[13]

Such considerations lead directly to, or perhaps stem directly from, a particularly thorny and widely recognized problem: Can we answer the question, "What is Gnosticism?" without asking, "Who were the Gnos-tics?"

The discovery of new manuscripts has produced a wealth of new infor-mation, but it is almost solely of one kind: myth. Although the texts illus-trate a wide variety of generic types—apocalypse, revelation dialogue, epistle, hymn, prayer, and so on—the content is primarily expressive of mythic and occasionally ritual language. The hesitancy to define Gnosti-cism is directly related to the paucity of sociological information and the accompanying liability of writing social or even intellectual history pri-marily from mythological sources.[14] We are left with little direct informa-tion about the identity of the individuals or groups that produced and read these texts.[15] We can only speculate whether they were produced by individual mystics, sectarian enclaves, or in school settings. Dating is sim-ilarly difficult to establish, except for the *terminus ad quem* supplied by the dates of the surviving manuscripts. What little information we do have from the ancient polemicists and the new texts is very scarce and must be read with an eye toward the rhetorical strategies and interests of both the polemicists and the texts' authors.[16] Even religious identity is a matter of hot dispute: Are these Christian heresies? Jewish heterodox writings? Evidence of a Platonizing philosophical underground? What do "heresy," "heterodoxy," and "underground movement" imply? In short, all the information basic to modern historiography is missing or in short supply, and this dearth seriously limits our ability to answer historical questions about the identity of Gnosticism.

Determining how to write social history from myth is surely one of the thorniest issues in ancient historiography. Although there is no direct relation between myth and social practice (that is, myths do not provide rules for behavior, let alone descriptions of actual behaviors), a cosmological myth, such as *The Apocryphon of John,* a work found in both the Berlin Codex and at Nag Hammadi, does provide a framework within which practices and choices can be oriented and made meaningful. Such a framework will make some practices more likely than others. For example, the use of powerful and positive female imagery of the divine could potentially have empowered women to play leadership roles, but it does not necessarily prove that they ever did; additional corroboration would be necessary to make that possibility into a historical probability.

Moreover, as Victor Turner cautions, myths are not merely "to be treated as models for secular behavior . . . What the initiand seeks through rite and myth is not a moral *exemplum* so much as the power to transcend the limits of his previous status, although he knows he must accept the normative restraints of his new status."[17] In *ApJohn,* the new status achieved through baptismal ritual and myth involves the reception of the Spirit, and with it the capacity to be free from the fetters of the counterfeit spirit who traps the soul through illegitimate domination, ignorance, and suffering. The new status confers ethical freedom and spiritual power, achieved both through baptism and through knowledge of the truth about the nature of the world and the True God.

How this new status would translate into actual behaviors is another matter. There are indications, however, that those who used *ApJohn* practiced exorcism for physical healing, encouraged sexual abstinence, and strove for *apatheia,* a state in which the psychic passions of desire, grief, anger, envy, and greed would be completely extinguished. Thus we can delve into a text like *ApJohn* to discover how it assesses the cultural values of its own day.[18] Surprisingly enough, at least in view of the usual stereotypes about "Gnostic rebellion," *ApJohn* presents a strong affirmation of its culture's values, along with a biting critique of their perversion.[19] Its attitude is less "rebellious" than idealistic and utopian.

Thus while there are decided limitations to using myth to describe social practices or construct group histories, it can be a fascinating indicator of how people were oriented toward certain behaviors, how those behaviors were conceptualized, and how patterns of meaning and belonging were constructed.

Nineteenth- and twentieth-century scholarship has been dominated by two methods for defining Gnosticism: (1) determining its historical origin and genealogical development; and (2) establishing its essential characteristics typologically.

The first method links origin with essence, assuming that if a particular phenomenon's point of origin can be identified, then we have learned something about its essential character and meaning as well as its history. Adolf von Harnack offers a good example of this approach, as we will see in greater detail in Chapter 3. He located the essence of Christianity in the earliest and purest form of the teaching of Jesus. Gnosticism arose when this pure form was contaminated by Greek religious and intellectual influences. Exposing this historical process, Harnack believed, allowed the original purity of true Christian piety to re-emerge in his own theology. Here essence coincides with origin, and development is figured as a process of decline and restoration.

Hans Jonas, by contrast, rejected the proposition that the origin of Gnosticism lay in a single historical site as the contamination of Christianity, arguing instead that it arose simultaneously in a variety of ancient Mediterranean locales as a distinct religion. Yet he, too, identified origin with essence. Gnosticism, he contended, arose from the existential experience of human alienation; it is therefore a possibility for every age and every time, despite the fact that it was clothed in the dress of antiquity. Jonas's understanding belongs to the demythologizing methods of the

German intellectual circles of his day, which allowed the essence of a phenomenon to be abstracted from the particularities of its historical expression. Yet the notion that essence and origin coincide remained fundamental to Jonas's definition of Gnosticism.

Despite their contradictory solutions to the problem of Gnostic origins, both Harnack and Jonas shared the presupposition that locating the origin of Gnosticism would simultaneously determine its essence and meaning. This shared assumption has been thoroughly confounded by the new materials, in part because of the variety of the materials classified under this compendious designation and in part because historical study cannot posit pure origins nor determine essences. To locate an original, pure form of Christianity, to chart the process of pagan contamination, or to find existential alienation in all the varied materials is simply not as easy as Harnack and Jonas supposed. Even if it were possible, the results would be dubious because, as George Eliot puts it so beautifully, "no retrospect will take us to the true beginning; and whether our prologue be in heaven or on earth, it is but a fraction of all-presupposing fact with which our story sets out." History can only trace continuity in difference; historians can only heuristically posit the origin of a phenomenon as a point of difference amid that continuity. And historical difference is never a matter of purity and essence, but a function of the relational possibilities produced in ever-shifting historical positions.

The second dominant approach, typology, uses phenomenological method based on inductive reasoning from a literary analysis of the primary materials. Gnosticism is defined by listing the essential characteristics common to all the phenomena classified as Gnostic. The most accomplished practitioner of this method was Hans Jonas. His greatest contribution was to shift the discussion of Gnosticism away from genealogy to typology. Rather than define Gnosticism by locating precisely where and how heretics deviated from true original Christianity, Jonas defined the essence of Gnosticism by listing a discrete set of defining characteristics.

Unfortunately, detailed study of the texts has led scholars to question every element of the standard typologies constructed by Jonas and others. In particular, specialists have challenged the cliché of Gnosticism as a radically dualistic, anticosmic tradition capable of producing only two extreme ethical possibilities: either an ascetic avoidance of any fleshly and worldly contamination (often caricatured as hatred of the body and the world) or a depraved libertinism that mocks any standards of moral behavior. In fact, the texts show a variety of cosmological positions, not only the presence of anticosmic dualism, but also milder forms of dualism, transcendentalism, and, most surprisingly, both radical and moderate forms of monism. The majority of the texts show a tendency toward ascetic values much in line with the broad currents of second- to fifth-century piety, and some argue for the validity of marriage, attack the human vices of greed and sexual immorality, and promote virtues such as self-control and justice—also ethical themes common in their day. That no treatises supporting libertinism have been found may of course be simply a matter of chance; it is nonetheless telling.

Part of the problem with typological definitions lies again with variety; part lies with the uncritical appropriation of the judgments of the ancient anti-Gnostic polemicists—for example, in making impiety one of the essential characteristics of Gnosticism. A greater stumbling block, however, is the conception of how ideas are related to practice. The assumption of demythologizing is that the essence of a phenomenon can be abstracted and removed from its "husk," that is, from the particular expressive form in which it appears. This view, however, is no longer tenable. Meaning and expression are indissolubly tied, and moreover meaning itself is local, specific, and socially constructed in the actual deployment of a myth or symbol in practice. Here again we run into the limits of what can and cannot be known about how Gnostic myth was performed in practice; acknowledging such limits is necessary for disciplining historical imagination. Moreover, the phenomenological distinction between thought and practice, essence and form, presupposes an untenable dualist epistemology. The work of sociologists such as Pierre Bourdieu clearly illustrates that thought is a kind of practice, that the formulation of social ideology has a practical link to social relations, economics, and politics. The evocation of a symbol, or telling an old story a new way, can in and of itself produce a practical social effect. In trying to interpret ancient texts, we do well not to essentialize their contents but to ask what work they are doing in practice, and for whom.

The ultimate problem in defining Gnosticism may lie with the nature

of definitions themselves. Both historical-genealogical (origins) and typological definitions take essentialist approaches to defining Gnosticism;
that is, in Raziel Abelson's terms, they assume that definitions provide
"precise and rigorous knowledge," "serve the purpose of providing de-
scriptive information about their objects," and offer "a causal explanation
of the thing defined."[20] Accordingly, "systematic classification is identical
with theoretical explanation."[21]

Bentley Layton has recently introduced a new, nominalist approach to
defining Gnosticism. Nominalism, in Abelson's words, is a "means of
clearing up and avoiding ambiguous, vague, and obscure language" by
"subjecting existing concepts to the test of definitional reduction to observable and measurable properties."[22] Nominalist (formalist) views further suggest that definitions are useful primarily as an economical short-
hand form of notation.

Layton begins by identifying cases where the terms "gnostic" and
"gnostics" are used in Greek texts to refer to a distinct social group. From
this strictly philological starting point, he then develops a set of methodological propositions for identifying "other, undenominated textual material [that] can be recognized as being Gnostic and thus added to the
Gnostic data base." The resultant term "Gnosticism" refers to this delimited set of data.[23]

Both essentialist and nominalist approaches to defining Gnosticism offer certain advantages and raise certain problems. Although the former
work strategically to stabilize definitions by pointing to the original meaning as the true meaning or by delimiting a fixed set of essential characteristics, they simultaneously tend to reify historical materials into static and
artificial entities, obscuring the rhetorical and ideological functions of defining Gnosticism. Moreover, insofar as the determination of origins remains general, obscure, or imprecise, so does meaning. Essentialist approaches are unable to cope with the variety of phenomena classified as
Gnostic; no one definition, no one solution to the question of origin, no
one set of typological categories can suffice.

Nominalism is extremely useful in pointing toward terminological clarity; nevertheless, this approach tends "to reduce definition to historical reports of linguistic behavior" or to derive inductive categories from linguistic behavior, so that it becomes necessary to look elsewhere to explore the
*meaning* of the phenomena beyond the arbitrary assignment of categorical

names to elements of a historical record.[24] Although categorization is a mode of definition, Layton's actual definition excludes from the category of Gnosticism the majority of the phenomena that have been classified as Gnostic. This suggests the need for recategorization of the excluded material, and in fact Layton's work points toward just such an alternative categorization.[25] A more serious difficulty is that Layton's nominalizing approach requires supplementary methods to establish larger contexts in which meaning can be explored, and is therefore compatible with the essentializing approaches of origins and typology. In short, we could end up back where we started.

Where do these observations leave us? Any definition is limited insofar as it calls attention to certain aspects or characteristics of a set of phenomena while ignoring or hiding others. Definitions tend to produce static and reified entities and hide the rhetorical and ideological interests of their fabricators. Nowhere has this reification been accomplished more comprehensively than with Gnosticism, which is much more often treated as a historical entity than as a definitional category. But despite these rather serious limitations, neither is it possible to give up definitions altogether.

Recognizing these difficulties, Abelson has offered a helpful suggestion in what he calls "a pragmatic-contextualist approach" to definition. In this approach, *definitions are formed and evaluated in terms of the purposes they are designed to serve.* He writes:

> Definitions are good if and only if they serve the purpose for which they are intended. Thus, an evaluation of a definition must begin with the identification of the point or purpose of the definition, and this requires knowledge of the discursive situation in which the need for the definition arises . . . The practical value of any account of the nature of definition is to be found in the clarity of the standards it provides for judging when a definition is good or bad . . . What must be stated in a definition varies with the definition's purpose.[26]

Because definitions and the criteria for determining their adequacy will vary depending on purpose and discursive situation, *definitions are to be regarded as both provisional and positional.*[27] From this perspective, definitions are treated as intellectual tools in the historian's workbox. The provisionality of each tool is tied to its having been crafted to suit some particular task; its adequacy is determined by its capacity to do its intended job. Recognizing definitions as positional requires analysis of the discursive situation in which a definition is constructed and deployed, including analysis of who is using the definition, for what ends, and in whose interests.

Abelson's approach immediately shows up one of the primary reasons that defining Gnosticism has become so muddled. The problem mainly arises because scholars have not clearly formulated what it is we want to know when we study Gnosticism. The nature of much historical discourse assumes that "the past" is a given, and the task at hand is simply to recover it; for example, to re-present Gnosticism through the disciplined practices of historical methods according to established standards. Once Gnosticism has been objectified and certain existing source materials such as papyrus manuscripts have been ascribed to it, it becomes possible to recover Gnosticism from the past. In this mode, what historians want to know is the truth about the past, the true past, the past as it actually was. The early twentieth-century historian of religion Wilhelm Bousset, for example, claimed that

> the actual historical course of events has always proved to be more strange, more diverse and richer than the theories posed in advance. The work in the history of religions certainly has not developed in this area out of preconceived theories; it has been shaped under the compulsion of the facts. And it can do nothing at all better than, in ever more intensive labor, to let the facts speak for themselves. Then the dispute over theories will clear up by itself and will come to an end. Whether in the present book I have succeeded in letting the facts speak for themselves and in approximating the actual course of events may be left to the judgment of those whose calling it is to form such judgments.[28]

This eschewal of any "preconceived theories," along with the invocation of "the compulsion of the facts" and the disciplining of the professional, makes it impossible to reflect on or articulate the purposes Bousset might have had in giving his account of Gnosticism.[29] It is the facts that are speaking, not the historian—assuming he or she is doing the job right. Few if any historians of Gnosticism today would make such a bald claim —for historians now recognize and acknowledge that the questions we ask are important determinants of the outcome of historical reconstruction. Nonetheless, the continuing lack of explicit conversation about the purposes of defining Gnosticism shows that the tendency to objectify the past is still operating.

The issue is not whether it is appropriate to use definitions to articulate particular identities; indeed, the very fact that definitions of Gnosticism are all tied to rhetorical and ideological practices is *in itself* no criticism. It is neither possible nor desirable to escape the world of practice and its politics. The sphere of practice is the social world that all humanity inhabits, in one way or another. Rather, the issue is whether it is possible to give a critical evaluation of a definition. When we view definitions as provisional and positional, their rhetorical and ideological uses can become more apparent and more readily visible for analysis and evaluation than is possible with essentializing definitions. In order to provide any adequate definition of Gnosticism, then, we must identify clearly the definition's purpose and provide standards for judging when the definition is good or bad, adequate or inadequate.[30]

In performing the task of definition for historical studies, it is crucial not to reify definitions by attributing to them a (past) reality that they have only in our (present) discourse about them; or, more precisely, by attributing to them the capacity to function as determiners of practice.[31] For example, we often hear that many elements of orthodoxy, including the doctrine of apostolic succession, the formation of a closed canon, and an exclusive rule of faith (creed), were shaped in reaction to the threat posed by Gnosticism.[32] In this model, the ability of Gnosticism to provoke a response from "the Church" is understood as a direct cause for the development of these crucial elements of orthodoxy. Here Gnosticism, a scholarly construct invented to define the origin and essential characteristics shared by a wide variety of ancient materials, has become an entity capable of acting in history and causing events. Understanding the term as a provisional category should help avoid such distortions.

Abelson's pragmatic-contextualist approach not only aids in formulating a direction for future attempts at defining Gnosticism but also helps to explain a final difficulty that contributes to some of the current confusion. One source of our problem may be that we are attempting to determine a single definition of Gnosticism that is adequate to serve the wide variety of purposes to which the term is put.

When defining Gnosticism was understood fundamentally to be the task of refining our knowledge of one prominent type of early Christian heresy, it was clear who wanted to know, what they wanted to know, and why: Christian polemicists wanted their readers to know where deception led people astray from the truth in order to help them avoid error. These motivations were and still are strong among historians of Christianity. Indeed, the fundamental and pervasive perception that Gnosticism is a heresy remains a crucial factor in both the ways it is defined and the actual content of the definitions. That is to say, the problem of defining Gnosticism has been and continues to be primarily an aspect of the ongoing project of defining and maintaining a normative Christianity.[33]

As long as defining Gnosticism was still primarily about determining the historical identity of Christianity, its purpose remained largely the same as that of heresy. Heresy appears to be a very tidy category—its purpose is to distinguish right and wrong belief and behavior, define insider-outsider boundaries, and establish clear lines of power and authority. Gnosticism has often performed these same functions. It has marked the erroneous, the heretical, the schismatic, as well as all things threatening, anomalous, esoteric, and arcane.

In the twentieth century, however, Gnosticism has come to serve a number of other purposes. For the philosopher Hans Jonas, it marked an episode in the history of human alienation. For the historian Bentley Layton, it locates the data to reconstruct an ancient religious group. Psychological and literary studies have employed it to refer to mysterious archetypes or dualistic themes. Plainly, using the same term for such different purposes has impossibly complicated our ability to define Gnosticism clearly.

So what do we wish to know from a study of Gnosticism? Christianity in all its variety? Why? To provide more options for contemporary theological reflection? To put normative Christianity on a firm historical foundation by showing the superiority of its particular structures and traditions? To legitimate changes to the definitional norms and practices of contemporary Christians (feminist, liberationist, evangelical)? To understand Gnostic phenomena as exempla of the religious experiences of humanity, and hence as possibilities for us? To plumb the depths of human intellectual folly? Or is the task more limited? Is it to distinguish a self-identified group and a complex of textual materials? To elucidate the meaning of obscure passages in ancient literature?

My purpose in this book is to consider the ways in which the early Christian polemicists' discourse of orthodoxy and heresy has been intertwined with twentieth-century scholarship on Gnosticism in order to show where and how that involvement has distorted our analysis of the ancient texts. At stake is not only the capacity to write a more accurate history of ancient Christianity in all its multiformity, but also our capacity to engage critically the ancient politics of religious difference rather than unwittingly reproduce its strategies and results.

# 2

# Gnosticism as Heresy

From the exact, unmisted reflection to the superposition of oneself on the other, the problem remains the same. The vanity of Metaphysics has the merit of marking time: it leads one straight back to the positivist dream of pure truth and pure presence. *Naked, but not naked enough,* I would say. The language of Buddhism sometimes speaks of the eighty-four thousand entrances to reality, and thinking reality versus non-reality may also lead to one of them as long as this chatter of the soul doesn't take the finger pointing at the moon for the moon itself.

*Trinh T. Minha*

Our discussion of Gnosticism begins with the ancient Christian polemicists. Chief among them were Justin Martyr, Irenaeus of Lyons, Clement of Alexandria, Origen of Alexandria, Tertullian of Carthage, Hippolytus of Rome, and Epiphanius of Salamis, all of whom lived in the Roman Empire during the first four centuries c.e. and wrote polemical treatises against other Christians.[1] In their refutations they supplied detailed if tendentious descriptions of their opponents' views and behaviors, and occasionally quoted long sections from their writings. Until recently, the study of Gnosticism has been based almost solely on this information. The works of the polemicists were carefully preserved largely because their perspectives won out in the struggles among early Christians.

Although the polemicists never used the term "Gnosticism," their detractions not only supplied most of the information about what we call ancient Gnosticism, but also established the strategies for defining and evaluating it. It is these strategies that have become entangled in modern discussions and constructions of Gnosticism such that the connections between the ancient construction of heresy and the modern construction of Gnosticism are neither ephemeral nor arbitrary.

The construction of heresy was only one part of the larger rhetorical enterprise of establishing the boundaries of normative Christianity, which also had to distinguish itself from other forms of belief and practice, notably Judaism and paganism. To this end, the polemicists wrote not only books against heresy but also polemical treatises against Judaism and apologetic works addressed to Roman authorities and Greek intellectuals. For example, the second-century polemicist and theologian Justin Martyr authored works of all three types: a lost treatise against heretics, two apologies addressed to Roman emperors, and an anti-Jewish tract titled *Dialogue with Trypho the Jew*. The aim of such treatises was at least as much to provide internal self-definition as to persuade heretics, Jews, or pagans that the polemicists alone held the keys to divine truth.

The important point for our topic is that the underlying strategies of refutation and defense in all three types of polemical exposition were remarkably similar, even though the themes differed depending upon the audience.[2] Twentieth-century historiography reproduces the discursive strategies of all three types of polemic, albeit with notable adaptations to contemporary social and intellectual conditions and discourses. Thus a discussion of the discourse of orthodoxy and heresy needs to include polemics aimed at pagans and Jews as well.

Of concern here is not a full analysis of Christian discourse on heresy, but rather the identification of those specific aspects of the polemicists' discourse that are reproduced in twentieth-century scholarship on Gnosticism.[3] Indeed, we can learn more about Gnosticism as a category by identifying the themes and strategies of the polemicists present in the works of modern scholars than by examining the content of the polemicists' descriptions of heresy. While lumping together all the polemicists' varied arguments does a disservice to their complexity and the specificity of their historical contexts, it does represent quite well the harmonized form in which the polemicists' views have been appropriated in the modern period. Although I offer here only an initial portrait of the intersections of ancient and modern discourses, it is one that I hope is sufficient to outline the contours of twentieth-century efforts to define Gnosticism.

## Christian Discourses of Identity Formation

Although ancient Christianity was theologically diverse and sociologically multiform, participating actively in ancient urban pluralism, the fourth and fifth centuries witnessed the formation and consolidation of a more uniform Christianity, under the guiding eyes of Christian emperors. A church headed by bishops, defined by creed and canon, and unified by increasingly standardized liturgical practices won out and for a time claimed the title of orthodoxy for itself. Although powerful controversies continued to mark the period and uniformity was never truly achieved, Christianity nonetheless attained a kind of stable and monolithic unity under episcopal authority and imperial patronage that had not existed before Constantine's conversion in the early fourth century.

Chief among its theological, political, and rhetorical tools was the capacity to brand opponents as heretics. Le Boulluec has suggested that the ecclesiastical capacity to enforce penitential discipline and excommunication, to define ritual purity and morality, and to defend the integrity and authenticity of doctrine against dissent progressively worked to consolidate ecclesiastical unity. The representation of heresy as a general and timeless notion became such a powerful tool in this cause that merely invoking it was sufficient to produce reprobation and exclusion.[4]

A second powerful, largely unrecognized tool was the rhetorical consolidation of manifold ancient religious practices into three mutually exclusive groups: Jews, Christians, and pagans. These categories became further reified in later centuries and continue to operate almost automatically in contemporary historiography, reinscribing and naturalizing the rhetoric of fourth- and fifth-century orthodoxy into a seemingly common-sense division of ancient religious life. Their tenacity demonstrates the success of Christian rhetoric in dominating the politics of religious identity up to our own day. Rather than assume that such categories represent historical givens, we need to ask how they were formed, what work they did, in whose interests they operated, and what was at stake.

The primary challenge for Christian self-definition was sameness, whether distinguishing the orthodox from heretics or Christians from non-Christians. Although the goal was to minimize actual differences within the group while maximizing the differences with outsiders, ironically the strategies were more or less the same, because in order to exclude Christian views the polemicists opposed, they needed to make their competitors look like outsiders, not insiders.[5] Real differences had to be fully exploited and even exaggerated, while similarities were best overlooked altogether or portrayed as malicious or superficial imitation. The polemicists succeeded so well that for us the terms "orthodoxy" and "heresy" imply only difference, not similarity.

Someone will rightly point out that the problems of internal Christian dispute were in fact matters of difference. True, but for distinguishing heretics from the orthodox, the pressing problem was that early Christians were all basing their theological positions on revelation from Jesus Christ. When they read Scripture and reproduced various streams of the ancient intellectual tradition, they used very similar hermeneutical methods, such as allegory, typology, and midrashic retelling.[6] It was not that the theologies were the same, but that the intellectual bases and discursive strategies for making truth claims were remarkably similar. Given that there was no universally recognized episcopal hierarchy, common creed, or New Testament canon in the first centuries, it was not easy to adjudicate whose Christology or whose reading of Scripture was right. It was this problem that the early polemicists took on. They developed a few distinctive and powerful rhetorical strategies to argue that they, and they alone, understood the revelation of Christ and interpreted Scripture correctly. It is these strategies that concern us here.

## Heresy

Ancient philosophical and medical writers employed the term *hairesis* to denote a coherent doctrine or tendency, often applying it to the variety of ancient philosophical teachings or "schools" of thought tied to a particular founder and his successors.[7] The polemicists similarly treated heresies as particular doctrinal tendencies and frequently presented a succession of heretics (usually beginning with Simon Magus) whom they described at some length biographically and doctrinally.

But for Christian polemicists, the term "heresy" was pejorative in a way that Greek usage was not. Le Boulluec suggests that Christians transformed the largely positive understanding of *haireseis* (pl.) into a negative

concept by applying the Greek antithesis between reality and naming to
the business of distinguishing between true and false believers. They reasoned that the heretics were not *in reality* Christians; they just falsely
*called* themselves by the name of Christian, despite the fact that their beliefs and practices were contrary to the precepts of Christ. From this logic,
Le Boulluec suggests, "the notion of 'heresy' is born."[8]

"Orthodoxy" and "heresy" are terms of evaluation that aim to articulate
the meaning of self while simultaneously silencing and excluding others
within the group. The power relations implied in the discourse of orthodoxy and heresy are firmly embedded in struggles over who gets to say
what truth is: the orthodox are the winners; the heretics, the losers. This
discourse not only determines the self but constructs the other as well.
The other is a rhetorical tool to think with and should not be confused
with the reality it is constructed to control intellectually and politically.[9]
Nor is it appropriate to understand such reflection as "really about" the
self. The construction of the self, as well as of the other, is, as Trinh puts
it, the "finger pointing at the moon, not the moon itself." Nor would
analysis of the pointing finger lead us to "the real, true moon," the "exact
unmisted reflection, the positivist dream of pure truth and pure reflection."[10]

Although processes of defining self and other are fluid, dynamic, and
ambiguous in practice, the basic pattern of the discourse of orthodoxy and
heresy has remained fairly stable from antiquity into the modern period,
exerting its power beyond religion to pervade other spheres of identity
construction such as nationalism, ethnicity, and race. It is my contention
that the strategies devised by early Christians to define orthodoxy and heresy are alive and well in the politics of religious normativity in the modern
world, albeit in forms modified to suit new and shifting situations. Claims
to be true to tradition, charges that opponents are contaminating the
original, pure form of the tradition with "secular," "modern," or "Western" ideas and mores, or eschewal of intellectual or moral questioning as
an unnecessary confusion of faith—such practices effectively replicate the
pattern of ancient polemics.

Calling people heretics is an effort to place *outside* those who claim to
be on the *inside*. As Jonathan Z. Smith suggests, it is the proximate, not
the distant, other who most urgently provokes the language of differentiation:

The issue of difference as a mode of both culturally encoding and decoding, of maintaining and relativizing internal as well as external distinctions, raises . . . the observation that, rather than the remote "other" being perceived as problematic and/or dangerous, it is the proximate "other," the near neighbor, who is most troublesome. That is to say, while difference or "otherness" may be perceived as being either LIKE-US or NOT-LIKE-US, it becomes most problematic when it is TOO-MUCH-LIKE-US or when it claims to BE-US. It is here that the real urgency of theories of the "other" emerges, called forth not so much by a requirement to place difference, but rather by an effort to situate ourselves.[11]

Heresy was a particularly disturbing case of proximity in that the heretics claimed to be Christians.[12] To exclude them denies something of what it means to be a Christian, to become estranged from some part of one's own tradition. To exclude those who claim to belong means to divide the corporate self against itself in the interests of power or purity. Hence the ambiguous rift of disturbing estrangement evident in the politics of exclusion.

The attempt to dominate one's opponents by calling them heretics has a reciprocal effect on the namer as well. As William Green points out, such naming "can reshape the naming society's picture of itself, expose its points of vulnerability, and spark in it awareness of, or reflection about, the possibility or the reality of otherness within."[13] Usually historians take note of this reciprocity by imagining that orthodoxy gained a firmer definition and shape in the process of confronting heresies. Henry Chadwick, for example, argued that the doctrine of apostolic succession, the development of the New Testament canon, and the formulation of a rule of faith were all weapons forged in the defense of orthodoxy.[14] We can turn this point around, however, and note that many elements that today are considered fundamental to Christian thought and practice, most especially canon and creed, were absent from earliest Christianity. There was no predetermined orthodoxy that was simply there, waiting to be more carefully defined.[15] Constructing a heretical other simultaneously and reciprocally exposes the partial, mutable, and irregular character of orthodoxy.

The works of the polemicists were carefully preserved largely because their perspectives won out in the struggles among early Christians. The writings of those they opposed were mostly lost, unless dry sand and fickle historical fortuity combined forces to preserve them for a later millennium.

The information supplied by the polemicists is historically significant, but it must always be read with a mind to their goal of detraction, and hence with an eye for ancient rhetorical conventions of refutation and intent to malign.[16] Moreover, the polemicists may sometimes have misunderstood those toward whom they had so little sympathy.[17] In any case, we cannot assume that they accurately represented the issues that were of concern to their rivals, since their refutations necessarily reflect the issues that concerned them.[18] The fact that such rhetorical practices have been little studied and little understood until recently has serious implications for any description of Gnosticism. Reading the evidence only through the tinted spectacles of its detractors has refracted our vision and obscured much crucial information.

Although the ancient polemicists did not actually use the term "Gnosticism," they did occasionally refer to groups of which they disapproved as Gnostics.[19] The term could also be used positively, however (for example, Clement of Alexandria used it to refer to Christians who had progressed far in their spiritual understanding); nonetheless, the polemicists were happy to suggest that the *gnosis* (knowledge) of their opponents was "falsely so-called." Indeed, the title of the major work by the second-century polemicist and theologian Irenaeus of Lyons was reported to be *Exposé and Overthrow of What Is Falsely Called "Knowledge."*[20]

A polemicist like Irenaeus of Lyons set out to exclude people he thought were heretics by emphasizing certain differences of theology and practice. He laid out his construal of the views of the heretics and then proceeded to refute them. He focused on three areas: cosmology, salvation, and ethics. The heretics, he claimed, rejected the God of the Hebrew Bible as the true God and creator of the cosmos. Against what he saw as the clear evidence of Scripture, they denied the divine goodness of both the creator and the creation. Moreover, they undermined salvation by denying both that Jesus had a physical body and that believers would physically rise from the dead even as Jesus had (a position called docetism). Instead, Irenaeus claims, the heretics presumptuously claimed that only a spiritual elite would be "saved by nature" owing to their heavenly origin; salvation came not by faith in Christ but through knowledge revealed only to them. In Irenaeus' view, such a position was arrogant as well as erroneous.

The polemicists further objected that such beliefs implied that humanity did not need a savior and that moral effort, instruction, purification, and good works were unnecessary. It was false belief, they claimed, that led the heretics to reject the authority of the legitimate successors of the apostles, that is, the bishops and priests of the true Church. Moreover, the heretics avoided martyrdom, an evasion which clearly demonstrated that they lacked true faith. This kind of theology, the polemicists claimed, could lead only to amoral or immoral practices, whether ascetic or libertine.

Although the polemicists' objections have become basic to the modern repertoire used to describe Gnosticism, their portrayals of heresy seriously distorted their opponents' views. The so-called Gnostic texts regularly portray the necessity for a savior (often Christ), and they portray the plight of humanity in terms of ignorance that must be enlightened with true teaching, impurity that must be cleansed, and evil that must be resisted and overcome. In short, moral effort was required. Further, there is evidence in the writings of the polemicists themselves that some heretics were martyred. A few of the so-called heretical works argue for the universal salvation of humanity, notably *The Apocryphon of John*, which excludes only apostates. Others limit salvation to those belonging to their own group, but the polemicists did the same, often condemning non-Christians to eternal punishment in hell. Still others deny that God is the cause of anyone's damnation and reject the notion of a final judgment.[21] Like other Christian writings, many of the recently discovered works base their authority on claims to an apostolic heritage, though they do advocate notions of authority undermining claims that only male bishops and priests could be the apostles' true successors.[22] Therein, perhaps, lay the real rub.

As for the charge that the heretics perverted Scripture, Tertullian, writing from North Africa at the turn of the third century, produced a book called *Prescriptions against Heretics,* in which he counseled his audience not to debate with heretics over the interpretation of Scripture because success would be far from certain. Tertullian's aim was not simply to dis-

courage open debate on the content of Scripture, but even more to set
limits on who could legitimately interpret it:

> What will you accomplish, most learned of biblical scholars, if the
> other side denies what you affirmed and affirms what you denied?
> True, you will lose nothing in the dispute but your voice; and you
> will get nothing from their blasphemy but bile. You submit yourself
> to a biblical disputation in order to strengthen some waverer. Will
> he in fact incline to the truth any more than to heresy? He sees that
> you have accomplished nothing, the rival party being allowed equal
> rights of denial and affirmation and an equal status. As a result he
> will go away from the argument even more uncertain than before,
> not knowing which he is to count as heresy. The heretics too can re-
> tort these charges upon us. Maintaining equally that the truth is
> with them, they are compelled to say that it is we who introduce the
> falsifications of Scripture and the lying interpretations. It follows
> that we must not appeal to Scripture and we must not contend
> on ground where victory is impossible or uncertain or not certain
> enough.[23]

The Christian works from Nag Hammadi illustrate just how frustrating
these types of debates must have been. Although all Christian exegetes
used similar types of interpretation, such as allegory or typology, they began with quite different premises, and so they came to widely varying
conclusions. All Christians appealed both to Scripture and to revelation in
Christ mediated through apostolic authority, but they did so differently.[24]

For example, *ApJohn* states that pure truth resides in the revelation of
Christ to his disciple John. In contrast, Jewish Scriptures have mixed
truth with error, so that without Christ's revelation to guide the reader,
Scripture by itself could be misleading or even deceptive. For Justin Martyr, by contrast, the truth of Christianity was demonstrated to the world
by showing how the events of Jesus' life fulfilled the prophecies of Scripture; indeed the truth of Scripture could only be fully illuminated by
Christ. In the end, both appealed to revelation and prophecy, but Justin
tied his Christology to the truth of Scripture, while *ApJohn* determined
Scriptural truth or falsehood on the basis of Christology. As a result, the

authoritative status of Scripture was essential for Justin in a way that it was not for those who wrote and used *ApJohn*. Both have to deal with problematic passages, but Justin treats them allegorically to avoid any imputation that Scripture is less than perfect, whereas *ApJohn* resolves similar difficulties by subordinating Scripture to the revelation of Christ. At stake was the very authority on which Christianity was based.

Despite this controversy over how to read Scripture, it was not yet fixed into a closed canon, as Tertullian obliquely notes: "Any given heresy," he writes, "rejects one or another book of the Bible."[25] He neglects, however, to give us his own list, perhaps because that was still an open question even for him; it was certainly an open question for many others in the second century.[26] Moreover, Tertullian suggests that it was hard to determine precisely who the heretics were, for they included people some considered to be "the most faithful and wisest and most experienced members of the church."[27] Tertullian sets a hedge around Scripture by insisting that there are limits to Jesus' injunction to seek and find. Once one has found, he says, it is time to quit seeking. Only as long as one adheres to the rule of faith, within the context of the group Tertullian sanctions, is it permissible to seek.[28] And yet he concludes:

In the last resort, however, it is better for you to remain ignorant, for fear that you come to what you should not know. For you do know what you should know. "Your faith has saved thee," it says, not your biblical learning. Faith is established in the Rule . . . To know nothing against the Rule is to know everything.[29]

Thus Tertullian's approach to Scripture was devised strategically to lessen the influence of his opponents: limiting who was allowed to interpret Scripture, reducing access to Scripture, establishing a rule of faith to regulate interpretation, and perhaps most important, equating the true Church with a hierarchical order of male authority, which he claimed stemmed from Jesus through the twelve male apostles. I would argue that these strategies were devised not in the face of a clear external enemy, but to deal with an internal crisis of differentiation. It was difficult for believers to determine who was right when matters of belief or practice were disputed. It is crucial, therefore, not to mistake Tertullian's own perceptions and rhetoric for reality. There were indeed matters under dispute; there were indeed crucial points of difference; but the polemicists can only guide us to what the polemicists thought the crucial issues were, not to a full range of the opinions under debate. The polemicists needed to create sharp lines of differentiation because in practice the boundaries were not so neat. The new primary sources discovered in Egypt show many unexpected areas of agreement in faith and practice, and at some points simply evince theological interests different from those of the polemicists.

The polemicists used a wide variety of additional strategies drawn from their cultural milieu and modified to suit their own purposes.[30] These included *ad hominem* attacks, accusing their opponents of such moral and mental malignities as arrogance, pride, jealousy, impiety, and sexual immorality—that is, the usual abuses of educated polemic. Another strategy was simply nominalist: they called their opponents "heretics" while reserving for themselves the name of true believer (true disciple, true Christian, and so on).

The term "heresy" does not necessarily need to be present for us to recognize this tactic; the polemicists could characterize heretics as such simply by claiming that their beliefs and practices were deficient. In this way, the polemicists' discourse produced heresy as the deficient and defective other in contrast to true Christianity. These characterizations took on a variety of forms, such as distinguishing the righteous from the unrighteous; the enlightened from the blind; the pure from the defiled; dry canals from channels that pass on true teaching, and so on. According to this discourse, true Christians are said to rely on God as creator; heretics, to reject God as creator and therefore to be godless. True Christians know they are saved through the grace of God by faith in Christ Jesus (*pistis*); heretics falsely believe they are saved by nature through the revelation of the Savior (*gnosis*). True Christians rely on the Scriptures as guides to faith and appropriate moral behavior; heretics pervert them for devious purposes and are incapable of truly moral behavior. True Christians are humble before God; heretics are arrogant. And so on. Whether heresy was represented as the absence of some positive element like piety or faith, or the presence of some theological error or moral deficiency, the point was the same: heretics lacked the truth and hence fell into error, immorality, and division.

Irenaeus in particular contrasted the unity of the true Church with the divisiveness of the heretics. He apparently thought that the best way to "show how utterly absurd, inconsistent and incongruous with the Truth" these heretical teachings were was to describe them and contrast them with the true teaching of Christ.[31] Thus his refutation was two-pronged: to describe the false teachings and to provide the true. In so doing, his work *Against the Heresies* not only laid the basis for what would later become Christian orthodoxy, but also set a pattern for attacking one's opponents that would persist to the present day.[32]

In describing the beliefs and practices of his opponents, Irenaeus was guided by two related strategies. One was to show that in contrast to the harmony and unity of the true Church and its one rule of faith, the heretics lacked any kind of social unity or doctrinal unanimity. Their opinions, he argued, were inconsistent and their leaders disagreed even among themselves. Their contentiousness alone showed that they were inspired by evil spirits.[33] Irenaeus' claim had a powerful impact in antiquity because it drew its rhetorical force from the widely shared supposition that truth is single and unified, whereas falsehood comes in many divergent forms. It was based on a fundamental ancient value that located unity and harmony in sameness; chaos and disorder in difference.

This claim flowed directly into Irenaeus' second strategy: constructing a genealogy of heresies from a single origin.[34] He strategically manipulated this genealogy to contrast the demonic origin of heretical groups with the apostolic origin of the true Church. His opponents, Irenaeus insisted, were not *really* fellow Christians; they were the agents of the Devil. Their teaching derived from the Devil through his minion Simon and his harlot Helen, whereas the teaching of true Christians came from God through Jesus and his chosen male disciples.[35] Hints at sexual pollution oppose pure patriarchal lineage in these genealogies of descent.[36]

In *AgHer* I.23–28, Irenaeus presents Simon the Samaritan as the heretic "from whom all heresies got their start" and traces all other arch-heretics from him.[37] He argues that heretical views are human inventions, surely inspired by the Devil but driven by the very human faults of jealousy, arrogance, and error. From Irenaeus' perspective, setting out the family ancestry of such heretics was sufficient to expose the true nature of their beliefs and practices, for origin revealed essence and character. You can know a good tree by its fruit; which means you can know what kind of fruit you will get from a poisonous plant. The teaching of the Church, by contrast, stemmed from God through Jesus to the twelve apostles; from such a source could only come inerrant truth.

Genealogy provided a powerful metaphor that allowed Irenaeus to lump all his opponents together under one rubric, heresy, despite the enormous variety of their beliefs and practices. Whereas diversity illustrated their falsehood, a common genealogy proved that they possessed a common root and essence in demonic error.

As Denise Buell has recently shown, the appeal to family genealogy, like the appeal to unity, had a powerful rhetorical impact in part because it drew upon notions of biological reproduction to naturalize the socially constructed view that "like produces like."[38] Although the most predominant language used by Irenaeus to describe the relationship among the heretics was that of a philosophical *hairesis* (a teacher with his disciples and successors), the metaphorical use of the language of procreation, genealogy, and kinship, like the image of a tree and its fruit, worked powerfully to naturalize the view that heretics could produce only other heretics. From Irenaeus' perspective, such distorted procreation could generate only monsters.[39]

Although the substance of Irenaeus' genealogy has not held up to critical scrutiny, modern scholarship has tended to keep Irenaeus' tactic alive by offering alternative genealogies.[40] Most important, the structural pattern Irenaeus set became the basis for the historical investigation of heresy well into the modern period: *describing various texts and teachings, emphasizing their differences from one another, while at the same time and despite clear recognition of their manifold differences connecting them in a linear genealogy to a single origin and a single essential character.* It is genealogy, not a common content, that continues to justify classifying all these varied persons, groups, practices, and mythologies under the common rubric of Gnosticism—despite the fact that scholars have not produced a consensus on any specific genealogy.

At the same time that heresies were said to be linked by a common origin and demonic essence, the polemicists treated them as the source of division within Christianity. They tended to focus explicitly on doctrinal matters, although, given that they considered immoral practices and schism to be the direct consequences of poor theology, the rhetoric ranged more widely. As a result of this association, heresy could be determined either by doctrinal variation or by social deviation. By insisting that group unity had to be rooted in a common doctrine, the polemicists furthered the view that adherence to the authority of the established leaders of the one institutional Church constituted orthodoxy. Those who disputed that authority would *by definition* be considered schismatics—whether they had actually left the group or not.

This kind of rhetoric worked to protect the polemicists from the charge that they were the ones who introduced schism. According to this reasoning, the polemicists' prescriptions to shun heretics would be recognized not as promoting division but rather as recognizing the schism that, from their perspective, the heretics had already established by being different.[41] Who may actually have first separated from whom—if or when they did—remains an open question, requiring evidence and argument beyond mere appeal to the rhetoric of the polemicists.[42]

The polemicists' rhetoric is further complicated by their claim that heresy was not in fact an *internal* issue but a problem of contamination from *outside.* In other words, the polemicists sought to redefine the situation rhetorically so that the problem of heresy was perceived as a matter not of internal dissension and struggle but of loose and leaky boundaries through which pollution had seeped. Polemicists such as Irenaeus and Tertullian, for example, insisted that heresies had arisen through the corruption of true Christian teaching by the introduction of pagan Greek thought.[43] Their rhetoric contains both implicit and explicit calls to secure the borders and shore up internal order, to "restore" (or rather to create) purity by exclusion.

We can understand this kind of reasoning by viewing it in terms of antisyncretism. Because determinations of syncretic practices can imply an *evaluation* of the authenticity of a tradition, and because that evaluation can be positive or negative or indeed ambiguous, Rosalind Shaw and Charles Stewart have argued that it is necessary to talk not only about discourses of syncretism but of antisyncretism as well. They define antisyncretism as

the antagonism to religious synthesis shown by agents concerned with the defense of religious boundaries. Anti-syncretism is frequently bound up with the construction of "authenticity," which is in turn often linked to notions of "purity." In Western religious discourses and scholarship in particular, the implicit belief remains that assertions of purity speak out naturally and transcendentally as assertions of authenticity . . . [T]he vocabulary of syncretism adopted is one of pathology, hazard, decline and loss: ominous references to "the problem" or "the dangers of syncretism," to "syncretistic tendencies" and to "forfeiting the essence of Christianity" recur.[44]

An especially pejorative use of the term implies "'inauthenticity' or 'contamination,' the infiltration of a supposedly 'pure' tradition by symbols and meanings seen as belonging to other, incompatible traditions."[45] This observation is extremely helpful in understanding charges of syncretism in the realm of apologetics and polemics. The discourse of antisyncretism functions primarily to define and defend boundaries. In the case of defining heresy, it is part and parcel of the polemicists' attempts to construct and position their brand of Christianity as normative and orthodox.

The main target of the polemicists' antisyncretistic discourse was pagan philosophy.[46] In this rhetoric, syncretism was construed both as the cause of heresy and as a feature that defined it. Examples abound in the work of Irenaeus, Hippolytus, and others, but the classic statement is found in Tertullian, who argued that certain heresies were instigated by the Devil through the influence of Greek philosophy on pure Christian faith.[47] He argued that although ultimately the source of all heresy was the Devil, "it is philosophy that supplies the heresies with their equipment . . . Heretics and philosophers propound the same themes and are caught up in the same discussions . . . From philosophy come those fables and endless genealogies and fruitless questionings, those 'words that creep like a cancer.'"[48] Valentinian errors, Tertullian claimed, came from Plato; Marcion's "better God" from the Stoics; false notions of the soul's death from Epicureans; the denial of the bodily resurrection from all philosophers together; the equality of matter with God to Zeno; the doctrine of a fiery god from Heraclitus; and dialectic, which Tertullian says makes true knowledge impossible, from Aristotle.

To support his claims, Tertullian pointed to the authority of the apostle Paul, who had already warned the Church to be on its guard against philosophy in Colossians 2:8. Paul, Tertullian said, had been to Athens and he knew what he was talking about.[49] In Athens, Paul "had come to grips with the human wisdom which attacks and perverts truth, being itself divided up into its own swarm of heresies by the variety of its mutually antagonistic sects." This observation culminated in Tertullian's famous declaration:

> What has Jerusalem to do with Athens, the Church with the Academy, the Christian with the heretic? Our principles come from the Porch of Solomon, who had himself taught that the Lord is to be sought in simplicity of heart. I have no use for a Stoic or a Platonic or a dialectic Christianity. After Jesus Christ we have no need of speculation, after the Gospel no need of research. When we come to believe, we have no desire to believe anything else; for we begin by believing that there is nothing else which we have to believe.[50]

It has often been pointed out that Tertullian did not really mean what he said, given that his own theology is deeply indebted to his classical Latin education.[51] This statement should be read not as a description of Tertullian's own theological practice but as an antisyncretistic assertion aimed at establishing the purity and authenticity of his creedal formulation of Christian faith. Tertullian consistently framed the issue of cultural amalgamation in terms of protecting the purity of the gospel revelation from contamination by false belief and practice.

Against the "human and demonic doctrines" of his opponents, Tertullian held up the rule of faith founded in the apostolic order as the basis for truth.[52] Because the content of the rule of faith, he argued, goes back to the apostles, truth has a historical basis and chronologically precedes falsehood. "Things of every kind must be classed according to their origin," he argued, for "truth comes first and falsification afterward . . . Our teaching is not later; it is earlier than them all. In this lies the evidence of its truth, which everywhere has the first place."[53] Note the tautology of Tertullian's reasoning: Because the rule of faith is true, it must stem from the apostolic period; because heresy is false, it must be later. As he put it:

> So these heresies may date their beginnings as they choose. The date makes no difference if they are not grounded in the truth. Certainly they did not exist in the apostles' time; they cannot have done. If

they had existed then, they too would have been expressly named, so that they too could be suppressed.[54]

In his short treatise, Tertullian succinctly articulated what became the normative treatment of difference within the history of Christianity. Origins were linked with unity, purity, essence, and truth. Heresies were later deviations caused by outside contamination of the original gospel truth. The story of Christian origin and development was plotted as one of decline, as the increasing encroachment of Satan's attacks against the purity of the Church's apostolic foundations. Tertullian contrasted the unity and simplicity of those foundations with the divisive diversity and confounding complexity of the heretics and their speculations. By the fourth century, this position had become foundational to the master story of Christian origins.[55] It remained largely unchallenged until the work of Walter Bauer in 1934. It is therefore particularly ironic that Tertullian, who so fully articulated the foundational paradigm for combating heresy, was himself later condemned as a heretic.

The polemicists added a powerful dose of rhetorical flourish to their descriptions of the views and behaviors of those whom they opposed. Description, after all, is not opposition unless it is framed in an oppositional discourse. Description only says "we believe and do this" whereas "they believe and do that." Oppositional discourse requires an explicitly rhetorical structure to become refutation. The polemicists developed a strong and enduring antisyncretistic thematics in their refutation of the views of other Christians, and these themes provided the rationale for claiming that "what we believe and do is right" and "what they believe and do is in error." They sought not merely to expose such views but to exclude them and the persons who held them from the groups to which they belonged. The degree to which they succeeded is another matter.

Although all Christians located the pure and original Truth in the revelation of Jesus Christ, they did so in varying ways.[56] The strategy of the polemicists was to insist that the essential truth of orthodox origins was encapsulated in the rule of faith and its purity guaranteed through apostolic succession. All who denied the rule of faith and opposed its male apostolic guarantors were heretics; they did not and rhetorically speaking never truly had belonged to the true Church. Heretics had another ori-

gin—not in Christ but in Satan—and that demonic inspiration exposed
their true identity as surely as the revelation of Christ determined the
Church's true identity. So claimed the rhetorical discourse of orthodoxy
and heresy. Yet we should not lose sight of the fact that this discourse generated considerable ambiguity, since opponents also claimed apostolic
roots and true revelation from Christ.

Ancient philosophical discourse identified truth with origin, purity,
and essence. In this way, ontology and epistemology were discursively
linked. True knowledge was knowledge of the beginning, and above all,
knowledge of the Divine.[57]

History was generally plotted as a story of decline from the moment of
pure origin. What was chronologically later or logically secondary could
be viewed as derivative and inferior, if not deviant. Hence to locate the development of a practice, idea, or phenomenon at some point subsequent
to pristine origins—in effect, to show that it was "new"—was tantamount
to casting suspicion on its value.

Purity, by contrast, was preserved by an uncontaminated genealogical
connection that traced an unbroken line from that pure origin to the present conditions of things. Identity was often articulated in terms of origin,
and common identity in terms of a common origin, whether one emphasized a monogenetic humanity over against beasts, privileged a more narrow ethnicity over against other groups, or deployed some correlative
strategy. How one defined that origin was critical, for it established proper
boundaries and relations and discursively defined the membership, mores,
and traditions of a group. For this reason, origins and genealogy were significant sites of struggle.

The textual remains indicate that all early Christians located the truth
of their beliefs and practices, and established their identity, by appeal to
origin, essence, and purity. As we have seen, Irenaeus and Tertullian elaborated this discourse in their refutation of the beliefs and practices of
other Christians. Their efforts were aimed at excluding unwelcome "others" from the fold, and at maintaining group purity. Irenaeus not only established distinct points of origin for orthodoxy and heresy (God and Satan), but also elaborated a genealogy for each: a unified succession of
apostles and their followers for the true Church; a succession of heretics
and their divided followers for the false perverters. He articulated a strong

theology for orthodox teaching and an even stronger refutation of the varied forms that perversion of the true teaching could take. Both were to have long and influential lives.

## Creating Outsiders: Jews and Pagans

The creation of heresy was only part of the project of Christian identity formation. Christians also had to create categories that distinguished themselves from outsiders.

The resulting categories are so well known as to be almost clichés: Christianity, Judaism, and paganism. Yet the validity of these categories is not as self-evident as their widespread usage might imply. Although Judaism and other religions of the Mediterranean world were around long before Christianity, Christians defined these groups in ways that suited their own project of identity construction, aligning Christianity with truth, Judaism with superseded truth now gone awry, and paganism with error. Here, too, the creation of an orthodox self simultaneously and reciprocally produced new categories of other.

In order to understand how these terms of religious designation and self-designation function in early Christian polemics, we need to view them as positional and provisional categories that do certain limited kinds of intellectual work. No matter how real and long-lasting their effects, the taxonomic classifications of religion function as much to produce distinctions among textual materials and social groups as they do to reflect them. The anthropologist Clifford Geertz has emphasized the constructed character of all ethnic and nationalist identities in the context of contemporary pluralism:

> When you look into them, their solidity dissolves, and you are left not with a catalogue of well-defined entities to be arranged and classified, a Mendelian table of natural kinds, but with a tangle of differences and similarities only half sorted out. What makes Serbs Serbs, Sinhalese Sinhalese, or French Canadians French Canadians, or anybody anybody, is that they and the rest of the world have come, for the moment and to a degree, for certain purposes and in certain contexts, to view them as contrastive to what is around them.[58]

So, too, the religious identity designations of antiquity.

Yet moderns and ancients do not shape religious identity in the same ways or with the same effects. Indeed, what religion is and how religious identity is conceived and shaped differ from place to place, even in the present day.[59] For many U.S. Americans, especially Protestants, religious identity is understood as a matter of individual choice. Christian identity is not supposed to be tied to any particular ethnicity, state, or legal system, although in practice this is not always the case.[60] In the United States, religious freedom is legally protected by distinguishing church and state, a system that tends to relegate religion to the private sphere and regard its presence in public with suspicion. This understanding of religious identity, however, is far from universal. In other places, religious identity sharply intersects ethnicity, law, and often nationalism. It is considered not a matter of individual choice but a natural consequence of birth and culture. In some places, the state may even enforce particular notions of belief and practice as law or state policy. Religion is thus no more stable an entity than identity itself, which is to say it is highly unstable, shifting, and multiform.[61]

Denise Buell has argued persuasively that identity in antiquity was shaped by appeal to constructed categories of gender, class, and ethnicity or race.[62] Ethnicity was determined by factors of place, blood, language, tradition, and way of life. Although Christians did not establish their identity primarily by gender or by class, they did appeal broadly to ethnicity, according to Buell. A few explicitly called themselves a "third race," but many more employed the logic of ethnicity in creating their sense of identity.[63] They would talk about becoming children of Abraham through faith, or belonging to the primordial seed of Seth or the undominated and kingless race. Blood, place, and language were of little use in Christian identity formation, but establishing a shared tradition and way of life was paramount.[64]

Christians were integrally a part of ancient Mediterranean culture and necessarily shaped their identity within it. Their challenge was determining how to distinguish themselves clearly from others and yet at the same time not appear to be a "new" group lacking an ancient and therefore respectable genealogy. In hindsight, we can see that in the early centuries different groups experimented with different strategies in attempting to establish their identity. Although there is some risk of caricature in overly homogenizing these diverse efforts, I would like to characterize some of the patterns and points of struggle that appeared as various Christians defined themselves over and against Jews and pagans.

## Judaism

Judaism, more than any other tradition in antiquity, supplied the resources for Christian reflection about identity, primarily through diverse appropriations of Jewish Scripture. Scripture often provided the means for constructing Christian epic, devising terms of Christian ethnicity, and establishing a respectably ancient past. As a result, forming the proper relationship to Judaism became the most crucial and accordingly the most hotly contested issue for Christian identity formation, as well as a central factor in defining orthodoxy and heresy. Within Christianity, the controversy raged almost solely around how to reinterpret Scripture and Judaism so that they could be used to serve Christian ends.

Judaism as a Christian rhetorical construction is not identical to Judaism as a description of the historical beliefs and practices of Jews, but neither are the two Judaisms entirely distinct since historical reconstructions to some degree constrain ideological constructions and vice versa. Christian rhetoric tended to establish Judaism and Christianity as quite separate and distinguishable entities, but this formulation ignores both the internal multiformity of Judaism and Christianity in antiquity and the multiple ways in which they intersected.[65] It also tends to hide the ways in which Jewish and Christian self-identity construction had mutual and reciprocal effects.[66]

Not all forms of ancient Christianity sought to create and define the same kind of relationship to the Judaism they constructed, however. Indeed, from one perspective, the two were never understood as distinct entities. Paul, for example, argued that Israel was made up of all who were reconciled to God through Christ's death and resurrection. While his intention was to include Gentiles among the people of God along with Jews, his construction of Judaism and his interpretation of Scripture effectively marked off a boundary from other types of Judaism by arguing that it was not necessary for Gentiles who were "grafted" into Israel to practice

---

circumcision or to obey the dietary laws in the face of Christ's death and resurrection.[67]

The Gospel of Matthew took another tack by connecting the Messiah Jesus with Hebrew epic, declaring that Jesus came to fulfill the law and the prophets.[68] Again the lines of contention were drawn around questions that were basically Jewish: What is the true meaning of the law and the prophets? Who is the true Israel? Is Jesus the promised Messiah? Despite conflict over these questions and despite the fact that the Church begins to appear as a distinct entity in Matthew's Gospel, there is still no clear boundary here between Judaism and Christianity. The stress is on continuity expressed as "fulfillment."

Until well into the third and fourth centuries, at least some followers of Jesus continued to attend synagogue, observe the commandments, including dietary laws and circumcision, and even emphasize a common, nonsupersessionist heritage.[69] There is no evidence that such people understood following Jesus to imply a definitive break with Judaism. This situation, however, was unacceptable to those who sought to establish a Christian identity distinct from Judaism.

The author of the early second-century treatise *The Epistle of Barnabas*, who seemed to be facing this kind of blurry-border situation, decried such ill-defined borders, and his opposition led to a sustained attack on Judaism.[70] He exhorted his readers: "take heed to yourselves now, and be not made like some, heaping up your sins and *saying that the covenant is both theirs and ours. It is ours*." He insisted that the Jews had lost the covenant by turning to idols while Moses was on the mountain. He argued that even Moses understood this fact "and cast the two tables out of his hands, and their covenant was broken, in order that the covenant of Jesus the Beloved should be sealed in our hearts in hope of his faith." In this way, the author of *EpBarn* filled his little book with the dichotomizing language of "us and them." To claim to possess Scriptural tradition meant dispossessing others of it. For this author, the covenant truly belonged only to Christians, not to Jews, who "are not worthy to receive it because of their sins."[71] He does not call his group "Christians"; he calls them the true Israel. The intra-Jewish problematics of Paul and the Gospel of Matthew have become vituperative and caricaturing polemics.

The anonymous author of the late first- or early second-century treatise *The Teaching of the Lord to the Twelve Apostles* (popularly called the *Didache*) goes so far as to suggest that difference should be created where none exists. He exhorts: "Let not your fasts be with the hypocrites, for they fast on Mondays and Thursdays, but you fast on Wednesdays and Fridays."[72] *EpBarn* and the *Didache* offer clear attempts, not only to rationalize the Christian appropriation of Jewish Scripture and tradition, but also to create markers of difference and sharpen boundary lines that were otherwise not so visible. In this process they eschewed those Jewish practices that most distinguished Jews from Gentiles: circumcision, dietary laws, Sabbath observance, and synagogue attendance.

Defining Christianity this way, however, led to other difficulties. A seeming contradiction arose when Christians claimed, on the one hand, to be the inheritors of Jewish Scripture and tradition while distinguishing themselves from Jews on the other. In appropriating too much Judaism, so to speak, they would be unable to distinguish themselves clearly; but in appropriating too little, they would lose their claim to the prestigious heritage of Judaism. The second-century theologian Justin Martyr walked this thin line in constructing a Judaism useful for Christian polemics.

Around 160 c.e., Justin wrote a polemical treatise that established the contours of a particularly influential Christian construction of Judaism and framed the rhetorical opposition of Christianity to it. He styled this treatise as a dialogue between himself and a Jew named Trypho, though of course Justin as author composed the lines not only of Justin the character, but of Trypho as well. In his treatise, Trypho mounts some serious criticisms of Christians: They claim to obey God, but they do not follow His commandments to practice circumcision, observe the proper festivals, and so forth. They even break the commandments by eating food offered to idols and saying it does no harm. Trypho goes on to say that Jesus cannot possibly be the true Christ because he was accursed by suffering a dishonorable and inglorious death. Moreover, by making him a God, Christians offend against monotheism. The character of Justin responds at length to each of these charges, countering them with an alternative interpretation of Scripture. He argues that the law was instituted because of sin and hardness of heart.[73] Although initially the law had the positive function of keeping Jews focused on God and protecting them from idolatry, now, because they misunderstood Scripture, killed Christ, and opposed

Christians, God has justly destroyed Jerusalem in order to show them the error of their ways. Those who accept Christ are the true Israel, possess the true covenant, and are a new people.[74]

He offered two proofs to demonstrate that those who follow Christ are right: first, he argued from Scripture that God had rejected Israel and offered universal salvation to the Gentiles; and second, he emphasized the Christian way of life, especially martyrdom.[75] These themes would have long histories in the anti-Judaism of the Christian West, where Christian universalism would be touted over against Jewish particularism, and the Christian ethos valorized as the highest form of moral life.

In constructing clear boundaries and defending Christianity, the authors of Christian polemical treatises reproduced many of the attitudes of the Gentile world toward Judaism. They ascribed those aspects of Jewish thought and practice that were most criticized to Jews and appropriated those aspects that were praised and respected for themselves. Gentiles had widely criticized Jews for their "barbaric" practice of circumcision, their "irrational" food laws, their anthropomorphic figurations of God (for example, walking in the garden in the cool of the day, or acting in jealousy and wrath), but especially for their exclusivism in rejecting the validity or even the existence of other gods.[76] All of these traits the polemicists attributed to Jews. By contrast, Jewish monotheism and ethics were widely praised in the ancient world. Moses was accepted as a wise law-giver and the prophets as voices of divine justice and revelation. Most especially, Judaism was accepted as an ancient tradition, and therefore was to be honored and respected. The polemicists attributed all these positive traits to true Christianity.

Their main line of argument was the claim that they alone properly understood the ancient Scriptures. The problem with this argument was that various Christians interpreted the Scriptures quite differently—an unacceptable situation given the apologetic and polemical importance of their exclusive claim to Scripture. Indeed, a single, true interpretation of Scripture was vital to the polemics of Christian theologians like Justin insofar as constructing a usable Judaism was rhetorically intertwined with the discourse of orthodoxy and heresy. The charge of "Judaizing" could be used not only to distinguish Christians from Jews, but also to identify heretics.

In her discussion of Ignatius, the bishop of Antioch, who was martyred in Rome sometime before 117 C.E., Joan Taylor argues that Christians who

> actively campaigned among the Christian community for a return to Jewish praxis, or maintenance of Jewish praxis . . . were dangerous not because they themselves practice Judaism, but because they pull away from episcopal authority and cause division by refusing to share table-fellowship with Gentiles.[77]

For Ignatius, the issue at stake was Christian unity. Defining Judaism was therefore not only a matter of drawing sharp lines between Christianity and Judaism; it also involved identifying heretics within. Ignatius of Antioch called such people "plausible wolves" and "poisonous weeds."[78] They were "plausible" precisely because they relied on Scripture to support their views.

When we look at early Christian interpretation of Scripture, a remarkable plurality of approaches and positions comes into view. Works like the *Gospel of Mary* or the *Gospel of Truth* built their theologies and Christologies with hardly any reference to Jewish Scripture at all. In contrast, the author of *EpBarn* sharply distinguished between Christian and Jewish interpretation of Scripture by insisting that the Jews misunderstood Scripture by reading it literally. For Barnabas, only the revelation of Christ provided the key to the true, spiritual meaning of Scripture through allegorical and typological interpretation. True fasting, for example, meant good deeds, but the Jews misunderstood Moses "owing to the lust of their flesh."[79] Although Barnabas accepts the truth and authority of Jewish Scripture, he argues that the true meaning of Moses and the prophets should lead, not only to true spiritual and moral practice, but also to seeing the necessity that Christ came in the flesh and died "that we should be sanctified by the remission of sin, that is, by his sprinkled blood."[80] He claimed that Scripture properly interpreted led to proper belief and practice, but incorrect (literal) interpretation led to sin and damnation. The line was drawn.

The problem with the so-called heretics, from the polemicists' point of view, was that they strayed to one side or the other of this narrow line, acting too much like Jews or not giving Scripture enough authority. For example, Marcion, a second-century Christian from Pontus in Asia Minor, was thought to be guilty of the latter. He agreed that a literal interpretation of Scripture led to an inadequate understanding of God's salvation, but whereas the author of *EpBarn* and others were content to invent or at least provide allegorical and typological interpretations to reconcile their beliefs with the literal sense of Scripture, Marcion read the Jewish Scriptures almost exclusively in a literal manner. When he did, it seemed to him that these writings were the work of an inferior creator God. Jesus and Paul had proclaimed the true higher God of Christianity, but their work had been perverted by those who mistook the creator God for this true God. Both Jews and misled Christians were the false followers of this lesser deity. So Marcion set out to reestablish the true message of Jesus by restoring the original, pure text of the Lukan gospel and Paul that had been contaminated with Judaizing interpolations. Again, the battle lines were drawn around the proper interpretation of Scripture, but in a radically different way.

Sethian Gnostics took a position toward Jewish literature akin to that of Marcion, though their tactic was not to expurgate but to retell the stories of Scripture to get them right.[81] Works like *ApJohn* or *The Hypostasis of Archons* appropriated select portions of Jewish Scriptures and retold them with novel twists, supposedly to bring out the real truth about the lower creator God and his role in the drama of salvation. In these retellings, Eve is not the primal sinner but the source of Adam's spiritual enlightenment. The knowledge of good and evil allows Adam and Eve to perceive that the creator of the world is but a jealous and vengeful pretender, not the true Deity who rules the transcendent realm of goodness and light.

The second-century Valentinian theologian Ptolemy took a middle road. In his *Epistle to Flora,* he argued that Scripture mixed together materials from three different sources—the true God, Moses, and the elders of the people—and he subsequently offered three divisions of Scripture:

- pure but imperfect legislation, such as the ten commandments, which the Savior came to fulfill;
- truth interwoven with the inferior and the unjust, which the Savior came to abolish;

- symbolic and allegorical materials, whose referent the Savior changed from the perceptible to the spiritual.[82]

For example, Jesus' teaching in Matthew 19.3–9 showed that the pure leg-islation from God forbade divorce, but Moses allowed divorce in cases of adultery as a concession to human weakness. The elders of the people also changed God's commandments, as Jesus pointed out in Matthew 15.4–9 concerning the commandment to honor one's father and mother. Simi-larly, the Savior showed that such teaching as "an eye for an eye" aimed at justice in that it held that the wicked should be punished, but it failed to achieve true justice because it demanded that another crime be commit-ted. Jesus corrected this mixed legislature by commanding people "to turn the other cheek" (Matthew 5:38–39). Finally, the Savior showed the true meaning of the commandments by interpreting them allegorically. True sacrifices and offerings were praise of God and good deeds. The Sabbath was meant to constrain people not from performing good deeds but from performing wicked acts.

According to Ptolemy, the Savior's teachings show that the God who made the universe and established the law is neither good nor evil but merely just. Above is a higher God who is completely good; the Savior re-veals this true God. Proper interpretation of Scripture again provided the key to the truth and was the field on which intra-Christian theological battles were waged.

It should be emphasized that Marcion, the author of *ApJohn,* and Ptol-emy did not reject Jewish Scriptures entirely; they elaborated their theolo-gies with extensive reference to it, but they privileged the revelation of the Savior and used it to critique Scripture. Like other Christians, they re-jected Jewish beliefs and practices that were widely denigrated in the Ro-man world, such as circumcision, animal sacrifice, and anthropomorphic portrayals of God. Unlike other Christians, however, they did not mind relinquishing the authority of Scripture in the process.

Despite the significant variations in how Christians read and valued Scripture, it is possible to discern a similar hermeneutical process at work, which involved three simultaneous steps: appropriation, negation, and erasure. Christians claimed that they alone could properly interpret Scrip-ture. They negated the claim of the Jews to their own scriptures by reading them differently, even counter to how (other) Jewish groups would read them.[83] They erased the processes of this appropriation by claiming that the Christian reading was in fact the ancient and original truth; the Jews had never understood the true meaning of their own Scripture. It is interesting to note, however, that when a purportedly heretical work employs these same strategic steps, both ancient polemicists and modern church historians make the same charge—impiety. They are best understood, however, as yet another exercise in the hermeneutical battle for control of this prestigious Scripture.

The appropriation of Jewish scriptures by Christians of all types did not go uncontested. Jews understandably opposed the various forms of Christian innovation as simply wrong and impious. Others, such as the Greek philosopher Celsus, tended to agree, charging Christians with innovation and impiety. Moreover, charges of improper interpretation of Scripture and impiety were flying within Christianity as well. Paul accused Peter and others of hypocrisy for following Jewish practices and misunderstanding Scripture. *EpBarn* warned against those who said that "the covenant is both ours and theirs." Irenaeus tells us that some so-called heretics charged the apostles with Judaizing! These heretics, he noted with astonishment, actually claimed that the apostles were influenced by the Jews because they taught people to worship the lower world creator rather than the true transcendent Father; in turning Gentiles away from the error of polytheism, the apostles had simply given them a new error![84]

A good example of such accusations is now available from the Nag Hammadi find. *The Testimony of Truth* charges that "many have sought after the truth and have not been able to find it; because there has taken hold of them [the] old leaven of the Pharisees and the scribes [of] the Law."[85] This charge that the apostles mistook the world creator for the True God is framed as a misreading of Genesis. But from our perspective, it is an example of identity politics operating through competing claims to hermeneutic truth; the battle over who could correctly interpret Scripture drew lines not only between Christians and Jews but among Christians as well. The result was division within Christianity, not to mention considerable violence to Judaism and to Jewish-Christian relations through the forcible creation of difference and the erasure of common ground.

## Paganism

How does one proceed when the goal is to deny continuity and yet appropriate the traditions of others? This is the problem Christian antisyncretistic discourse faced in defining itself in terms of Mediterranean traditions other than Judaism.

Such traditions are often collectively referred to by modern scholars as paganism. "Pagan" was a term of colloquial usage whose first written record can be found in Christian inscriptions from the fourth century. There pagan referred to persons who had not been baptized, in short, to non-Christians. Classical historians invented the derivative, "paganism," primarily to describe the cultic aspects of ancient Mediterranean religious practices. The term covers a wide geographical area and an enormous diversity of beliefs, practices, and material goods (temples, cultic implements, statuary, and so forth). If anything, paganism encompasses phenomena much more varied than either Judaism or Christianity.[86]

If the term "pagan" was used only colloquially and appeared relatively late (fourth century), how did Christians refer to pagans before that time? Their language varies. Conceptually, paganism is a Christian construct in which Christians sometimes identified themselves as a "third race."[87] Jew and Christian were the constants in the triad; the third party varied, depending on who was speaking or who was being addressed. The designation of Christian was sometimes added to the Jewish terminology of Jew and Gentile ("the heathens" and "the nations," respectively), hence, "Jew, Gentile, Christian." Or merging with Greek terminology ("Greek and barbarian"), it could result in the triad of "Greek, Jew, Christian," which Adolf von Harnack took to be "the church's basal conception of history."[88] Moreover, the terminology could alternatively be "Roman, Jew, Christian." In this way, though the designation for pagans could shift rhetorically, it always referred to anyone who was not Jewish or Christian. It was a general category, a shorthand term for "others."[89]

From the household codes to *logos* theology, examples of how Christians were fully a part of ancient Mediterranean society and culture are sufficiently numerous and well known that they need not be rehearsed here.[90] And while various hybridizing practices were usually accompanied by overt antisyncretistic discourse, in practice the polemicists' attitudes were varied, ranging from unequivocal rejection to ambiguity and even ambivalence.[91] Still, for the sake of brevity we can characterize three main strategies used to set the boundaries between Christians and pagans: outright rejection, hierarchical subordination, and transformation (*spolatio*).

Christians' dominant position on Greco-Roman religions was in fact quite unambiguous. With regard to worship of other gods, the attitude was one of complete rejection: no compromise was to be made with any form of activity that could be construed as participation in the worship of other gods, especially if it involved sacrifice. Christians' attitude is adamantly and vociferously antisyncretistic. This position posed few if any problems for Christian self-definition; indeed, it was Christians' refusal to participate in the civic and imperial religious activities of their day that most clearly set them apart from their fellows and most powerfully served to create clear boundaries of Christian identity.

At the same time, the polemicists recognized that there were a number of ineradicable similarities between certain elements of Christian theology and Greco-Roman philosophy. As with discourses of heresy and Judaism, the more intractable problem proved to be similarity, not difference. Thus when pagan philosophical and moral elements accorded with Christian teaching, the strategy was to treat them positively under the rubric of natural theology or *preparatio evangelica*.[92] Christian theologians admitted that pagan philosophy sometimes disclosed truth, albeit in a partial and veiled way; Christianity, however, was superior in that it possessed the full truth through revelation.[93] This strategy accommodated similarity, but only under the guise of preeminence. This hierarchical subordination veiled the implications that similarity and syncretism might be compromising Christian purity and claims to uniqueness. As we will see in the following chapters, in the nineteenth and twentieth centuries this strategy was reworked under the new theories of social evolution or unilinear typology, in which Christianity appeared as the "most developed" form of religion.[94]

Ancient examples of this strategy may be found in Athenagoras' apologetic treatise addressed to the emperors Marcus Aurelius and Lucius Aurelius Commodus, titled *A Plea Regarding Christians*. Athenagoras' purpose was to refute charges that Christians were atheists who engaged in incest and cannibalism. He took two related tacks. The first was to demonstrate that Christian teaching agreed with but surpassed the highest convictions of the pagans regarding proper philosophical views of God and standards of moral conduct. The second was an open attack on paganism at some of its most intellectually vulnerable points: the crude portrayal of the gods' immoral behavior, the gods' desire for sacrifice, and the worship of images. Athenagoras' defense used many of the same arguments that the polemicists were using against their fellow Christians: they had missed the true God and been led into immoral and impious conduct under the influence of demons; their conflicting doctrines further demonstrated that the philosophers had missed the whole truth. Athenagoras' explicit acknowledgment of similarities to the most prestigious intellectual and moral traditions of paganism served apologetic purposes.[95] But such acknowledgment was inevitably accompanied by the affirmation of Christian preeminence, even to the very best of Greek and Roman philosophical traditions.

Moreover, borrowing of any kind was explicitly denied. For example, opponents of Christianity charged that any similarities between their views and those of Christians were the result of defective imitations by Christians of their own more ancient religious practices and philosophical beliefs. In defense, Athenagoras argued that while some poets and philosophers may have had a limited "sympathy with the divine spirit," Christian prophets had not learned from them, but had received their teaching directly from God:

> Here as elsewhere the poets and philosophers have proceeded by conjecture. They were driven each by his own soul and through a sympathy with the divine spirit to see if it were possible to find out and to comprehend the truth. They were able, indeed, to get some notions of reality, but not to find it, since they did not deign to learn about God from God, but each one from himself. For this reason they taught conflicting doctrines about God, matter, forms, and the world. We, on the contrary, as witnesses of what we think and believe, have prophets who have spoken by the divine Spirit about God and the things of God.[96]

Other Christian apologists countered the charge of inept borrowing by tracing Christianity's origins back to creation itself, and by charging that

demons had imitated Christian rites in order to discredit Christian practice.[97] Christian beliefs and practices were touted as the true model of
which pagan practices were but a distorted copy. This argument turned
the tables on the apparent chronological priority of Greco-Roman philosophy and religion. In this way, even explicit acknowledgment of similarity
could be fully embedded in antisyncretistic discourse that denied borrowing of any kind.

A third but less common strategy was that of *spolatio.* The term is taken
from Origen's apologetic interpretation of Exodus 12:35–36, where the Israelites despoil their neighbors as they depart from Egypt. Origen has provided a classic Christian reading of this text as a cautionary story: any appropriation of the goods of others should be *transformed* by dedication to
God, lest those goods become a cause for idolatry. After all, the spoils
taken by the Israelites were meant to build the tabernacle of God, not the
golden calf. Wendy Helleman summarizes the point:

> Critical appropriation . . . allows for a positive model of transforma-
> tion of cultural treasures as these are assimilated *into* a Christian po-
> sition. On the other hand it is also possible that Christians adapt
> their own positions *to* such gifts; this may result in idolatry or other
> forms of contamination.[98]

The rationalization of *spolatio* exposes all the ambiguity of early Christian
discourse about the appropriation of Greco-Roman materials: they have
the potential to be transformed for Christian use, but they also represent
real dangers because of their potential to contaminate Christianity. The
rhetoric of this position accounted for similarity and appropriation not as
borrowing but as transformation. Moreover, by designating such appropriation as "spoils" or "gifts," the language of *spolatio* masked the political
dynamics of cultural synthesis—that is, the struggle over the right to say
who "owns" a tradition. After all, one group's "spoils" can be another
group's "theft." It also masks the aims of antisyncretistic discourse to introduce new distinctions and divisions into previously unmarked (or differently marked) social territory.

As history demonstrates, not only did various Christians mark the
boundaries between themselves and others differently in practice, but the
boundaries had to be constantly renegotiated, and indeed are still under

negotiation.[99] Even though the polemicists recognized and accepted some appropriations under certain conditions, it is clear that the predisposition of their discourse is antisyncretistic in tone and implication. Having constructed paganism explicitly as a category for exclusion, normative Christianity could not tolerate admitting that it had appropriated much from pagan thought and practice. The problem for Christian self-definition was not difference but similarity; not distance but proximity.

## Heresy in the Modern Period

In the last century, scholars of Gnosticism have struggled to come to terms with the strategies bequeathed by the polemicists, while charting both subtle and not-so-subtle shifts in modern discourses. They have also debated how to incorporate new source materials into the study of ancient Mediterranean religion.

The chapters that follow will show that many elements of the polemicists' discourse have been thoroughly interwoven in twentieth-century scholarship's discussions of Gnosticism. But that is hardly surprising. It was, after all, the polemicists who provided almost all of our information until recently. The situation has changed dramatically with the discovery of new texts, occurring in the wake of European colonialism. But the discourses in which the study of Gnosticism have been embedded are changing much more slowly. Scholars are only gradually coming to realize the inadequacy of older models and methods, and beginning to formulate new approaches.

Despite important shifts, the polemicists have reigned supreme for most of the twentieth century; scholars have tended to evaluate Gnosticism negatively, and on nearly the same grounds as the polemicists did heresy.[100] Gnosticism has been described as theologically inferior and ethically flawed; as an artificial and syncretic parasite; as an individualistic, nihilistic, and escapist religion incapable of forming any kind of true moral community. Scholars have included an increasingly wide range of diverse materials under the category of Gnosticism, and yet they have chafed at the problem of defining its essential characteristics. But above all, we have been mistakenly preoccupied with determining its origin and tracing its genealogical relation to orthodox Christianity because we have unwittingly reified a rhetorical category into a historical entity.

The discoveries in Egypt have yielded ancient texts apparently written by the kinds of Christians the polemicists were denouncing. Scholars now have new opportunities to assess the polemicists' portraits of their opponents. The polemicists did not directly falsify these portrayals, but they did focus on those aspects of their opponents' beliefs that were most unappealing or differed most sharply from their own. It seems that they took their rivals so seriously and denounced them so emphatically precisely because their views were in many respects so similar to the polemicists' own.

Another problem is that the discourse of orthodoxy and heresy created a rhetoric that tended to bifurcate and polarize early Christianity by implying that it offered only two opposing alternatives, orthodoxy and heresy; but scholars now recognize that this characterization is a vast oversimplification. For example, literary works from the Nag Hammadi finds, such as *The Apocalypse of Peter* and *The Testimony of Truth,* make it clear that, despite the polemicists' contention that true Christians were unified against the diverse heresies, charges of heresy were flying in multiple directions by the third century. Indeed, the polemicists would surely have regarded the radically docetic and ascetic teachings of *TestTruth* as archheretical and yoked its author to the Valentinians and other such "heretics." The author of *TestTruth,* however, lumps together the teachings of both the heresiologists and the Valentinians as of one and the same ilk. He considers both to be utterly wrongheaded about the teachings of Christ and the nature of salvation, given that they both allowed marriage, a practice contrary to the author's belief that Christ came "to end the dominion of carnal procreation." This example hints at the complexity of the situation in the first few centuries of Christianity, illustrating that accusations were flying not merely between two sets of opponents, but in multiple directions and configurations. Possibly the most serious disadvantage to modern scholars' appropriation of the discourse of orthodoxy and heresy, however, lies in the ways in which similarity and difference are noted and treated. The discourse of orthodoxy and heresy has been employed to construe the relationship of Gnosticism to Christianity almost solely in terms of difference, and the relationship of widely varying so-called Gnostic materials to each other almost solely in terms of similarity. This discourse has almost impossibly obscured and confused the historical study of the ancient materials and their relationships, whether classified as heretical or orthodox, Gnostic or Christian.

When modern historians adopt the strategies as well as the content of the polemicists' construction of heresy to define Gnosticism, they are not just reproducing the heresy of the polemicists; they are themselves propagating the politics of orthodoxy and heresy. We should therefore not be surprised to observe twentieth-century historians employing the category of Gnosticism to establish the bounds of normative Christianity— whether in Protestant anti-Catholic polemic, intra-Protestant debate, or the colonial politics of Orientalism. As I have argued, specialists in Gnostic studies now clearly recognize the problems in defining Gnosticism, but the ways in which the ancient discourses about heresy are threaded through contemporary historiography is much less clear.[101]

The language, themes, and strategies of orthodoxy and heresy proved to be a powerful discourse, persisting in various forms up to our own day. My purpose in this book is to show how twentieth-century scholarship on Gnosticism has simultaneously reinscribed, elaborated, and deviated from this discourse. The first revisionary step was the one that has perhaps had the greatest effect: by substituting the term "Gnosticism" for one type of heresy, Henry More and those who followed him established this theme as a perennial topic of church history.

The following chapters selectively survey some cases in which the older discourses of orthodoxy and heresy are still operating in twentieth-century scholarship, as well as some of the shifts in the discourse brought about by changing historical conditions, the intersection with alternative discourses, and discoveries of new textual evidence. This discussion is also meant to serve as an occasion for reflexive analysis of the way scholarly practices and historical-intellectual positions affect the questions we bring to these materials, how those questions are framed, and how we might approach the materials from a fresh angle.

# 3

## Adolf von Harnack and the
## Essence of Christianity

### Gnosticism as the "Acute Hellenization of Christianity"

There can be no more intriguing a place to begin the discussion of contemporary attempts to define Gnosticism than with the work of the radical Protestant church historian Adolf von Harnack. Writing in Germany at the threshold of the twentieth century, Harnack was a scholar of staggering erudition who produced an impressive range of enduring works in church history and theology.

In *Dogmengeschichte* (1885), his multivolume work on the history of Christian thought, Harnack famously described Gnosticism as "the acute Hellenization of Christianity." By this characterization he meant that Gnosticism "was ruled in the main by the Greek spirit and determined by the interests and doctrines of the Greek philosophy of religion."[1] It would seem, then, that Harnack was taking the same position as Tertullian, claiming that heresy was an "acute" condition resulting from the alien influence of Greek thought on Christianity.[2] Yet despite the basic and crucial similarity, the demands of German historiography and Protestant apologetics led Harnack in another direction. What he meant by Hellenization was quite different from anything Tertullian imagined when he declared: "It is philosophy that supplies the heresies with their equipment . . . Heretics and philosophers perpend the same themes and are caught up in the same discussions."[3] Harnack meant something at once much broader in influence, more precise in effect, and more complex in its interactions with Christianity. The terseness of his sound-bite formula belies

its grandiloquence, for the enormous burden it bears is nothing less than
the key to the whole development of Christianity.

For Harnack, the term "Hellenization" described the inescapable background of all intellectual and cultural life in the Eastern Mediterranean.
The conquests of Alexander had set in motion a synthesis with Greek
(Hellenic) culture so pervasive that nothing was left entirely untouched
in the territories he conquered. As a result, Harnack could not acknowledge that the distinction between Athens and Jerusalem, between Greek
thought and the Gospel, was as simple as Tertullian's rhetoric would have
it. In his opinion, Christianity arose in "the general spiritual atmosphere
created by Hellenism." The New Testament documents could not be understood apart from that background:

> There is indeed no single writing of the New Testament which does
> not betray the influence of the mode of thought and general condi-
> tions of the culture of the time which resulted from the Hellenising
> of the East: even the use of the Greek translation of the Old Testa-
> ment attests this fact. Nay, we may go further, and say that the Gos-
> pel itself is historically unintelligible, so long as we compare it with
> an exclusive Judaism as yet unaffected by any foreign influence.[4]

How, then, could Harnack *also* write: "But it is just as clear that specifically Hellenic ideas form the presuppositions neither for the Gospel itself, nor for the most important New Testament writings"?[5] Or later in his
lectures on the essence of Christianity: "We cannot say that the earliest
Christian writings, let alone the Gospel, show to any considerable extent,
the presence of a Greek element."[6] How could he make such apparently
contradictory claims?

The answer lies in his understanding of Christianity and its historical
development. For Harnack, the essence of Christianity is transhistorical;
none of the forms that it takes in history is identical with the Gospel itself or even necessary to it. Therefore, because Harnack conceived of
Hellenization as only the background of the Gospel, as the mere scenery
against which the drama is set, he could also affirm the fundamentally
non-Greek character of the Gospel without feeling any contradiction.[7]

What, then, is "the essence of Christianity"? Harnack answers this question with great vigor in *Das Wesen des Christentums* [What Is Christianity?"]. As religion, he says, Christianity consists in a life lived in the presence of God: "The Christian religion is something simple and sublime; it means one thing and one thing only: Eternal life in the midst of time, by the strength and under the eyes of God."[8] According to Harnack, this life is characterized by inwardness and enthusiasm, and it is expressed in the teachings of Jesus, which he calls simply "the Gospel." He gave a compendious summary of the Gospel in three points:

> Firstly, the kingdom of God and its coming.
> Secondly, God the Father and the infinite value of the human soul.
> Thirdly, the higher righteousness and the commandment of love.[9]

In determining these essential elements of the Gospel, Harnack insisted that Christians must distinguish between "what is traditional and what is peculiar, between kernel and husk" in order to grasp "the deeper knowledge that (Jesus) spoke and taught."[10] A good example of Harnack's method in practice is his treatment of Jesus' teaching about the coming of the kingdom of God, understood in Harnack's day to be the core of Jesus' message.[11] He writes:

> There can be no doubt about the fact that the idea of the two kingdoms, of God and of the devil, and their conflicts, and of that last conflict at some future time when the devil, long since cast out of heaven, will be also defeated on earth, was an idea which Jesus simply shared with his contemporaries. He did not start it, but he grew up in it and he retained it. The other view, however, that the kingdom of God "cometh not with observation," that it is already here, was his own . . . If anyone wants to know what the kingdom of God and the coming of it meant in Jesus' message, he must read and study his parables. He will then see what it is that is meant. The kingdom of God comes by coming to the individual, by entering into his soul and laying hold of it. True the kingdom of God is the rule of God; but it is the rule of the holy God in the hearts of individuals; *it is God himself in his power.* From this point of view every-

thing that is dramatic in the external and historical sense has van-
ished; and gone, too, are all the external hopes for the future. Take
whatever parable you will, the parable of the sower, of the pearl of
great price, of the treasure buried in the field—the word of God,
God himself, is the kingdom. It is not a question of angels and devils, thrones and principalities, but of God and the soul, the soul and
its God.[12]

Note the method in Harnack's passion: he begins by separating the ideas
of the times (the "traditional") from the message that is distinctive to Jesus
("the peculiar") in order to distinguish the inner meaning of the teaching
(the "kernel") from its external form (the "husk"). As a result, Harnack rejects any interpretation of kingdom in terms of the apocalyptic eschatology of "Late Judaism" in favor of spiritualizing the kingdom as the interior relation of the soul to God.[13]

   This method allowed Harnack to insist repeatedly, not only that the essence of Christianity is neither Greek nor Jewish, but also that it is not
historically bound. He went so far as to insist that "none of the forms in
which (the Gospel) assumed intellectual and social expression—not even
the earliest—can be regarded as possessing a classical and permanent character."[14] Indeed, it is precisely because the Gospel is not tied to any particular form of expression that it continues to signify.[15]

   In the face of this powerful transhistorical essence, Harnack could
hardly concede to any historical phenomenon, including Hellenism, a determinative influence on the Gospel. Hence he could claim paradoxically
both that the New Testament documents cannot be understood apart
from Hellenization, and that Hellenization is not present to any great extent in the Gospel the New Testament proclaims. The first statement concerns the husk; the second, the essence.

   The meaning of Hellenization was not yet exhausted, however. Indeed,
for Harnack, locating the essence of Christianity was only part of the task,
however crucial; it remained to lay bare the history of its "husk." The
most significant event in that history was Hellenization.

   The early Christians, Harnack wrote, breathed deeply from the spirit of
the Old Testament psalms and prophets, as well as from "Late Judaism."
Following the conquests of Alexander, this Judaism imbibed some of

the Greek spirit, allowing "Judaism to free itself from its limitations and start upon its development into a religion for the world."[16] Despite this breath of Greek universalism in Judaism, Harnack claimed, in the second century Christianity left the "particularism" of Judaism behind in order to embrace more fully Greek thought as a path to universalism. Here Harnack reflected the limited perceptions and prejudices of his day, which contrasted the strategic communalism of Judaism with the "classical" universalizing impulses of Greece and Rome that undergirded European expansionism.[17] He specifically associated the universal claims of Hellenization with the realization of the universal message and mission of the Gospel.[18] As he put it:

> Even had this youthful religion not severed the tie which bound it to Judaism, it would have been inevitably affected by the spirit and the civilization of that Graeco-Roman world on whose soil it was permanently settled. But to what a much greater extent was it exposed to the influence of this spirit after being sharply severed from the Jewish religion and the Jewish nation. It hovered bodiless over the earth like a being of the air; bodiless and seeking a body. The spirit, no doubt, makes to itself its own body, but it does so by assimilating what is around it. The influx of Hellenism, of the Greek spirit, and the union of the Gospel with it, form the greatest fact in the history of the Church in the second century, and when the fact was once established as a foundation it continued through the following centuries.[19]

For Harnack, a study of Hellenism was necessary to understand the history of Christian dogma but not the essence of Christianity.[20]

Harnack did not, however, unequivocally associate Hellenization with progress; for the story of Christianity in its first 120 years, he wrote, was one in which "*the original enthusiasm,* in the large sense of the word, *evaporates,* and the religion of law and form at once arises." At the heart of Harnack's personal belief was a piety that rejected all religion in which "doctrines, regulations, ordinances, and forms of public worship" were "treated as the thing itself." He railed against changes in Christianity in which the living faith seems to be transformed into a creed to be believed; devotion to Christ, into Christology; the ardent hope for the coming of "the kingdom," into a doctrine of immortality and deification; prophecy, into technical exegesis and theological learning; the ministers of the Spirit, into clerics; the brothers, into laymen in a state of tutelage; miracles and miraculous cures disappear altogether, or else are priestly devices; fervent prayers become solemn hymns and litanies; the "Spirit" becomes law and compulsion.[21]

This transformation, or rather this deformation, was in Harnack's view only the beginning, for Hellenism transformed the Gospel into dogma: "Dogma in its conception and development is a work of the Greek spirit on the soil of the Gospel." Dogma, Harnack argued, stood between Christianity as a living experience and Christianity as a superstition tied to cult, sacraments, ceremony, and obedience.[22]

This intellectualizing "influence of Hellenism on Christianity" took place in three stages, according to Harnack. The first stage, which "went straight to the centre" of the new religion, occurred in the early second century, with the appropriation of Greek philosophy, but without any trace of Greek myth or religious practice. Harnack warmly and effusively welcomed it:

Who can deny that elements here came together which stood in elective affinity? So much depth and delicacy of feeling, so much earnestness and dignity, and—above all—so strong a *monotheistic* piety were displayed in the religious ethics of the Greeks, acquired as it had been by hard toil on the basis of inner experience and metaphysical speculation, that the Christian religion could not pass this treasure by with indifference.[23]

In the early third century, however, Christianity entered a second stage through the appropriation of the Greek mysteries and other aspects of Greek civilization. Only a century later, in its third stage, polytheism and mythology entered the Church with the rise of "worship of the saints."[24] Thus as positive as the initial influence of Hellenization was, Harnack thought its continued influence led to the degeneration of Christianity into an empty religion of form and polytheistic saint worship.

Harnack's view of the complexity of Hellenization ought to make us cautious about his characterization of the essence of Christianity as a "bodiless spirit," capable of embodiment in any number of different cultural forms. That image would seem to imply that Christianity could take on new styles of dress without being itself touched or affected in any essential way. But such a perspective would not accord with the intricacy of what he is proposing. William Rowe's thoughtful formulation is of great help in clarifying the matter:

> What at first appears to be nothing more than the transmigration of the Christian spirit to another body is really its alliance with another spirit. Hellenization suddenly seems much more dangerous than transmigration, for transmigration is a process in which we can imagine—to the extent that we can imagine transmigration—a spirit retaining its integral and personal identity while simply taking up residence at a new bodily address. What we called transmigration now looks more like the dangerous arrangement of parasitism in which one life form attaches itself to another, and the latter functions as the "host" of the former. The parasite appends itself to its host in such a way that the host becomes partly a new environment for the parasite, partly an extension of the parasite's bodily organism, and partly the very principle of the parasite's life. The parasite "lives" off its host's body; and this is closer to Harnack's concept of Hellenization.[25]

Hellenization was therefore not mere window-dressing; the very survival of Christianity was at stake. It was possible, Harnack believed, for Hellenism to have entirely overwhelmed the Gospel. Fortunately enough, from his perspective, this did not happen. But the early centuries were dangerous times. The Greek spirit was a powerful force that had already overwhelmed the ancient cultures of the East. Now, Harnack said, this spirit was drawn to Christianity.[26] At this point Gnosticism enters into the story:

The epoch-making significance of Gnosticism for the history of dogma must not be sought chiefly in the particular doctrines, but rather in the whole way in which Christianity is here conceived and transformed. The decisive thing is the conversion of the Gospel into a doctrine, into an absolute philosophy of religion, the transforming of the *disiplina Evangelii* into an asceticism based on a dualistic conception, and into a practice of mysteries.[27]

On the basis of descriptions given by the polemicists, Harnack listed eleven items that he suggested constituted the *regula fidei* of Gnosticism.[28] They may be summarized as follows:

1. Gnostic thought distinguished between the supreme God and the creator, and hence between redemption and creation.
2. The supreme God was separated from the God of the Old Testament, and hence at least some parts of it could no longer be accepted as revelation of the supreme God; the Old Testament did, however, give an essentially accurate portrait of the world creator.[29]
3. Matter was considered to be independent and eternal.
4. The created world was conceptualized either as the product of an evil being or intermediary acting out of hostility to the supreme God, or as a "fall of humanity."
5. Evil was understood as a physical force, inherent in matter.
6. The absoluteness of God was dispersed in Aeons ("real powers and heavenly persons").
7. Christ revealed a previously unknown God.
8. Gnostic Christology distinguished Jesus in his human appearance from the heavenly Aeon of Christ, resulting in the belief that (a) Jesus was only a human being because he and Christ were entirely unrelated; *or* (b) Jesus' soul was formed in heaven and only appeared to pass through Mary's womb; *or* (c) Jesus' earthly appearance was a mere phantasm. The saving action of Christ was to reunite to God everything that had been severed from Him by an unnatural connection to matter.
9. Humans were divided into two or three classes, depending on whether they possessed spirit and soul or only a material nature.

Only the spiritual were "capable of Gnosis and the divine life . . . in virtue of their constitution" (that is, the spiritual were saved by nature).

10. Christian eschatology, including the second coming, the resurrection of the body, and the final judgment, was rejected entirely. Instead, Gnostics thought the spiritual person enjoyed immortality here and now, while waiting for future delivery from the sensuous world and entrance into heaven.

11. As an addendum, Harnack noted that Gnostic ethics were based on a contrast between the "sensuous and spiritual elements of human nature," and therefore Gnostics were capable of only two kinds of practice: strict asceticism or libertinism.

Although Harnack identified Gnosticism proper with the "great systems of Basilides and Valentinus," he offered a very complex picture of Gnostic origins. Before the development of these systems, he envisioned preliminary stages in which a number of "sects, schools, and undertakings," only partially related to Gnosticism, were grouped together with it. All of these he called "heresy" and "Gnosticism." Although Harnack fully recognized the heterogeneity of these classifications, he argued that grouping such a motley crowd together was justified "if we will understand by them nothing else than the world taken into Christianity all the manifold formations which resulted from the first contact of the new religion with the society into which it entered."[30]

The character of this world, Harnack asserted, was syncretistic. Although Gnosticism "was ruled in the main by the Greek spirit, and determined by the interests and doctrines of the Greek philosophy of religion," Hellenism had already "assumed a syncretistic character."[31] Thus, despite the appearance that Gnosticism brought Christianity into contact with Oriental cults and Asiatic mythologoumena, these were already part of the syncretistic character of Greek philosophy. Included in this amalgam were Assyrian and Babylonian religious philosophy and myth, popular Greek religion, the mysteries, astrology, and so on, all of which had spread across Syria and Palestine before Christianity was born. According to Harnack, this syncretism had affected even Judaism, leading to a lessening of Old Testament authority. Under the influence of the Gospel, some like Simon

Magus attempted to establish new religions; others infiltrated already established Christian communities. But in Harnack's view, the primary impetus for the rise of Gnostic Christianity was the disparaging interpretation of the Old Testament that arose by merging the Gospel with Greek
philosophical ideas. As Harnack put it:

> There appeared, about the transition of the first century to the sec-
> ond, a series of teachers who, under the impression of the Gospel,
> sought to make the Old Testament capable of furthering the ten-
> dency to a universal religion, not by allegorical interpretation, but by
> a sifting criticism . . . They conceived the creator of the world as a
> subordinate being distinct from the supreme God, which is always
> the mark of a syncretism with a dualistic tendency; introduced spec-
> ulations about Aeons and angelic powers, among whom they placed
> Christ; and recommended a strict asceticism.[32]

The impetus, then, for the creation of Gnostic myth was *exegetical,* a
point that would be repeated often in subsequent scholarship.[33]

According to Harnack, Christian theologians made a significant ad-
vance toward "the great Gnostic systems" when they "philosophically manipulated" these mythologoumena by means of allegory and forced them
to serve Pythagorean, Platonic, and "more rarely" Stoic philosophy.[34] The
result was the first transformation of Christianity into a system. For
Harnack, then, *the Gnostics "were, in short, the first theologians of the first
century."* Given Harnack's opinion that theological dogma arose only with
the degeneration of true religious enthusiasm, this achievement was not to
their credit. He explained:

> They were the first to transform Christianity into a system of doc-
> trines (dogmas). They were the first to work up tradition systemati-
> cally. They undertook to present Christianity as the absolute reli-
> gion, and therefore placed it in definite opposition to the other
> religions, even to Judaism. But to them the absolute religion, viewed
> in its contents, was identical with the result of the philosophy of reli-
> gion for which the support of a revelation was to be sought. They are
> therefore those Christians who, in a swift advance, attempted to

capture Christianity for Hellenic culture, and Hellenic culture for Christianity, and who gave up the Old Testament in order to facilitate the conclusion of the covenant between the two powers, and make it possible to assert the absoluteness of Christianity.[35]

Against this attempt, Catholic Christianity arose:

If by "Catholic" we mean the church of doctrine and of law, then the Catholic church had its origin in the struggle with Gnosticism . . . *The struggle with Gnosticism compelled the Church to put its teaching, its worship, and its discipline, into fixed forms and ordinances, and to exclude everyone who would not yield them obedience* . . . It had to pay a heavy price for the victory which kept that tendency at bay; we may almost say that the vanquished imposed their terms upon the victor: *Victi victoribus legem dederunt.* It kept Dualism and the acute phase of Hellenism at bay; but by becoming a community with a fully worked out scheme of doctrine, and a definite form of public worship, it was of necessity compelled to take on forms analogous to those which it combated in the Gnostics . . . How much of its original freedom the Church sacrificed![36]

Remarkably, Harnack did not yet depict Gnosticism as a great evil or even entirely as heresy. On the contrary, he was able to recognize its positive contributions as well as its negative ones:

All those who in the first century undertook to furnish Christian practice with the foundation of a complete systematic knowledge, she [Catholic Christianity] declared false Christians, Christians only in name. Historical enquiry cannot accept this judgment. On the contrary, it sees in Gnosticism a series of undertakings, which in a certain way is analogous to the Catholic embodiment of Christianity, in doctrine, morals, and worship. The great distinction here consists essentially in the fact that the Gnostic systems represent the acute secularizing or hellenizing of Christianity, with the rejection of the Old Testament; while the Catholic system, on the other hand, represents a gradual process of the same kind with the conservation

of the Old Testament . . . It is therefore no paradox to say that
Gnosticism, which is just Hellenism, has in Catholicism obtained
half a victory.[37]

In this way, Harnack distinguished Gnosticism and Catholicism as two
types of interaction with the Greek spirit, interactions that were different
not in kind but only in degree.

The analogy was not entirely flattering to either. While Harnack could
praise Catholicism for its role in slowing down the process of Hellenization, primarily by keeping the Old Testament, he felt that in the end Catholicism had to give up too much and eventually fell too far under the
influence of Hellenism. By contrast, while clearly recognizing that Gnosticism had to be combated, he nonetheless maintained a very positive attitude toward some of its teachings. In particular, his opinion of Marcion
was very high. He went so far as to suggest that Marcion might be called
"the first Protestant"—high praise indeed! Harnack liked the way Marcion interpreted the Old Testament and Paul, and the way he properly
tried to reduce the Gospel message, church organization, and ritual to
their bare core in order "to know nothing save Christ the crucified one."
Harnack even agreed with Marcion in suggesting that Protestantism did
not need the Old Testament anymore; it had served its purpose in slowing
down Hellenization, he argued, and could now be dispensed with.[38]

This observation brings us to the function of church history as an apologetic for Protestantism. As part of his Protestant heritage, Harnack de-
murred to anchor the essence of true Christianity in apostolic succession
and a rule of faith, as Tertullian had done, no doubt because those positions were in his day closely associated with Roman Catholicism. Instead
he located the essence of Christianity in "the original enthusiasm" of the
Gospel in the primitive Church.[39] Necessary as its transformation into a
religion of rule and law may have been to the survival and success of
Christianity, in the context of his own pietist background Harnack could
not help casting it in terms of loss and rigidification, the hedging round of
the fire of the Spirit.

For Harnack, neither Catholicism nor Gnosticism contained the original Gospel enthusiasm, which he claimed as the heritage of his own Protestantism. Both went astray, albeit in differing degrees. The success of

Protestantism for Harnack lay in the return, as far as possible under the conditions of his own day, to the original vitality of the Gospel faith, before Christianity became a religion of law and superstition clothed in syncretic dress.[40]

William Rowe has pointed out quite insightfully that despite the self-congratulatory tone of Harnack's presentation of the Protestant Reformation, his criticism was aimed less at Catholicism than at his own Protestant tradition. His efforts to expose the negative effects of ancient Hellenization were targeted against what he saw as a similar hardening of his beloved Protestantism into an authoritarian and defensive orthodoxy in his own day.[41] Hence his appeal to pure Gospel origins was aimed not so much at rebuking Catholicism as at turning fellow Protestants toward what he saw as the heart of the Reformation.[42]

It is hard to know what Tertullian would have thought of all this. Harnack's scholarship was contoured by his Protestant perspectives and was couched in the highly sophisticated terms of the critical-historical methods of his day. But it followed a pattern not dissimilar to that of Tertullian in that Harnack considered the problem with Gnosticism (heresy) to be the fact that it suffered from an acute overdose of Greek philosophy.[43] Moreover, this position functioned polemically for Harnack, as it did for Tertullian, within the context of intra-Christian controversy over what constitutes the true identity of Christianity and who holds the keys to that truth. Although Harnack posited Greek influence to be much earlier and much more pervasive than Tertullian had reckoned, he could still envision and characterize an original Christianity barely touched by Hellenism. Harnack rearranged the particulars rather severely and elaborated quite extravagantly, but in the end he maintained the structural core of the polemicists' position.

## Identity Discourses in Harnack's Historiography

Harnack appropriated many elements from the ancient Christian discourses of identity formation, but he adapted significant variations on these themes as well. He followed the polemicists' pattern of allowing a singular term—now "Gnosticism" instead of "heresy"—to encompass with ease considerable heterogeneity. He was well aware of the lack of in-

ternal uniformity in the phenomena classified as Gnostic, yet he held that
these phenomena shared a common culture and a common function: "the
acute Hellenization of Christianity." Like heresy, Gnosticism was not a
living entity, but rather a rhetorical tool that worked to produce a normative version of Christianity.

Moreover, for Harnack "Hellenization" clearly implied pagan contamination, and he engaged in a thoroughly antisyncretistic discourse in treating this contamination. Where he diverged from the polemicists' approach was in his evaluation of that contamination. Fully a man of the
Enlightenment, Harnack valued universalism as a great good and applauded Christianity's appropriation of the rational universalism of ancient philosophy. He warmly welcomed the monotheistic piety displayed
in the religious ethos of the Greeks. In keeping with Enlightenment values, Harnack denigrated those aspects of human thought and practice regarded as irrational and superstitious, especially polytheistic myth and
cultic practice. He lamented the assimilation of these elements into true
Christianity through the introduction of the worship of the saints in
Catholicism, and he contrasted Christianity as a living experience in
true Protestantism with Christianity as a moribund superstition tied to
cult, sacraments, ceremony, and obedience in Catholicism. In this way,
Harnack tended to associate Catholicism with paganism, even as Henry
More had when he coined the term "Gnosticism" in the seventeenth century, an association firmly rooted in the context of Protestant anti-Catholic polemics.

Harnack appears to have done with paganism what the polemicists did
in the Christian construction of Judaism: appropriated all the positive
characteristics of pagan thought (such as universalism, rational philosophy, monotheistic piety, and ethics) for true Christianity, while attributing all the negative characteristics (superstition, myth, polytheism, cultic
practice) to his opponents, in this case Catholics.

Harnack also showed his debt to Romanticism in contrasting the rigidification of religion in doctrine and law with the living enthusiasm of
immediate feeling and inner experience. The Romantics had posited the
purity and naturalness of the primitive or the "savage" in contrast to the
corruption of civilization.[44] Harnack does not go so far, but he does extol
the depth of feeling, dignity, and simplicity of primitive Christianity.

Underlying this portrayal was the philosophical distinction between the spiritual kernel of Christianity and its historical husk. Although his radical historicism did not allow for a truly transcendent, disembodied Christianity, this distinction allowed Harnack to mark off an arena of stability for true Christianity safe from the vicissitudes of historical change.[45] Moreover, by identifying the kernel of Christianity with the life of the primitive Church, Harnack reinscribed Tertullian's polemical identification of true Christianity with its chronologically original form. The appeal to the primitive Church as site of the pure origins of Christianity had a political purpose analogous to that of Tertullian—the authorization of a particular set of views.[46] But the deployment of that appeal pointed in a new direction, in this case toward the authorization of a particular form of liberal German Protestant pietism.

By conflating Catholicism with paganism, Harnack could exploit the polemicists' strategies of heresy to further this aim. Even as Irenaeus or Tertullian had treated heresy, so Harnack characterized Catholicism as the contamination of pure Christianity by paganism, while Protestantism occupied the ancient polemicists' position of original orthodoxy. Despite the chronological discrepancies—most notably that Protestantism is demonstrably later than Catholicism—Harnack rhetorically portrayed the goal of Protestantism as the ideal approximation of the original form of Christianity.

Harnack's treatment of Judaism also resembled that of his heresiological predecessors, but again with a twist. Justin and those who followed him had characterized Judaism in terms of a literal misreading of Scripture in contrast to the true spiritual (allegorical and typological) reading of Christianity. According to Justin, this literalism had led the Jews to such particularistic practices as circumcision and kashrut, and kept them from seeing Christ as the key to the true spiritual meaning of their own Scripture. Harnack pursued a similar strategy, but its themes were in line with Enlightenment values. He identified Judaism with particularism, in contrast to Christian universalism. Moreover, he identified the apocalyptic elements of Christianity as a mythological contamination from degenerate "Late Judaism," and he insisted that apocalyptic myth had no part in Jesus' original Gospel.[47] Harnack attributed the positive aspects of Judaism that Justin had appropriated to Greek thought, especially monotheism and the ethics of love and justice.

The differences between Harnack's history of Christianity and the or-

thodox form of the master narrative of Christian origins are many.
Harnack's disciplined, historical analysis encompassed a stunning breadth
of early Christian materials and resulted in many innovative and important insights. But we need to be aware of the ways Harnack utilized many
of the rhetorical strategies of ancient Christian identity formation to anchor his own views of normative Christianity in liberal Protestantism. We
also need to be mindful of the intersections between the ancient discourses of heresy with the new values and traditions of the European Enlightenment and the Romanticist movement that appear in Harnack's historiography. Gnosticism as "the acute Hellenization of Christianity" was a
product of all these historical insights and rhetorical intersections.

# 4

# The History of Religions School

At about the same time that Harnack was writing, another group of scholars had begun to reconsider the long-established consensus that the roots of Gnosticism lay in a Christianity gone awry. Like Harnack, these scholars held that the New Testament and early Christianity could only be understood against the background of the culture and religion of the Hellenistic world from which they arose. But unlike Harnack, they turned to the Orient rather than to the Greek world to provide the keys for that understanding.[1]

Whereas Harnack had located the impetus for the development of early Christian dogma in the Greek spirit, scholars in the history of religions school would turn increasingly to the folk religion of Iran, Babylonia, and even India for the keys to the origins of a pre-Christian Gnosticism that would unlock the meaning of the Gospels and Paul.[2] Moreover, they were interested precisely in those aspects of Christianity that Harnack had dismissed peremptorily as "husk." They were fascinated by the fantastic myths and took ritual practice, no matter how crude they considered it to be, very seriously as an important generative locus of religious community.

History of religions scholars came to the astonishing conclusion that Gnosticism was an independent religion whose origin lay, not in deviant Christian heresy, but in pre-Christian, Oriental myth and cultic piety. This perspective significantly changed the way the relationship of Gnosticism to Christianity could be conceptualized. Scholars could now explore how Gnosticism may have exerted a formative influence on Christianity at its very origin. They focused on three particular topics: tracing the title

"Son of Man" back to its origin in Iranian folk religion, the Gnostic influence on Paul, and the Gnostic background to the Christology of the Gospel of John.

The primary method of the history of religions school was motif history, which involved tracing the origin and genealogical development of a particular motif such as Son of Man from its earliest manifestation to its most developed form. This progression was often said to involve a geographical-cultural shift from Oriental origin to Occidental development. Here we can see the nineteenth- and early twentieth-century discourse of evolutionary progress intersecting the new fields of comparative religion, history, and philology, as well as the accompanying colonialist identity politics of Orientalism.[3]

In their use of motif history, these scholars were very much drawn to the methods and presuppositions of the study of Germanic religion, folklore, and ethnology (race). Even so, the case for the pre-Christian origin of Gnosticism could never have been made without rich infusions of new manuscripts from Africa and Asia, especially Coptic, Manichaean, and Mandaean texts. It would be impossible to imagine the work of the history of religions school in the area of Gnosticism and Oriental religions apart from the advances made in philology and the rich new archaeological and textual finds that were coming to light at the turn of the century. The new materials and the shifting discourses in which their study was framed all pointed history of religions scholars in directions different from those Harnack had pursued, and they revolutionized the portrait of Gnosticism and Christian origins.


## Intellectual Context

The distinctive intellectual character of the history of religions approach lay in the conjunction of old and new discourses: heresy and antisyncretism with Enlightenment historicism, developmental models of cultural progress, and Orientalism. Like Harnack, history of religions scholars were steeped in the contemporary discourses of Enlightenment historicism and colonialism, but in their work Orientalism and evolutionary models of cultural development were markedly more pronounced.

They expressly promoted their scholarship as a science, *Religions-*

*wissenschaft,* which would free the study of Christianity from dogmatic limits by making it the object of scientific-historical investigation.[4] The investigation of religion moved from the field of theology, connected with the institutional structures of church, to the field of science and the institutional structures of the secular university.[5] The overt discourse of orthodoxy and heresy became submerged, although its effects continued to operate through fascination with origins and pervasive attitudes of antisyncretism.

The origins of language, race, and religion were major preoccupations of European scholarship from the eighteenth to the twentieth centuries. As Tomoko Mazusawa points out, however, the term "origin" could be conceived several ways: "the true meaning, the essential being, the real thing, or the genius of the author-creator."[6] However used, the term implied that a unitary origin lay behind the representation of every phenomenon. History of religions scholars used two primary modes of determining origins: the typological-structural and the chronological-historical.[7] The structural tended to treat origin as the ever-present cause; the historical, as the first beginning of a phenomenon. Structural approaches privileged similarity, tending to treat varied cross-cultural religious expressions as differentiated forms of the same essential transhistorical and transcultural phenomenon—religion. In this approach, religion was conceived as universal or innate in human experience. Distinctions among religions were generally organized in hierarchical stemma, with particularistic, natural, and superstitious nature religions at the bottom, and universal, ethical, and rational monotheism at the top. Christianity generally capped the pyramid as religion's highest expression. As J. Z. Smith points out, "Often mistermed evolutionary, these theories conceded no historical dimensions to those being classified but rather froze each ethnic unit at a particular 'stage of development' of the totality of human religious thought and activity."[8]

Historical approaches, by contrast, were used to explain difference in terms of developmental processes. This method presupposed the historicist notion that phenomena are historically determined by the time and place they occupied and the role they played within a process of development.[9] Information was ordered into chronological narratives according to one of two plots: decline from pure origins or stages of progress from

primitive origins to ever higher forms of synthetic development. History
was often conceived as operating in a teleological mode toward its own
ends. The connections among events were figured in terms of causal links
in a linear chronology. In this discourse, the historical marked the contingent representations of a phenomenon; the typological marked its essential characteristics.

In the work of history of religions scholars, the two approaches were
often used simultaneously or at least in tandem. The result, as J. Z. Smith
notes, "had the effect of blurring the distinctions between questions of
truth and questions of origins."[10] As we will see in the next chapter in the
discussion of Hans Jonas's work, there was considerable tension between
these two approaches.

History of religions' methodology was further complicated by the application of the geographical politics of Orientalism, which tended to
map the dichotomy of nature religions and ethical monotheism onto the
geographical territory of East and West, and link both the map and the
territory to typological classifications and historical constructions of language, race, and ethnicity. Although it is not possible in the brief compass
of this discussion to lay out a full exposition and critique of these intellectual enterprises, it is necessary to offer at least a brief overview of those
aspects that most affected the history of religions' construction of Gnosticism.

The most obvious connection was with the new and prestigious field of
philology. Indeed a philologist, Max Müller, is generally credited with
founding the study of comparative religion (history of religions).[11] Philology provided the methods for locating the origin of religion and the presuppositions for connecting it with ethnicity and race. Linguistics and
comparative philology had made tremendous advances in the eighteenth
and nineteenth centuries. A series of brilliant studies by scholars such as
William Jones (1786), Franz Bopp (1810), and Karl Verner (1876) had succeeded in showing the inter-relatedness of Indo-European languages and
had classified them into language families. These new surges in philology and linguistics drew heavily on the rich archaeological and textual
finds of the nineteenth and twentieth centuries, which formed the basis
for philological-historical study.

Adolf Deismann, for example, relied almost entirely on new papyrus finds for his study. In his pioneering philological work *Licht vom Osten* (1908), he used newly discovered Greco-Roman papyri to prove that the language of the New Testament writings was not a unique, inspired Greek but rather *koine,* the language of the marketplace and the home. Deismann argued that primitive Christianity began with the living spoken word ("the gospel, but no gospels") and only over time developed a literature that attempted "a flight from its native levels into the higher region of culture." Like Harnack, he identified true religion with pious fervor and argued that Christian historiography wrongly focused on the literary upper classes and ecclesiastical politics. To a greater degree than Harnack, however, he emphasized that in its origin, when Christianity "was still sustained by inspiration," it was a popular movement with a living connection to its contemporary world. Deismann's work stimulated the search for the keys to Christian origins in the linguistic and literary *koine* of the Hellenistic conceptual world. The origin of religion lay at the primitive roots of popular piety with its everyday language, not in its developed cultural forms. Thus when Richard Reitzenstein turned to Iran to seek the origin of the Primal Man myth, it is perhaps not surprising that he sought it in Iranian "Volksreligion."[12]

Philologists also tied religion to race. Using typological-structural methods, they classified languages into two families: Aryan (Indo-European) and Semitic. Historical approaches arranged the resulting genealogical stemma of language families geographically and chronologically, associating them with two basic types of culture and religion, each tied to a particular place and people ("Volk"). As Maurice Olender summarizes:

To the authors who used it, the notion of "a family of languages" meant demonstrating the existence of affinities among different language groups. These linguistic affinities were then justified either by historical and geographical connections between peoples (with a consequent implication of systematic borrowings) or by the idea of descent from a common ancestor to account for the existence of common word roots and grammatical structures. Some authors combined both arguments, and to this day the ambiguity persists in the form of a tension between typological models and historical arguments.[13]

In his brilliant study *The Languages of Paradise: Race, Religion, and Philology in the Nineteenth Century*, Olender has demonstrated how these developments in philology were intertwined with European nationalist awakening and colonial politics. The search for the origin and development of language was directly tied to nationalist discourses of "the Volk." As he notes, "The concept (of 'Volk') involved religion, nationality, culture, society, and politics, all bound together by a common language." This implied a conceptuality in which "language is a kind of grid structuring thought and molding national character. Equally common are variations on the theme of language as a mirror, which reflects the images that form the soul of a people."[14]

Ubiquitous but ambiguously defined, the term "race" became increasingly central to such conceptuality, as did religion. In his discussion of the work of Adolphe Pictet (1799–1875), Olender provides an example of how the two were linked. For Pictet, the goal of historical philology was to uncover the design of Providence in bringing the Aryan and Semitic traditions into their final and most exalted synthesis: "the radiant future of humanity in Christianity." Each brought what it possessed to that synthesis:

> The Hebrews possess the authority that preserves; the Aryans, the freedom that allows for development . . . On the one hand is a single compact nationality, on the other a vast race divided into a host of diverse peoples. In both we find exactly what was needed to accomplish the providential designs.[15]

In Pictet's mind, their providential meeting destined Christians to rule the entire globe.[16]

We have already encountered one variation on this theme in the work of Harnack, who characterized Hellenism as containing the seeds of universalism required for Christianity to expand beyond the isolating nationalism of the Jews.[17] We encounter it again, but in a different guise, in the Orientalism of the history of religions school, which maintained a tight association of language and location with race, religion, and culture.

By the beginning of the twentieth century, Europeans had been involved in colonial enterprises for a long time, and they had constructed a highly developed set of intellectual rationales that supported their colonial politics. Chief among them was the discourse about race and religion, which postcolonial studies often refer to as "Orientalism." Orientalism is, according to Said,

> a way of coming to terms with the Orient that is based on the Orient's special place in European Western experience. The Orient is not only adjacent to Europe; it is also the place of Europe's greatest and richest and oldest colonies, the source of its civilizations and languages, its cultural contestant, and one of its deepest and most recurring images of the Other.[18]

Developed primarily in the context of British and French colonialism, Orientalism takes many forms and appears in a broad array of genres and milieus. Its essence, however, is defined by the "ineradicable distinction between Western superiority and Oriental inferiority."[19] This expression of superiority did not preclude strategies that acknowledged the former greatness of Oriental civilizations or the importance of their previous contributions to the West; indeed, it placed the Orient in a developmental scheme culminating in Western culture. In this way, such strategies could be central to the appropriation of "the East" for the purposes of "the West."[20]

Orientalism intersected most prominently with philology through the conceptual linkage of the two basic language groups (Aryan and Semitic) with culture and "Volk." Each culture or people was said to be characterized by a particular "soul," expressed in its particular language. Semitic (Oriental) culture was figured in terms of passivity, stagnation, and stability, whereas Aryan (Indo-European, Western) culture was said to be characterized by rationality, dynamism, and creativity. Note that in this typological schema, the actual geography of East and West, which varied from author to author, was less important than the typological characteristics assigned to each.

The explicit aim of history of religions scholars was to study the religious traditions of the Orient in order to demonstrate their value and contributions to the formation of Western culture, above all to Christianity.[21] Yet even these attempts to appreciate Oriental religions were burdened by an inadequate sociological model of cultural interaction (syncretism) and by the Orientalist framework in which their work was embedded. These limitations are particularly evident in scholarship dealing with Gnosticism.

In tracing the origin of Gnosticism from Oriental myth and ritual to its most developed expression in the so-called Gnostic redeemer myth, history of religions scholars transformed the polemicists' theology of origins into "a history of the primal."[22] While retaining the conviction that the task of history was to trace the origin and development of a phenomenon, they revised the older view of the ontological and epistemological superiority of origins by plotting the story as one of progress, not decline. They bought deeply into the new comparative-typological study of religion that associated true but primitive religious intuition with humanity's earliest condition in nature. They concluded that this intuition aroused primitive feelings (of fear or awe) that were expressed in magical, cultic practices or fantastic myths.

In many of these discussions, myth was distinguished from other types of narratives by determining its origin typologically, not historically. According to this model, myth originated in the primitive mind and was said to belong to societies at the beginning (that is to say, at the bottom) of the evolutionary scale.[23] Hence the later and higher developments of scientific logic and Christian ethics lacked myths. Because they were often fantastic and scandalous in nature, myths were dismissed as confused expressions or incorrect explanations about natural phenomena, or as products of diseased language.[24] In contrast to scientific thinking, which sought to explain the world, myth was a kind of social ordering of the universe that functioned to account for what could not be explained, to guard frail humans against fears of the unknown, or to legitimize social institutions.[25]

These discussions relegated mythic thinking to uncivilized others or to the abandoned past—though the discerning investigator could still detect remnants of myth in contemporary Western society. From such humble origins, scholars were able to trace the development of primitive religious impulses through increasingly complex forms of expression to their final culmination in the exquisite moral, intellectual, and aesthetic sensibilities of Christianity. Once this development was shown, little more needed to be said. Primitive cults and myths required little or no interpretation, be-

yond noting their essentially primitive character. In short, origins and genealogy explained all. Unfortunately, they interpreted little; questions of
truth and questions of origin blurred and coalesced.

Although the associative genius of the history of religions scholars was
intellectually brilliant, it was a disaster sociologically and historically.[26]
They understood cultural interaction basically in terms of syncretism, by
which they meant the borrowing of a discrete element ("motif") from one
culture by another. The goal of motif history was to identify the original
location of the motif in some primitive nature religion, and then trace its
path through various stages of syncretic borrowing. In practice, the analysis started from the later work, determined which of its elements belonged
to earlier pure traditions (Iranian, Greek, Jewish, and even Gnostic), and
then worked backward to posit the site of primitive origin. The result,
however, was presented in terms of a genealogical schema beginning at the
origin and tracing the sequential addition of each discrete element forward to its culmination in the fully developed phenomenon. Scholars
accounted for differences between the original motif and its later occurrences by suggesting that the primitive element had been disguised, transformed, or somehow altered in the process of its development. It was the
task of the history of religions scholar to unmask the primitive form,
reveal its concealed development, and represent the true history of the
motif.

The early history of religions scholars who investigated Gnosticism focused almost solely on locating original Gnostic motifs and tracing their
genealogies to the developed forms of second- and third-century systems.
They emphasized the syncretistic character of Gnosticism, arguing that it
was made up of motifs drawn from a wide variety of ancient cultures
stretching from the Eastern Mediterranean to the Tigris-Euphrates valley
and even into India. Structurally, their work fits the old mold in which
original purity (the primal) is transformed by alien influences (syncretic
contamination); but they altered this framework by organizing the transformations typologically and plotting the trajectory in terms of progress,
not decline.

Scholars now consider the historical method of tracing motifs to be ir-
remediably flawed because the analysis did not give sufficient attention to
the shifting meanings and uses of motifs throughout shifts in their histori-

cal, intellectual, and sociological contexts. In hindsight, most of the genealogical stemma produced by early history of religions scholars appear to
be more or less arbitrary. The association of a motif in one context with a
similar motif in another context did not expose the dynamics of historical
change; rather, it masked them by recasting the data into static nine-
teenth- and twentieth-century frameworks that classified the primitive, irrational other over against the advanced, rational civilization of the West.

## The New Discoveries

The greatest single stimulus to the work of history of religions scholars
was the recovery of texts believed to stem from the Gnostics themselves,
untouched by the dubious mediation of their polemicist detractors.[27] Together with other non-Gnostic materials that were becoming known from
the Orient, especially from Iran and India, these texts were mined to determine the origin and development of Gnosticism. Without these discoveries, it is impossible to imagine how history of religions scholars could
have constructed Gnosticism as a pre-Christian, Oriental religion. Among
the textual finds, the most important for our topic were the recoveries
from Egypt, Central Asia, and Persia (Iran-Iraq).

Three codices containing works considered to be Gnostic had been discovered in Egypt before the turn of the twentieth century. The earliest was
the fifth-century Codex Brucianus, found in upper Egypt near Medinet
Habu and purchased by the Scottish traveler James Bruce about 1769. It
contained two works in Coptic considered to be of Gnostic provenance,
the *Books of Jeu* containing teachings of Jesus to his disciples, and an untitled work on theogony and cosmogony (now charmingly called *The Untitled Text*). Another codex was purchased in 1772 by A. Askew, the London
physician after whom it was named (Codex Askewianus). Its date of discovery and specific provenance are unknown. It is a large fourth-century
parchment codex, containing an extensive revelation dialogue between
Jesus and his disciples, titled *Pistis Sophia*.[28] A third codex was purchased
in Egypt in 1896 and taken to Berlin, whence it has come to be known as
the Berlin Codex (Codex Berolinensis). This fifth-century papyrus book
contains four works: the *Gospel of Mary, ApJohn, The Sophia of Jesus
Christ,* and an *Act of Peter*.

Owing to a variety of unfortunate circumstances, including burst water pipes, two world wars, and the untimely death of the first editor, Carl Schmidt, a printed edition and German translation of the Berlin Codex did not appear until 1955.[29] As a result this codex did not exert any real influence on the study of Gnosticism in the first half of the century. The materials of the Bruce and Askew codices were known, but they seemed to scholars to represent a late and degraded form of Gnosticism, and thus to reveal little of real importance about Gnostic or Christian origins. Hence none of the three codices received serious attention from scholars who were interested primarily in the question of Christian origins. Another set of discoveries was to prove more significant.

Between 1902 and 1914, four German archaeological expeditions explored the old silk routes from Persia to China and returned to Berlin with a huge number of texts from the Central Asian area of Turfan (on the northern fringe of the Taklamakan desert). Included among these finds were the first original Manichaean documents known to modern Europeans. Mani was already well known as the third-century founder of a religion that had penetrated deep into the Roman Empire and influenced such pivotal Christian figures as the great Latin theologian Augustine. The new Manichaean texts, while potentially fascinating and of widespread interest, presented a formidable challenge to philologists, representing as they do seventeen languages from Syriac to Chinese, of which two (Sogdian and Tocharian) were previously altogether unknown. Even today, the Manichaeism scholar Hans-Joachim Klimkeit reports, only about one-fourth of these texts have been published. In addition, the more recent discovery and 1988 publication of the *Cologne Mani Codex*, containing information about the early life of Mani, located the root of Mani's religious background among the Jewish-Christian baptizing sect of the Elchasites, whose founder preached around 100 C.E. in Syria.[30] This codex clearly demonstrated that Manichaeism is not of particular interest for the earliest period of Christian beginnings. That fact, however, was much less apparent to the history of religions scholars in the first half of the twentieth century than it is today. For them, the Manichaean materials were an important resource for understanding the origin of Gnosticism, and they were widely used in the construction of the Gnostic redeemer myth.

And yet the sources that were to have the greatest impact in shaping the direction of early history of religions scholarship on Gnosticism came

not from Turfan but from the literature procured from the living community of the Mandaeans in the area of Iran and Iraq. For centuries the
Mandaeans had lived in the marshy areas along the lower Euphrates and
Tigris Rivers and in Khuzistan along the Karun River. There they survived, forced to sequester themselves from various afflictions by Persian
and Islamic rulers. Today their situation has become increasingly precari-
ous.[31]

Europeans had known of the existence of the Mandaeans since the thirteenth century. Around 1250, the Italian traveler Rialdus drew upon his
travels in the area to produce an accurate account of Mandaean life and
practice. In the late sixteenth century, a Jesuit mission from Portugal came
in contact with an extensive community living in Basra and the neighboring area of Khuzistan in Iran whose members called themselves *Nasoraiê
d'Yahya* ("Nasoreans of John"), or *Mandayi* (which might be translated as
"Gnostics," "people of the Manda," or "believers in Manda d'Haiya").
From them scholars coined the name "Mandaeans."[32]

Although Mandaean studies have never attracted a large number of
scholars, their importance was evaluated quite differently in the first half
of the twentieth century than it is now. Mandaean literature, though extensive, had reached the West only slowly, in bits and pieces, over a period of approximately three centuries. The Maronite Orientalist Abraham
Ekchellensis had Mandaean manuscripts in his possession as early as the
seventeenth century. By the nineteenth century, codices could be found in
the libraries of Paris, London, Oxford, Leiden, Munich, and Berlin. With
these textual resources, Mandaean studies began in earnest.[33]

The nineteenth century witnessed the publication of the first Mandaean grammar, texts, and translations.[34] The early twentieth century was
dominated by the work of Mark Lidzbarski, an Oriental philologist at
Göttigen whose accurate and reliable translations of Mandaean texts into
German provided a sound basis for history of religions study. In 1905, he
published the *Book of John;* in 1920, the Mandaean liturgy; and in 1925, a
new translation of the *Ginza.* Over the next thirty years only a few minor
magical texts were published, but beginning in 1949, works by the ama-
teur anthropologist Lady Drower began to appear. Drower was the first
Westerner to gain the confidence of a Mandaean group, and with it access
to a wealth of unpublished literature. She also secured the rare opportunity to observe Mandaean ritual and cultic practices.[35] Her work contin-

ues to play a central role in the study of Mandaean religion. Together, these materials provided history of religions scholars with the resources for a generation of industrious labor, including the invention of the Gnostic redeemer myth.

## The Oriental Roots of Pre-Christian Gnosticism

The impact of these new sources on the study of Christianity was felt almost as soon as knowledge of them became available in European scholarly circles. In 1750 Johann David Michaelis published an *Introduction to the Divine Scriptures of the New Covenant*. The book was primarily concerned with a discussion of the historical problems of the New Testament, including textual and source problems, but his discussion of the Gospel of John led him to suggest "that John had taken 'the word' as an expression for the divine Person 'from the Gnostics' and had written 'against the disciples of John the Baptist, the Sabians (Mandaeans)."[36] He was thus the first to note the affinities between the Gospel of John and Gnosticism, and to propose that the Mandaeans, styled as disciples of John the Baptist, had come into conflict with the earliest Christians.

Further consideration of the relationship of Mandaeism to Christianity awaited the publication of the Mandaean texts themselves. Wilhelm Brandt, in *Die Mandäischen Religion* (1889), published the first critical-historical study to make extensive use of the Mandaean materials, especially the *Right Ginza*. He argued that the oldest layer of Mandaean tradition was pre-Christian. Because of the strong anti-Christian and anti-Jewish polemic in the Mandaean writings, he felt that this tradition must have originally been pagan, a polytheistic type of "Semitic nature religion" that contained various water rites, including baptism, that eventually merged with "Chaldaean philosophy."[37] He envisioned a Babylonian rather than a Jewish or Christian origin for the sect, arguing that the Greek, Jewish, Gnostic, and Persian conceptions had been added during the long history of its development. The Jewish contribution included the tendency to monotheism, which is present in various sections of the texts. The final result was Mandaeism. In a later work Brandt proposed that the original home of the Mandaeans should be sought between the Jordan and Aleppo.[38]

As a result of the work of Brandt and others, scholars saw in Man-

daeism an early form of Gnosticism, if not precisely its sole or most pristine origin. In addition to Brandt, twentieth-century philologians such as
Mark Lidzbarski and Rudolf Maçuch proposed that Mandaeism originated in first-century Palestine from a pre-Christian, Jewish-pagan baptizing sect. The pre-Christian date, the connection with heterodox Judaism,
and the location in Palestine all indicated to them that Mandaeism could
have influenced the origin of Christianity.[39]

In a series of pivotal works aimed at determining the background and
history of the Christian Son of Man, Pauline theology, and Johannine theology, history of religions scholars drew heavily on Mandaean materials to
form a thesis about the Oriental origin of Gnosticism and its influence on
Christianity.[40] Both the early dating of the Mandaean material and the
scholarly acceptance of motif history as a basic methodological tool were
fundamental to the creation of an Oriental, pre-Christian Gnostic redeemer myth. We can illustrate further development of this line of scholarship by examining the work of three preeminent scholars in the German
history of religions school: Richard Reitzenstein, Wilhelm Bousset, and
Rudolf Bultmann.

## Richard Reitzenstein

The most radical of the three scholars was the classical philologist Richard
Reitzenstein. He was also—perhaps because of his training in classics, not
religion, and the radical character of his conclusions—the one least willing to discuss the implications of his work for Christian theology. He can
be credited with laying the foundations for the construction of the Gnostic redeemer myth in his work on the Iranian Primal Man (German:
*Urmensch*).

Reitzenstein slowly built up a full portrait of this redeemer myth in a
series of brilliantly imaginative studies, beginning with his analysis of the
Egyptian Hermetic tractate *Poimandres* (1904). In this work, he claimed to
have found the basic outline of a non-Egyptian myth of the Primal Man
(Greek: *anthropos*) that could be traced back to an Oriental Gnosis and
connected to the New Testament Son of Man.

In particular, Reitzenstein pointed out the influence of Oriental myth
on early Christianity. The theme appeared in his next work, *Die Helle-*

*nistische Mysterien-religionen* (1910), in which he proposed that the basic language and conceptuality of Greek *pneuma* ("spirit"), *psyche* ("soul"), and *gnosis* ("knowledge") came from the terminology of the Mysteries: they are pre-Christian and Oriental in origin.[41] He argued that Greek philosophy and Judaism adopted this conceptuality, and from them it passed to Paul and early Christology.[42]

The concept that had the greatest influence on Christianity and other religions, according to Reitzenstein, was the Iranian view of the soul and its connection with the Primal Man: "Since the Primal Man abides with his members in matter and since he himself abides in the kingdom of Light, he is the soul and at the same time its Savior, and is moreover the entire Divinity since he has unified himself with it."[43] In his next work, *Das mandäische Buch des Herrn der Grösse und die Evangeliumüberlieferung* (1910), he supported this thesis with evidence from Mandaean texts. He equated the Mandaean Savior Manda d'Hayje ("knowledge of Life") with the Primal Man, who is in all people (as soul) and who must be saved: he is the "redeemed redeemer."[44] By identifying the soul with the Primal Man, and the Primal Man with the redeemer, Reitzenstein constructed a myth in which the fall of the Primal Man into matter was equated with the situation of the soul in the world.[45] But since the Primal Man and the redeemer were the same figure, it also meant that the redeemer himself was in need of redemption! The divine soul, he argued, found itself in an analogous situation: it was already divine by nature, but it required a redeemer to awaken it to knowledge of itself. In this notion of a redeemed redeemer, Reitzenstein presents the core of what would become known as the Gnostic redeemer myth.

Reitzenstein continued to enlarge upon these ideas in "Iranischer Erlösungsglaube" (1921), in which he considered especially the new Manichaean and Mandaean materials.[46] Here the genealogical direction of his thesis became entirely clear. Reitzenstein posited that the basis of both Manichaean and Mandaean religion lay in Iranian popular religion (*Volksreligion*).[47] Their teaching on the soul and salvation was Iranian in all its essential aspects, including the myth of the redeemed redeemer:

For the Mandaeans and Manichaeans, salvation is basically only the coming of the messenger and his proclamation; he is the Light. That he descends into darkness (earth and hell converge in the concept) is the decisive thing. So he himself falls into their misery and can leave again only by calling upon God. The Primal Man (or Primal Soul) is both redeemed and redeemer, according to the Manichaeans. This is shown too in a number of Mandaean texts: he reserves for himself the sending of a helper who calls him if he is sleeping, heals him if he is wounded, frees him if he has been imprisoned. When he has fulfilled his task, he receives as a reward a lordship which he had not previously possessed.[48]

Having thus established the decisive influence of Iranian salvation teaching on Mandaeism, at least to his own satisfaction, Reitzenstein next turned to the problem of the origin of Mandaeism and its relationship to early Christianity. Although he depended on Lidzbarski's philological work in attributing a West Semitic, pre-Christian origin to Mandaeism, he insisted that Iranian influence was still the most decisive factor.[49]

Here Reitzenstein stands in sharp opposition to Harnack, who posited that the ruling force in Gnosticism was the Greek spirit.[50] Reitzenstein argued that philosophy took its ideas from religion, not the contrary:

It is in fact clear that philosophy does not create these ideas, but takes them over from religion, at first as mere figures, in order to offer assurance that it can vouchsafe the same gifts as can religion, and later of course as its own ideas, but always without significantly influencing their essence.[51]

Reitzenstein was even willing to suggest that Plato was "influenced by Iranian feeling."[52]

Reitzenstein concluded that however much these concepts were modified and their origins obscured when they were absorbed into Judaism and Greek thought, they nonetheless still drew nourishment from their Oriental roots and profoundly influenced the cultures they penetrated.[53] According to Reitzenstein, an enormous task faced the history of religions scholar: "to demonstrate on the one hand the Oriental origin, and on the other hand the stages of the occidentalizing of this thought-world by the Jewish, the Greek, and finally the general Western feeling. It is not Christian by birth, but it has become Christian through powerful religious personalities."[54] This statement encapsulates Reitzenstein's vision for the entire history of religions field. He affirmed the fundamental contributions of the Orient to the West, but at the same time reproduced the discourse of colonialism by proposing that the primary task of the history of religions should be to chart the intellectual colonization of the Orient by the West.

In order to demonstrate how early Oriental influence had penetrated into Palestine, Reitzenstein focused persistently on the prominent anti-Jewish and anti-Christian polemic of Mandaean literature, which told of the destruction of Jerusalem by the Mandaean savior Hibil and the expulsion of Jesus from the Mandaean community. For Reitzenstein, this anti-Jewish polemic proved that Oriental influence was pre-Christian: "Only hate that is close at hand in time and place can speak in such a manner."[55] In addition he would argue, contra Brandt and Lidzbarski, that the anti-Christian material in Mandaean literature was not a later fourth- or fifth-century insertion, but derived from the time of Christian origins. He held that the Mandaean texts prove that Jesus, like John the Baptist, was once a member of that baptizing heterodox Jewish sect! Lidzbarski, he claimed, had already demonstrated that fact when he argued on philological grounds that the ancient designation Jesus *ho Nazôraios* cannot be derived from Nazareth. Rather it must, said Reitzenstein, signify the members of the Nasorean sect, that is, the early Mandaeans.[56]

According to Reitzenstein, the anti-Christian polemic in Mandaean myth arose from the view that Jesus was a false messenger who worked by the lordship of the aeonic demiurge, Yahweh. When he persisted in his bogus role of a great magician, the Mandaeans broke away from him. This rupture was the cause and explanation of the strife between the disciples of John and the early Christians illustrated in the Gospels. But—and this is the crucial point—although the early Christians split off from the Nasorean (Mandaean) group, they took over many of the Iranian conceptions that had already influenced Judaism.[57]

Reitzenstein was now in a position to answer the question of where the Christian title Son of Man (*bar nascha,* or simply Man) had come from and how it was to be understood. Not surprisingly, he suggested that the

origin of the title was to be sought in Iran, since "Son of Man" was the
Christological designation used by the Hellenistic Jews from whom Paul
first learned of Christianity, and Iranian belief had heavily influenced
Hellenized Judaism.[58] In a similar fashion, he argued that the Gospel of
John's proclamation of the divine messenger's descent from God was
based on the Iranian redeemer myth. The real meaning of the title Son of
Man could be understood by this origin:

> If we understood the form of the Iranian Anthropos as it is presented
> in Mandaeism, and focus it sharply, it offers not the transcendental
> Messiah who has come down in order to judge, but the homeless cit-
> izen of the world of light, who while standing in connection with the
> Father yet has fulfilled a mission on earth under stress and persecu-
> tions, who seeks to return homeward and is certain of magnification
> in his home world. Thus also do our Gospels, especially Q, point to
> the self-designation as *bar nascha* in those places in which the earthly
> lot of Jesus or the expectation that the enemies will hold him in
> their power is described; they have, as Welhausen once observed, a
> religious (super-human) significance to dispute the self-designation.
> That he in other places had power can hardly be doubted any longer.
> But I conclude through this that the rock-hard faith of the disciples
> in the resurrected one is only conceivable if they had in life already
> plainly seen in him more than a man, so that the *bar nascha* in him
> became *ho Christos*. If they later remembered the ancient formula
> and ascribed it to Jesus as a self-designation, then the simplest expla-
> nation is that he really had thus designated himself . . . Though John
> in his preaching had meant Enosh, yet Jesus called himself *bar
> nascha*.[59]

There are two extremely important points to note here. First is the way in
which the determination of origin and the question of meaning are vitally
linked for Reitzenstein. The passage above illustrates well how the history
of religions school argued that tracing the genealogy of a motif like Son of
Man would provide insight into its true historical and theological meaning. Reitzenstein often insisted that even though form changed radically,
this essential meaning was never lost.

The second point to note is that although Reitzenstein often spoke of influence in a very general fashion, in fact he could not conceive that such influence occurred other than through written texts. His argument for the Mandaean origin of the Son of Man designation presents a good example. He based this astonishing thesis primarily on an apocalypse that he reconstructed from portions of the *Ginza* on the basis of a comparison with Matthew 23:34–39 and 11:5 (cp. Luke 7:22). He claimed this apocalypse was a literary precursor *(Vorlage)* of the synoptic gospel source Q.[60] As we will see in the next chapter, this source analysis was seriously flawed.

Reitzenstein's work had placed him in the midst of a theological debate over the meaning and use of Son of Man. His concluding words, in which he expressed an apparent intention to withdraw from the theological issue that he had brought into such sharp focus, indicate his awareness that he was treading on sensitive ground:

> Clearly these conclusions deal with historical explanation, not religious valuation. Something completely different had sprung from the Enosh of John to the deepest being of a new religious personality who is no longer the judge of the world who can spare the individual, but the Savior who led humanity back to God through his example and teaching about the living Father. We have only explained the formula and the connection of apparently wider tendencies of the form. And that is indeed enough.[61]

No doubt it was more than enough for some. After all, Reitzenstein had concluded that Jesus had originally been a Mandaean Gnostic, at least until the Mandaeans rejected him as a bogus magician. Basic components of Christian conceptuality in Q, Paul, and the Gospel of John were said to stem from Oriental mystery piety and Iranian popular religion. According to Reitzenstein, Gnostic heresy lay at the foundations of Christian tradition.

Reitzenstein's disavowal should not lead us to think that he was uninterested in Christian origins; his interest in Gnosticism lay precisely in how it could illuminate them. By reversing the chronological precedence of Gnosticism and Christianity, he increased the importance of non-Jewish materials for understanding early Christianity. He also explicitly argued that his "historical explanation" was not "religious valuation." The very fact that he thought the two could be separated suggests a conscious attempt to distance himself from the discourse of heresy, in which the two are most intimately linked.


## Wilhelm Bousset

Wilhelm Bousset was a contemporary of Reitzenstein, and their scholarly production intersected at various points. Bousset, however, was neither a classical philologian nor an Orientalist, but a New Testament scholar.[62] His interests in the new Mandaean and Manichaean materials stemmed from their potential to elucidate certain obscurities in early Christianity. Again, chief among these was the title Son of Man.

Bousset's starting point was the observation in *Die Religion des Judentums* (1903) that the New Testament use of the title Son of Man could not be adequately explained in terms of Jewish conceptions of the Messiah. Even Philo's portrait of the heavenly Adam could not have been based solely on the Genesis narrative. So Bousset turned to Gnostic, Mandaean, Manichaean, and Kabbalistic sources to determine the term's origin and meaning. He concluded that behind the Son of Man title lay a more general Primal Man conception that belonged to the sphere of "Hellenistic religious syncretism."[63]

In his next book, *Hauptprobleme der Gnosis* (1907), he surveyed the entire range of materials then available, including Mandaean sources, linking them together to construct a history of the origin and development of the Primal Man figure. The result was a linear genealogy stretching from ancient India to the New Testament gospels.[64]

The starting point for Bousset's genealogy was a cultic hymn, the song of Purusha from the *Rig Veda,* which he suggested may have been connected with a magical fertility cult. He claimed that this song contained the original form of an ancient myth telling how the world arose through the sacrifice of the Primal Man and was formed from his body. From this starting point, Bousset traced the Primal Man motif through a variety of mythic developments in its journey toward the New Testament Son of Man. Persian religion associated the Primal Man figure of the song with Gayô-Maretan, the first creature made by the good God. As in the ancient

Sanskrit song, the world was said to be born from the body of the Primal Man, but according to the Persian myth creation occurred only after he had suffered death at the hands of the evil spirit Ahriman. In this way, an element of conflict between the divine powers of good and evil was introduced into the story.

According to Bousset, contact with the Greek world brought further modifications to the original myth, and it took yet another new turn. The Primal Man was split into two figures: the *proto-anthropos* and the *deuteros theos*. The first became the creator and model for humanity, whereas the second formed the world by sinking into the primordial matter, giving it form and life. This split, claimed Bousset, was exemplified in Plato's *Timaeus,* with its two divine creative forces, the Demiurge and the World-Soul, and it could be traced through the Hermetic *Poimandres,* Plotinus' Gnostics, the wild speculations of Zosimos, the Naassenes, and the mysteries of Attis. In his opinion, these conceptions also deeply affected the cosmology and soteriology of various Christian Gnostic systems—in the Valentinian myth, for example, the fall of Sophia led to the imprisonment of light in matter.

Another decisive shift in the myth took place when the Primal Man figure was transformed from a universal prototype of the cosmos into the figure who brought spiritual substance to humanity. Bousset noted, for example, that in Valentinian myth it is not the newly created world that is divine, but only the substance of light enclosed in humanity. Despite these changes, he insisted that up to this point in its development the myth had shown a fundamental continuity:

> Basically the same myth is under consideration, and the idea of a higher being who enters the body of the first created man is originally hardly different from the idea, which has now changed anthropologically, of the Primal Man, who calls the world into existence through his descent into matter.[65]

Yet another major twist was added, Bousset declared, when the Primal Man speculation came into contact with Judaism, but this time the twist so changed the myth that "it was hardly recognizable." In Judaism "the Primal Man became an eschatological figure." His primary activity was accomplished not in the Beginning but at the Endtime, so that he gradually coalesced with the Jewish figure of the Messiah. This twist takes us a full turn back to Philo. It is now comprehensible, said Bousset, that the *deuteros theos,* a prominent figure in the Primal Man speculation of Philo, should appear in Hellenistic Jewish theology. Moreover, this eschatological figure may have been further influenced by the Indian Yama or Iranian Yiman sagas, in which the "first man" was the prince of the underworld and judge of the dead. This development, Bousset claimed, may thereby have further influenced the depiction of the Son of Man as judge of the world.[66] With this final refinement, we have arrived at the New Testament Son of Man: a divine, cosmic figure who comes in the Endtime to bring salvation and to judge the world.

In this way Bousset traced the genealogy of the Primal Man figure from its "dark origins" in Oriental fertility rites toward the New Testament Son of Man:

> Thus the links of the chain are united throughout and we can actually survey a great interconnected sphere of speculation of a related kind. And only when we first penetrate and go through this entire chain can we bring a unified significance and coherence into these individual confused phantasmata and Baroque fancies.

These phantasmata and Baroque fancies were all "branches on the same tree," a tree whose roots reached far into the "syncretistic soil of the withered religions of antiquity."[67]

Bousset only partially associated the meaning of a motif like the Son of Man with its origin, for its full meaning necessarily included the sum total of its historical developments. In other words, he did not intend genealogy to *reduce* the New Testament Son of Man merely to an ancient magical fertility rite; rather, genealogy *enriched* the motif's field of meaning by supplying it with a complex of connotations and references vastly beyond its usage in specific New Testament literary contexts. The narrow incomprehensibility of Son of Man was replaced by "a great interconnected sphere of speculation of a related kind."

What difference does this Orientalizing focus make for defining Gnosticism and its relation to Christianity? Bousset's answer is seen most clearly in his comprehensive work *Kyrios Christos* (1913), a remarkable

book devoted to tracing "a history of the belief in Christ from the beginnings of Christianity to Irenaeus."[68] In the foreword to the fifth edition,
Rudolf Bultmann lauded it as an "indispensable" work of New Testament
scholarship.[69] It remains utterly fascinating reading, not only for its own
insights but also for the influence it had on later scholarship of the New
Testament and the history of early Christianity, including the problem of
the relationship to Gnosticism.

At first Bousset's conclusions do not appear to differ significantly from
those of Harnack. Although the book's aim was to construct a history of
how Christians have perceived Jesus rather than a portrait of the historical
person, Bousset did fashion a fairly clear profile of Jesus and his message.
His Jesus was a heroic figure with a daring faith in God that led him to
stand uncompromisingly against the false piety of his day, living in simple
trust of God with a relatively carefree attitude toward the things of the
world. Jesus preached the kingdom of God, taught an ethical religion of
forgiveness, and advocated human relationships of righteousness, love,
mercy, and reconciliation.[70]

Where, then, did the Gospel portrait of Jesus as the miracle-working
Messiah, the heavenly Son of Man, the Lord and Judge of the world, and
the fulfillment of prophecy and history come from? Bousset suggests that
these mythic inflations were invented by Jesus' first disciples because their
age was not ready for this simple and compelling figure and his teaching.
The "purely historical actuality" of Jesus alone would not have made an
impact. People needed to have a touched-up glossy photo of Jesus because they lived in a time when eschatological fantasies, miracle-workers,
prophets, devils, and demons reigned in the imagination. But Bousset ex-
cused these excesses, claiming that despite all the fabrication and elaboration, the "eternal and universally valid" remained visible in the foreground
of this fantastic Jesus. People merely "accepted the Eternal in it in the colorful wrappings of temporal clothing."[71]

Thus Bousset, like Harnack, held that the "eternal and universally
valid" still resided in the "colorful wrappings of temporal clothing." Bousset, however, makes no claims to exempt this "eternal" element from historical analysis, though he comes close to implying just that:

That religion is something original on its own basis: the relation of
the human soul to God—this *tu nos fecisti ad te, ac cor nostrum*

*inquietum est, donec requiescat in te*—and again, that all religious ut-
terances about God and human nature have to take their departure
from this point, all this [the apologists] did not recognize. To them
religion was a bundle of truths accessible to human knowledge, a
sensible world view.

Besides, the apologists too were firmly rooted in "the community dogma
and community cultus" so that while the "simple ethical content of gospel
has shone forth anew" in their work, nonetheless, "the time was not ripe
for the interpretation of religion or of Christianity as an eternal and universally valid necessity of the human soul; perhaps it will never be altogether ripe."[72] Here Bousset affirmed that even though he could show the
historical background of Christian ideas in the pre-Christian Orient, that
fact did not imply that Christianity lacked a unique originality, one that
humanity had yet to grasp fully in history.

In *Kyrios Christos,* Bousset was less interested in distinguishing the eternal elements of Christianity from its dogmatic forms than in determining
what the Palestinian primitive community *meant* when it said that Jesus
was the Messiah. The dominant expression of that view, he wrote, was
Son of Man.[73] It is true that Jesus never understood himself in terms of eschatological messianic expectation; that conviction was the belief of the
primitive community, which arose on the soil of Jewish eschatology and
messianic expectation. But—and here Bousset finds the decisive historical
significance of the term—the Christian concept of the Messiah–Son of
Man was shaped decisively not by any intellectual process but by the historical event of the crucifixion. Bousset is very firm in this conviction:
"The Jewish transcendent Messiah picture of the Son of Man and the historical experience of Jesus' suffering and death completely suffice in and
by themselves to account for the messianic faith of the first Christian
community in its genesis."[74] In Bousset's view, it was precisely this affirmation of the crucified Jesus as the Messiah–Son of Man that defined the
confession of the primitive Palestinian church and marked both its deepest intimacy with Judaism and its most decisive departure from it.

But at this point, Bousset hesitated. His genealogy of the Son of Man
in *Hauptprobleme der Gnosis* had tied the title's use in Judaism to Oriental
speculations about the Primal Man. In *Kyrios Christos,* Bousset chose to

leave open the question of whether "gnosticizing extensions" of Jewish eschatology, along with "all sorts of speculations of Oriental origin about
the semi-divine figure of the Primal Man," had already influenced Judaism and the Palestinian Christian community, or whether these elements
entered first with the decisive move of Christianity out into the Hellenistic world.[75] At other places in the book, however, it is clear that Bousset
regarded Judaism, at least *qua* the Old Testament, as part of "the genuinely Christian milieu" in a way that excluded "Hellenistic piety."[76] In the
end, then, his position closely approached that of Harnack, though for
different reasons and on different grounds. Both ultimately privileged the
gospel of Jesus and the primitive community from any Hellenizing or
Orientalizing influence and managed to set them at an ambiguous distance from Judaism.[77]

Bousset was more definite than Harnack in distancing Jesus from Judaism; he even reserved judgment about whether the primitive church had
been correct in identifying Jesus the Jew with the Jewish Messiah.[78] Like
Harnack and Christian culture in general, Bousset described Judaism as
ignorant and crude, and he caricatured it with negative stereotypes. In
an earlier work titled *Jesu Predigt in ihrem Gegensatz zum Judentum*
(1892), Bousset had associated "Late Judaism" almost solely with a limited
politico-nationalism, legalism, and "pathological" apocalyptic myth, and
as a result he claimed that "Judaism and Jesus are at completely opposite
poles to each other."[79]

The real parting of ways, however, came with the reconstruction of
the development of Christianity after Jesus. Poking at Harnack, Bousset
quipped: "If we wish to choose our *termini* following a famous example,"
we should see in Gnosticism not the acute Hellenization of Christianity,
but its "acute Orientalizing."[80] What does the reconstruction of Christian
and Gnostic origins look like from this "acute Orientalizing" perspective?

The intellectual world of early twentieth-century Europe tended to
dichotomize the geography of East and West into Oriental and Greek cultural divisions. Neither the geographical nor the cultural boundaries were
very precise, but in general Bousset followed the discourse of Orientalism,
in which the Greek, Western side tended to be characterized as rationalist,
historical, and universalizing; the Eastern, as nonrational, mythical, and
cultic. Thus for Bousset to suggest an "Orientalizing" rather than a "Hel-

lenizing" of Christianity was intended to maintain that it was not ratio-
nalizing forces that shaped the origins of Christianity but myth and cult.
Insofar as Harnack had relegated the forces of Oriental syncretism to a
very minor role in the drama of Christian origins, Bousset insisted that he
was quite mistaken:

> Rome and especially Greece, in spite of all the syncretistic currents,
> are not the Orient. What breaks forth into the open here in the sec-
> ond half of the second century has a long prehistory which has tran-
> spired especially in Syria (Asia Minor) and Egypt. But Christianity
> came out of the Orient, and the intellectual home base of the Gen-
> tile Christian church was first Syria (Antioch) and southern Asia Mi-
> nor (Tarsus), and in the second place from the earliest times onward,
> Egypt. And further, in its beginnings, to which especially Paul, John,
> and Gnosticism belong, Christianity has nothing, nothing at all, to
> do with the truly philosophical literature of the educated circles and
> its historical development. What here first begins to climb up the
> ladder in the course of the second century can have been lively for a
> long time in a lower stratum.[81]

Bousset recognized that he would meet resistance in taking the study of
Christian origins beyond the study of Judaism into the Hellenistic world,
and even more resistance to moving outside the Roman Empire into the
Hellenistic Orient.[82] But he insisted that Christianity would otherwise remain incomprehensible.

The decisive point, and indeed one of the distinguishing features of
Bousset's approach, was his insistence on *the primacy of cultic community
as the generative matrix for religious thought.* Remember that Bousset began
his genealogy of the Son of Man with a cultic hymn. So, too, he took
Christian community to be the primary generative matrix for Christian
theology.[83] This perspective led him to reject Harnack's view that intellectual speculation and metaphysics were secondary features of Christian development that arose when its "original enthusiasm" was rigidified into
dogma. Instead, he insisted that "speculation and myth accompanied
Christianity from the outset." The break with Jesus and his teaching arose
not through rational systematizing but in cult: "If one insists upon wish-
ing to point to the place where the development of the gospel of Jesus suf-

fered the break one finds it in the very beginnings, in the emergence of the Christ cult." This break took place very early with the shift to "Hellenistic territory": "The great and decisive turning point in the development of Christianity is marked by its transition to Gentile-Christian territory in its very earliest beginnings. No other event approaches this in importance."[84]

This decisive shift to Hellenistic territory was already visible in both Paul's and John's Gospel, and therefore with them attention ought to shift to the larger history of religions context of the whole Greco-Roman world. For although Paul was a Jew, he was a diaspora Jew, and his Gospel of the *Kyrios Christos* was permeated by ideas and influences from Oriental piety. So, too, the Gospel of John: its conceptuality was "rooted in the soil of Hellenistic, Oriental piety."[85]

At this point Gnosticism becomes an important issue. Bousset devoted ten pages of *Kyrios Christos* to describing the basic nature and content of Gnostic thought, which may be summarized as follows:[86]

- *sharp dualism,* formed when "motifs which stem from Greek philosophy of a Platonist or Neoplatonist tendency are combined with specifically Oriental, mythologically determined dualism." Here Gnosticism shows itself to be "non-Greek" and sharply at odds with Hellenistic piety, which understood the stars to be the visible manifestation of divinity, not of the demonic, as the Gnostics would have it;
- *radical pessimism* toward the lower world;
- *alienation:* "the Gnostic feels homeless, an alien in an alien world. Again and again this key word of alienation sounds through the deepest and most personal confessions of the Gnostics";
- *a theology of the alien God;*
- *an elitist anthropology,* that is, "the foolish dream that *one belongs alone in the immediate entourage of God*";[87]
- *a radical religion of redemption,* "not the ascent from the lower to the higher but wholly the liberation from the absolutely inimical, the absolutely different."[88] Bousset suggested that this "unrestrained yearning for redemption" was an expression of "an age tending toward bankruptcy";
- *salvation by nature, through revelation, initiation, and sacrament:* On

the one hand, he states: "If the divine higher nature is from the first something native to the elect, then to a certain degree the absolute necessity of a redemption occurring at a definite time disappears. At least no longer is something absolutely new introduced into the human race by means of redemption." On the other hand, Bousset insightfully perceived that such redemption is by no means automatic merely because divinity is "native to the elect": "It is not the opinion of the Gnostics that the half-extinguished spark could, from its own nature and power, again be fanned and burst into flame. The elements of light, the fallen Sperma, the ἀπόρροιαι are in hopeless captivity here below. A redemption is required that comes down from above and comes in from without. Gnosticism is not the reflection of the intellect or of the better spiritual ego upon itself; Gnosis is mysterious revelation and redemption brought about in vision and ecstasy through initiation and sacrament. It is not the philosopher who is the guide of the Gnostics but the mystagogue, and it is not philosophical study that saves the soul but participation in the mystery society and the initiation";

- *esoteric:* "Gnosis is rather mysterious wisdom which rests upon secret revelation . . . Gnosticism is the world of vision, of ecstasy, of secret revelations and mediators of revelation, of revelational literature and of secret tradition";
- *mythic:* "in Gnostic redemption theology, myth everywhere takes the place of the historical";
- *docetic Christology:* "For [Gnosticism's] basic outlook the idea was indeed unendurable that Jesus had lived as a real man in a genuine human existence. Such a contact of the upper celestial world and of an aeon stemming from that world with the filth of lower matter must have appeared to them once and for all impossible. The most ancient answer which the Gnostics gave to this question was simply to cut the knot. It was roundly declared that Jesus on earth had possessed only an illusory form. This view of Docetism was one of the earliest manifestations of actual Christian heresy."

Most of these characteristics derive more or less directly from the views of the ancient polemicists. Two, however, belong to the modern age: the association of religion with feeling (alienation), and the particular way in which myth is contrasted with history.

Bousset held that Gnosticism was a pre-Christian religion, existing alongside of Christianity.[89] It was an Oriental product, anti-Jewish and un-Hellenic, that became attached to Christianity when it moved out into Hellenistic territory.[90] Gnosticism, he claimed, is essentially mythic and thereby distinct from Christianity's historically rooted theology: "in Gnostic redemption theology, myth everywhere takes the place of the historical."[91] It could not, therefore, absorb the most basic elements of Christianity, especially the earthly Jesus:

> Only with difficulty and gradually was Gnosticism able to draw the figure of Jesus of Nazareth into its mythological basic outlook, and one clearly senses, throughout, the compromise character of the resultant view. For this reason Jesus has surprisingly limited significance for the practical piety of many Gnostic sects, as is best evidenced in the ancient Valentinian source document in Irenaeus and in the *Excerpta.*[92]

The real attraction of Gnosticism to Christianity was not, then, the figure of Jesus; it was the theology of Paul, which contained "the basic outlook of its own piety."[93] Bousset listed the major affinities of Gnosticism to Paul: "his radical anthropological dualism and pessimism . . . his theory about the inferior nature of the first man, his demonizing of almost the entire world of spirits, the tendency of his ethic to a dualistic asceticism, his spiritualistic doctrine of the resurrection, his anthropological terminology."[94] Yet, Bousset notes, Paul would have recognized little of his own theology once the Gnostics were done,[95] largely because Paul's "idea of a unique redemption taking place at one point in history" is lost when redemption becomes pure myth.[96] It was not that Gnosticism had twisted Paul into something he was not; rather, Gnosticism had taken Paul's theology in the direction of "acute Orientalizing."[97]

Bousset was quite clear that the greatest danger Christianity faced from Gnosticism was its legitimate connections with Pauline thought. In order for Gnosticism to be defeated, Paul had to be reinterpreted along ecclesiastical lines.[98] This feat, Bousset argued, was accomplished by Irenaeus, though not without a very high price, "the price being that in a grandiose manner he distorted the genuine Pauline ideas and divested them of their essential nature."[99] The result of this intricate process, however, was that the distorted interpretation of Paul functioned to define the boundaries or limits of orthodox Christianity. By wresting Paul from the Gnostics, Irenaeus had "struck a fatal blow" to the elements in Gnosticism most dangerous to Christianity.[100]

Why was Gnosticism so dangerous? Because its unfettered, utopian, spiritual enthusiasm threatened "to explode and annihilate an old world," Bousset suggested, though it lacked the capacity of ecclesiastical Christianity to "build a new world-embracing fellowship."[101] Gnosticism's spirituality ran to ground on its sociological failure.

In the end, the history of religions method, which aimed to set out the meaning of Christianity apart from dogmatic and ecclesiastical limits, fell into the business of showing the originality and superiority of Christianity.[102] However muted this tendency was in Bousset's work, the final note he sounded was the triumph of ecclesiastical Christianity over the dangers of Gnostic heresy.

## Rudolf Bultmann

It is no exaggeration to call Rudolf Bultmann the greatest German New Testament theologian of the twentieth century. Though perhaps most famous for his theological project of demythologizing and his pathbreaking work on the history of the synoptic tradition, Bultmann also wrote extensively on the Gospel of John, placing important emphasis on its relationship to Gnosticism. It is here that his connection with the history of religions school is most apparent.

As early as 1750, Johann Michaelis had recognized the relationship of the Gospel of John to the Gnostic thought world; Reitzenstein's work on the Gnostic redeemer myth and Bousset's connection of the Gospel of John with "Hellenistic, Oriental piety" only brought the issue into greater focus and broader acceptance.[103] Bultmann took the results of these earlier scholars as a starting point and set out to ascertain that relationship in finer detail in order to elucidate the meaning of John's Christology.

In 1923 he published a study on the Johannine prologue in which he argued that "a *Vorlage* was used in the prologue in the statement of v. 9–13 and 1–5 which pertains to a preexistent divine being." The difficulty, he said, lay in the use of such language by a Christian author to refer to Jesus:

> It is in any case not intelligible in what sense a Christian author would have spoken of the preexistent Jesus, since he came into the world, his property, but the world did not know him from whom it had taken its being. On the other hand, pre-Christian and non-Christian speculation of this sort is known to us.[104]

Through a study of Jewish wisdom literature, for example, Bultmann found that the *logos* figure of the prologue had been heavily influenced by speculation on the cosmic role of the preexistent Wisdom. The fact that the Johannine tradition used the term *logos* instead of *sophia* would seem to indicate that the roots of the *Vorlage* lay in "Alexandrian Jewish speculation" because there we see, for example in Philo, that *logos* and *sophia* are presented as "parallel figures." With this much assured, Bultmann contended, it was necessary to determine "the origin and type of this Wisdom speculation" in order to "place the Johannine prologue in its proper history of religions' context." The work of Bousset and Reitzenstein convinced him that a much older and non-Jewish mythological speculation stood in the background. Its precise origin, however, was unclear. He found illuminating parallels in Babylonian and Persian literature where the term "wisdom" occurred, but he concluded that "the name wisdom for the revelatory deity is no more essential than the feminine gender." Because focus on the term itself was not particularly helpful, he turned to an examination of the Iranian Primal Man tradition cited by Reitzenstein and to a study of the role of messenger figures in Manichaeism and Mandaeanism. Although he found many similarities between these figures and Wisdom-*logos* speculation, in the end he wrote that the connection of all this remains "unclear to me."[105]

Undeterred, Bultmann sought an answer in the work of Reitzenstein: "There is, however, yet a further notable proof: how very much *the Christology of the entire Gospel of John* stands in relation to" Reitzenstein's presentation of Iranian speculation concerning the saved Savior, that is, his presentation of that divine being, the heavenly "Man" who descended to the earth as the messenger of God, the revealer. The revealer took on the position of a human being and then, after completing his revelatory message, returned to Heaven, where he will be raised up, honored, and become the Judge of all. Bultmann wrote: "I do not believe that Reitzenstein was correct in understanding the synoptic Son of Man in this context, but the Johannine words *uios tou anthropou* are based in this [mythological] view."[106] In the Gospel of John, Jesus is presented as (1) preexistent, (2) honored and raised up, and (3) a judge. Like the heavenly "Man," he has the same nature as those he came to save, so that they are assured of salvation by his being raised up.

Bultmann concluded that the Johannine prologue must have stemmed from "the baptizing sects, in whose circles are included John the Baptist." He claimed that this view was supported by the role of John as a witness to Jesus. Bultmann's final conclusion was entirely speculative and rested, not on his own investigations, but on the work of Reitzenstein: "If my supposition is correct, then the Gospel of John is in a new sense a proof for the extraordinarily early penetration of Oriental Gnostic speculation in early Christianity."[107]

Two years later Bultmann published a second article on the Gospel of John, titled "Die Bedeutung der neuerschlossenen mandäischen und manichäischen Quellen für das Verständnis der Johannes Evangeliums" ["The Significance of Newly Discovered Mandaean and Manichaean Sources for the Understanding of the Gospel of John"]. In it he argued that the Gospel of John presupposed a Gnostic salvation myth and could be understood only against that background. To describe that myth, Bultmann drew primarily on Mandaean and Manichaean texts, but he also referred to material from Jewish Wisdom literature, the Odes of Solomon, and so-called Gnostic texts, especially the apocryphal acts of the apostles.[108] He offered a full sketch of the Gnostic redeemer myth, based on Reitzenstein's myth of the Primal Man:

> The soul, imprisoned on the earth, is brought a revelation by a messenger who comes from heaven about its heavenly origin, its home, and its return. The messenger appears in earthly, human clothing; in glory, he rises upward. Parallel to this soteriological myth runs a cosmological myth: the state of the messenger expresses the state of the

heavenly Primal Man, who descended in primordial times from the heavenly world into matter by which he was overcome and imprisoned. Now the state of the messenger is assimilated to that of the Primal Man, and the messenger in his earthly form appears imprisoned and distressed, and his ascension is also his own salvation: he is the redeemed redeemer. Furthermore the fate of the Primal Man is the same as the fate of the individual soul; the salvation of the soul is the liberation of the Primal Man and the end of the earthly world whose origin and condition was made possible by the imprisonment of the light particles of the Primal Man in chaotic substance. So then, in the end, the fate of the messenger and the soul are the same; indeed the messenger is no more than an image of the soul which recognizes itself in him. Therefore it is not always possible to be sure about whom the text is referring to: the Primal Man, the messenger, or the soul. It is also therefore possible under certain circumstances to use texts which refer to the Primal Man or the soul to draw the picture of the messenger which is necessary for an understanding of the form of Jesus in the Gospel of John.[109]

It cannot be doubted, Bultmann claimed, that this Gnostic redeemer myth in its essential outline is older than the Gospel of John: "No one . . . could possibly think that many-branched and many-formed mythology . . . could have developed from the Gospel of John." In his opinion, the fact that the Gospel of John lacks so many elements of the myth proves that the author must have presumed the myth, and indeed knew it so well that he did not need to repeat it in full. There were other shifts as well, for John's own concern was not the fate of the soul but cosmology and anthropology. For one, the vital connection with cultic practice was lost.[110]

Bultmann then asked the question, "Was there a particular religious community that stood in a decisive literary relationship with and under the influence of Johannine Christianity?" He answered in the affirmative and suggested that "perhaps" that community was the Mandaean sect. This is possible, he argued, because "the origin of the Mandaeans falls in an earlier period than the literature belonging to us."[111] He cited evidence from Lidzbarski and Reitzenstein to support this view.[112]

In his influential commentary on the Gospel of John (1941), Bultmann again drew on the Gnostic redeemer myth to describe the basic content of Gnostic belief.[113] Given this starting point, he concluded that the "relationship of John's Gospel to this Gnostic view of the world is twofold." On the one hand, Gnosticism forms an important influence on the Gospel of John; on the other hand, the Gospel of John is anti-Gnostic, especially in its teaching of the Word made flesh, and may have been written in part to convert Gnostics to his view.[114]

Bultmann's most systematic comparison of Christianity and Gnosticism is laid out in *Das Urchristentum im Rahmen der antiken Religion* (1949, translated as *Primitive Christianity in Its Contemporary Setting*). After presenting a description of Gnosticism, he compared it with Christianity in order to illuminate not only what the two religions have in common, but at what points they diverge. The points of divergence mark the boundaries between the two and, in Bultmann's opinion, demonstrate the superiority of Christianity. Note that his primary method of proving this preeminence was comparison, not genealogy, for he viewed Gnosticism as an Oriental competitor of Christianity.[115]

He could not establish superiority on the basis of chronological priority, since he held that Gnosticism was pre-Christian in origin. Neither did he believe that the preeminence of Christianity over Gnosticism could rest on the view that Gnosticism is syncretic, while Christianity is not.[116] Bultmann fully affirmed that Christianity is "a remarkable product of syncretism," by which he meant that it is "no unitary phenomenon" but is "full of tendencies and contradictions." He followed Bauer in claiming that some of these early "tendencies and contradictions" were later condemned "by orthodox Christianity" as heretical.[117]

But then Bultmann switched tactics. After affirming that Christianity is a syncretistic religion, he asked: "Is Christianity then really a syncretistic religion? Or is there a fundamental unity behind all this diversity? . . . Does primitive Christianity contain a single, new and unique doctrine of human existence?"[118] The most significant word in this statement is "or"; by juxtaposing syncretism with uniqueness and simultaneously proving that Christianity offered something entirely new, Bultmann could deny its essentially syncretic character. His construction of Gnosticism, however, could not pass that test. The assumption that makes this kind of logic appear reasonable is linked to the nineteenth-century temporal economics of social evolution in which "new" means unique and original, not chronologically prior. Truth does not necessarily precede error, as Tertullian would have it; rather, Christianity was the culmination of scattered and half-successful attempts at reaching the highest stage of religion:

> It is obvious that an unbroken connection exists between Christianity and the non-Christian religions, if we consider the Christian faith to be a *religious* phenomenon at all and if, thinking we are making a Christian judgement, we see it as the highest of religious phenomena. A consideration of the history of religion seems to confirm this judgement, for we can indubitably regard the heathen religions as first steps towards the Christian religion, or as phenomena parallel to it; and it may be that we can establish that what exists in them only in initial stages has reached its full development in Christianity or that what grew into a less complete or distorted form in them through faulty development has reached its consummation in it.[119]

Hence for Bultmann, calling Christianity a syncretic religion poses no problem, since that assertion can simultaneously be dismissed by showing the superiority of Christianity in its uniqueness. Syncretism no longer excluded the possibility of purity.

Comparison was the method Bultmann used to prove that uniqueness and superiority. For example, he argued that Christianity and Gnosticism had the same understanding of the situation of humanity in the world, and both presumed the need for divine salvation in an event outside oneself.[120] They differed, however, in what each conceived to be the root cause of the problem. For Gnosticism, it was fate; for Christianity, sin.[121] As a result, salvation was also conceived differently, and it is here especially that Gnosticism failed the test, falling into cosmological dualism and a view of salvation by nature that nullified authentic historical existence.[122] The Christian proclamation of the Cross led (and still leads), Bultmann said, to a positive life of love grounded in faith; Gnosticism could lead only to denial of the value of all historical existence: "It was a point from which every possible human action and experience was denied." Hence Gnosticism was inadequate because of its cosmological dualism, its doctrine of salvation by knowledge, and its world-denying ethics. Comparison therefore affirmed that Christianity is not "really a syncretistic religion" because it contains "a single, new and unique doctrine of human existence," one which involves "a new existential understanding of Self," a complete freedom which is nothing less than "simply a radical openness for the future."[123]

Bultmann's comparison of Gnosticism and Christianity was still about defining true Christianity. Whether or not the other is called Gnosticism or heresy, its function is still the same, the players are still the same, and the terms of the engagement are still much the same. To be sure, Bultmann connected the genealogy of Christianity to Gnosticism much more intimately than Irenaeus could have tolerated, and he rejected Tertullian's thesis that truth always precedes error—still nothing in his results would much disappoint either. Both Irenaeus and Tertullian found Gnosticism objectionable, and on precisely the same grounds: its cosmological dualism rejected the true God as creator; its doctrine of salvation by nature seemingly made nonsense of the Cross; and far from a positive ethics of love and reconciliation, it maintained only a negative attitude toward the world and its creator. By articulating this perception in terms that could grip the contemporary imagination and stir the desire for authentic existence, Bultmann demonstrated how thoroughly he comprehended the polemicists. His was a new strategy suited for a new age, but the result was much the same for Gnosticism. Bultmann's conclusions were completely normative—for in this intellectual economy, Gnosticism can only play the inferior role of primitive, incomplete, or faulty development, whether prior to Christianity or parallel to it.

The plot of Christian history had shifted from a narrative of original purity and subsequent deviance to a comprehensive account of the whole history of religion, one that aspired to map humankind's progress from incomplete or distorted religion to its fullest and highest expression in Christianity. The method, too, had shifted: from genealogy to comparison. Only the results remained the same.

And yet, the shift to comparison brought an overtly theological note to the process of determining the relative value of Gnosticism. Before, the historian had determined the purity of Christian origins and its chronological priority to heresy; now the theologian determined the religious adequacy of Christianity through comparison. In the past, the overt deployment of theological norms was considered to be suspect in what was supposed to be an "objective" or at least an impartial historical enterprise.[124] What Bultmann did was to exemplify in his own practice the conviction that the evaluation of Gnosticism is a theological enterprise. Here I must agree; the overt discussion of value and meaning opens the door for critically engaged scholarship, whether by theology, philosophy, ethics, or cultural criticism.

## Reflections on the History of Religions School

Taken collectively, the impact of scholars from the history of religions school on the twentieth-century conceptuality of Gnosticism is hard to overestimate. Their greatest achievement was to extend the study of Christianity beyond the parochial borders of church history by exploring more widely the possible intersections between Christianity and the surrounding cultures of its formative matrix. And they asked historians to consider the meaning of Gnostic myth as a phenomenon worthy of study in its own right. No longer the product of heretical tendencies in Christianity, Gnosticism was reconceptualized as a pre-Christian, Oriental religion that influenced Christianity in its most formative period of development. By framing their historical reconstruction in terms of typological or chronological models of hierarchical development, these scholars put into question the secondary and derivative character of Gnostic thought, challenged the chronological priority and purity of Christianity, and openly reconfigured the relationship of Gnosticism and Christianity to their cultural environment, enlarging the scope to include a wide range of literature, especially Iranian and Mandaean materials.

Their work constituted a significant challenge to the centuries-old understanding that Gnosticism originated as a Christian heresy. And yet normative definitions of Christianity remained strangely unaffected by this seemingly radical assault. History of religions scholarship did not undermine basic commitments to the ultimate superiority of Christianity, and it did not challenge the view that Christian Gnosticism was a secondary and derivative heresy. As Bultmann accurately perceived, history of religions methods required a different basis for the devaluation of Gnosticism than had been offered by polemicists. It was no longer a matter of locating where and why some forms of Christianity had gone amiss. What had to be established was an alternative basis for articulating the widespread belief in the superiority of normative Christianity. In this enterprise, Gnosticism, deployed comparatively in a colonialist and evolutionary framework, remained a reliable tool for the articulation of orthodoxy. As Rudolph summarizes:

> It is the undeniable merit of the so-called "religionsgeschichtliche Schule" of German Protestant theology to have done pioneering work here. One of its most important results was the proof that the gnostic movement was originally a non-Christian phenomenon which was gradually enriched with Christian concepts until it made its appearance as independent Christian Gnosis. This development, which we know in rough outline only, is equivalent to the development of Gnosis from a relatively independent Hellenistic religion of later antiquity to a Christian "heresy." Its link with Christian ideas, which began at an early stage, produced on the one hand a fruitful symbiosis which greatly helped its expansion, but on the other hand contained a deadly germ to which sooner or later it was to succumb in competition with the official Christian Church.[125]

As this statement shows, the history of religions school did not put into question the identity of normative Christianity ("the official Christian Church") or the heretical character of Gnosticism.

Wilhelm Bousset had regarded Gnosticism as an Oriental pre-Christian religion that at its roots was anti-Jewish and un-Hellenic. It was more utterly "other" than anything we have yet encountered. But this "other" was in fact none other than the product of nineteenth- and twentieth-century European Orientalism. Gnosticism had merely become less a heretical other than a historical and cultural other. It became possible to see Gnosticism not as the systematizing, intellectual enterprise of the first Christian theologians, as Harnack had, but as an esoteric, mythic religion of the Orient, incapable of historical consciousness and thus of higher religious sensibility.[126] Gnosticism ultimately failed, Bousset claimed, not because of any systematizing rigidity but because its excessive enthusiasm made group stability impossible. In this way, the construction of Gnosticism as pre-Christian and non-Christian opened a path to imagining Gnosticism not as the product of an alien influence on Christianity, but as itself the alien parasite whose infestation produced the heresies of Christian Gnosticism.

History of religions scholars left an influential legacy of innovative misconceptions and misleading characterizations of Gnosticism. Of these, possibly the greatest mischief was done by the invention of the Gnostic redeemer myth, that staple of two-page summaries of Gnosticism.[127] This stirring narrative is the product of motif history viewed synthetically. It was constructed by taking bits and pieces from particular motifs from a variety of historical and literary contexts, and combining them into a single, coherent narrative. The impression that this artificial narrative actually existed gained support from the fact that so many literary artifacts could be interpreted to fit at least some part of the myth. They then appeared as evidence for the whole story—even though in reality *there is no single existing ancient literary source that gives "the Gnostic redeemer myth" as scholars have "reconstructed" (i.e., invented) it.* We might also note the irony that contemporary scholars have often explicitly characterized this myth as "artificial," but they have seen this artificiality as the product, not of twentieth-century methods of historical reconstruction, but of the "half-educated" minds of ancient "Gnostics." In this case I would say that historians have been guilty of precisely what they accused the Gnostics of: the creation of *Kunstmythen.* The fact that current scholarship has thoroughly undermined any foundation for this artificial construction has not stopped it from continuing to exert considerable influence.

# 5

# Gnosticism Reconsidered

The year 1934 was remarkable for scholarship on Gnosticism and Christianity, signaled as it was by the publication of the two most important books on the topic in the twentieth century. In that year both Walter Bauer's *Rechtgläubigkeit und Ketzerei im ältesten Christentum* and the first volume of Hans Jonas's *Gnosis und spätantiker Geist* appeared.[1] The two works were written independent of each other, and indeed they took quite different approaches to the topic.

Bauer's work stood within church history and challenged the long-standing assumption that heresy was a secondary development in the history of Christianity. Bauer was disturbed by what he saw as the overweening and distorting influence of normative theological categories on what were supposed to be impartial historical studies. Jonas agreed at least in principle, noting that within the whole question of the relationship of Gnosticism to Christianity was "nested a rat's maze of problems that arose out of concern about the originality and uniqueness of Christianity."[2] But Jonas chose not to be led into those debates; what disturbed him was not the influence of theology but the inadequacies of motif-historical research used by the history of religions school to explain the origins and meaning of Gnosticism.

## Walter Bauer

In his pioneering book translated into English as *Orthodoxy and Heresy in Earliest Christianity,* Bauer suggested the following working hypothesis: "certain manifestations of Christian belief that the authors of the church renounced as 'heresies' originally had not been such at all, but, at least here and there, were the only form of the new religion—that is, for those regions they were simply 'Christianity.'"[3] Bauer's reconstruction of the evidence pointed toward the need to abandon the dominant master narrative of Christian origins, which he called "the ecclesiastical position." He summarized this position in four points:

(1) Jesus reveals the pure doctrine to his apostles, partly before his death, and partly in the forty days before his ascension.

(2) After Jesus' final departure, the apostles apportion the world among themselves, and each takes the unadulterated gospel to the land which has been allotted him.

(3) Even after the death of the disciples the gospel branches out further. But now obstacles to it spring up within Christianity itself. The devil cannot resist sowing weeds in the divine wheat field— and he is successful at it. True Christians blinded by him abandon the pure doctrine. This development takes place in the following sequence: unbelief, right belief, wrong belief. There is scarcely the faintest notion anywhere that unbelief might be changed directly into what the church calls false belief. No, where there is heresy, orthodoxy must have preceded . . .

(4) Of course, right belief is invincible. In spite of all the efforts of Satan and his instruments, it repels unbelief and false belief, and extends its victorious sway even further.[4]

"Scholarship," according to Bauer, "has not found it hard to criticize these convictions."[5] There was no pure doctrine stemming from Jesus that later generations merely fixed in creedal form. Rather, the ecclesiastical doctrine and institutional structures of fourth- and fifth-century orthodoxy developed slowly and amid significant controversy. Questions about the meaning of Jesus' teachings, the significance of Jesus himself, especially his death and resurrection, the relationship to Judaism and the Old Testament, the legitimate basis for organization and authority, the roles of women and slaves, and other significant issues were all under hot debate and were addressed in different ways by various groups of Christians.

All early Christian texts without exception show evidence of being shaped in the forges of those controversies. In the first centuries, the appeal to apostolic genealogy, to Scripture, to revelation and ecstasy, or to a rule of faith did not settle matters, since groups made such appeals to support diverse positions. Marcion was the first to develop a canon and Heracleon the first to write a commentary, and both were "heretics" in the eyes of Irenaeus and Tertullian. The Spirit spoke to many different Christians, to so-called Montanist heretics as well as to Paulinists, and Christians of all stripes died as martyrs to the faith.

Bauer insisted that scholars face these facts without blinking or turning away and without recourse to predetermined judgments. But he was discouraged about his own day:

> For my tastes, [criticism] all too easily submits to the ecclesiastical opinion as to what is early and late, original and dependent, essential and unimportant for the earliest history of Christianity. If my impression is correct, even today the overwhelmingly dominant view still is that for the period of Christian origins, ecclesiastical doctrine (of course, only as this pertains to a certain stage in its development) already represents what is primary, while heresies, on the other hand, somehow are a deviation from the genuine. I do not mean to say that this point of view must be false, but neither can I regard it as self-evident, or even as demonstrated and clearly established. Rather, we are confronted here with a problem that merits our attention.[6]

Despite the disclaimer "I do not mean to say that this point of view must be false," he spent the rest of the book working to prove that it indeed was false.

Bauer's approach involved three important innovations. First, he focused on local histories. Rather than seeing the rise of Christianity as a uniform development from Jesus to the orthodox Church of the post-Constantinian period, Bauer emphasized that Christianity did not look the same everywhere or develop through the same stages; it took different directions in theology and practice in different areas at different times. His model would result, not in a single homogenized history of Christianity, but in a set of distinct local histories that would illustrate the variety of early Christianities.

Second, Bauer refused on methodological grounds to take the New

Testament as the starting point for writing the history of Christianity. Because the New Testament was produced precisely to undergird ecclesiastical doctrine, to take it as the starting point would be to concede at the outset a good deal to the validity of hindsight.

Third, he regarded the ominous silence of the New Testament and apostolic fathers regarding particular geographical areas (notably Edessa and Egypt) to be highly significant. Bauer asked what might lie behind their silence: might it indicate that the earliest forms of Christianity in these areas were not orthodox? Bauer has repeatedly been criticized for relying too heavily on arguments from silence. Yet if the subsequent discovery of heterogeneous works at Nag Hammadi has taught us anything, it is that a lot more was going on in the first centuries of Christianity than traditional sources had previously allowed. How much to rest on silence is of course another matter. But we can no longer consider the silence to be without significance.

Bauer argued with great learning and imagination that the earliest forms of Christianity in Edessa, Egypt, and Asia Minor only later came to be viewed as heretical. Regarding Edessa, Bauer noted that the older portion of the *Edessene Chronicle* could not offer more than three names for the early period of Christianity there: Marcion, Bar Daison (Bardesanes), and Mani—all representatives of heretical Christianity. He concluded:

> The inclusion of these names in a *Chronicle* from Edessa thus must be due less to the relationship of their persons to this city than to that of the doctrines that they advocated. If these three, and *only* these—with no "ecclesiastical" "bishop" alongside of them—are specified by name in a Christian *Chronicle* of Edessa, that indicates that *the* form of religion and of Christianity which they advocated represents what was original for Edessa. Ecclesiastically organized Christianity with cultic edifice, cemetery, and bishop, first appears at the beginning of the fourth century—the time of Eusebius and of the Emperor Constantine—and from then on, it unremittingly determines the course of things for the chronicler.[7]

For Egypt the situation also seemed to indicate that the earliest forms of Christianity there were varied, though they were not neatly divided along the lines of orthodoxy and heresy:

> At the beginning of the second century—how long before that we
> cannot say—there were Gentile Christians alongside Jewish Chris-
> tians, with both movements resting on syncretistic-gnostic founda-
> tions . . . There is every reason at least to raise the question whether
> distinct boundaries between heretical and ecclesiastical Christendom
> had been developed at all in Egypt by the end of the second century.[8]

The situation in Asia Minor was even more complicated, for strands of
Christianity competed there in complex interchanges. Before Bauer it had
often been suggested that the opponents of Paul in Greece were Gnostics,
and Bauer was able to build his case in part on that basis.[9]

What continues to make Bauer's book so important is not the precise
conclusions he reached in his reconstruction of early Christianity (later
scholarship has found much to criticize, as well as to praise); it is rather
that the main point has remained remarkably firm and provided real insight into early Christian historiography.[10] Bauer insisted that writing the
history of Christianity backward through the lenses of the later ecclesiastical position distorted the evidence.

Bauer's most lasting contribution was the fact that his work pointed the
way toward an alternative model of Christian historiography. Bauer directly challenged Tertullian's thesis that orthodoxy chronologically preceded heresy. Of course the history of religions school had already declared Gnosticism to predate Christianity, but Bauer's work offered a
more profound challenge to normative definitions of Christianity because
Bauer did not consider Gnosticism to be a non-Christian religion. From
Bauer's perspective, the early heresies, including those classified as Gnostic, were Christian. As a result, his construction of early Christian history
directly challenged the normativity of orthodox Christian identity in ways
that the history of religions school had not. In its own way, Bauer's work
has had a more lasting impact than that of Jonas. Despite the considerable
criticism of his book, Bauer provided the conceptual tools for thinking
about what all historical-critical scholars of Christianity now quite rou-
tinely refer to as "the varieties of early Christianity." Largely for this reason, his book remains one of the most important works in the history of
Christianity in the twentieth century, and may well point the direction for
early Christian historiography in the twenty-first.

Although Bauer sought to undermine the insinuation of theological interests into historical reconstruction, his continued use of the terms "orthodoxy" and "heresy" to refer to distinct forms of early Christianity
tended to reinscribe the normative view and marginalize anything labeled
heresy. Bauer himself suggested that these terms would be inadequate because the multiformity of Christianity cannot be comprehended by only
two categories. What he did not say, but what seems implicit in his work,
is that the relationship between Gnosticism and Christianity would never
yield a single solution—not just because that relationship varied from
time to time and place to place, but because our very understanding of
Gnosticism and Christianity requires rethinking.

## Hans Jonas

In 1934, the German Jewish philosopher Hans Jonas published the first
volume of *Gnosis und spätantiker Geist,* a systematic rethinking of the origin and meaning of Gnosticism. Soon after, matters of world significance
would lead Jonas to leave Europe and eventually take an academic position at the New School for Social Research in New York City. For the re-
mainder of his career he wrote in English.

Jonas's work was imbued with the simple but profound insight that the
methods of origins and genealogy that had dominated—and indeed continue to dominate—the study of Gnosticism were inadequate to explain
the meaning of Gnosticism or account for its origin.[11] Jonas proposed instead a methodological shift toward a typological (phenomenological) delimitation of the essential characteristics of Gnosticism as a way both
to define Gnosticism and to explain its existential meaning. This shift
resolved the most serious tensions between typological-structural models and chronological-genealogical historiography by unlinking them. He
continued to use both typological and historical approaches, but each was
substantially transformed. Typology became subject to phenomenological
methods. Motif history with its chronological stemma was banished. History remained important to his thinking, but it was viewed less diachroni-
cally than synchronically. Historical analysis in Jonas's view primarily involved interpreting a phenomenon in its social and political context, not
charting its linear evolution through time.

An example of the methodological shift Jonas proposed is found in his critique of Bousset.[12] Bousset supposed that Gnostic dualism arose by adding Platonic ideas to Persian dualism; Jonas considered Gnostic dualism to have been formed through a synthesis of Platonic and Persian conceptions in accordance with the Gnostic experience of self and world.[13] The difference in the two positions is clear: Bousset believed that both origin and meaning could be established by tracing the genealogy of a motif or idea. Jonas correctly pointed out that even if such a genealogy could be accurately plotted, it would still not be sufficient to account for the origin of Gnosticism and certainly not the meaning of its language and myth.[14]

Jonas did not reject the possibility of identifying relationships among motifs, but he cautioned that a metaphor (such as that of a valuable pearl) may be used to express a variety of meanings.[15] Whether an image like the pearl is the product of specific exegetical transformation has to be determined from comparison of the contexts in which it appears. Motif history obscured the processes by which new tradition is generated; according to Jonas, "it is the meaning context, taken in its wholeness and integrity, which matters, and not the traffic in single symbols, figures, and names."[16]

Jonas criticized the search for genealogical dependence insofar as it tended to obscure the possibility that Gnosticism (or any other tradition) might have been a living force and not merely a sponge sopping up whatever tradition lay at hand: "And once we grant this as a living force, we might even credit it [Gnosticism], *horribile dictu,* with the invention of some of its own symbols."[17] His own method analyzed "recurrent elements of expression" that revealed "something of the fundamental experience, the mode of feeling, and the vision of reality distinctively characteristic of the gnostic mind." The alien, the beyond, the stranger's sojourn in the world below, light and darkness, fall and capture, forlornness, dread, sleep, intoxication, call and awakening—these and other images and symbolic language bespoke "a level of utterance more fundamental than the doctrinal differentiation into which gnostic thought branched out in the completed systems" of Marcion, Valentinus, and Mani.[18] Analysis of this symbolic expression grappled with the conceptual elements of Gnostic myth on its own terms, and it led the investigator to grasp the unity of the experience, feeling, and worldview fundamental to all the various systems of Gnosticism.

Throughout his work, Jonas argued that a Gnostic myth must be seen, not merely as a conglomeration of disparate elements, but as a unified whole. Indeed, his goal was to account for the whole, not merely the forms of its expression, and he found that unifying and originating principle in the Gnostic experience of the self and world: "Thus it appears that a genuine Gnostic principle of origination, which has done whatever it wanted with that material of a polyform tradition, is indispensable for the genesis of the 'central Gnostic teaching.'"[19] Gnosis, he insisted, did not arise merely through the process of binding together disparate elements lying idly about in antiquity. Rather, *the origins of Gnosticism must be sought in the peculiarly Gnostic experience of self and world that lay behind the ordering of those elements.* The genealogical practices of motif history were not useful in locating that experience. Although Jonas agreed that Gnosis drew upon a variety of elements whose ultimate origins might lie in the Orient (Iran), Egypt, Palestine, Greece, or elsewhere, he stressed that this fact did not explain the origin of Gnosis or account for the fact of its existence. His main objection to genealogy was that "the chronological *arche* is equated with the hermeneutic as the basis for illuminating an interpretation."[20] By conflating chronology and hermeneutics, genealogical analysis could appear sufficient to interpret meaning—but that is precisely the fallacy against which Jonas lodged his most strenuous objections.

Indeed, Jonas argued, no product of syncretism can be reduced to its ostensible constituents. One can, he conceded, often identify the origin of the individual components by recognizing Persian, Babylonian, Jewish, Egyptian, or Greek influence, but the meaning conveyed by the present cultural-historical situation is not the same as its antecedents, and to that degree its meaning cannot be derived from them. For in identifying the antecedent components, one has said nothing about the existential center that determines the sense of the whole ("sinnbestimmendes Daseinszentrum"). Rather, one must account for the new attitude to existence ("Daseinshaltung") that provides an order and systematization to these disparate contents. To understand the essential, unmediated character of the new phenomenon, scholars would need to explain this new attitude rather than trace the chronological history of the individual antecedent motifs and determine all their inter-relationships.[21] For Jonas, Gnosticism was still a single phenomenon; however, its unity lay not in a common origin or genealogy but in a common attitude toward existence. Not history but existential essence was the key to defining Gnosticism.[22]

Nonetheless, Jonas's own thinking remained firmly entrenched in the history of religions tradition; to a large degree he relied on and assumed the correctness of its scholarship.[23] For his database he used the same materials as history of religions scholars, and he gave a strong priority to Mandaean imagery and symbolic language.[24] The *Poimandres* of Hermes Trismegistus and Mani took their places alongside the "Hymn of the Pearl," Marcion, and Valentinus. Jonas's criticism of Harnack's formulaic description of Gnosticism as the "acute Hellenization of Christianity" was based on the work of history of religions scholars. He assumed that the Oriental elements in Gnosticism were fundamental.[25] He agreed that Gnosticism was neither essentially Christian nor acutely Hellenized, but instead was an original phenomenon independent of Christianity altogether.

Thus, Jonas's insistence that Gnosticism had its own essential unity led him to reject the attribution of Gnostic origins to either Hellenism or the Orient.[26] Instead, he developed a scenario in which something quite new arose, appearing at once in the Greek language and clothed in the terminology of Greek conceptuality, but expressing a new attitude:

> In the centuries around the turn of the millennium a new attitude toward the world (Weltgefühl) grew up, extending from the areas east of the Mediterranean deep into Asia. So far as we can see, it arose spontaneously at the same time across a wide area, breaking in with colossal might and all the confusion that belongs at the beginning of an enterprise, and striving quite naturally to find its own expression.[27]

Because of the time and place this new attitude arose, it was necessarily preserved for the most part in the Greek language, such that Hellenism adopted a tradition that had grown up in Oriental soil while obscuring its origin. But neither is the origin of Gnosticism properly Oriental. Although the Orient (meaning the whole territory of Alexander the Great except Greece) correctly designates the geographical origin of Gnosticism, using the term "Oriental," like using the category "Hellenistic," obscures the fact that a radical new attitude had appeared.[28]

Jonas imagined a situation in which all the spiritual elements of former ages had broken loose from their moorings and been set free for deployment in a new expression of existence. Such a thing could happen, he said, only in a situation where the cultural deterioration of existential meaning had left a vacuum needing to be filled.[29] When these "loose elements" were reformed under the impulse of the new attitude toward existence, they did not carry with them their previous meanings. It was, therefore, not entirely accurate to say that the new meanings derived from earlier tradition. Charting the diachronic history of a motif did not necessarily help one understand its meaning in its new historical context, viewed synchronically.

How, then, is this new thing to be described? Like his predecessors, Jonas continued to define Gnosticism in terms of origin, but origin no longer carried the same meaning as it had for history of religions scholars like Reitzenstein or Bousset. For Jonas, origin did not point toward the earliest historical moment in which a motif appeared nor toward its most primitive form. Rather, it referred to the existential experience that made a particular arrangement of motifs meaningful. To get at that experience, Jonas turned toward philosophy, psychology, and social history.[30]

Jonas used philosophical method to develop a typology aimed at describing the essential characteristics of Gnosticism on its own terms (phenomenologically), not in terms of the prior meanings of the elements it had absorbed (motif-historically). A historical element was still present in his work, but only to describe the general conditions in which Gnosticism as a new attitude toward existence arose and was experienced.[31]

The substance of Jonas's typological categories was not particularly new.[32] Most if not all of his points could be found in earlier summaries of the primary teachings of Gnosticism. That is not surprising since he, too, necessarily had to rely on the same sources as earlier scholars had. But he interpreted those sources in terms of existential philosophy and psychology, giving a new and enriched sense of the meaning of Gnostic myth.

## Typology

The essay that most clearly and decisively presents Jonas's typological understanding of Gnosticism is "Delimitation of the Gnostic Phenome-

non—Typological and Historical."[33] In it Jonas proposed seven characteristics to encapsulate the essence of Gnosticism: *gnosis,* dynamic character
(pathomorphic crisis), mythological character, dualism, impiety, artificiality, and unique historical locus. Each of these characteristics will be discussed in turn.

## GNOSIS

By *gnosis,* Jonas meant "the peculiar status of knowledge," which appears
both as "secret, revealed, and saving knowledge" and as "theoretical content." The content of this knowledge included theology, cosmology, anthropology, and eschatology. Theology narrated the transcendent genesis
of the divine world above, including the drama within it that led to the
origination of the lower world, which was structured along a vertical axis,
emphasizing antithesis and distance between the upper and lower terres-
trial worlds. The condition of humanity was determined by this structure,
for humanity had its origin in the precosmic divine realm, but had fallen
into the world below. At the end, however, humanity would be restored to
the divine world, for the Gnostic principle of salvation held that the end
would be like the beginning, the fall would be reversed, and all things
would return to God.[34]

Jonas never considered the content of this *gnosis* to be the sole distinguishing characteristic of Gnosticism or to apply exclusively to Gnosticism. Indeed, in *The Gnostic Religion,* he stated quite explicitly that the
content of *gnosis* (as "a dualistic transcendent religion of salvation") was
not characteristic of Gnosticism *per se,* but rather was "the prominent
characteristic of the second phase of Hellenistic culture in general."[35]

## DYNAMIC CHARACTER: PATHOMORPHIC CRISIS

From the Gnostic perspective, Jonas wrote, history was conceived myth-
ically in terms of the movement of mind: "the whole can be considered
as one grand *movement* of 'knowledge,' in its positive and its privative
moods, from the beginning of things to their end." For Jonas, this characterization was critical since it determined the peculiar status of *gnosis* in
Gnosticism that set it apart from Hellenistic culture generally:

Time, in other words, is actuated by the onward thrust of a mental life: and in this thoroughly *dynamic* character which makes every episode productive of the next, and all of them phases of one total evolution, we must see another distinctive feature of Gnosticism.

Yet Jonas noted that this dynamic view of generation was shared by "all the 'vertical' schemes of late antiquity," including especially the Alexandrians and Plotinus. What sets Gnosticism apart from these schemes, he argued, is its "catastrophic character": "The form of its progress is *crisis,* and there occur failure and miscarriage. A disturbance in the heights starts off the downward motion which continues as a drama of fall and alienation. The corporeal world is the terminal product of this epic of decline." Thus in the end, it is not its dynamic character as such but *crisis* that distinguishes Gnostic myth. Jonas called this crisis-driven dynamism "the *pathomorphic* form of gnostic emanationism."[36]

## MYTHOLOGICAL CHARACTER

Directly connected with this "pathomorphic form" was the essentially mythical character of Gnostic thought. Unlike Plotinus' theory of emanation, Gnosticism told a dramatic story that required "concrete and personal agents, individual divinities." In form and substance, it is nonphilosophical by nature. But again the mythological character of Gnosticism, however essential, was not sufficient to distinguish it from the many other types of ancient religious expression that could also be considered mythological. Jonas, therefore, went on to provide a synthetic account of "the typical gnostic myth," in many respects a variant of the Gnostic redeemer myth:

The typical gnostic myth . . . starts with a doctrine of divine transcendence in its original purity; it then traces the genesis of the world from some primordial disruption of this blessed state, a loss of divine integrity which leads to the emergence of lower powers who become the makers and rulers of this world; then, as a crucial episode in the drama, the myth recounts the creation and early fate of man, in whom the further conflict becomes centered; the final theme, in fact the implied theme throughout, is man's salvation, which is more than man's as it involves the overcoming and eventual dissolving of the cosmic system and is thus the instrument of reintegration for the impaired godhead itself, or, the selfsaving of God.[37]

Jonas made four additional points that became crucial for subsequent understandings of Gnostic thought. They brought out the philosophical and psychological implications of the Gnostic myth:

One is the identity, or consubstantiality, of man's innermost self with the supreme and transmundane God, himself often called "Man": utter metaphysical elevation coincides, in the acosmic essence of man, with utter cosmic alienation. Another point is the conception of the created world as a power system directed at the enslavement of this transmundane self: everything from the grand cosmic design down to man's psychophysical constitution serves this fearful purpose—such is the uniquely gnostic *Weltanschauung* (worldview). A third point is that enslavement is "ignorance" actively inflicted and maintained, i.e., the alienation of the self from itself as its prevailing "natural" condition; and the fourth point, consequently, is that the chief means of extrication, the counteraction to the power of the world, is the communication of knowledge.[38]

Here the theme of alienation is particularly prominent—alienation from God, from the cosmos, and from the self. Knowledge is the means to overcome the acute pain and distress of the human situation in the world.

In this context Jonas also articulated the particular Gnostic understanding of human history as the story of salvation. History was the site of revelation, the vehicle for meaningful movement and direction toward ultimate salvation, but this history was tied to a narrative of pathomorphic crisis. An alienated and ignorant humanity was in dire need of revelation, but the divine messengers were themselves engaged in a struggle with those who would thwart their purpose and keep humanity enslaved. All that Gnosticism offered to historical understanding was this mythic narrative of crisis. But that was apparently a great deal, for Jonas called this narrative "a metaphysic of pure movement and event, the most determinedly 'historical' conception of universal being prior to Hegel."[39]


## DUALISM

Dualistic patterns of thought were widespread in antiquity. What made Gnosticism distinctive, Jonas argued, was its expressly *cosmological* dualism: "a world-*God* opposition which sprang from the immanent disunion of *man* and the world." Its "cosmic pessimism" and "radical mood," reflecting a human condition of alienation, set it apart from less extreme dualistic positions. In Gnostic thought, Jonas contended, dualism is "an invariant, *existential* 'first principle'" that must be distinguished from the "variable *speculative* first principle employed in its representation."[40] It was, in short, not a result of philosophical speculation, but the reflection of existential alienation.

Later scholars of Gnosticism distinguished among types of dualism on the basis of the value each attributed to the created world: Gnosticism was anticosmic because it regarded the world as evil; Zoroastrian dualism regarded the world favorably; while Greek philosophy represented the constitution of the world as a dialectic of two irreducible and complementary principles.[41] The principle of Gnostic dualism was thus reduced to regarding the material world as evil. Jonas would seem to agree, for he stated that "the complete absence of any such symbol (as the Demiurge) for an inferior or degraded cause of the world, or of its particular order, or of its matter, would make one greatly hesitate to accept a doctrine as gnostic."[42]

The polemicists had portrayed Gnostic ethics as either ascetic or libertine; Jonas uncritically accepted this depiction, but he interpreted it in terms of anticosmic dualism. He suggested that the Gnostic devaluation of the world had left only these two options of behavior open to adherents:

> Generally speaking, pneumatic morality is determined by hostility toward the world and contempt for all mundane ties. From this principle, however, two contrary conclusions could be drawn, and both found their extreme representatives: the ascetic and the liber-

tine. The former deduces from the possession of gnosis the obligation to avoid further contamination by the world and therefore to
reduce contact with it to a minimum; the latter derives from the
same possession the privilege of absolute freedom.[43]

His point was that Gnosticism was incapable of promoting a positive ethics because its dualistic worldview could only negate any kind of moral
life in this world. Even ascetic practice, which elsewhere is deeply tied to
ethics, in Gnosticism "is not strictly speaking a matter of ethics but of
metaphysical alignment."[44] The only possible result is a kind of depraved
moral revolt, whether ascetic or libertine in expression.

Jonas also accepted the polemicists' statement that Gnostics believed
they were saved by nature; in Jonas's opinion, this position further undermined the possibility that Gnostics could develop a positive ethics.[45] Jonas
assumed—wrongly, as it turns out—that Gnostic belief in the consubstantiality of the self with the divine led them to conclude that moral effort as such was unnecessary for their salvation.

Although libertinism and asceticism are seemingly at opposite ends of
the ethical spectrum, underlying both is the view that the moral life was
just another trap set by the wicked world rulers to tie Gnostics to the
body and further entrap them in the material world.[46] The Gnostic response to every invitation to join in the life of the world, with all its de-
lights and duties and disappointments, Jonas said, was a resounding refusal. Libertinism and asceticism were equally capable of expressing that
refusal. Hence, he claimed, these two very different types of behavior actually arose from a single principle: anticosmic dualism.

IMPIETY

Jonas felt that the elements of the typology presented so far were as yet inadequate to catch the mood or tone of the phenomenon. So he added
three additional characteristics: impiety, artificiality, and syncretism.
These more than anything else show Jonas's own negative evaluation of
Gnosticism:

The gnostic mood, apart from the deadly earnest befitting a doctrine
of salvation, has an element of rebellion and protest about it. Its re-

jection of the world, far from the serenity or resignation of other nonworldly creeds, is of peculiar, sometimes vituperative violence, and we generally note a tendency to extremism, to excess in fantasy and feeling. We suspect that the dislocated metaphysical situation of which gnostic myth tells had its counterpart in a dislocated real situation: that the crisis-form of its symbolism reflects a historical crisis of man himself. Such a crisis, to be sure, shows in other phenomena of the period as well, Jewish, Christian and pagan, many of which betray a deeply agitated state of mind, a great tension of the soul, a disposition toward radicalism, hyperbolic expectations, and total solutions. But the gnostic temper is of all the least restrained by the power of traditions, which it rather treats with peculiar *impietas* in the cavalier use it makes of them: this lack of piety, so curiously blended with avid interest in ancient lore, must be counted among the physiognomic traits of Gnosticism.[47]

What is this distinctive "cavalier use" and how does it indicate a "lack of piety"? Jonas offered two revealing examples. In the account of the creation of humanity, Gnosticism drew on both the Genesis creation account and the Platonic teaching that the demiurge shaped humanity according to a divine archetype. Both narrate that humanity was created according to a divine pattern or image, and in both cases, Jonas argued, the understanding of creation lent humanity a "share in perfection and justifies its being." But Gnosticism, he said, turned homage into opprobrium: "Biblical and Platonic lore are perverted at the same time," by figuring the creation of humanity as the perverted act of a wicked creator. Or again, Jonas wrote that Gnosticism's account of the fall of Adam made Gnostics "unable to assimilate any serious meaning of the incarnation and the cross." Here Gnosticism is implicitly contrasted with normative Christian theology, in which the incarnation and cross occupy central positions in the doctrine of salvation. In the end, Gnostic impiety was delineated by comparing it unfavorably with normative interpretations of Platonism, Judaism, and Christianity.[48] Impiety is not a phenomenological nor historical characterization but a theological judgment.

It was, however, the Gnostic attitude toward Judaism that Jonas thought was most distinctively impious. Gnostic myth clearly used Jewish sources, but, he asked,

What is the spirit of this use? Why it is the spirit of vilification, of parody and caricature, of conscious perversion of meaning, wholesale reversal of value-signs, savage degrading of the sacred—of gleefully shocking blasphemy . . . Is this merely exuberant license, pleasure in the novel and bizarre? No, it is the exerciser of a determined and in itself thoroughly consistent tendency.[49]

Jonas concluded that the "nature of the relation of Gnosticism to Judaism—in itself an undeniable fact—is defined by the *anti-Jewish animus* with which it is saturated."[50] In his opinion, Gnostic impiety so consistently denigrated and abused notions of the sacred—whether directed at Platonic, Jewish, or Christian materials—that this tendency could be regarded as an essential characteristic of Gnosticism.

### ARTIFICIALITY

Another characteristic that Jonas considered essential to the character of Gnosticism was its artificiality, that is, the lack of originality in its form. Gnostic myth was consciously constructed, secondary, and derivative. He argued that "primary" myth, in contrast, is "naïve," "natural," and "nondeliberative"; it arises "without choice" from the "imagination" and is "prior to thought and abstraction."[51] Although Jonas insisted that the "gnostic theme" was "genuinely original," nonetheless, the "means of its representation" was unmistakably "contrived" and "second-hand."[52]

As noted in the last chapter, in eighteenth- and nineteenth-century Europe, myth was understood to be prelogical, prephilosophical, and prescientific—if not chronologically, at least typologically. Most important, the location of myth's origins in the primitive mind had obviated the need for further elucidation. "That barbarism brings with it silence of interpretation," remarked Detienne. Jonas's work, however, belonged to later discussions that attempted to rehabilitate myth and restore it to the realm of intelligibility, and hence interpretability. Durkheim, for example, understood myths to be expressions of underlying social reality. In his view, it is through myth that society makes and remakes itself. Yet at the same time, he suggested that mythology masks this truth, veiling its references to nature, humanity, and society under a cloak of mystery.[53]

In a similar vein, Freud held that myth is the key to an underlying reality: it belongs to the earliest stages of psychic development, childhood.[54] Myth is an expression of the human subconscious, whether a veiled expression of repressed desires or infantile wish-fulfillment. For both Durkheim and Freud, myth is an expression of some fundamental reality (society or human consciousness), and therefore worthy of interpretation. But for both, interpretation is understood as demystification, as the reduction of illusion.

Lévi-Strauss changed the terms of the conversation in his structural analysis of myth. Structuralism could see in myths a truly logical, binary mode of thought equivalent to scientific thought, but differing from it in that myth deals with a different set of problems, such as the resolution of conflict or ambiguity. Jung similarly gave myths a positive function in the communication of the unconscious to the conscious, but for him, myths are not mystifications of some other reality but archetypes of the collective unconscious necessary for maintaining a healthy psychological balance. For Cassirer, mythical thinking is a specific form of consciousness that relates not to the objective world or even to society but to the organizing principles of the human mind—that is, myth is an early stage of the self's experience of its own consciousness. Its substratum is feeling. Victor Turner understood myth to belong to episodes of social transition, both for individuals and for groups. As he put it, "Myths treat of origins but derive from transitions." For Lévi-Strauss, Jung, Cassirer, and Turner, then, myths have significant and irreducible functions in their own right, and as such they reveal (rather than merely veil or conceal) important aspects of human mental life.[55]

Thus through a variety of strategies, myth was rehabilitated from scandalous entertainment or deluded, confused thinking and elevated to scientific thought or social action of the highest, most subtle kind. It could be conceived as the expression of a particular reality, such as the human unconscious or human society. Such understandings not only allowed for the interpretation of myths; they insisted on it.

Where are we to place Jonas in this discussion? Clearly, elements of this debate are reflected in his characterization of Gnostic myth as "artificial." He continued to distinguish between myth and philosophy by appealing to origins.[56] For him, Gnostic myth has a philosophical, speculative component that distinguishes it from true mythical thinking, which is prior to thought and abstraction. Authentic myth is natural and naïve, a characterization that belongs to discourses on the primitive origins of myth. Here the distinction between nature and culture clearly comes into play. In this discourse myth, like primitive societies, is closer to the simplicity of nature—artless, ingenuous, and credulous. In its "sophistication," Jonas says, Gnostic myth betrays its ties to the complexities of education and civilization. It is therefore "not naïve," but the product of literate, albeit "half-educated intellectuals."[57] Again there is an implicit appeal to origins (in nature, not culture) as a mode of defining authentic myth. Moreover, Gnostic myth is not original (despite the "genuine originality" of its "theme") because it has clearly "borrowed" from others ("syncretism").

In Jonas these ideas are not configured in evolutionary models of human social and psychological development. By locating the origins of myth in the "imagination," his views fit at least in part into later psychological and philosophical discussions of myth. Most important, myth demands interpretation. He was interested in exploring the meaning of Gnostic myth and undertook to probe the symbolic structures of the myth to understand its existential impulses. There was very little room for sociological aspects of myth in his phenomenological approach, however, since only the *form* of Gnostic myth is historical; its essence and originality are rooted in the experience of alienation.[58] From this perspective, the essence of Gnosticism lies in its existential originality, not in the flow of history (which only demonstrates its "second-hand" character). Jonas clearly belonged to the era of "demythologizing" in which it was believed that one could liberate the existential meaning of a myth from its (primitive or artificial) form. That form, however, had a particular historical location.

UNIQUE HISTORICAL LOCUS

In identifying the final essential characteristic of Gnosticism, Jonas shifted from typology to synchronic historical description. He argued that it would be incorrect to think that typological delimitation, which dealt primarily with doctrine, mood, and style, could be carried out apart from historical reference. All the characteristics of the typology listed above "one way or another involve the factual situation in which gnostic thought was born and carried on." In this manner, the "unique historical locus (of Gnosticism) . . . injects itself into the typology itself." In order to understand the specificity of Gnosticism as a distinct phenomenon, we must ground its typology in the historical situation in which Gnosticism existed.[59]

Historical analysis supplied the specific context within which Gnosticism could be comprehended. Without an understanding of that context, it would not be possible to grasp what irreducibly distinguished Gnosticism from similar phenomena at other times and places. The historical factor is irreducible precisely because history itself is unique and non-repeatable. Only in "the hellenistic-oriental world of the first Christian centuries" could Gnosticism have arisen, Jonas claimed. Only there were certain conditions present:

> All this is possible only in a historically "late," distinctly literate, and thoroughly syncretistic situation, which thus belongs to the phenomenology of Gnosticism, over and above its doxography. This situation includes the freefloating availability of traditions that were no longer binding, but pregnant with redefinable meaning; and those who availed themselves of them in the gnostic manner were "intellectuals" (half-educated, perhaps) who knew what they were about.[60]

At this point sociological and psychological factors, especially syncretism, enter into phenomenological description. For Jonas, syncretism indicated not merely a particular cultural situation, but a deterioration of existential meaning that was experienced as alienation. In turn, the alienation expressed in Gnostic dualism must have been based, he claimed, in a historical crisis. This crisis, he argued, was reflected by other non-Gnostic phenomena of the period as well; but in Jonas's view the Gnostic reaction, the total rejection of the world, had in it a special mood of rebellion and protest that needed "to be counted among the physiognomic traits of Gnosticism."[61] Metaphysical dualism exposed existential alienation, and alienation pointed toward social-historical crisis and rebellion. By means of a circular logic, Jonas rooted the sociological description of the Gnostics' historical situation (of crisis) and their reaction to that situation (rebellion).

But, he went on to ask, how is it that such a historical situation came about in the first place? How is it that traditions came loose from their moorings and floated free? What crisis, what rebellion, could provoke these impieties and perversions of meaning?

In the introduction to *The Gnostic Religion,* Jonas set Gnosticism within a historical framework that he titled "East and West in Hellenism," and here we find a classic example of Orientalist discourse at work.[62] His starting point appears to have been a version of Droysen's classic study *Geschichte des Hellenismus* (1836), which represented Hellenism in the Eastern Mediterranean as a syncretic "merging of cultures": the Western Greek empire under Macedonian rule with the Eastern empire of the Persians. The conquests of Alexander politically unified these two areas and set in motion a process of cultural syncretism. There were basically two major phases to this process in Jonas's view: the manifest domination of the Greek over the Eastern, and the reactionary reemergence of the East that provided a spiritual renewal for the West.[63] It was in the second phase that Gnosticism arose.

At first, Jonas opined, the new political unity established by Alexander went hand in hand with a new cultural unity—the culture of the conqueror. The dominance of Greek culture was not merely a result of military conquest—Jonas reminded his readers that many conquered peoples have culturally overwhelmed their overlords—rather, it was due to the West's development of a rational and universalist ideology, and the East's "apparent or real passivity, docility, and readiness for assimilation," a condition he related to the conquests preceding those of Alexander.[64] They "had broken the political backbone of the local populations and accustomed them passively to accept each new master in the change of empires." Nevertheless, Jonas insisted that the "literary sterility" and "petrifaction" of Oriental civilization at the time of Alexander's conquest should not be interpreted as a judgment against its former greatness; rather, "the inertia of formidable traditions" could be "regarded as a mark of the perfection which a system of life has attained."[65]

The political unity of empire in fact disguised what was actually a cultural plurality. Part of the reason for the apparent "muteness" of the East was its assimilation of Hellenism. Under Alexander, Hellenization of the natives proceeded primarily through education, so that "one born a barbarian could be become a true Hellene."[66] Because Oriental thought became cloaked in Greek, the earliest contributions of the East to the merging of the two cultures is hard to identify. Jonas wrote that

> the muteness of the East cannot be construed as a lack of intellectual vitality on the part of its individuals: it consists rather in its not speaking for itself, in its own name. Anyone who had something to say had no choice but to say it in Greek not only in terms of language but also in terms of concept, ideas, and literary form, that is, as ostensibly part of the Greek tradition.[67]

Although Jonas acknowledged that the hegemony of Hellenism "was made possible by catastrophes overtaking the original units of regional culture," he nonetheless regarded the ultimate outcome for the "East" to be positive, not only because assimilation offered "equal rights" to the "native" population, but also because "the Greek conceptual form offered to the Oriental mind an entirely new possibility of bringing to light the meaning of its own heritage."[68] "Oriental thought," wrote Jonas, was at bottom "mythological," that is, it "had been non-conceptual, conveyed in images and symbols, rather disguising its ultimate objects in myths and rites than expounding them logically." It was freed from this "imprisonment" and "rigidity" by the liberating force of the Greek *logos,* "the abstract concept, the method of theoretical exposition, the reasoned system—one of the greatest discoveries in the history of the human mind":

> Thus the Greek spirit delivered Eastern thought from the bondage of its own symbolism and enabled it in the reflection of the *logos* to discover itself. And it was with the arms acquired from the Greek arsenal that the East, when its time came, launched its counteroffensive.[69]

This offensive came not from the assimilated barbarian-turned-Hellene, but from the "other," the "radically different and inassimilable" that "was excluded and went underground": "Thus the spiritual monopoly of Greece caused the growth of an invisible East whose secret life formed an antagonistic undercurrent beneath the surface of the public Hellenistic civilization."[70]

When the East did regain its voice, Jonas said, that voice was religious—by which he meant that it was primarily focused not on the social-political-economic world but on transcendental, spiritual concerns. Among these Oriental responses he listed Hellenistic Judaism, astrology and magic, mystery cults, Christianity, Gnostic movements, and the transcendental philosophies of Neopythagoreanism and Neoplatonism. Despite their great diversity, Jonas argued that they all shared "characteristic mental attitudes," expressed in a spiritual principle that found its "most radical and uncompromising representative" in Gnostic literature.[71] Thus the Gnostic religion, for Jonas, was a representative, although radical, expression of renascent Oriental thought in the context of a thoroughly syncretic Hellenism.

Still, from Jonas's perspective, the origin of Gnosticism could not be found in its Oriental roots, any more than in its Hellenistic dress. From the very beginning, his point had been that it was not possible to reduce the origin and meaning of Gnosticism to the determination of its antecedents; the fact of syncretism only made this point all the more pressing:

> The most conflicting theories have been advanced in the course of time and are still in the field today. The early Church Fathers and independently of them Plotinus, emphasized the influence upon a Christian thinking not yet firmly consolidated of Plato and of misunderstood Hellenic philosophy in general. Modern scholars have advanced in turn Hellenic, Babylonian, Egyptian, and Iranian origins and every possible combination of these with one another and with Jewish and Christian elements. Since in the material of its representation Gnosticism actually is a product of syncretism, each of these theories can be supported from the sources and none of them is satisfactory alone; but neither is the combination of all of them, which would make Gnosticism out to be a mere mosaic of these elements and so miss its autonomous essence.[72]

Syncretism meant that elements of Gnostic representation had been drawn from a variety of traditions, and hence evidence existed for locating the origin of Gnosticism in any or all of those traditions. But to repeat Jonas's point, Gnosticism did not arise merely through the process of binding together disparate elements lying freely about in antiquity; the origins of Gnosticism were to be sought in the peculiarly Gnostic experience of self and world that lay behind the ordering of those elements. That experience could not be defined by its own expressions because they were only the "outer aspect and not the essence of the phenomenon."[73] Nonetheless, he insisted: "It is also our opinion that the factual living conditions of people are a decisive constituent in their thinking; and further, that external events and patterns can play a significant role as well."[74] The content and mood of Gnosticism disclosed the world as it was actually experienced, and as such it expressed the particular historical conditions of that specific time and place.[75]

Jonas noted that there was an unavoidable circularity in this kind of thinking, given that the transcendental Spirit of an age is already a constituting factor contained in the real conditions themselves. At the same time, he did not want to fall into the trap of reducing thought to sociology. As he amusingly put it, a few bad days are not sufficient to generate the foundational principles of a new meaning of the world.[76]

### Relation to Christianity

Although Jonas's work did not focus on the relationship of Gnosticism to Christianity, the issue was in some ways unavoidable. Yet, Jonas produced the only extensive study of Gnosticism that did not take up the question of the relationship to Christianity as a decisive starting point or goal. From his point of view, the question of whether Gnosticism existed in pre-Christian times was indeterminable and nearly irrelevant; what mattered was only that the two were roughly contemporaneous and hence had much in common. Because they were responding to the same general situation, "there was vigorous interpenetration of the two which provoked the well-known reactions in the Church."[77]

Yet, as noted above, Jonas did not prevaricate about the implications of his approach for the relationship of Gnosticism to Christianity. Although he acknowledged that Christian claims to originality and uniqueness were at stake, he noted that scholarship had already established that there were foreign, Greek influences at work in the New Testament. He cited the Johannine *logos* doctrine and the Pauline concept of spirit as examples.[78]

Thus the issue as he saw it was not whether or not there were "foreign influences" on New Testament literature; the issue was whether these influences had touched on the inner core of Christianity itself. In the case of
the Greek examples just cited, Jonas responded no; these are cases of one-
sided dependence by Christianity on already well-formulated elements of
Greek thought.

The case with Gnosticism, however, was quite different, in Jonas's
opinion, for both it and Christianity arose during the same period and as
expressions of the common spirit of the age. They "sustained the same impulses and moved on the same, albeit contested field, and were in the
same way the symptoms of a fundamental, deeply agitated situation of the
contemporary existence (*Dasein*), which first fought for its representation
in these different forms."[79] This close kinship put Christianity and Gnosticism in competition with each other, as claimants to the revolutionary
movement of the spirit that was nourished by the powers of their common environment.

Their close kinship also meant that they should be treated as truly contemporaneous. A genuine light could be shed on the inner being of Christianity by studying Gnosticism, Jonas argued, precisely because of the
close relationship between the two. It was even possible to argue not simply that Christianity may have "taken over" something from the pagan-
Gnostic world, but that it had an original and legitimate claim on that
legacy. In this case, it was no longer proper to speak of "foreign influence"
at all. Christianity, Jonas argued, was not a passive recipient of elements of
Hellenistic syncretism that were already fully formed and at hand; rather,
it was an active player in negotiating its environment and bringing the elements to maturity. Its appropriations, he wrote, should be regarded not
as secondary carry-overs but as elements whose mature manifestations
first appeared in Christianity.[80] The same can be said of Gnosticism.

It is not that Christianity arose out of Gnosticism or from Gnostic influences *per se,* and even less that Gnostic influences on Christianity
could be considered secondary influences on a Christianity otherwise untouched by the spirit of the age. Jonas argued that Christianity, not only
in its heretical forms such as Marcionism, but also "in the thought forms
of certain layers of the New Testament (in sections outside the synoptic gospels)," should be counted as belonging to the Gnostic domain.[81]
Christianity and Gnosticism therefore are two species of the same genus.

## *Jonas's Contribution to Gnostic Studies*

Jonas's clarity of thought and philosophical insight brought to Gnostic studies a breath of fresh air that makes his work still the classic starting point for exploring this topic. He fed the growing dissatisfaction with the more arbitrary aspects of motif history and offered a highly attractive alternative. His approach was in keeping with the spirit of history of religions scholarship, but it charted exciting new intellectual ground; for though Gnosticism remained a religion in its own right, now scholars could perceive that its deepest religious impulses and feeling were rooted in existential alienation and revolt.

Yet Jonas insisted on seeing Gnosticism as a unitary whole. While recognizing the variety of its discrete manifestations, he considered its essence to constitute an overwhelming and distinctive core. In fact, he deplored "the atomizing, dismembering methods of previous research that leave one feeling the lack of a unified sense of the whole, a matter which was utterly left out of consideration."[82] Yet by directing his research at uncovering that unified sense of the whole, he contributed spectacularly to the reification of Gnosticism as an independent religion and a singular, monolithic phenomenon. This aspect of his legacy continues to haunt the study of Gnosticism.

Moreover, though Jonas passionately promoted Gnosticism as a phenomenon with its own creative impulses and religious integrity, he maintained the traditional negative evaluation of it intellectually, morally, and religiously. This is clear from his list of the characteristics that most readily distinguish Gnosticism from the other types of the "Oriental wave": pathomorphic crisis, cosmic pessimism, impiety, artificiality, and amorality or immorality. Gnostic mythmaking, he wrote, was "arbitrarily high-handed," a "degradation of the Old Testament God . . . performed with considerable venom and obvious relish"; a "ruthless derogation," it is not "tolerant" and shows a "ruthlessness of deployment," "bold and scandalizing exegesis"; it stays "unblushing in the tradition of pagan polytheism"; it "perverts" Biblical and Platonic lore; and so on.[83]

His evaluation of Gnosticism reproduced many of the elements of the polemicists' discourse of heresy, and he constructed it as the deficient "other" of true religion. Its ascetic or libertine ethics demonstrated an incapacity for a positive ethics. It displayed impiety in the lack of proper reverence for God and tradition, whether Jewish or Greek. Its mythical character was intellectually deficient in comparison with higher "historical" religion. The artificiality and syncretic character of its myth exemplified its secondary nature and demonstrated a lack of originality, purity, or authenticity. Its anticosmic dualism stood in contrast to proper monotheism. It was pathomorphic, demonstrating a negative attitude toward life, characterized by alienation and rebellion. Moreover, the Gnostics were arrogant and lacking in proper humility, especially in their claim to possess a divine nature that ensured their ultimate salvation.

These are not impartial descriptions of the phenomena but evaluative judgments based on largely unarticulated assumptions about what constitutes true religion and piety. Jonas's own commitments to philosophical rationalism and ethical monotheism intersected with discourses of heresy and Orientalism. They could remain largely unarticulated only because they were widely shared among scholars of religion.

One further aspect of Jonas's work should be mentioned here. According to Jonas, Gnosticism offered a direct and intentional challenge to "the long-established moral and mental attitudes" of its day, because the revolutionary character of Gnostic myth produced a highly critical representation of the world:

> What it reveals is unenlightened and therefore malignant force, proceeding from the spirit of self-assertive power, from the will to rule and coerce. The mindlessness of this will is the spirit of the world, which bears no relation to understanding and love. The laws of the universe are the laws of this rule, and not of divine wisdom. *Power* thus becomes the chief aspect of the cosmos, and its inner essence is ignorance.[84]

Because the demands of law stem from this will to rule and coerce, they could be perceived as "part of the great design upon human freedom." Jonas characterized the Gnostic resistance to this ruthless domination as libertinism: "the brazen expression of a rebellion no less against a cultural tradition than against the demiurge."[85]

Where did this new attitude come from? Jonas suggested that it arose as a result of the demise of the independent city-state. The ideology of the city-state, which defined the individual within the social-political whole and made possible the meaningful life—indeed the good life—lost "the conditions of its concrete validation" with the absorption of the city-state into the monarchies of the Greek successors of Alexander and finally the Roman Empire. The classical ideology, Jonas maintained, "was kept in force even though it no longer reflected the practical situation of man." This disintegration of thought and practice resulted in a forlorn and desolate attitude toward existence that Jonas felt had much in common with the existential nihilism of the twentieth century.[86]

I was profoundly affected by this passionate exposition when I first read *The Gnostic Religion*. But more and more my own acquaintance with texts like *ApJohn* has led me to think that Jonas emphasized the psychological aspects of the myth too strongly, focusing almost exclusively on alienation at the expense of what may have been a profound element of social critique in some of the works classified as Gnostic. He himself had suggested a social-political component to Gnostic myth when he characterized it in terms of the demise of certain political institutions. What if the myth of *ApJohn* was not so much an expression of the intellectual and moral vacuity arising when ideology became divorced from social reality as it was an evaluation of political rule? What if the "experience" underlying estrangement were to be analyzed less in terms of psychology than in terms of the social-political conditions of imperial violence? How then might we read a myth that describes the powers that rule the world as malignant forces motivated by the will to dominate and coerce? How then might we understand the representation of these powers as evil and ignorant? What hope might Gnostic revelation of divine knowledge and salvation then be seen to offer its recipients?

## The Demise of the Gnostic Redeemer Myth

Bultmann, Jonas, and other scholars who worked within the framework of the history of religions school could accept the pre-Christian Gnostic redeemer myth as a given. Subsequent work, however, has made this position untenable. Its demise rests on three fundamental grounds: (1) The dating of the source material, especially the Mandaean materials, could not support a pre-Christian origin for Gnosticism. (2) Reitzenstein, Bous-

set, and many who followed them were not themselves Orientalists and
were not acquainted with the languages in which their sources were written. They relied on the work of philologists, such as Lidzbarski and
Maçuch, but in so doing they made mistakes that would prove devastating to their philologically based motif history. (3) The abstraction of particular motifs from their literary and historical contexts had led to serious
misunderstandings, resulting in an artificially constructed myth that had
never existed as such in antiquity. The pre-Christian Gnostic redeemer
myth was the invention of modern scholarship; it is inadequate, when not
entirely misleading, for reading the ancient materials.

## Later Assessment of Mandaean Origins

The entire construction of the Gnostic redeemer myth, and not just
Bultmann's thesis about the Gnostic background of the Gospel of John,
was based on an early dating of Mandaean materials. Criticism of that
dating thus constituted the first major blow against the history of religions
construction of a pre-Christian, Oriental origin for Gnosticism.

In 1930 Hans Lietzmann published a short article titled "Ein Beitrag
zur Mandäerfrage," in which he argued very simply and cogently against
the prevailing thesis that the Mandaeans originated in the West in pre-
Christian times. Basing his critique primarily on the indisputable observation that the existing Mandaean texts were written 1,600 years after the
New Testament writings, he argued that the Christian elements in Mandaeanism were due to a late seventh-century influence of Christianity on
Mandaeanism—not the reverse. He concluded:

> The Mandaeans have nothing to do with the disciples of John in the
> early Christian period. Rather all the Johannine stories in the Man-
> daean literature were created from the New Testament and Christian
> legends, and were first introduced into the images of this sect in Ara-
> bian times, at the earliest in the seventh century. The [Mandaean]
> celebration of Sunday makes it probable that the present form of
> their religion took its decisive impulse from Christianity. The ritual
> of their primary sacrament, baptism, is a copy of the East Syrian
> Christian liturgy . . . An older Oriental Gnostic religion in later

times—perhaps first in Arabian times—is forced into further advances by a Nestorian Christianity that has been emptied of its content and has been remoulded into a Christian syncretistic gnosis. This exhorts [the scholar] to a cautious analysis of the texts and forbids unconditionally the now-common uncritical use of all layers of Mandaean literature to explain the New Testament. With reference to the Mandaeans we are able to study the Christianizing of an Oriental gnosis, not the Gnostic foundations of early Christianity.[87]

Although there are notable difficulties with Lietzmann's thesis, he clearly set the chronological order of the texts back into line and demonstrated that the previous work of Reitzenstein, Bultmann, and others had rather flagrantly and uncritically used texts that were centuries older than the New Testament texts to explain Christian origins.[88]

This critique reopened the debate about the date of Mandaean origins. Scholars had proposed a first-century Palestinian origin for the Mandaeans on the basis of a variety of archaeological and linguistic evidence.[89] Although the oldest dated manuscript of Mandaean literature takes us back only to the sixteenth century, it seemed correct to suppose that the Mandaeans possessed a written literature before the Arab invasion of Persia because they received the Islamic status of a tolerated group as a "people of the book." In addition, Theodore bar Konai, an eighth-century Syrian Christian theologian, listed the sect of the "Dostaiê" (also called Mandaiê or Nazoriê) in his book of *Scholia,* and he included several quotes from the *Ginza.* Archaeological discoveries have added further evidence to the discussion. A Mandaic bowl discovered at Nippur has been dated to approximately 600 C.E., and the Semiticist Mark Lidzbarski published a lead tablet that he dated to the beginning of the fifth century on the basis of the script.[90]

Many specialists in Mandaean studies still argue for an early Western origin for Mandaeanism, preeminent among them Maçuch, Lady Drower, Kurt Rudolph, and Lupieri, but they generally reject a pre-Christian date and argue for great circumspection in using Mandaean texts to explain the genesis of New Testament literature.[91] Maçuch argued that the discovery of inscriptions on Babylonian coins of the second and third centuries C.E. in Elymaean, a script that closely resembles Mandaean, presupposes the existence of Mandaean writing. He contended that this evidence lends strong support for the view that the Mandaeans migrated from the West and were settled in Babylonia by the second century C.E. Rudolph, however, pointed out that the existence of a proto-Mandaean script may not presuppose in any way a Mandaean community. Yet he, too, argues for an early date, but on the basis of his literary analysis of the Mandaean texts, especially by comparison with other mythological motifs from second- and third-century works.[92]

Another stimulus to establishing the age and origin of the Mandaeans was the publication of additional Mandaean manuscripts by Lady Drower.[93] Of special interest to the question of origins is the *Haran Gawaita* ["Inner Haran"], published by Drower in 1953 from two extant manuscripts dated to the early eighteenth century, but with colophons indicating a source from the early Islamic period. This document contains evidence within the Mandaean tradition itself that has been used to support the hypothesis of a Palestinian origin for the sect, followed by a subsequent migration into Mesopotamia. It begins as follows:

> And Haran Gawaita received him and that city in which there were Nasoreans, because there was no road for the Jewish rulers. Over them was King Ardban. And sixty thousand Nasoreans abandoned the Sign of the Seven and entered the Median Hills, a place where we were free from domination by all other races.[94]

The text would seem to indicate that the Mandaeans migrated from Jerusalem into northwestern Mesopotamia as a consequence of persecution by the Jews. Depending on how one identifies "King Ardban," this could have taken place early in the first century C.E.[95] Yet because of its clearly confused and legendary nature, the historical value of this information is debatable, and it would be questionable to use it to establish the age and origin of the Mandaeans without corroboration from other types of evidence. Nevertheless, it is difficult to give up the information entirely because it fills an important gap in Mandaean history.

Recent research supports the view that some Mandaean traditions may go back as far as the second or third century C.E. The colophons trace some works back at least into the early Islamic period and provide an important source for the history of the Mandaean community.[96] The colophons contain lists of the scribal lineage for each manuscript, and often short descriptions of the current situation of the Mandaeans in the scribe's region. They are therefore important, not only for the issue of origin, but also for the two-thousand-year history of this remarkable tradition. Jorunn Buckley has been able to trace select texts back as far as the second and third centuries, including Book I.1 of the *Right Ginza* (third century) and the colophon of one copy of the *Left Ginza*, which dates back to a second-century woman priest named Ulama, daughter of Qidra. Her work provides a firm evidential foundation for reconsidering the early history and development of Mandaeism. Lupieri has also attempted to construct a reliable history of Mandaeism on the basis of the available colophon evidence, as well as other Mandaean sources, concurring in the early second- or third-century dating.[97]

Once Mandaean materials no longer were thought to provide the key to the problem of Christian origins, Western scholars shifted their attention decisively away from Mandaean materials. It is as though the Mandaeans disappeared from the face of the earth, so completely have they slipped from the notice of scholarly literature.[98]

## Carsten Colpe

Credit for the final demise of the pre-Christian Gnostic redeemer myth belongs primarily to the German history of religions scholar Carsten Colpe. In *Die religionsgeschichtliche Schule: Darstellung und Kritik ihres Bildes vom gnostischen Erlößermythus* (1961), Colpe brought the results of recent scholarship in Iranian studies to bear on the work of Reitzenstein, Bousset, and others. The results proved to be devastating.

Colpe identified several crucial philological mistakes that early history of religions scholarship had made in the construction of the Gnostic redeemer myth. For example, Reitzenstein had claimed to have located a "fragment" from a Zarathustrian writing in an early Manichaean hymn, and he had used this "fragment" to establish the Iranian basis of Manichaeism and Mandaeism. Colpe determined that this so-called fragment was in fact "a pure Manichaean song" of post-Christian date.[99] It had not been based on a separate hymn, but rather belonged to the last section of the Parthian hymn cycle *angad rosan.* Reitzenstein had considered the topic of the hymn to be the soul and had argued that its concept of the soul, derived from Iranian "folk religion," had greatly influenced Judaism, Christianity, and even Plato. But Colpe showed that when the hymn is read in the context of the whole hymn cycle, the topic is humanity, not the soul. Thus both on chronological grounds and in terms of content, this "fragment" exerted no influence whatsoever on the development of Jewish, Christian, or Platonic notions of the soul.

Reitzenstein had also used this hymn to argue that in Gnostic myth, the Savior and the soul are consubstantial. Colpe examined the contents of the hymn cycle in order to determine how humanity was conceived and whether the Savior and humanity were indeed identified. He put three terms under his exacting philological lenses:

1. *Gyan* is the name for humans in the physical body. This designation cannot be used to establish consubstantiality or identity with the Savior because it is not only the soul, as Reitzenstein believed, but humans as embodied beings who are saved. Since the Savior nowhere called himself *gyan, gyan* is no redeemed redeemer, but is merely the person who is called to salvation.[100]

2. *Griw* is the inner essence (*Wesenheit*) of a person that is separated from the body at death. It is the *griw* that has sunk into sleep and been bound and that therefore laments and cries out. Unlike *gyan,* this essence is identified with the Light-*nous* and is consubstantial with it. As such, it is the potential saving spiritual power in a person. This capacity, however, is also found in evil people, and thus possession of *griw* in no way guarantees salvation for the individual.

3. *Manuhmed* represents the fundamental soteriological potentiality; it clearly refers both to the person who is to be saved and to the Savior.[101] Reitzenstein used this concept, which Andreas translated as soul, to construct the Iranian teaching on the soul. Yet it is clear that *manuhmed* is not the Savior; rather, as Lentz writes, "the Savior is consequently *griw* and *manuhmed,* but not *gyan.* Rather he speaks to *gyan,* who for his part possesses *griw* and *manuhmed . . .* This yields the essential form of the soul expressing the double

> function of *manuhmed* as . . . the sleeping organ that is suscepti-
> ble to the call of the divine and further is the Savior who comes
> to it."[102]

Colpe concluded that the sum of these nonbodily substances (*griw* or *manuhmed*) constitutes the soul. There is no single term corresponding to the Greek concept of the soul to be found in the hymn cycle. Yet it is clear, Colpe pointed out, that the Parthian hymn does view the nonbodily essence of a person as in some way consubstantial with the Savior, though the equation of the two is only seldom made and then only indirectly.[103]

On the basis of these and other observations, Colpe targeted Reitzen-stein's notion of the redeemed redeemer. Reitzenstein had argued that a key feature of the Gnostic redeemer myth was the shared identity of the Savior with the saved. According to Colpe's analysis, Reitzenstein had ar-gued variously that the Primal Man and the Savior are identical in that (1) they have the same origin; (2) they consist of like substance; (3) they have covered the same path down and up (by the fall of the Primal Man and the sending of the Savior on the one hand, and by the collection of the light particles and the rise of the Savior, on the other hand); and (4) they both have a human form (the Primal Man as the preexistent Anthropos; the Savior, because he is clothed in the cloak of the earthly human body).[104] Because of this identification, the redeemer appears to need re-demption; he is, in short, the "redeemed redeemer."

Colpe's evaluation of this argument is complex. On the one hand, he argued that it is possible to speak accurately of a redeemed redeemer in four senses: (1) The Primal Man–Savior may save himself by collecting to-gether the particles of light or (2) by paving the path upward to the Light world; (3) the Primal Man can only save others because he is himself saved; (4) and further, the Savior can be saved in that he cannot himself rise and pave the way upward, but must be raised by the high God above. It would seem, then, that the texts do establish some kind of identity be-tween the Savior and the saved in terms of *substance*. Yet on the other hand, the term "redeemed redeemer" itself never appears in any primary text, and its content was determined only by reference to the Gnostic sal-vation myth constructed by Reitzenstein, Bultmann, and Jonas—and that myth itself exists nowhere in the idealized form presented by those authors. No single figure ever appears in the myths who comprises the four-fold sense of "redeemer redeemer" described above; rather, various figures play roles that at different points intersect one or another of these senses.[105] Not only the formula but the concept itself is basically a modern interpretive construct; it tends to collapse the myths' careful distinctions among the various mythological figures into one character—the redeemer redeemer—with the result that salvation appears to be unnecessary:

> The formula is tautological; it excludes all hypostasizations that Gnosis is compelled to view again and again; it springs over the tragic and dramatic end of the world as being merely the background for the act of salvation and allows the prayer of the Gnostic to become a monologue . . . [because] all differences between humanity and God have been abolished. Thus this formula turns the problem of salvation—with which Gnosis is so thoroughly imprinted—into something banal.[106]

Colpe's own solution is terminological. He suggests that scholars distinguish between the concept of the redeemed redeemer—which wrongly collapses all the dramatic characters of the Gnostic redeemer myth into a single principle—and the *salvator salvandus,* which would indicate only the substantial identity between the Savior figures and the particles of light that are to be saved. This latter formula might then be added as a "proper Gnostic category" to those already established by Jonas.[107]

Another example of the mischief done by abstracting elements out of their literary and social contexts is illustrated by Colpe's reevaluation of Reitzenstein's theory of the relationship between the Gnostic Urmensch and the Son of Man.[108] Reitzenstein had constructed a geneaology of Primal Man figures, beginning with the Iranian Gayomart, moving toward the Gnostic Urmensch, and culminating in the figure of the Son of Man. Colpe began his disassemblage of Reitzenstein's construction by arguing that Zoroastrian dualism can be clearly distinguished from Gnostic dualism. By portraying the two opposing principles, Ohrmazd and Ahriman, as twin sons of a common father, the Infinite, Zoroastrianism actually resolved its dualism into a monistic solution. Thus the situation of the Gnostic Urmensch, tied as it was to a strict cosmological dualism, was significantly different from that of Gayomart. The same criticism was also applied to the supposed connection between the Gayomart of the *Great Bundahisa* and the anthropos of the *Poimandres*.[109]

There were also problems in genealogically connecting the Gnostic Urmensch in Manichaean and Mandaean traditions to the Son of Man in "late Judaism."[110] The Jewish figure lacked important Gnostic elements, especially the descent of the messenger into the lower world and the constitutional relation of the human soul and the Urmensch. It is true that there are analogies in Jewish literature to the so-called return of "the Man." But even there, differences exist as to whether these instances refer to "the return of the same figure or the appearance of a soteriological 'successo prophetica.'" It seems "more than doubtful," wrote Colpe, "that the late Jewish Son of Man was conceived as the returning protoplast."[111]

It is also necessary, Colpe argued, to ask what type of saving deed was accomplished by the "return." In Iranian thought, the Savior effected the renewal of a mythical primordial state of the world; in Judaism, he brought the End of Days or, in another context, the dissolution of the world and humanity into its original preexistent state.

All we can say for sure, concluded Colpe, is that the Jewish Son of Man and the Oriental soteriological myths belong to a common circle of thought—but they may not be resolved into a teleological or linear genealogy. For example, though we find a figure in the Iranian Yima-Yaga saga who ruled in the time of origin (Urzeit) and will bring in the salvific conditions of the end time (Endzeit), Colpe maintained that this is

> yet merely a typical example of the common Oriental Urzeit-Endzeit schema, inside of which the Biblical schema forms a special case, but it should not be set in historical dependence upon it. Even if someone should succeed in pointing out parallels to the Son of Man, on the one hand, and Gayomart and Yima/Yaga respectively on the other—which we have shown would be most difficult—the historical dependence of the first upon the last would not thereby be settled. The Son of Man (and by the way also the Gnostic anthropos) could not be grasped as the end result of a history which had been discharged from the Indo-Iranian myth; for that the mediating hymns are lacking.[112]

These kinds of considerations led to an all-out attack by Colpe on the validity of a motif-historical model for determining the origin and development of the Gnostic salvation myth:

> What appears to me to be directly false concerning this model is that it is *de facto* burdened with the whole claim of archaic weight, as though the Gnostic salvation myth arose sometime in a grey archaic period, somewhere in the far wide East (whose location can't seem to be specified more precisely than "Iran"). Then it wandered throughout time and space, appearing now in this, now in that circle of tradition, such as Wisdom poetry, in Philo, in Adam speculations, and in apocalyptic. These left behind a scattering of mosaic pieces which Manichaeism once more gathered together into a grandiose unity, but which finally disintegrated with the Mandaeans.[113]

In the end, vague origins and scattered traces say little or nothing about where Gnosticism began and how it developed. Only by letting go of this "Willen zur Genealogie," Colpe argued, can we arrive at "the possibility of seeing these concepts, traditions, or types of expression in a different way," namely, that they arose as part of a structural change in the basic, underlying *Weltanschauung*.[114]

The strains of Jonas's composition can be clearly heard in Colpe's work, but they are played in a new key. Although he agreed with Jonas that the origin of Gnosticism lies in a particular attitude toward the world, Colpe understood its content differently. At its base is the idea that there is "a certain definite relation between the transcendental and the contingent world." That idea was expressed by the concept that the world soul is present in the individual as well as in the cosmos; or that there is a consubstantiality of identity between the cosmic powers on the one hand and humanity on the other; but particularly that there is a relationship between the heavenly Savior and humanity. In all these cases, the basic object of Gnosis was founded on the transcendental concept that the true being of humanity is identical with its spiritual essence.[115]

Thus in the end Colpe placed no value on determining whether Gnostic myths originated through reinterpretation of older myth (like Helen in the Simonian system), or by transforming older tradition through allegory, or even whether they had borrowed older materials or discovered new ones themselves. Rather, his concept of Gnosis led him to assert, like Jonas, that the determination of various elements that may have played an important role in the expression of Gnosis does not necessarily explain its origination. We are dealing here not with influence, he argued, but with confluence: Gnosis is the product of a West-Oriental Zeitgeist. "It seems possible," he wrote, "that in the history of religion we must reckon with as many occurrences of origin as we have types of origin."[116] The real task of the scholar is therefore not to construct genealogies that explain nothing, but rather to analyze individual texts and specific concepts in order to elucidate their "phenomenological determination of essence [Wesenbestimmung]," which, for Colpe, shows itself to be Gnostic above all by the presence of the *salvator salvandus* concept.

Colpe pointed out that focusing on determining the essence of Gnosticism usually led scholars to accept the view that Gnosticism predated Christianity, while attempts to date Gnosticism by the presence of the "Gnostic salvation myth" naturally led to the opposite view. This controversy could easily be resolved, he argued, if scholars were to realize that

> the constitution of Gnosis as a common human religious phenomenon and its historical localization are two different things, and that there can be a "Gnostic attitude toward existence" and "saving Gnosis" with or without a salvation myth. Then a common basis of discussion might be found for both fields of research.[117]

It was precisely such a distinction that Colpe put forward at the Messina Congress on the origin of Gnosticism in April 1966 and that participants adopted in the "Proposal for a Terminological and Conceptual Agreement on the Theme of the Colloquium."[118] It is unfortunate that his dehistoricized and essentialized category of Gnosticism was so fully accepted, whereas his crucial and devastating critique of genealogy had little impact.

## Reflections

Many scholars have contributed in various ways to the critique of the modern construction of Gnosticism, and in so doing they have posed serious challenges to the normative story of Christian origins. Those who appear in this chapter illustrate some of the crucial points that have been made: despite all the problems with Bauer's work, he has established that chronological priority can be no sure determinant of theological ortho-doxy; normativity must be determined on some other basis. Jonas's work sought to put an end to genealogical and motif history as a method to de-termine the origins and nature of Gnosticism. Mandaeism scholars have demonstrated that there is no sure evidence for the existence of pre-Chris-tian Gnosticism. Finally, Colpe has shown that the Gnostic redeemer myth is an artificial and composite synthesis that misconstrues the mean-ing of the actual texts it purports to describe.

At the same time, however, these scholars at points have further com-plicated the problem of understanding Gnosticism. Because Bauer con-tinued to use the terms "orthodoxy" and "heresy," he tended to reinscribe a later view of Christian orthodoxy onto the early period of Christian be-ginnings. Jonas has probably done more than anyone else to reify Gnosti-cism into an objectively existing entity and religion in its own right through his typological delimitation of it as a singular phenomenon, though perhaps Colpe has helped somewhat by insisting on distinguish-ing Gnosis (as a human phenomenon) from Gnosticism (as its historical localization)—and thereby continuing to traffic in the discredited world of demythologizing.[119]

Despite these criticisms, the enduring work of church historians and history of religions scholars has been to emphasize the multiformity of early Christian phenomena, as well as to demonstrate irrefutably that Christianity and Judaism are integrally entwined in a wider historical and cultural matrix. They, too, began to expose an increasing awareness of the ways in which the ancient discourse of orthodoxy and heresy has been en-tangled with modern historiography. It fell to the next generation of scholars to understand these insights more fully. They had not only the shoulders of great predecessors to stand on, but also the resources of a fab-ulous discovery of new Egyptian manuscripts.

# 6

# After Nag Hammadi I:
# Categories and Origins

In 1945, two Egyptian peasants quietly set out on a short journey that was to change the study of Gnosticism forever. At the foot of the Jabel al-Tarif, a cliff near the town of Nag Hammadi in Middle Egypt, they made an astonishing discovery.[1] Digging for fertilizer, they uncovered a sealed clay jar containing a hoard of papyrus manuscripts. These fourth-century C.E. papyrus codices, known as the Nag Hammadi Codices, included a wealth of ancient religious literature, a total of forty-six different works, almost all of which were previously unknown. The manuscripts had probably been in the possession of the nearby Pachomian monastery, until someone hid them for reasons we can only surmise.[2]

The rediscovery of the works in 1945 was overshadowed by events in the aftermath of World War II; thus they are far less famous than the Dead Sea Scrolls. For the few specialists into whose hands these manuscripts fell, however, the excitement was immediate and overwhelming. It seemed that now for the first time, books written by the Gnostics themselves were available for study. No longer would the writings of their polemicist detractors dominate the field. The Gnostics would be able to speak for themselves, and the problem of defining Gnosticism would finally be resolved. A new chapter in the history of Christianity could be written.

Alas, that has not proved to be the case. The new riches did not provide quick or easy solutions. Indeed, the surprise is that for decades little has changed. The problem of defining Gnosticism is as intractable as ever.[3] Why?

We can no longer blame a lack of evidence. Given that the evidence available to scholars has increased so dramatically, it is reasonable to expect at least some resolution. So far, however, the new materials have served more to highlight the problems than to resolve them. And that must give us pause. The reason for the continued confusion, I would argue, is not the lack of material evidence but the continued entanglement of heresiological discourses in the scholarly study of Gnosticism. Exegetes have found it increasingly difficult to get the texts to fit neatly into the old typological and genealogical frameworks. The tensions are becoming increasingly acute.

In this chapter I chart some of those tensions and point out the directions in which scholarship is moving. One crucial impact of the Nag Hammadi codices has been to force scholars to reconsider our current frameworks and methods. More data have not resulted in more certainty; rather, they have exposed the implausibility of explanatory frameworks that may be elegant but are too simplistic to deal with the historical complexity of the pluralistic religious life of the ancient social world.[4] The Nag Hammadi codices have only added to that complexity. But that is quite acceptable, because the complexity of our own lives requires resources to think with that match the untidy perplexities we ourselves must negotiate. Far from unmaking Christianity or denigrating theological enterprises, elucidating this complexity will ground theological reflection in more accurate historical and theological readings of the ancient materials. It may also provide resources for reflection on a wide range of deeply felt issues in cultural studies, not least of which are the processes of identity formation wrought in conditions of religious pluralism.

## The Current State of Research

The decades since the discovery near Nag Hammadi have seen a flurry of scholarly activity. The sheer volume of the material and its intellectual complexity have required enormous efforts. Painstaking studies focused on the philological and exegetical problems of specific works initially constituted the bulk of the research. Work on Coptic language and codicology, as well as on questions of composition, use of sources, and genre, has made significant advances. Three groups of scholars in particular have focused on these problems. The first and most truly collaborative is the Berliner Arbeitskreis für koptisch-gnostische Schriften, under the leadership of Hans-Martin Schenke. This group produced many of the first modern-language translations of the Nag Hammadi texts, as well as critical editions, commentaries, and studies.[5] The most comprehensive project was done by an international team led by James M. Robinson in conjunction with UNESCO, which by 1996 had produced a facsimile edition, English translations, and critical editions of the entire Nag Hammadi corpus.[6] The third collaborative effort is a French-language project centered at the University of Laval in Quebec, now under the leadership of Louis Painchaud. This group is producing an impressive set of critical editions, French translations, commentaries, and concordances, as well as specialized studies of the Nag Hammadi and related Coptic texts.[7] Numerous other editions and studies by independent scholars have appeared as well. A full and reliable bibliography of work on the Nag Hammadi literature has been laboriously compiled by David Scholer.[8]

Although analysis of the Nag Hammadi texts is still in its early stages, these detailed studies are providing exciting new insights and a sound basis for rethinking every issue related to the study of Gnosticism. From the beginning, discussions of the new find have clustered around a set of related topics. A great deal of conversation, for example, has been directed toward assessing the adequacy of the pre–Nag Hammadi portrait of Gnosticism and its relation to Christianity. In particular, scholars have addressed the possible relationship of Nag Hammadi texts to the New Testament, not least of all because they believe that one of the Nag Hammadi texts, *GosThom,* contains previously unknown, authentic sayings of Jesus.[9] Other texts, such as *DialSav, ApJames,* and the Berlin Codex *GosMary,* also contain evidence of early stages of the Jesus tradition.[10] The question of the Gnostic character of these works is being hotly debated. The answer, of course, depends very much on how Gnosticism is defined—and that itself remains a vexing problem.

Certain Nag Hammadi works appear to be closely related to heresies described by the early Christian polemicists. There are, however, some significant discrepancies between the descriptions of the polemicists and the contents of Nag Hammadi works; such discrepancies indicate where and how the rhetorical strategies, theological interests, and ecclesiastical

politics of the polemicists may have shaped their descriptions of heretical
groups and affected the reliability of their "reports."[11] In addition to
prompting a reevaluation of the early Christian polemicists as historians,
this investigation has simultaneously had the unexpected but happy effect
of stimulating renewed interest in the polemicists' own distinctive contributions to Christian theology.[12]

The Nag Hammadi works have also challenged scholars to reconfigure
the boundaries of orthodoxy and heresy, and indeed to rethink the useful-
ness of that distinction for reconstructing the history of the early period.
Whereas we might have expected these works to solidify the ancient distinctions between orthodoxy and heresy, they have instead supported
Bauer's thesis that distinct varieties of Christianity developed in different
geographical areas, at a time when the boundaries of orthodoxy and heresy were not at all fixed. As Robinson argues, both what came to be "orthodoxy" and what came to be "heresy" in the debates of the second and
third centuries had roots in "a common body of tradition." As he puts it:

> There seems not yet to be a central body of orthodox doctrine distin-
> guished from heretical doctrine to the right and to the left, but
> rather a common body of beliefs variously understood and translated
> or transmitted . . . To this extent the terms *heresy* and *orthodoxy* are
> anachronistic.[13]

Early Christian literature does not divide neatly into orthodox and heretical camps; there are unexpected overlaps and surprising similarities, and
crucial points of difference are not always where we expect them to be. As
a result, scholars have come to realize that the diverse forms of early Christianity were much more entangled than previously thought.

Helmut Koester recognized the implications of this position for the
study of Gnosticism, and he insisted that "the line between heretical and
orthodox cannot be drawn by simply using the term *gnostic* for certain developments customarily designated in such fashion." Accordingly, some
texts that have been classified as Gnostic (that is, heretical), such as
*GosThom,* need to be considered "historically of equal value with the canonical writings."[14] This means, Koester insisted, not that the categories
of orthodoxy and heresy are theologically invalid, but rather that "true
faith" must be determined on the basis of criteria other than origins: "In

the quest for criteria, the task of the historian and of the theologian cannot be divided into the free inquiry of the one and the dogmatic security of the other." For Koester, the two are linked:

> The theological search for the decisive criterion for distinguishing between true and false belief coincides with the historical quest for the essential characteristics of early Christianity as such. We have to do here with a religious movement which is syncretistic in appearance and conspicuously marked by diversification from the very beginning. What its individuality is cannot be taken as established a priori.[15]

By centering his analysis on the earliest layers of the Jesus tradition from Nag Hammadi (especially on *GosThom, ApJames,* and *DialSav*), Koester went to the heart of the issue. He recognized with unusual frankness that the problem of defining Gnosticism is intimately bound up with establishing the identity of Christianity.

Other studies have focused on the relationship of certain texts to the Platonic tradition. The Neoplatonist Plotinus had written against the Gnostics in the third century, and it is now widely accepted that the Nag Hammadi collection probably contains treatises known to him, chief among them *Allogenes.*[16] Other Nag Hammadi texts evince complex relations to the Greek philosophical tradition. Numerous studies, a conference, and now a seminar have been devoted to exploring these relations.[17]

Predictably, the Nag Hammadi manuscripts have provoked considerable discussion about the adequacy of prior theories about the origin and typological characterization of Gnosticism, as well as the social character and location of the Gnostics. They have provided a new basis for testing previously held theses and for developing new resolutions for old problems. While the heritage of past methods, frameworks, and discourses continues to shape how scholars interpret the new materials, scholars are also forging new avenues. We turn to these now.

## The Trouble with Variety

The enormous diversity of materials contained within the Nag Hammadi collection poses an immediate problem for scholarship, and the problem of categorization has become particularly urgent. The wide variety of perspectives regarding cosmology, theology, ethical orientation, anthropology, spiritual discipline, and ritual practice requires that some distinctions be made lest the discussion remain hopelessly muddled.

## Rethinking Classification

Some scholars have addressed the issue of variety by organizing the disparate materials into subcategories. The earliest attempts placed individual works within categories drawn from the catalogues of the polemicists. With the notable exception of Valentinus and his school, such attempts were largely unsuccessful. In the case of Valentinus, however, scholars grouped together a substantial amount of the literature from Nag Hammadi largely on the basis of comparison with testimonies from polemicists. Although lively discussion continues about the precise boundaries of the Valentinian literature, the following seven works from Nag Hammadi are most often considered to belong to Valentinian circles: *The Gospel of Truth, The Prayer of the Apostle Paul, The Treatise on the Resurrection, The Tripartite Tractate, The Gospel of Philip, The Interpretation of Knowledge,* and *A Valentinian Exposition.* Scholars have argued for the inclusion of several other works with varying degrees of enthusiasm: *I and II Apocalypse of James, The Letter of Peter to Philip, The Testimony of Truth,* and *The Apocryphon of James.*[18]

By all accounts, Valentinus was a poet and theologian of considerable talent and persuasion. Born in Egypt, he was a prominent Christian teacher in second-century Rome. The polemicists relate that Valentinus' theology extended through the activities of his followers, among whom were several significant teachers, including Florinus, Heracleon, Marcus, Ptolemy, and Theodotus. They did not merely pass on Valentinus' teaching rotely but were themselves often innovative thinkers. This fact has raised questions about how to define Valentinian thought, given the discrepancies between Valentinus' own writings and the other writings categorized as Valentinian (especially the system of Ptolemy described by Irenaeus and the *Tripartite Tractate* from Nag Hammadi).

For example, Valentinus' own work, the *Gospel of Truth,* tells how God's transcendence resulted in human ignorance of Him, a situation

that was corrected by the sending of his Son, Jesus.[19] Jesus showed the way
to knowledge of the Father, but he is persecuted for his teaching and
nailed to the tree of the cross. Valentinus interprets this event allegorically
in terms of Genesis and the Gospel of John: Jesus is the fruit of the true
Tree of Knowledge that brings life when one eats of it (perhaps a reference
to a sacramental meal); he is the divine Word of revelation, posted like a
public notice on a wooden pole and read like the Book of Life. Through
his teaching and resurrection, the Son reveals the Father and restores the
souls to restful unity with Him, as they are refreshed by the Spirit and attracted to Him like a sweet fragrance, participating in His nature "by
means of kisses." It is incorrect, *Gos Truth* admonishes, to think of the Father as harsh or wrathful; rather, he is without evil, imperturbable, and
sweet.

The account of Valentinian thought written by Irenaeus tells a quite
different story. It begins with the divine Father's generation of fourteen
pairs of male-female aeons who together constitute the heavenly world.
The youngest of these is the female aeon, Sophia (Wisdom). In her desire
to be like the Father, she creates a being out of herself without the permis-
sion of her male counterpart and without his participation. The result is a
deformed creature, living but void of divine spirit. Together with his
mother Sophia, this imperfection is cast forth from the divine world like
an abortion, and finds himself in darkness and chaos. This ignorant and
weak being is the creator God of Genesis. He proceeds to create the lower
world, but mistakenly boasts that he is "the only God" with none above
him. He and his angels create humanity according to the image of God,
but in their own likeness. At the instigation of the mother, Sophia, humanity is endowed with Spirit and becomes superior to the creator God.
In his ignorance, God tries to keep humanity from the knowledge of good
and evil, but Eve is instructed by the serpent to eat of the fruit, so that she
and Adam become the first Gnostics. The humans, however, are cursed,
and thus plunged back into ignorance. Now Christ the Savior is sent to
teach these lost souls about their heavenly origin and divine nature, so
that they may escape the bonds of the world ruler and return to their
heavenly home and the blessed rule of the true Father. Although quite different in its particulars and much more elaborate, *TriTrac* presents a story
more congruent with Irenaeus's account than with *Gos Truth*.

The considerable differences between these accounts have generated discussion about whether *GosTruth* was written before the development of the full-blown Gnostic system with its heavenly aeons and the story of Sophia's "fall," or whether it presupposes the myth so that one needs to know the entire myth in order to understand the obscure allusions to it in the text.[20] Another approach, offered by Einar Thomassen, suggests taking *TriTrac* as the clearest case of a Valentinian work owing to its congruity with the descriptions of the polemicists; from this perspective, however, works like *GosTruth* conform only in part to the criteria he establishes. To complicate matters further, Thomassen suggests that Valentinians may have adopted non-Valentinian works and adapted them to suit their own purposes. Such, he suggests, is probably the case with *PrayerPaul* and *Eugnostos*.[21]

Most recently the discrepancy has led Christoph Markschies to question whether Valentinus was a Gnostic at all. He has argued that if we compare the theology in the extant fragments of Valentinus' own work with the Messina Congress definition of Gnosticism, Valentinus cannot be considered a Gnostic. The same cannot, however, be said for followers of Valentinus such as Ptolemy.[22]

An alternative method has been to privilege Valentinus' own work as the basis for inclusion, but that approach eliminates most of the literature corresponding to the polemicists' descriptions. Some have attempted to define the essential elements of Valentinian thought and ritual practice typologically, using that definition as the basis for delimiting the range of what should be included. Others have attempted a genealogical model, tying later individuals and schools of thought to the founder Valentinus, however distinct and original their own mythological speculations may be. The most solid consensus among scholars is that Valentinianism is a category whose boundaries are relatively permeable and unfixed, no matter how solid the core may be. The category needs to include both the works of Valentinus and those of his apparent successors.

A second, highly influential and useful subcategory of the Nag Hammadi materials was proposed by Hans-Martin Schenke, who argued persuasively for grouping a set of Nag Hammadi works under the heading of "Sethianism." Although the name "Sethian" was derived from the polemicists' literature, Schenke based inclusion on a set of shared mythic elements:[23]

- The Sethians understand themselves to be "the seed of Seth."
- Seth is the Gnostic savior, or alternatively, Adam is the savior of his son Seth. Both may have a heavenly and/or an earthly aspect.
- The heavenly place of rest for Adam, Seth, and the seed of Seth is the four aeons and illuminators of Autogenes: Harmozel, Oroiael, Daveithe, and Eleleth.
- Autogenes is a member of the divine triad as the Son of the Father (often named the Invisible Spirit) and the Mother, Barbelo. This triad is itself specifically Sethian.
- "Man" (Adam) in his primal form is connected with this heavenly triad.
- Beneath the four lights is the realm of the Demiurge, Yaldabaoth.
- The appearance of the divine Man is a result of the arrogance of Yaldabaoth and the punishment for his hubris.
- Finally, Sethian mythology contains a distinctive periodization of history: the age of Adam, the age of Seth, the age of the original Sethians, and the present time.

To these mythic contents, Schenke added consideration of the intertextual relations among the works and, above all, evidence for the practice of two cultic mysteries: baptism and a ritual of ascent.[24] This method resulted in the following list of Sethian works: *The Apocryphon of John, The Hypostasis of the Archons, The Gospel of the Egyptians, The Apocalypse of Adam, The Three Steles of Seth, Zostrianos, The Thought of Norea, Marsanes, Allogenes,* and, from the Bruce Codex, *The Untitled Treatise.*[25] On the basis of Schenke's list of texts and characteristics, others have suggested also including *Trimorphic Protennoia, On the Origin of the World, Melchizedek,* and *Hypsiphrone.* Schenke himself included the parallel to the first part of *ApJohn* in Irenaeus, *AgHer* I, 29; and the doctrines of the so-called Gnostics, Sethians, and Archontics in Epiphanius (*Panarion* I.26, 39, 40).[26]

Like the Valentinian literature, the Sethian works evince considerable internal diversity. In this case, however, that diversity has sparked debate about whether in fact any distinct social group lies behind this literature. John Turner attempted to overcome this problem through a "literary history of Sethian Gnosticism," accounting for the internal diversity by positing changes in Sethian interactions with Christianity over a period of three centuries.[27] His main insight, that these texts evince diverse relationships to Christianity, is intriguing, though his treatment of Sethianism in terms of a linear history is less persuasive.[28]

Although Schenke based the contours of Sethianism on an analysis of mythic materials within the Nag Hammadi corpus rather than on the descriptions of the early Christian polemicists,[29] he did include the polemicists' accounts as supplemental evidence. Alisdair Logan has further argued that there is significant continuity between Schenke's list and a distinct set of materials described by the polemicists. Moreover, Logan has insisted that the ritual aspects of Sethianism, identified by Jean-Marie Sevrin in his excellent study of baptism, are foundational for seeing Sethianism as a distinct phenomenon. He attributes the basic Sethian myth to "the work of a hitherto unknown visionary or visionaries," comparable to religious geniuses known from later history, such as Valentinus and Mani.[30] By insisting that Sethian Gnostic myth was generated in religious experience and especially in ritual, Logan offered a further basis on which to establish Sethianism as a distinct subcategory of Gnosticism.

Bentley Layton has proposed yet another approach, suggesting that we focus on common internal self-designation as an indication of social distinctiveness. As noted above, he began with the use of the term γνωστικόι ("Gnostics") and from there generated a list of textual materials that may be associated with that self-designation in antiquity. It should not go unnoticed that Layton's final database corresponds very closely to Schenke's delineation of the Sethian corpus; his list includes all the materials designated "Sethian" by Schenke, but adds the following: *The Book of Zoroaster, Trimorphic Protennoia, Thunder Perfect Mind,* and *Melchizedek.* The fact that approaches as different as those of Schenke, Logan, and Layton arrived at largely the same collection of materials, I submit, adds significantly to the persuasiveness of the category, both as a sociological grouping and as a coherent set of intellectual materials. Of course, the question remains as to how much this grouping belongs to a level of historical "factuality" (that is, to what degree it delimits an actual distinct historical group of persons) and how much belongs to the categorizing processes.

The considerable similarities between Valentinian and Sethian myths argue for some connection, but the precise contours of that relationship remain unclear. Rather than attempt to solve the problem of their relationship, let me offer a brief comparison of the two. It should be clear by now that Sethian mythology and Valentinian Christianity are neither uniform nor monolithic. Both show considerable diversity of thought and mythmaking. Hence a comparison of the differences identified below only reflects directions or tendencies of thought and mythic expression; the real situation was certainly much more complex.

Valentinian myth and thought are more decidedly Christian than is Sethian mythology, and this shows up in a number of ways. In Valentinian mythology the primary role of savior is played by Christ, whereas Sethian myth presents a number of saviors, including many female figures. While the tendency to identify saviors with Christ is observable in Christian Sethian texts as well, Christ is still not as central a figure as he is in Valentinianism.

Valentinian myth tends to portray the world creator in a partially positive light, while Sethian myth paints a more sharply critical portrait of him. Whereas in Sethianism the world creator appears arrogant, ignorant, and evil, in Valentinianism he is more sympathetically portrayed as a character who is not truly wicked but simply lacks complete understanding— not good but merely just. The Valentinian myth therefore does not stress the spiritual inferiority of the creator God as completely as Sethian myths tend to do. This tendency puts Valentinian thought somewhat more in line with other forms of Christianity that viewed the world creator of Genesis as the true God.

These differing portrayals of the world creator also have a significant impact on understanding the condition of humanity in this world and the nature of salvation. Sethian myths emphasize the active malevolence of evil more than Valentinian theology does, for example, in the tyranny of the world rulers against humanity, in the Sethian stories of the rape of Eve, or in the interpretations of Genesis 6 as a general deception and enslavement of humanity. Hence for Sethians the situation of humanity in the world is envisioned as a battle against the forces within (worldly desire and passions) and without (the powers that rule the world and establish Fate and death) that seek to enslave the divine/human spirit. Salvation stresses an ethic of ascetic self-rule that offers protection against the demonic forces until the light below is reintegrated into the world above by the savior. Valentinian myth tends to portray the situation of humanity more in terms of ignorance and error, where suffering and death are illusory conditions that can be overcome through saving knowledge (*gnosis*). The Son is able to effect salvation by overcoming the deficiency of creation, which is ignorance of the Father. Thus even in Christian Sethian myth, the meaning of the savior on the cross is portrayed as yet another episode in the struggle of the spirit against the foolish world rulers, while in Valentinian thought the crucifixion is a revelation (a "publication") of the Son's knowledge of the Father.

Views about the nature of the world are affected as well. The *Gospel of Truth* in particular shows the tendency toward radical monism in which there is only one ultimate principle of existence. This monism is implicit in the view that suffering (death) is illusory and evil (ignorance) is only a "deficiency" that needs to be "filled up." In the end, Sethian thought is more decidedly dualistic in its conceptuality of the world, evil, and salvation than is Valentinianism. A qualification is necessary, however, since two Sethian texts, *Marsanes* and *Allogenes,* exhibit a less radical philosophical monism.

The differences in Sethian and Valentinian views of humanity in the world also have a significant impact on ethics. Even though we know very little about the actual behavior of either Sethians or Valentinians, the Sethian literature seems to point toward a more staunchly ascetic lifestyle than does the Valentinian. There may have been considerable variety among the Valentinians in this regard, but it seems that at least some Valentinians accepted the legitimacy of marriage. Valentinians also clearly talked about sin, viewing it largely as Paul did, not only as a matter of right and wrong acts but as the faulted condition of the self in the face of divine perfection.

Their different ethical emphases can be illustrated by comparing statements about the ideal life in the Valentinian *Gospel of Truth* and the Sethian *Apocryphon of John*. Both texts make it clear that salvation is manifest in one's life in the world and both emphasize the importance of purifying the self from evil. The Valentinian text emphasizes the need to proselytize and reach out to others in their suffering, while the Sethian text stresses attaining an ideal spiritual and moral state in which one can persevere until the end. Thus these ideal characterizations of morality reflect the tendencies noted above: Valentinianism emphasizes overcoming ignorance and suffering (death), while Sethianism emphasizes that life in the world is a spiritual battle waged against actively malevolent foes. It is worth noting in this context that the oft-repeated cliché that Gnostics are "saved by nature," with the result that Gnostic theology is considered incapable of providing a rationale for ethical behavior, is an error based on the polemicists' misunderstanding of the texts' emphasis on the providence of God. Even when the texts emphasize the spiritual nature of humanity and God's providential care for humans, they clearly see the need for persons to strive for moral perfection.

Another difference lies in their treatments of "history." Whereas Sethian mythology sometimes has room for a scheme of salvation history (traced from Adam and Eve through the descendents of Seth and Norea down to the present-day Sethians), Valentinian myth tends to dissolve the temporal divisions of the narrative into a timeless portrayal of the soul's situation in the world. This tendency is particularly evident in the *Gospel of Truth*.

Sethians, like most Christians and indeed most social groups, divide humanity into only two categories (those who will be saved and those who will not, that is, insiders and outsiders), while Valentinians have three categories (spiritual humans and psychic humans—both of whom will be saved—and material persons who will not). Valentinians may have come up with this tripartite division of humanity as a compassionate way to rationalize their presence within a Christianity that rejected them, by making a place in the scheme of salvation for their less spiritually advanced Christian fellows, whom they considered to be psychics.

Different emphases can also be noted in the gender symbolism of the two mythologies. While both largely share in the patriarchal gender construction of ancient Mediterranean society, Sethianism tends to portray the female in more active and positive roles, and in a few places even critiques the illegitimate domination of women by men (for example, by portraying the subordination of women to men in Genesis 3:16 as part of the wicked God's attempt to enslave the Spirit). Valentinian myth and ritual make more use of androgyny as a symbol of primal unity (for example, in the *Gospel of Philip*'s portrayal of the separation of woman from man as the cause of death, making the mission of Christ to reunite the two and restore them to life).

Finally, significantly different ritual practices might be inferred from the two sets of texts. This is particularly tentative ground given that references to the ritual practices of Sethians and Valentinians are obscure. Both apparently practiced baptism, but their understandings of these rituals may have differed considerably. In addition, Sethians may have practiced a ritual of ascent and Valentinians a rite of the bridal chamber. These differences, along with the notable distinguishing features listed by Schenke for Sethianism, justify separate categories for classifying Valentinian and Sethian texts.

Early on, a third and smaller group of works were deemed Hermetic on the basis of comparison with known Hermetic materials, and this category has remained essentially unchallenged. It includes *Asclepius, The Discourse on the Eighth and Ninth,* and *The Prayer of Thanksgiving.*

A few scholars have begun to recognize a fourth grouping as yet another distinct category: Thomas Christianity. In this class they include two works from Nag Hammadi, *The Gospel of Thomas* and *The Book of Thomas,* along with the previously known *Acts of Thomas.* This category, however, is beginning to come under serious fire and in my opinion will probably not stand the test of scholarly scrutiny.[31]

These four subcategories (Valentinianism, Sethianism, Hermeticism, and to a lesser degree Thomas Christianity) have become well established within the field.[32] Their status with regard to Gnosticism, however, has become increasingly unclear. Should they be regarded as subcategories of Gnosticism or of Christianity, or as distinct religious phenomena, comparable to Mandaeism and Manichaeism?

If we opt for the former, the question arises of how the categories are related to one another. Several scholars have connected Sethianism and Valentinianism genealogically. Relying at least in part on Irenaeus' comment that Valentinus "adapted the principles from the so-called Gnostic heresy to his peculiar system of doctrine," Layton has suggested that Valentinus was a Christian reformer of a classical Gnostic system. Markschies, however, thinks Christianity developed in a Gnosticizing direction only within later Valentinianism.[33] The French scholar Simone Pétrement, in contrast to Layton, has argued that Valentinianism influenced Sethianism.[34] After all, Tertullian had argued—in contradiction to Irenaeus—that "the doctrines which have grown up amongst the Valentinians have already extended their rank growth to the woods of the Gnos-

tics."[35] None of these genealogical schema has achieved any wide acceptance, at least partly because any such linear formulation is much too
simplistic to account for the complexity of the phenomena, especially
given the diversity within the subcategories themselves.

And how are we to classify the texts that do not fit into any of the four
categories, such as the texts relating to the early Jesus tradition (for example, *GosThom, GosMary, ApJames, DialSav,* and *GosSav*)? Are there more
streams of Gnosticism yet to be determined? Or are such "left-over" works
to be considered "generically Gnostic"? Or not Gnostic at all? Should the
fact that a work was found within the Nag Hammadi cache or the Berlin
Codex be a factor in determining whether it is Gnostic? For example,
what about the badly mangled translation of a section of Plato's *Republic*
in Codex VI, or the collection of Jewish wisdom sayings, *The Sentences of
Sextus,* in Codex XII? Surely they cannot be classified as Gnostic solely on
the basis of the other contents of the jar or codex in which they were
found. Or can they? These works had evidently been taken up as grist for
the mill of Gnostic hermeneutics. Have they then become Gnostic in
much the same way that the Hebrew Scriptures became Christian—by
hermeneutic appropriation? What does it mean that the Nag Hammadi
collection was once in the possession of the supposedly orthodox
Pachomian monks? Does that context suggest that the works should be
considered orthodox? Or that the monks should be considered heretics?

The problem of classification was explored with particular care at a
Laval conference in 1993.[36] Paper topics concerned the collection as a
whole (linguistic, codicological, or doctrinal groupings), where to place
documents that had been subject to revision (such as *Eugnostos* and the
*SophJesusChr*), how to understand the possible coherence of apparently
varied materials within single codices (ancient rationales for inclusion),
which criteria to use in delimiting certain categories (Valentinian, Sethian), and where to place individual texts.[37] The fact that ancient scribes
put into the same codex works that scholars have included in different
subcategories is particularly disconcerting. Codex II, for example, contains works classified as Sethian, Valentinian, Thomas Christianity, and
two miscellaneous works—a fact which illustrates that ancient practices of
collection (and hence ancient criteria for categorization) do not correlate
with the categories delimited by late twentieth-century scholarship.

On the basis of this discussion, Louis Painchaud and Anne Pasquier, the editors of the conference volume, concluded that "given the actual state of our knowledge, it would not be possible to retain a satisfactory principle of classification for the collection of these tractates without risking hardening them into categories of classes that have been insufficiently established."[38] The very process of classification tends to reify its own categories, often at the expense of understanding how individual works cross and blur definitional categories. The variety of ways that texts can be categorized reflects the variety of interests and perspectives of those doing the classifying. For example, a reader interested in linguistics will group the texts in one way; a reader interested in the history of varieties of Christianity in the second century would make a very different list, excluding a number of works from consideration altogether. The point is that though categories and categorization are useful for particular ends, any classification system is provisional and positional.

This point can be illustrated by looking at another, even more pervasive mode of classifying the Nag Hammadi works that concerns their relationship to Christianity, Judaism, and paganism. Most of these works have been classified as one of the following: Christian Gnostic (for example, *GosTruth*), Jewish Gnostic (*Apocalypse of Adam*), or philosophical-pagan Gnostic (*Allogenes*). Indeed, scholars often argue about "how Jewish" or "how Christian" or "how philosophical" a work "really" is, or what kind of Judaism, Christianity, or paganism it might be.[39] Might we just as well regard Valentinianism, Thomas Christianity, or some of the Sethian works as subcategories of Christianity as of Gnosticism? Is the point of these discussions less to make categorical sense of the textual diversity than to (re)establish the boundaries of normative Christianity, Judaism, and paganism?[40] If so, at every turn the Nag Hammadi collection confounds these basic categories of religious classification.

The pertinent question is whether categorization is able to place a work in a fixed and permanent intellectual and historical location, which then ought to govern its interpretation and determine its historical significance. Surely works can and do move around, and as they do, their meaning and historical significance shift as well. Hence the categories themselves do not represent fixed, essential, or mutually exclusive entities. Religions are always in flux, but particularly so under the conditions of ancient pluralism that obtained in the eastern Mediterranean during the first centuries c.e. Although categorization is an important hermeneutical tool, it is necessary to articulate clearly the purposes of such classification, and above all to note the provisional status of all categorization.

Another approach to sorting out the muddle caused by treating Gnosticism as a monolithic category has been to eliminate the term, or at least limit the range of materials designated as Gnostic.[41] As early as 1935, ten years before the Nag Hammadi discovery had even been made, R. P. Casey had questioned the adequacy of Gnosticism as a category. After reviewing the ancient literature then available (Greek, Latin, Syriac, Armenian, Coptic, and Mandaean), he concluded:

> There is no trace in early Christianity of "Gnosticism" as a broad historical category, and the modern use of "Gnostic" and "Gnosticism" to describe a large but ill-defined religious movement, having a special scope and character, is wholly unknown in the early Christian period.[42]

Whereas the term γνῶσις (gnosis; "knowledge") was used broadly in antiquity, the term γνωστικός ("Gnostic") appeared infrequently, Casey argued, and was used only by Clement of Alexandria, Irenaeus, Tertullian, and Plotinus. Clement used it to refer to spiritually mature Christians who had attained an advanced philosophical understanding of Christianity. Irenaeus, and Tertullian following him, used the term to refer to "a group of related sects otherwise known as the Ophites or Naassenes." According to Casey, it is difficult to know whom Plotinus had in mind, unless the term was merely a disparaging reference to "know-it-alls."[43]

Given this information, Casey asked "whether the modern conception is justified." His answer was somewhat ambiguous. On the one hand, he noted that modern attempts to define Gnosticism have not been particularly illuminating. "It should be clear," he wrote, "that all attempts to define Gnosticism have darkened counsel by emphasizing some one aspect of particular systems [such as Greek philosophy, Oriental religion, or failed eschatological hopes] at the expense of the wide variety of interests and speculations and fancies found in the evidence." On the other hand, Casey did not insist that we eliminate the category altogether:

In dealing with them [Gnostics] it would no doubt be unwise to abandon the terms "Gnostic" and "Gnosticism" which have so long been current in historical literature, but the implication of these words should be clearly understood. It should be recognized that "Gnosticism" is a modern, not an ancient category, that its use has frequently obscured more than it has illuminated the picture of early Christianity, but that behind it lies a definite historical reality: a group of theologians and sects characterized (a) by their obligations to Christianity, (b) by the autonomous quality of their systems which made them rivals of orthodox Christianity rather than modifiers of it in points of detail, and (c) by a demand for theological novelty which their frequent appeals to a remote antiquity have obscured but not concealed.

The best solution Casey could offer was to make a call to "clear the air of a mystery which the unhappy grouping together under a spurious category of theological speculations so widely diverse has tended to create."[44] Needless to say, his call went mostly unheeded.

In his discussion entitled "The History of the Term Gnostikos" at the 1978 Yale conference on "The Rediscovery of Gnosticism," Morton Smith made much the same point as Casey, albeit with a much sharper rhetorical tone. He left the outcome much less ambiguous: in his opinion, the term should be employed only in conformity with the ancient usage. Although Smith considered a broader range of Greek literature than did Casey, he largely came to the same conclusion—that the term γνωστικός ("Gnostic") in ancient usage had a very limited range of reference, largely polemical and "primarily a phenomenon of later Platonism." Given that we know very little about the ancient use of the term and to whom it may have referred, Smith counseled that reticence would be the best policy.[45]

Bentley Layton has now taken up Smith's challenge to determine the precise usage of γνωστικός ("Gnostic") without saying more than is warranted by the evidence. He began by stating quite clearly that the best historical practice is to use the name that a social group applies to itself; he then added an even stronger caveat: "Furthermore, the modern historian must avoid using that word in any other sense, because ambivalent usage would introduce disorderliness into the historical discourse."⁴⁶ This practice would restrict the term "Gnosticism" to a nominalist designation.

Layton aimed to develop "a means of identifying the data that can be used to write a history of the Gnostics, and thus to define the term Gnosticism." His starting point was the observation that the term γνωστικός ("Gnostic") is used to designate people, not a particular kind of doctrine. The goal, then, is to locate a social group in antiquity that used the term γνωστικός as a self-designation. But right at the beginning he encountered a significant obstacle: the direct testimonies to γνωστικός or γνωστικόι ("Gnostics") occur only in literature written by the enemies of the Gnostics. At this point, Layton made a crucial move. He noted that the polemicists associate the Gnostics with a particular cosmological myth. This myth, in his view, can be considered a relatively reliable pointer to the distinctive character of the group. Thus, wherever one finds this myth, one has encountered Gnostics, even when the myth is not explicitly attached to the self-designation γνωστικόι (Gnostics). Working from this premise, he applies five steps aimed at including additional materials in his database:

1. The direct testimonies are collected and analyzed.
2. They are compared with other ancient Christian literature to discover corresponding materials, which are then added to the database.
3. The distinctive features of the materials added in step 2 are analyzed. They then become the basis to look for further corresponding materials, which are in turn added to the database.
4. The enlarged collection is compared with other Christian literature. If materials under different designations (for example, Barbeloites or Ophites) are shown to have features corresponding to the distinctive features determined in steps 1 and 3, then those groups or persons are added to the database.
5. All information about the groups registered in step 4 is included in the database, regardless of whether or not it corresponds to the distinctive features determined by steps 3 and 4. Step 5 implies that "the inclusion of information under names other than Gnostikoi

may mean that the result of the survey is a species containing several varieties. It may, of course, also mean that the survey contains some irrelevant data."

According to Layton, the results of this survey should produce the only data on which the social and intellectual histories of the Gnostics are to be based.[47]

Although this approach offers a certain clarity, it limits the category of Gnosticism to a relatively small portion of those materials that had previously been so designated. What about the rest of the works? If no longer to be called "Gnostic," what are they? The answer is not clear.

Michael Williams has recently made an argument for the elimination of the term "Gnosticism" altogether. Although he notes that it is incongruent to classify such a diverse range of phenomena together, it is not the variety of the phenomena that bothers him so much as the inadequacy of the standard typological characterizations of Gnosticism. This focus leads Williams to suggest jettisoning the term "Gnosticism" and replacing it with "biblical demiurgical," a designation that would, nonetheless, still classify "most of the same myths together for study and comparison." It is hard to see how this suggestion helps us deal with the classification problem, as it merely substitutes a new (and cumbersome) term, while keeping the range of material included in the category basically intact.[48]

In the end, whether specialists work to construct subcategories, argue to eliminate the term "Gnosticism" altogether, or use it to designate a more limited range of phenomena than the discussion portends—they all recognize the inadequacy of the term to encompass the variety of phenomena that have been assigned to it. That at least remains an assured result of current scholarly work on the Nag Hammadi literature.

The problem with variety is not variety itself; the problem is trying to force multiform, irregularly shaped objects into square essentialist definitional holes. As Chapters 1 and 2 illustrate, the categories of Judaism, Christianity, paganism, and heresy are products of identity discourses shaped during the first centuries of the Common Era. So, too, Gnosticism in the modern period. By definition, such categories are intended to be essentializing, working to establish religions rhetorically as well-bounded and mutually exclusive entities. But historiography requires positional and provisional categories, functioning as analytic tools to do certain kinds of delimited intellectual work. Such a position recognizes that there are multiple legitimate means of classifying particular works, depending on what it is the investigator wishes to show. Given the "syncretic" and mobile character of religious literature in the ancient Mediterranean world, it is unhelpful to insist that texts belong to one (and only one) tradition. Instead, we ought to be exploring the field of late antique cultural hybridity in order to illuminate their overlapping themes, strategies, and discourses, as well as their distinctive practices.

## Rethinking the Origins of Gnosticism

Not surprisingly, the perennial question of the origins of Gnosticism has received sustained attention from scholars who study the Nag Hammadi texts.[49] In 1966, an international congress convened in Messina with the express purpose of addressing this issue. Although twenty years had passed since the discovery, the conference papers (published by Ugo Bianchi in *Le origini dello Gnosticismo*) pointedly illustrated how little agreement existed. In an attempt to resolve the diversity of scholarly opinion, the congress put forth a joint proposal "for a terminological and conceptual agreement with regard to the theme of the colloquium." In retrospect, it seems that the aim was less to solve the problem than to create a protocol acceptable to all. Rather than trying to resolve the areas of disagreement, the congress organized various solutions under different terminological categories. Participants proposed distinguishing among four terms:

- *Gnosis:* "knowledge of divine mysteries reserved for an élite."
- *Gnosticism:* "a certain group of systems of the Second Century AD . . . The Gnosticism of the Second Century sects involves a coherent series of characteristics that can be summarized in the idea of a divine spark in man, deriving from the divine realm, fallen into this world of fate, birth and death, and needing to be awakened by the divine counterpart of the self in order to be finally reintegrated. Compared with other conceptions of a 'devolution' of the divine, this idea is based ontologically on the conception of a downward movement of the divine whose periphery (often called Sophia or Ennoia) had to

submit to the fate of entering into a crisis and producing—even if
only indirectly—this world, upon which it cannot turn its back,
since it is necessary for it to recover the *pneuma*—a dualistic conception on a monistic background, expressed in a double movement of
devolution and reintegration."
- *Pre-Gnosticism:* "the pre-existence of different themes and motifs constituting such a 'pre-' but not yet involving Gnosticism . . . Generally
  speaking, scholars who speak of *pre-Gnosticism* usually emphasize
  Jewish apocalypticism, Qumran, or Pharisaism, as well as the atmosphere of crisis within Judaism following 70 AD; certain currents of
  Christian thought; and the importance, in such a 'pre-' context, of
  Egypt or Mesopotamia."
- *Proto-Gnosticism:* "the essence of Gnosticism already in the centuries
  preceding the Second Century AD, as well as outside the Christian
  Gnosticism of the Second Century . . . Those who speak of *proto-
  Gnosticism* point especially to Iran, or to the Indo-Iranian world, or
  to the India of the Upanishads, or the Greece of Platonism and Or-
  phism (and the Pythagoreans)."[50]

In practice, the proposal merely categorized the various types of solutions
to the problem of Gnostic origins that had been proposed over the last
century. The primary designation "Gnosticism" was reserved for the systems directly related to those assailed by the Christian polemicists, and it
was defined largely in terms of the Gnostic redeemer myth. The introduction of three other terms allowed for very broad conceptual usage
(*gnosis*), for establishing genealogical connections with other traditions
(pre-Gnosticism), and for comparative history of religions approaches
(proto-Gnosticism).[51]

Although this approach sincerely aimed to bring some order to the discussion, it proved ineffectual because in the end nothing was resolved. Every thesis about Gnostic origins received a place, while the basic categories
and methods of analysis remained intact and unexamined, suggesting that
the problem was terminological confusion, not substantive disagreement.
By including everything, nothing was decided. In the end, the congress's
"terminological and conceptual agreement" did more to expose the problem of origins than to solve it.

The final proposal did, however, take a clear and strong stand on one issue: the relationship of Gnosticism to Christianity. The congress participants had already signaled their position by agreeing to reserve the unqualified term "Gnosticism" for the systems described by the polemicists as heresy. They went further, however, adding that their definition makes it "impossible to classify (Gnosticism) as belonging to the same historical and religious type as Judaism or the Christianity of the New Testament and the *Grosskirche*."[52] In short, they settled the issue by distinguishing Gnosticism not only from the New Testament but also from normative Judaism and ecclesiastical Christianity: they declared that Jewish or Christian forms of Gnosticism are not really Jewish or truly Christian; they are of a different "historical and religious type." The effect was to settle the relationship of Gnosticism to Christianity *definitionally* rather than sociologically, historically, or theologically.

The Messina definition, as it became known, did not work any better in practice than in theory. Debate over the origin of Gnosticism has continued with unabated vigor, and the basic terms of the discussion have remained the same.

Even before the Nag Hammadi discovery, the whole question of a pre-Christian Gnosticism had stalled because of the late date of the Mandaean and Manichaean sources. The new texts did little to resolve the chronological problem, for they did not yield any sources that were indisputably pre-Christian. Definitive proof one way or another for a pre-Christian dating of Gnosticism was lacking, so the problem of the chronological relationship to New Testament literature remained as ambiguous as ever.

Although Jonas had made a sustained case against the methods of genealogy, arguing passionately that the identification of the earliest occurrences of particular themes and motifs was insufficient to provide the keys to the origins of Gnosticism, his argument bore little fruit. Scholars have indeed largely shunned the crass and inaccurate form of genealogy practiced by Reitzenstein and others, but not its underlying supposition. Despite continuing criticism, the assumption that the literary sources or intellectual precedents of specific Gnostic texts will reveal the origin of Gnosticism continues to operate unabated.[53]

Scholars did pick up Jonas's notion that Gnosticism originated in some kind of crisis situation. Some radical originating event must account for the invention of its radical theology. But rather than view crisis as the general situation of antiquity, as Jonas had, they tried to locate specific events or conditions that might account for the formation of Gnosticism *as distinct from* other religious traditions of antiquity.

Similarly, the normative definition of Christianity continues to be the main issue at stake in the debate over Gnostic origins.[54] This point is easily illustrated by the fact that the various proposals for the origins of Gnosticism can be readily categorized according to how they understand the relationship of Gnosticism to Christianity. In the interest of brevity, these proposals can be organized in four categories, each of which appeals to one portion of the evidence for support:

1. Gnosticism is a Christian heresy. Logically and chronologically, it developed at a secondary stage, deviating from established norms by introducing alien elements into primitive Christianity. The evidence focuses on the testimony of the heresiological (polemicist) sources and Valentinian texts.

2. Gnosticism is one variety of Christianity with claims to antiquity equal to those of other varieties of Christianity. The evidence focuses on Paul and his supposed opponents, the *Gospel of John*, and texts closely related to the early Jesus tradition, such as *GosThom* or *GosMary.*

3. Gnosticism is a pre-Christian or proto-Christian religion that influenced or competed with Christianity in its formative development. The evidence focuses on "non-Christian" traditions, texts, or materials, such as *ApocAdam*, Jewish materials in the *ApJohn*, or Mandaeism.

4. Gnosticism is an independent tradition, so essentially different from Christianity that the two should be regarded as distinct and separate religions, which may nonetheless have exerted some mutual influence on each other. Evidence focuses largely on the Sethian materials.

Each of these proposals makes Gnosticism's relationship to Christianity the central factor in defining the origin of Gnosticism. The first two proposals presuppose that Gnosticism originated within Christianity, but they evaluate that origin differently. In accord with Tertullian's view that truth is prior to falsehood, option number 1 has left intact the view of Gnosticism as heresy. To my knowledge, those who take Gnosticism to be chronologically secondary to Christianity have never suggested that Gnosticism might nonetheless be a theologically legitimate option for Christian belief and practice. They have instead taken a variety of routes in determining precisely where Gnosticism deviated from established Christian norms, usually by identifying where alien elements were introduced into Christianity or where it became "radical" and "rebellious" (that is, impious).

Those who argue that Gnosticism arose simultaneously within Christianity (category 2) thereby open the possibility that Gnosticism might be viewed as a legitimate theological option for Christian thought and practice. Walter Bauer's work laid the historical foundation that made this perspective thinkable, though he never made that argument explicitly in theological terms. Pétrement, however, identified the Gnostic (Christian) attack on "*the religion of the world*, the boundless adoration of that which is nothing but might" as a central and essential characteristic *of original Christianity*. Although this view is radical in regarding Gnosticism as theologically legitimate, it nonetheless reinscribes Tertullian's claim that legitimacy must be tied to origins. I would argue that Bauer's work should undermine chronology as a determinant of legitimacy; theological legitimacy should be determined on other grounds. Koester, for example, argued that relationship to the historical Jesus should be the prime criterion, though other theological and ethical criteria could be proposed as well.[55]

In the third and fourth categories the origins of Gnosticism are to be located outside of Christianity, though they differ in their assessments of the significance of Gnosticism for understanding Christianity. If, for example, Gnosticism is a pre-Christian religion, it may have influenced Christianity's early development. In this case Gnosticism can be figured as an alien influence on Christianity. The implications could be staggering for the identity of Christianity, in particular for the question of its theological uniqueness. Yet for the most part scholars have limited their inquiries to asking how a pre-Christian Gnosticism might illuminate such obscure New Testament motifs or passages as the Son of Man, the Johannine prologue, elements of Paul's anthropology, or the character of Paul's "opponents." A recent exception is Jean Magne, who argued that Jesus first appeared in Gnostic speculation as the (mythical) divine Son of God identified with the serpent instructor of Genesis; later, under the influence of Judaism, Jesus became figured as a human being and was identified as the Messiah.[56] Christianity put these two traditions together—despite protest from Gnostics—inventing Jesus the God-Man. From this perspective, Gnosticism is the originating source for the representation of Jesus, not as a historical person but as a mythological figure.

As the contemporary literature shows, scholars can be torn between the explanatory value of Gnosticism for New Testament interpretation and a sometimes strong aversion to thinking that heresy had influenced anything of importance in the foundational development of what has become the normative canon of Christian literature. Identifying the opponents of Paul with Gnostics or other unsavory types is a less controversial matter, of course (though no more easily resolvable). Whatever position one takes, however, a major sticking point continues to be the dating of source materials. The extant materials simply do not support a pre-Christian dating of Gnosticism, however it is defined.

If, by contrast, Gnosticism is an independent religion so essentially different from Christianity that any similarities between the two are merely superficial or secondary—owing, perhaps, to common traits of shared Mediterranean culture or Gnostic attempts to ride piggy-back on Christianity's success—then Gnosticism poses no threat at all to the normative definition of Christianity. Indeed, it is then completely irrelevant for determining the identity of Christianity, except insofar as comparative studies may serve to demonstrate the superiority of Christianity to Gnosticism, either theologically, ethically, or sociologically.

In trying to resolve which of these proposals has more merit, scholars have tended to focus on determining the following: which of four possible sources for Gnosticism is the most crucial to its origins (Christianity, Greek philosophy, Oriental religion, or Judaism); the appropriate chronological relation of Gnosticism to Christianity (pre-Christian, post-Christian, simultaneous, or coterminous origins); and the correct morphological relation of Gnosticism to Christianity (deviant form, proto-form, pre-form, variant form, or no morphological relation).[57] My four-fold categorization is intended to illustrate that the question of the relationship of Gnosticism to Christianity lies behind each of these explicit considerations; and further, that this question is bound up with the historical and theological identity of Christianity. The pervasive concern with Christian normativity has meant that almost unavoidably the study of Gnosticism has been caught up with various apologetic enterprises.

All four of these views had proponents before the Nag Hammadi discovery. Since then, the most significant shift is simply that the quest for Gnostic origins in "acute Hellenization" or "Oriental syncretism" has subsided considerably. Although strong arguments have recently been made for reconsidering the origin of Gnosticism within Christianity, the hot new contender for the locus of Gnostic origin is Judaism.

## The Jewish Origin of Gnosticism

How did scholars arrive at the thesis of the Jewish origin of Gnosticism?[58] As early as 1898, Moritz Friedländer had proposed the existence of a pre-Christian Jewish Gnosticism based in antinominian circles in Alexandria.[59] These circles were made up of Jews whose interpretation of Scripture resulted from the "Hellenization of Judaism in the Diaspora," that is, from the effect of pagan contamination on Judaism.

The logic of this thesis has roots extending back into early intra-Christian debates, and it is worthwhile to explore them here. The Christian construction of Judaism was a central factor in defining orthodoxy and heresy among early Christians, even as it is for modern historians. Ignatius, for example, warned his readers against both Judaism and docetism. In his epistle to the Magnesians, he admonished against "living according to Judaism,"[60] in contrast to the divine prophets, who "lived according to Jesus Christ."[61] But in his epistle to the Smyrnaeans, he warned against docetists, "whom neither the prophecies nor the law of Moses persuaded, nor the gospel even until now, nor our own individual sufferings."[62] His problem with both the "Judaizers" and the "docetists" (whom church historians identify all too often as Jewish Christians on the one hand, and Gnostics or "Gnosticizers" on the other) was that they did not understand the Jewish prophets and writings.[63] That is, Ignatius framed

the question of orthodoxy and heresy in terms of the correct interpretation of Jewish Scripture and tradition.

So, too, Friedländer located the origins of Gnostic heresy in improper
Jewish interpretation of Scripture.[64] Unlike the ancient polemicists, however, he accounted for that error by suggesting that Jews had already gone
astray from the truth of their own tradition by misreading their own
Scriptures, at least in part because of Hellenization. In taking this step, he
combined two elements of ancient heresiological discourse with powerful
effectiveness: heresy is due to misreading of Scripture, and heresy is due to
pagan contamination. No longer did one have to posit outside contamination (from Greek philosophy or Oriental myth) of correct Christian
reading of Jewish Scripture; Jewish error could be seen as the locus of heresy. Hence Gnosticism could be conceived at once as pre-Christian (sociologically if not chronologically) and non-Christian, a view conforming
with the basic premise of the history of religions school. Much of the persuasive power of this position lies in how it coalesced so many elements of
both ancient and modern heresiological discourse.

Friedländer's thesis, however, did not receive much attention until after
the Nag Hammadi discovery. The real excitement began when scholars
identified several works that were replete with Jewish material.[65] Just as
history of religions scholars, like Bousset, had argued for a Hellenistic
(that is, a non-Christian, non-Jewish) origin for Gnosticism by positing
the existence of a "purely Hellenistic Gnostic literature," so now scholars
pointed to Jewish Gnostic works from Nag Hammadi to argue for the
Jewish origins of Gnosticism.[66]

The hypothesis of Jewish origins was aided by Colpe's critique of the
Oriental thesis of the early history of religions school, and by arguments
like that of Gilles Quispel that the anthropos figure found in Gnostic
myth is not Iranian but Jewish. More important, a number of detailed
studies by George MacRae, Birger Pearson, and others have left no doubt
as to the critical importance of Jewish texts and traditions in the intertextual and hermeneutic enterprises of many Nag Hammadi works.[67] On
this point, these scholars are compelling and surely correct. Their work in
identifying the Jewish resources is of lasting importance. The affinity with
a wide range of Jewish traditions—including not merely Genesis and

other texts of canonical status but also Philo's works, wisdom literature, apocalyptic literature, midrashic traditions, so-called apocryphal literature, and the Qumran sectarian literature—indicates more than a superficial acquaintance with Judaism. No merely passing acquaintance would have reflected such intellectual wealth. Yet this conclusion has not ended the debate over the origin of Gnosticism. It remains to be determined what the presence of all this Jewish material means with regard to sociological origin, historical context, or literary production, and whether it means the same thing for all texts.

Scholars have identified a number of serious problems with positing a Jewish origin for Gnosticism.[68] It is not clear precisely what this hypothesis implies since it can support a considerable range of possibilities for understanding the interactions of Judaism and Christianity. For instance, Judaism can be seen as the common point of origin for both Christianity and Gnosticism, in which the two would appear mutually exclusive or in competition with each other. Or Judaism in its heretical Gnostic form can be seen as the alien influence leading to the development of Christian heresy (by tracing a genealogy from authentic Judaism, to Jewish Gnosticism, to Christian Gnosticism). Or Jewish Gnosticism can be seen as just one more form of the same "spätantiker Geist" that had already infected Christianity with gnosticizing heresy.[69] Each of these hypotheses has been proposed at one point or another, but all of them rest on an inadequate understanding of how traditions interact within a pluralistic setting, where they are constantly implicated in mutual and reciprocal definition and self-definition, such that no one tradition can be said to originate another.

It is also questionable whether any purely Jewish Gnostic texts exist. The strongest case has been made for *ApocAdam*,[70] but even there discussion continues about whether the "Illuminator" is a Christ figure.[71] If so, scholars argue, that would suggest a Christian context. Another candidate for a purely Jewish Gnostic work is *ThoughtNorea,* whose only definitely Jewish features are the names of Adam and Norea; otherwise it is most clearly Sethian in character.[72] Besides, it consists of only fifty-two lines, a fragile basis on which to build so weighty a theory.

Moreover, Bentley Layton has challenged the premise that the absence of Christian features implies a non-Christian provenance.[73] Christians did, after all, appropriate Jewish Scripture and tradition for themselves. This point immediately raises the question of how to define the boundaries between Judaism and Christianity (or Platonism). Layton proposes that they be distinguished on sociological grounds, not in terms of literary works. After all, both Jews and Christians could have used the same work.

The other crucial examples used to posit the existence of Jewish Gnosticism, *ApJohn* and *BookThomas,* rely on contested literary arguments that they have been secondarily Christianized; in their current forms, both are framed as dialogues between the Savior and his disciples.[74] In other cases, scholars have used source criticism to identify hypothetical Jewish sources beneath the finished text, positing that such sources point to an original setting for the work in Judaism. The problem with this approach, however, is that it requires us to dismantle a work into hypothetical parts and disregard the existing whole—a procedure Jonas discredited decades ago.

Let us look briefly at one example of this method. In the introduction to his edition of *TestTruth,* Pearson attributes the work to a Christian author writing in Alexandria or its environs in the late second or early third century.[75] It is a manifestly Christian document concerned with the presentation and work of Jesus and is aimed at promoting radical asceticism and denigrating other Christians who are led astray to embrace marriage by "those under the law." The author condemns both Valentinians and "catholic Christians."

In a later article, Pearson isolated two "foreign bodies" (*TestTruth* 45, 23–49, 10; and 70, 4–30) that "exhibit considerable contact with Jewish haggadic traditions"; he calls them "midrash."[76] He extracts them from the work, having determined that the "Christian" elements are secondary additions to the original midrash. By comparing these midrashim with normative Jewish literature (primarily Rabbinic sources, but also Philo, as well as wisdom and apocalyptic literature), Pearson declares them to be a "perversion" of Scripture. Finally, he takes the midrashic excerpts out of their literary context within *TestTruth* and interprets them in terms of Jonas's typology of revolt and alienation—in the process giving them a meaning manifestly at odds with their literary context. Within *TestTruth,* they express not an "echo of existential despair" coming from Jews abandoned by their God, but a condemnation of Christians who accept the Law that commands them to procreate. Further comparison with descriptions by the polemicists leads Pearson to assign the hypothetical original source of this "anti-Jewish" writing to (pre-Christian?) Ophites, even though none of the polemicists had treated the Ophites as anything but Christian heretics.[77]

Pearson's method is a version of the old genealogically based motif-history (albeit now in the form of a more sophisticated source criticism) that takes materials out of their literary contexts in order to construct a genealogy that serves to point, not to the literary (intertextual) production of the works in question, but to the supposed origin and essence of Gnosticism. Moreover, in locating the primary element defining Gnosticism as a kind of perverse, crisis hermeneutics, this framework reinscribes the Christian discourse of orthodoxy and heresy in which the proper (or improper) interpretation of Scripture, as determined by Christian polemicists, sets the boundaries of religious identity.[78] In my opinion, this kind of method is unable to support the Jewish origin of Gnosticism.

The remaining non-Christian texts from Nag Hammadi are also non-Jewish and therefore do not aid in positing a Jewish origin for Gnosticism.[79] But they have to be dealt with anyway. The usual method is to construct a linear genealogy, privileging Jewish materials as chronologically earlier or logically prior to Christian or pagan-philosophical works. Scholars on this track posit an originally non-Christian Sethian myth, derived from Jewish circles, at the beginning, and then relegate Christian and Platonizing works to later stages of development.[80]

This position has recently been challenged by Simone Pétrement. In *Le Dieu séparé: les origines du gnosticisme,* she revived the view that "the Gnostics were originally and essentially Christian heretics":

> Gnosticism sprang from Judaism, but not directly; it could only have sprung from a great revolution, and at the time when Gnosticism must have appeared, such a great revolution in Judaism could have been nothing other than the Christian revolution.[81]

In the second part of her book, Pétrement proposes a linear genealogy of the origin and development of Gnosticism, with multiple branches stemming from the original trunk.[82] Contrary to the reconstructions of those supporting the Jewish hypothesis of Gnostic origins, she argues that the Sethian materials, such as *ApJohn,* are not the source for Valentinian Christianity but the reverse: Sethianism relied on Valentinian traditions.[83] The Christian elements are primary; the development of Gnosticism as an independent tradition comes later.

More recently, Alastair Logan has made an alternative argument. Although he disagreed with Pétrement concerning the relationship between Sethianism and Valentinianism (arguing for the dependence of Valentinus and his followers on Sethian myth), he did agree that the earliest expressions of Gnosticism, including the connection to baptism, "cannot be understood apart from Christianity." He located the original Gnostic myth in Antioch among "a Christian group reacting to Jewish (and 'orthodox' Christian?) rejection of them and their claims, with a characteristic form of initiation based on their own experiences or (more likely) those of the creative genius responsible for their myth."[84] Pétrement convinced him of the Gnostics' essentially Christian character. Yet though he regarded Gnosticism "as a basically Christian phenomenon," he also saw it as "one that has a claim to being a religion in its own right, with its distinctive understandings of God, the world, humanity and salvation, and its cultus and forms of communal life." What this seeming contradiction implies, he argued, is that

> one is justified in seeking both a central core of ideas, a myth or myths based on and concretely expressed in a rite of initiation as a projection of Gnostic experience, which holds it together, and in treating it as a valid form (or forms) of interpreting Christianity.[85]

Perhaps Logan does not fully realize that what he is really suggesting is that Christianity historically encompasses more than one religion.[86] At any rate, he considers the myth that he reconstructed from *ApJohn* and identified as the foundation of Sethian Gnosticism as basic to all later forms of Gnosticism, even those that appear to be more thoroughly

Christian, and thus argues that a linear genealogy beginning with Seth-ianism does not necessarily support the thesis of the Jewish origin of Gnosticism. But it does not quite support a Christian origin either.

Whether one argues for a Jewish or a Christian origin of Gnosticism, the method is the same: genealogy privileges one set of materials as the original locus of Gnosticism and derives all other forms from it.

## ANTI-JEWISH ANIMUS IN GNOSTIC MYTH: THE ORIGIN OF THE EVIL WORLD CREATOR

Although many arguments for the Jewish origin of Gnosticism are framed genealogically, in fact the crux of the argument lies elsewhere: how to ex-plain the anti-Jewish animus in Gnostic myth. This question is particu-larly poignant for those supporting the Jewish origin of Gnosticism. If the origin of Gnosticism is to be found in Judaism, what kind of Judaism could this have been? How could Jews have produced a religion in which the creator God of Genesis was portrayed as a weak, arrogant, malicious, and inferior deity? Such a position appears so anti-Jewish as to be impossi-ble to attribute to devout Jewish imagination; hence scholars resort to Jonas's notion of crisis and alienation.

Robert M. Grant, for example, proposed that Gnosticism arose out of "the failure of Jewish apocalyptic hopes," basing his argument primarily on certain similarities between Gnostic themes and motifs and Jewish apocalyptic, in particular new materials from Qumran. He imagined that bitterness arising from the disappointment of apocalyptic expectations could have led some fervent Jews to a reactionary reinterpretation of their own tradition, and he described this kind of behavior in terms of "the usual symptoms of social maladjustment."[87] Yet what historical disap-pointment could be so severe as to provoke such a radical response? In Grant's opinion, only a crisis of significant proportions could have pro-duced such a radical turn, a crisis like that triggered by the series of defeats at the hands of the Romans, culminating in the destruction of the Jerusa-lem Temple and the tragic losses of the Bar Kochba revolt. Perhaps sensi-tive that his thesis might perversely seem to imply Jewish responsibility for anti-Judaism, Grant lessened the force of his point by insisting that this anti-Jewish tendency gained force as Gnosticism spread to include Gentiles, since "the most militant anti-Semites were gentiles."[88] While Grant later retracted his view about the singular importance of disappointed apocalyptic expectations as the impetus for the generation of Gnosticism, the notion that Gnosticism originated in a Judaism in crisis is still widespread.

George MacRae agreed with Grant that Gnosticism was an independent religion with Jewish roots and a strong syncretizing tendency, but he located its origin in Jewish wisdom as well as apocalyptic circles, and he placed both in the Hellenistic milieu. According to MacRae, two heretical movements arose out of Judaism at about the same time: Christianity and Gnosticism. Because of their common genealogical origin, a "natural affinity" led to rivalry between the two. But not only were they rivals; Christianity also assimilated non-Christian Gnosticism to produce an "authentic Christian Gnosticism."[89] There is little new here except the emphasis on Hellenized Jewish wisdom and apocalyptic as the matrix for Gnostic myth-making, but it is there that MacRae's contributions have been of enduring importance, especially in connecting Gnostic cosmology to Jewish wisdom speculation.[90]

Birger Pearson, too, has argued that there must have been some kind of historical crisis within Judaism to lead Jews into Gnostic revolt.[91] Following Grant and MacRae, he holds that Gnosticism was an independent religion with roots in heterodox sectarian Judaism; thus it is non-Christian and possibly pre-Christian.[92] He differs, however, in insisting that Gnosticism is not essentially Jewish, not even as a Jewish heresy:

> The Gnostic attitude to Judaism, in short, is one of alienation and revolt, and though the Gnostic hermeneutic can be characterized in general as a revolutionary attitude vis-à-vis established traditions, the attitude exemplified in the Gnostic texts, taken together with the massive utilization of Jewish traditions, can in my view only be interpreted historically as expressing a movement of Jews away from their own traditions as part of a process of religious self-redefinition. The Gnostics, at least in the earliest stages of the history of the Gnostic movement, were people who can aptly be designated as "no longer Jews."[93]

This statement seems to imply that Jews ceased to be Jews when they became Gnostics by revolting from their own tradition. Pearson actually states this explicitly: "In my opinion the sources we now have tend to show that this revolt did indeed arise from *within* Judaism, though it is axiomatic that once Gnosticism is present Judaism has been abandoned." Thus the anti-Jewish elements in Gnostic hermeneutics are part and parcel of a critical and revolutionary process of leaving Judaism behind. The crucial element of revolt, Pearson finds, is hermeneutic—and here he comes closest to Friedländer's thesis that Gnosticism came about as a result of improper interpretation of Scripture.[94] In his discussion of *TestTruth,* Pearson states this point directly:

> Historical existence in an age of historical crisis, for a people whose God after all had been the Lord of history and of the created order, can, and apparently did, bring about a new and revolutionary look at the old traditions and assumptions, a "new hermeneutic." This new hermeneutic arising in an age of historical crisis and religiocultural syncretism is the primary element in the origin of Gnosticism.[95]

Pearson links revolutionary hermeneutics with a general sense of "existential despair" provoked by "historical crisis"; in combination, these are taken to account for the origin of Gnosticism.

As an alternative thesis, several scholars have advocated locating the Jewish matrix of Gnosticism among Samaritans.[96] Pheme Perkins, for example, attributed the origins of "the early gnostic mythology" to alienated Samaritan Jews:

> The Samaritans were among the groups alienated from the purified race of Jews returning to their sacred land. According to the Apologists, two early gnostic teachers, Simon Magus and Menander, carried on their activities in Samaria. Writings like *Apocalypse of Adam* invert the Jewish traditions about the pure race of Seth. Finding themselves excluded as "impure seed" by those with whom they continued to dwell, gnostic mythologists turned the Jewish tradition against itself.[97]

Here Jewish policies of exclusion in doctrine, purity laws, and other sepa-
ratist social relations are made responsible for the Samaritan creation of
Gnostic anti-Judaism.

Although there is clear evidence for hostilities between Samaritans and
Judaean Jews, there is no proof that the Samaritans were led by this *to vil-
ify their own traditions.*[98] The fallacy in this approach is that it presumes
an anachronistic definition of Jewish normativity that results in two unlikely imaginations: first, that Samaritans necessarily felt alienated from
their own traditions simply because other Jews rejected them; and second,
that the boundaries between Jew and Gentile were so definitive that
Gentiles could not have known enough about Jewish tradition to create a
wickedly anti-Jewish cosmological myth. Yet in certain contexts, such as
Alexandria of the first and especially the second century, both knowledge
of Jewish tradition and animus toward it can be clearly documented. Another difficulty is that Perkins seems to correlate Gnostic rejection of sexuality with Jewish exogamy based in purity law. Yet it is not at all clear why
a group would reject *all* sexual relations and reproduction as a reaction
against exclusion from inter-marriage. The general climate of asceticism
found in the cultural milieu offers closer parallels than does anything
within Judaism.[99]

Alan Segal, in turn, has suggested that the Gnostic Demiurge was created out of the "two powers" tradition in Judaism by bifurcating the second power into a Gnostic Savior, on the one hand, and an evil Demiurge,
on the other. This distortion of the Jewish tradition, he suggests, "can be
seen in response to the aggravated atmosphere created by the rabbinic polemic on the one side and incipient orthodox Christian polemic on the
other."[100] This thesis has the advantage of locating the Gnostic creator,
neither in Judaism nor Christianity, but in the dynamics of their interaction. It flounders, however, on chronology: both Rabbinic polemic and
the development of Christian orthodoxy presuppose dates too late to account for the early second-century myth of the evil Demiurge.

Gilles Quispel stands out in insisting that the anti-Jewish animus of
Gnosticism is no impediment at all to locating its origins among Jews.[101]
He sees no need to regard the process as one of leaving Judaism behind, as
Pearson argued.[102]

Hans Jonas—as usual—has offered several compelling clarifications in response to this thesis that anti-Jewish animus arose with Judaism.[103] He suggests that there are three hypotheses about the relationship of Judaism to Gnosticism that require further examination, "each more specific than the preceding one":

1. Gnosticism as an evolving state of mind *reacted* against Judaism when and where it encountered it.
2. Gnosticism *originated* out of a reaction (that is, *as* a reaction) to Judaism.
3. It was so originated *by Jews*.[104]

The first hypothesis he finds uncontroversial. The second is more problematic in that "it takes too narrow a view of Gnosticism" and "is an inadequate view of its autonomy as a spiritual cause." Nevertheless, "in some such polemical sense, Judaism may have been a focal fact in the genesis of Gnosticism." The third point Jonas finds even more problematic because he regards anti-Jewish animus as the defining characteristic of the relationship of Gnosticism to Judaism.[105] Certainly, he says with some irony, positing anti-Jewish Jews is the most radical solution to this problem, especially given the specific evidence for anti-Jewish sentiment elsewhere![106] Jonas concedes that Jewish anti-Judaism is not impossible, but what, he asks, is the evidence for it?[107] Do any Hebrew Gnostic writings exist that would support such a view? Do we know of any specific Jewish persons who are known to have been Gnostics, whether as teachers or as writers? The answer to the first question is completely negative; the second yields only one figure: Simon Magus, and his shoulders are rather frail, in Jonas's opinion, to have "started the mighty gnostic tide."[108]

How, then, might we properly frame the relationship? Jonas suggests:

All this is not to deny that Judaism was a powerful factor in the formation, perhaps even in the nativity of Gnosticism. In a sufficiently loose and non-committal sense of "fringe" one may safely say (but it says little) that it did originate "at the fringes" of Judaism. I prefer to say: in a zone of proximity and exposure to Judaism, where the Jew-

ish share—besides the contribution of much transmissible material—was in essence *catalytic* and *provoking*.[109]

Thus Jonas proposes that, instead of "Jewish origins," we might better
speak of "Jewish antecedents"; instead of an origin within Judaism ("at the
fringes"), we might better speak of a "zone of proximity and exposure"; instead of a crisis among Jews, we might better imagine that the encounter
of Judaism by (antagonistic) non-Jews was "catalytic and provoking."[110]
This thesis points away from crisis and social maladjustment or impiety
and rebellion, toward the intertextual practices of cultural hybridity and
conflict as the site for the origins of Gnosticism.

In 1978, MacRae could assert confidently that the majority of scholars agreed that the new texts from Nag Hammadi had effectively ruled
out the possibility that "Gnosticism is to be seen as heretical offshoot
[sic] from Christianity," and indeed it seemed he was right.[111] But in
1984, Simone Pétrement sharply challenged this consensus. To be sure,
she tended to assume the anachronistic notion of the New Testament as
the standard of normative Christianity, to emphasize the witness of the
church fathers, and to interpret counter-evidence with a heavy hand, but
despite these shortcomings, she succeeded in disturbing the reigning consensus about the Jewish origin of Gnosticism.[112]

Pétrement pointed out that there is no firm evidence of any kind for a
pre-Christian Gnosticism. The existence of non-Christian texts does not
imply the existence of pre-Christian Gnosticism, and there are no unam-
biguously pre-Christian sources. Neither is it necessary to posit the origin
of Gnosticism outside of Christianity in order to account for the absence
of explicitly Christian motifs in some works.[113] But as with other Gnosticism scholars, the weight of her argument rested on her portrayal of
Christian anti-Judaism. It makes more sense, she argued, to see Gnosticism's negative portrayal of the Genesis creator God coming out of Christian anti-Judaism than out of Judaism itself, however heterodox. In fact, it
could *only* have developed out of Christian ideas, she argued, since the
fundamental mark of Gnosticism is "the distinction between God and the
Demiurge . . . that is, the distinction between the God of the Gospel and
the God of the Old Testament."[114] Such an idea was not present in the

New Testament but could arise only from it, especially out of the Gospel of John and Paul.[115] She writes:

> What the Gnostics blamed in the Demiurge, that is, the power that for them dominated and symbolized the world, was that it wished to be God and even to be *the only God.* Thus, it was not exactly the world that they attacked but *the religion of the world,* the boundless adoration of that which is nothing but might . . . The Gnostics said that humanity must be liberated from the religion of the world and that this was not possible except by a revelation that was not of this world. What did Christianity say but this? What did the Gospel of John say other than this? . . . I certainly do not defend everything the Gnostics say. Who could do that? . . . I do not defend the anticosmic attitude of the Gnostics, in the sense that, wishing to overcome the religion of the world, they seemed to overcome the world itself. I defend their docetism even less . . . I do not defend the excesses of Gnosticism, but it must have had some meaning. It seems to me that the Gnostics of the first half of the second century wished to be faithful to Paul and John, and that in certain ways they were more faithful to them than their orthodox contemporaries. (In other respects, it is true, they were less faithful.)[116]

But with the increasingly anticosmic attitude in Christianity came increasing anti-Judaism, for the Jewish God was the cause of the world and the giver of "Old Testament Law." For Pétrement, this double development could have occurred only in Christianity. No other tradition that has been posited as the source of Gnosticism—neither Hellenism, Persian religion, Judaism, nor anything else—takes up the problems of human freedom and the relationship of the New Testament to the Hebrew Scriptures. Christianity alone was posing these problems that shaped Gnostic theology.[117]

This discussion illustrates a definite tendency in current scholarship to reduce the origins of Gnosticism to the production of an evil Demiurge

even though many of the Nag Hammadi texts have no biblical Demiurge.
And even in those that do, it is not possible to choose *one* feature of a
complex myth to determine its historical context and positionality. The
entire complex of literary and thematic resources, the rhetorical goals and
strategies of the work as a whole, must be taken into account. When we
do this, Jewish materials—no matter how integral—appear as part of a
heterogeneous complex.

Given that by the second century there is strong evidence that Jewish
literature and hermeneutical traditions were well known among certain
groups of non-Jews—for example, in certain philosophical-religious circles in Alexandria, by Marcion in Rome, and by Gentile Christians in Asia
Minor, all of whom were engaged in anti-Jewish polemics—the thesis of
Jewish origins of Gnosticism is not required to account for the central
place of Jewish materials in Gnostic myth-making. What is required is "a
zone of proximity and exposure to Judaism, where the Jewish share—besides the contribution of much transmissible material—was in essence
catalytic and provoking."[118]

To be clear, my point is not to locate the origins of Gnosticism apart
from Judaism; indeed, that would be impossible, both because Gnosticism is not a monolithic phenomenon with a single point of origin, and
because ancient cultural hybridity does not allow for one tradition to originate wholly within or outside of another. Although I am arguing against
the Jewish origin of Gnosticism, I do not intend to defend some other
essentialized religion as an alternative site for Gnostic origins. As Jonas
emphasized decades ago, every work is constituted in the integral intersection of all its resources. It is the whole that elicits interpretation, not the
parts. It is not possible to pull out any one stream of tradition from a literary work and make it the "origin" or the "essence" of Gnosticism.

These literary works did not all use the same cultural resources nor deploy them to the same rhetorical ends. Moreover, ancient works traveled
happily among groups and individuals, across geographical territories and
linguistic boundaries. The historian's task is not to determine essence but
to analyze practice. When we look to practice, what we see are the dynamics of ancient cultural hybridity. This mixing, however, is not everywhere
the product of homogeneous gloom, characterized by the age of anxiety,

failed apocalyptic hopes, or alienated existence. Rather, as Virginia Burrus puts it,

> there is an incredible energy and creativity and vitality that comes out of "mixing" which is also a "resistance" and everywhere tense with unequal relations of power . . . Jonas' (suspiciously orientalizing) syncretism and alienation are pointing toward what might be reframed as hybridity and ambivalent resistance to empire/colonization, characteristics which arguably mark all products of early Roman (and earlier) Hellenism, yet differently and to different degrees.[119]

When we peruse the texts of Nag Hammadi for signs of alienation and resistance, we find they mark a variety of attitudes: ascetic withdrawal, utopian hope, compassion, and not least parody and satire with their biting critiques of power relations in the world. Such variety does not have a single origin or even a single generative logic.

The fixation on origins has tended to distort the actual social and historical processes of literary production because the purpose of determining the origin of Gnosticism is less historical than rhetorical: it is aimed at delimiting the normative boundaries and definition of Christianity.[120]

Any attempt to resolve the multifarious materials into a single origin and linear genealogy is doomed to fail on its own premise. Such an approach cannot solve the problem of the origin of Gnosticism because no such monolithic entity ever existed. Many scholars now posit multiple origins for these materials; Jonas had suggested that "the gnostic movement—such we must call it—was a widespread phenomenon in the critical centuries indicated, feeding like Christianity on the impulses of a widely prevalent human situation, and therefore erupting in many places, many forms, and many languages."[121] This point of view has found supporters among scholars of Nag Hammadi works as notable as Hans-Martin Schenke and Carsten Colpe.[122] The notion of multiple origins challenges the reification of Gnosticism, but even this position does not go far enough. Because the core problem is the reification of a rhetorical entity (heresy) into an actual phenomenon in its own right (Gnosticism), the entire question of origin is a non-issue whose seeming urgency arises only because of its rhetorical function in the discourse of orthodoxy and heresy. We can and should feel free to set it aside and move on, turning instead to analysis of the practices of literary production and social formation.

# 7

# After Nag Hammadi II: Typology

Most summary definitions of Gnosticism continue to describe it as a Christian heresy.[1] They usually recount a version of the Gnostic redeemer myth and refer to Gnosticism as a religion of redemption through knowledge (*gnosis*). They state that the radically anticosmic dualism of Gnosticism is demonstrated by the belief that the world was fashioned by an ignorant and wicked demiurgic creator. Gnosticism is commonly said to exhibit an attitude of alienation and rebellious protest, as well as a belief that Gnostics are saved by nature—two views that, when combined, led to either an ascetic or a libertine rejection of the world and hatred of the body. Sometimes accounts of Gnosticism indicate that it is a syncretistic religion or the product of some historical crisis, proof of which can be found in the impious hermeneutic that reverses and mocks the traditions of Jews and Greeks alike.[2]

Despite the prevalence of such descriptions, some specialists are beginning to realize the difficulties of squeezing the new materials into these old molds, not to mention the impossibility of finding a single list of essential characteristics that adequately represent the enormous variety of the materials grouped under the terminological canopy of "Gnosticism." For these reasons, scholars have become increasingly reluctant to define Gnosticism or use the old typological categories. This chapter illustrates the problem with typology by examining three of the supposedly "essential characteristics" of Gnosticism: dualism, ascetic or libertine ethics, and docetism.

## Dualism

Contrary examples of almost every supposedly essential element of Gnosticism abound. For example, radical anticosmic dualism is said to be a fundamental and essential characteristic of Gnosticism. But this characterization is problematic, in part because of the fluidity and imprecision with which the term "dualism" itself is used, and in part because the works from Nag Hammadi document such a wide range of attitudes toward the cosmos, as the following examples illustrate.[3]

*GosTruth,* a writing from the mid-second century thought by many scholars to have been written by "the arch-heretic" Valentinus himself, is an excellent example of a work that defies classification as a "Gnostic" text.[4] This remarkable work exhibits none of the typological traits of Gnosticism. That is, it draws no distinction between the true God and the creator, for the Father of Truth is the source of all that exists.[5] It avows only one ultimate principle of existence, the Father of Truth, who encompasses everything that exists.[6] The Christology is not docetic; Jesus appears as a historical figure who taught, suffered, and died. Nor do we find either a strictly ascetic or a strictly libertine ethic; rather, the text reveals a pragmatic morality of compassion and justice:

> Say, then, from the heart that you are the perfect day and in you dwells the light that does not fail. Speak of the truth with those who search for it and (of) knowledge to those who have committed sin in their error. Make firm the foot of those who have stumbled and stretch out your hands to those who are ill. Feed those who are hungry and give repose to those who are weary, and raise up those who wish to rise, and awaken those who sleep. For you are the understanding that is drawn forth. If strength acts thus, it becomes even stronger. Be concerned with yourselves; do not be concerned with other things which you have rejected from yourselves. Do not return to what you have vomited to eat it. Do not be moths. Do not be worms, for you have already cast it off. Do not become a (dwelling) place for the devil, for you have already destroyed him. Do not strengthen (those who are) obstacles to you who are collapsing, as though (you were) a support (for them). For the lawless one is some-

one to treat ill rather than the just one. For the former does his work as a lawless person; the latter as a righteous person does his work among others. So you, do the will of the Father, for you are from him.[7]

Whatever we may think of these sentiments, they do not express a hatred of the world and the body, which can lead only to either libertine or ascetic ethics. Neither do they reveal an elitist view that only some are saved by nature. It may very well be the case that the basis for salvation is the fundamentally spiritual nature of humanity, but if so, such salvation requires enlightenment and moral practice. Moreover, it can be argued that, according to *Gos Truth,* all of humanity will be saved.

*Marsanes,* a work of Platonizing Sethianism probably written in the early third century, is another clear example of the failure of "anticosmic dualism" to describe all these works.[8] While recognizing a distinction between the transcendent Divine sphere and the lower corporeal world that derives from it, *Marsanes* unequivocally declares that "in every respect the sense-perceptible world is [worthy] of being saved entirely." The text conceives of the Divine as completely transcendent, and yet in some fashion (which is difficult to discern because of the fragmentary condition of the one surviving manuscript) everything that exists comes from God, for all "belong to the One who exists."[9] The active principle of this transcendent Being maintains a basically monistic scheme, while admitting a kind of dualism into the lower world. Nonetheless, matter is clearly not evil by nature because it has the capacity to be saved.

Closely related to *Marsanes* is the Sethian tractate *Allogenes,* also a Platonizing work dating to the early third century. *Allogenes* may be classified a bit differently from *Marsanes* only because of its extreme emphasis on the utter transcendence and unknowability of God and its complete lack of interest in the material world.[10] The work provides one of the earliest examples of a thoroughgoing negative (apophatic) theology.[11] Yet despite the utterly transcendent character of the Unknowable God, everything that exists derives from It through the mediation of a hierarchy of divine beings. There is no ignorant or wicked Demiurge responsible for the creation of a lower, material world. Neither does the work advocate either an ascetic or a libertine ethic; rather, it concentrates on the spiritual

development of the inner self through philosophical study and moral labor. The culmination of this process is portrayed as an out-of-body ascent
attained only after a long period of preparation that involves overcoming
fear, turning away from the distractions and misconceived loyalties and
opinions of "the multitude," shaping an internal quiet and stability of
character, and learning about the true nature of Reality from a spiritual
guide. Preparation may also have involved ritual and theurgic practices,
such as baptism and the invocation of divine names.[12] Although the work
suggests that its teaching belongs to all who are "worthy," it warns against
offering that teaching to those who are "uninstructed."[13] It is difficult to
read into this commonplace adage any kind of doctrine that "Gnostics are
saved by nature." Here again we find no particular disparagement of the
lower world except as a distraction from spiritual contemplation, and no
lower creator figure set in opposition to the Unknowable God.

*Book Thomas,* an early third-century Christian work framed as a revelation dialogue, contains enough fiery rhetoric denouncing the body and its
evil deceptions to satisfy any characterization of Gnosticism as world-
denying and body-hating. It illustrates a radical anthropological dualism
with strongly pro-ascetic ethics. For example, the resurrected Savior tells
his disciple Thomas:

> "O blessed Thomas, of course this visible light shines on your (pl.)
> behalf—not in order [that] you remain here, but rather that you
> might come forth—and whenever all the elect abandon bestiality,
> then this light will withdraw up to its essence, and its essence will
> welcome it, since it is a good servant."
>
> Then the Savior continued and said, "O unsearchable love of the
> light! O bitterness of the fire that blazes in the bodies of men and in
> their marrow, kindling in them night and day, and burning the limbs
> of men and [making] their minds become drunk and their souls be-
> come deranged . . . For the males [move . . . upon the females] and
> the females upon [the males. Therefore it is] said, 'Everyone who
> seeks the truth from true wisdom will make himself wings so as to
> fly, fleeing the lust that scorches the spirits of men.' And he will
> make himself wings to flee every visible spirit." . . .
>
> There are some who, although having wings, rush upon the visi-

ble things, things that are far from the truth. For that which guides them, the fire, will give them an illusion of truth, and will shine on them with a [perishable] beauty, and it will imprison them in a dark sweetness and captivate them with fragrant pleasure. And it will blind them with insatiable lust and burn their souls and become for them like a stake stuck in their heart which they can never dislodge. And like a bit in the mouth it leads them according to its own desire. And it has fettered them with its chains and bound all their limbs with the bitterness of the bondage of lust for those visible things that will decay and change and swerve by impulse. They have always been attracted downwards: as they are killed, they are assimilated to all the beasts of the perishable realm.[14]

This passage confirms an attitude of encratic "hatred of the body." The question is whether this ascetic dualism is tied to a radical anticosmic dualism. That appears not to be the case, for there is no hint of a wicked or ignorant demiurgic creator who has imprisoned souls in bodies of flesh to entrap them. Instead, the dualism of the text lies largely in the opposition between divine light and truth on the one hand, and the fire and deception of the body and its passions on the other. Men have the choice of following the light by taking up a path of ascetic practice or following the fire by indulging in all the false pleasures of the body:

Watch and pray that you not come to be in the flesh, but rather that you come forth from the bondage of the bitterness of this life. And as you pray, you will find rest, for you have left behind the suffering and the disgrace. For when you come forth from the sufferings and the passions of the body, you will receive rest from the good one, and you will reign with the king, you joined with him and he with you, from now on, for ever and ever. Amen.[15]

Following the light leads to release from bondage and suffering and to the attainment of rest and ruling power, while following the fire leads to bondage to malevolent forces that drag a person down to the level of any other beast. The force of the opposition lies in the contrasting portraits of wise and foolish men.[16] The wise reject the temptations and evils of the flesh that have ensnared the foolish.

*Book Thomas*'s portrait of the elect in the world, trapped in the body and in need of a Savior to lead them into the light, would appear to correspond to several of the typological characteristics of Gnosticism: hatred of the body, radical ascetic ethics, and a redeemer myth in which the Savior brings teaching to lead the soul to the light, away from the domination of the body and malevolent forces. But the text lacks other crucial characteristics, notably a distinction between the true God and the creator, and the view that Gnostics are saved by nature rather than through moral endeavor. Here ascetic practices are essential in separating the elect from the damned. The Savior offers two clear alternatives and insists that people make a choice. One is saved not by nature but by following the light and engaging in ascetic practices. Nor is there any notion of a redeemed redeemer or a consubstantiality between the Savior and the elect.

*GosThom,* a first- or second-century collection of Jesus' sayings, lacks the vigorous condemnation of the body as the locus of evil that can be found in *Book Thomas.* While the body is inferior to the spirit, flesh is not antithetical to spirit. Indeed, the spirit has made its home in the body, and in doing so has bestowed the benefits of its wealth upon the poverty of the flesh: "Jesus said, 'If the flesh came into being because of spirit, it is a wonder. But if spirit came into being because of the body it is a wonder of wonders. Indeed, I am amazed at how this great wealth has made its home in this poverty.'"[17]

It may be the case that *GosThom* advocates sexual celibacy, if the frequent references to becoming a "single one" or "solitary" are interpreted as a call to celibacy or virginity.[18] The clearest expression of renunciation of the world, however, regards not sex but wealth and power: "Whoever finds the world and becomes rich, let him renounce the world."[19] Other ascetic practices, such as fasting, prayer, almsgiving, and keeping dietary regulations, are regarded with considerable ambivalence.[20] For example, when the disciples suggest that they pray and fast, Jesus asks them what sin has been committed.[21] *GosThom* also contains a variety of more widespread wisdom material, for example, sayings about good and evil people bringing forth good and evil fruit; about the impossibility of serving two masters; and about the vanity of trusting in wealth.[22] There is little here to suggest a radical asceticism (let alone libertinism!).

Neither does *GosThom* express any kind of cosmological dualism, as is illustrated by saying 113:

His disciples said to him, "When will the kingdom come?" [Jesus said,] "It will not come by waiting for it. It will not be a matter of saying 'Here it is' or 'There it is.' Rather, the kingdom of the Father is spread out upon the earth, and people do not see it."[23]

This saying makes clear that the world itself is capable of communicating the presence of God, and other passages also suggest that *GosThom* understands salvation as "paradise regained."[24] Creation offers the pattern for salvation. No wicked Demiurge here.

The closest that *GosThom* comes to fulfilling any of the usual categories for a definition of Gnosticism is in its teaching that salvation comes through knowing one's true identity. Jesus tells his disciples:

When you come to know yourselves, then you will become known, and you will realize that it is you who are the children of the living Father. But if you will not know yourselves, you dwell in poverty and it is you who are that poverty.[25]

Jesus insists on the need to look inward and outward (in creation) to achieve enlightenment, not upward toward the world of light.[26] *GosThom* understands Jesus' redemptive role to be that of a teacher who shows the way to others: "His disciples said, 'Show us the place where you are, since it is necessary for us to seek it.' He said to them, 'Whoever has ears, let him hear. There is light within a person of light, and he lights up the whole world. If he does not shine, he is in darkness.'"[27] The light is within and it shines within the world itself. Jesus himself takes a role akin to the figure of Jewish Wisdom, descended to call her children to their created purpose.[28]

Yet scholars have argued that other sayings in *GosThom* allude to Gnostic myth. A frequent example is saying 50:

Jesus said, "If they say to you, 'Where did you come from?,' say to them, 'we came from the light, the place where the light came into being on its own accord and established [itself] and became manifest through their image.' If they say to you, 'Is it you?' say, 'We are its children, and we are the elect of the living Father.' If they ask you, 'What is the sign of your Father in you?,' say to them, 'It is movement and repose.'"[29]

This saying is frequently interpreted in terms of the myth of the soul: descended from the world of light, trapped in the world, and in need of enlightenment from a redeemer sent from above to give it knowledge (*gnosis*) of its true condition so that it might escape the powers by giving correct answers on its ascent from the body to the world of light.[30] It is questionable, however, whether this slim saying can sustain reference to a fully developed Gnostic redeemer myth, especially given the lack of correspondence to the myth in the rest of the sayings collection. Its positioning in the collection between sayings 49 and 51 provides a better clue to its contextual meaning:

49. Jesus said, "Blessed are the solitary and elect, for you will find the kingdom. For you are from it, and to it you will return."
50. Jesus said, "If they say to you, 'Where did you come from?,' say to them, 'we came from the light, the place where the light came into being on its own accord and established [itself] and became manifest through their image.' If they say to you, 'Is it you?' say, 'We are its children, and we are the elect of the living Father.' If they ask you, 'What is the sign of your Father in you?,' say to them, 'It is movement and repose.'"
51. His disciples said to him, "When will the repose of the dead come about, and when will the new world come?" He said to them, "What you look forward to has already come, but you do not recognize it."[31]

In these sayings, the emphasis is not so much on the soul's ascent back to the world of light at death as on the existing presence of the kingdom for those who understand their identity as children of the living Father. Even the future saying "to it you will return" implies "as soon as you recognize that what you look forward to has already come."

*GosThom* yields only ambiguous and forced support for the Gnostic redeemer myth, and even less for the thesis of a radical asceticism based on hatred of the body and the world. It contains no evidence of a division between the true Father and the creator of the world. It is even questionable whether it advocates ascetic practices to any appreciable extent. To the contrary, Stephen Patterson grasped the fundamental import of *GosThom* when he wrote:

> For the Gospel of Thomas, the significance of Jesus was that when he spoke, the Reign of God became a present reality for those who heard and understood what he was saying. What he said, according to the Gospel of Thomas, was that a person's worth as a human being does not depend upon how one fares in the world. The concerns of the world: home, family, business, synagogue, temple—all of these are relatively unimportant. One's worth as a human being is inherent, and fully realized simply and only when one truly knows oneself to be a child of God.[32]

Nothing here suggests the necessity of a Gnostic redeemer sent to free spiritual humanity from a malevolent creator who has trapped people in the prison of the world and the fleshly body. People's ignorance of their essential nature is due to an overweening preoccupation with the things of the world, which keeps them from cultivating the presence of the light within themselves and seeing it in creation.

If we are looking for an example of anticosmological dualism, we can find no better example than *ApJohn*. This work fits Jonas's requirements for a radical dualism between God and world and between humanity and world. The true God is utterly transcendent, even alien to the world. He neither created it nor governs it. *ApJohn* portrays the relationship between the lower world of darkness and the divine world of light as one of antithetic (parodic) imitation and conflict. The lower powers who created the world are ignorant of their own origins and seek at every turn to obstruct the attempts of the divine realm to instruct the soul in knowledge of God and truth. Moreover, the plot of *ApJohn* fits well with most versions of the Gnostic redeemer myth, and it can easily be characterized as belonging to a religion of redemption. Its protest against the powers that govern the world is fundamental to its mythic structure, and it shows a clear tendency to sexual asceticism and rejection of worldly values. Its mythic imagination is highly "syncretic" (I would say hybrid) in its intertextual use of a wide variety of materials. And from the perspective of the polemicists, it is most certainly heresy.

Yet even in this grand drama of malevolent creation and heroic rescue, we would do well to exercise some caution in applying the typological categories typically used to define Gnosticism. For although *ApJohn* probably resembles Jonas's model more closely than any other among the Nag Hammadi Codices, even this clearly dualistic work does not figure a Savior himself in need of salvation ("a saved Savior"). Nor does it regard the body and the world as evil *per se,* but only as the battleground on which the struggle between good and evil is waged.[33] Indeed, the longer version of *ApJohn* gives a great deal of space to listing the demons that control the body—not in order to prove that the body is evil, but to provide a magical resource for healing the body of illness through exorcism. Although believers are saved by nature (because their spirits are divine and destined to return to the realm of the transcendent divine Totality), salvation still requires moral effort, ritual practice, and acceptance of the Savior's teaching. Moreover, *all of humanity* is destined for salvation—all, that is, except apostates. There is no elitist notion that only a select few will be saved. Even the reservation about apostates reveals more of the bitter disappointment at human betrayal than it does a theological position of arrogant elitism and immorality, as the polemicists charged. The rebellion and protest of the work's oppositional dualism can be read as impiety and alienation—we know for a fact that they were read that way from antiquity well into the modern period—but more can be said about how those who wrote and read this text may have understood what they were up to, for their myth expresses a strong utopian desire for divine goodness coupled with a biting critique of unjust power relations in this lower world.

These examples do not exhaust the range of cosmological views to be found among the Nag Hammadi texts, but they are sufficient to illustrate my point: as a group, Gnostic texts do not supply consistent evidence of the extreme anticosmic dualism for which they so often stand as the most famous example in Western history. The variety of perspectives represented by the works classified as Gnostic confounds any attempt to treat them adequately under the single theme of radical anticosmological dualism.

Nonetheless, broad generalizations about Gnostic dualism persist:

> As theologically seriously as the Stoic cosmos was an object of love, veneration, and confidence, so seriously is the gnostic cosmos an object of hate, contempt, and fear.[34]

> The identification of "evil" and "matter," which is not to be found in Iranian and Zoroastrian thought, occurs in Gnosis as a fundamental conception.[35]

> Gnostic dualism, with its anti-cosmic stance and uncompromising rejection of the beauty and positive aspects of the cosmos, is to be placed at the opposite end of the spectrum of ancient thought . . .[36]

Such statements imply a much more negative view toward the world on the part of Gnosticism, and a much clearer distinction of Gnosticism from other kinds of ancient dualistic thought, than is warranted by the evidence.

These caricatures are, however, still the staples of summary definitions of Gnosticism. Too often the result is that any cosmological or anthropological tendency toward dualism within any text classified as Gnostic is immediately read (and usually misread) in terms of an extreme anticosmic dualism.[37] Trying to force all these works into the same typological mold can do considerable violence to their interpretation.[38]

## Gnostic Ethics: Asceticism and Libertinism

The study of Gnostic ethics does not begin without a history, one that demonstrates considerable influence from the ancient Christian polemicists. The most common contemporary descriptions tend to follow Jonas, indicating that Gnostic anticosmism and its doctrine of salvation by nature left open only two options of behavior to their adherents: libertinism or asceticism.[39] Neither was considered capable of producing a positive ethic; rather, anticosmic dualism could only negate any kind of moral life in this world.

This widespread stereotype of Gnostic ethics raises three points for investigation: (1) the accuracy of the description of Gnostic belief (especially anticosmism and the doctrine of salvation by nature); (2) the historical basis for and accuracy in describing Gnostic moral behaviors; and (3) the judgment that Gnostic myth is incapable of generating positive ethics. All three points can be questioned in light of the new textual discoveries. But first we must ask how this dichotomized view of Gnostic ethics arose in the first place.

The characterization of Gnostic ethics as either libertine or perverted asceticism relies heavily on the early Christian heresiological tradition.[40] The polemicists stated that Christian heretics, specifically Valentinians, believed that they were saved by nature owing to their heavenly origin.[41] The polemicists objected that such beliefs meant that a Savior was unnecessary, as were instruction, purification, and good works.[42] They described heretical ethical behavior in terms of either a false asceticism based on pride and impious hatred of the creator or a libertine immorality by which the Gnostics flaunted their superior spirituality and "knowledge."[43] In short, they held that Gnostic beliefs could not support an authentic ethic.

This caricature of Gnostic ethics, which derives directly from the ancient polemicists, continues to influence the judgment of modern scholars. For example, Irenaeus wrote that

> the so-called Encratites, who sprang from Saturninus and Marcion, preached abstinence from marriage and so made void God's pristine creation, and indirectly reprove Him who made male and female for generating the human race. They also introduced abstinence from what is called by them animal food, being thus ungrateful to the God who made all things.[44]

A contemporary commentator interprets this passage as follows:

> St. Paul had foretold the coming of this heresy in Col. 2.16. It was an abuse of Christian asceticism. Christ and Paul taught a sane and sav-

ing spirit of asceticism. In the middle of the second century, how-ever, Cerdo and Marcion taught both that creation was from the just, that is, the bad God, and that all creatures were bad. As a conse-quence, they imposed complete continence and abstinence from meat and wine on all Christians and insisted that Christ's counsels were of precept and necessary for salvation. In the last quarter of that century some Christians observed continence and abstinence out of pride. Then they lined up with the Gnostics and insisted on absti-nence from all meat and wine and the use of sex and also forbade marriage . . . Because of their supposed holiness they misled even good Christians, among whom were some bishops. But they were opposed from the beginning by Irenaeus, Tertullian, Hippolytus, and especially Clement of Alexandria.[45]

Here the commentator has elaborated Irenaeus' denunciation of the Encratites into a characterization of Gnostic ethics more generally, and opposed it to the whole tradition of Christian orthodoxy.

Yet while most of the Nag Hammadi texts tend toward asceticism, there is no evidence in the corpus for libertine views or practices. Indeed, as we have seen, at least one of these texts, *TestTruth*, accuses "the ortho-dox" of immoral libertine behavior in their continued practice of mar-riage! It is often repeated that Gnostic ascetic practices—which looked identical to other Christians' ascetic practices of abstinence from meat, wine, and sex, as well as vows of chastity and virginity—were motivated by bad theology and pride. Such assertions are reinscriptions of the po-lemicists' discourse, not impartial analysis. The texts themselves indicate that the motive for abstinence was the desire for spiritual development and purification. Although in antiquity similar kinds of ascetic practices could be rationalized from differing theological perspectives, that fact ought to be a matter for historical description, not normative imputation of bad theology or perversity. If, by contrast, the negative judgment about Gnostic ascetic practice is the product of a theological judgment, then theological argument is required. Confounding historical description with theological judgment produces neither good history nor good theology.

Moreover, it is clear that the new texts show a variety of ethical posi-tions, including sharp sexual and alimentary asceticism, a modified (Stoic) ethic of apatheia, wisdom teaching, and a social ethic of care for the poor and hungry. The point is that no single attitude can account for this variety. Again, it would seem, Gnosticism cannot be viewed as a uniform, monolithic phenomenon, and certainly the wide variety of its ethical orientations cannot be accounted for by anticosmic dualism.

Clearly, the inferences drawn by the ancient polemicists do not accurately reflect the views of the Nag Hammadi authors themselves. Even an anticosmological treatise like *ApJohn* regularly portrays the necessity for Savior figures (often Christ). It depicts the plight of the "divine spark" in humanity in terms of ignorance that must be enlightened with true teaching, impurity that must be cleansed, and evil that must be overcome through intellectual, moral, and ritual efforts. Although positions vary considerably from text to text, attitudes toward the body and the world are suffused with moral views, moral attitudes, and moral feelings. Contrary to the opinions of their opponents, the authors of these works were deeply concerned with ethical issues.

Most astonishing of all, there is mounting evidence that the Sethian Gnostics were interested in the healing of the body as well as the soul. The fact that some Sethians thought the body was created and controlled by demonic forces is universally given as an example of how "Gnostic" ascetic ethics are motivated by self-hatred rather than self-discipline and love of God. Yet as pointed out above, analysis of a catalogue of demons connected to parts of the body in the longer version of *ApJohn* suggests that the text could promote control of demons in order to cure the body and soul of its ills, and thereby free the self for communion with God. Far from providing evidence of self-hatred, the work's preoccupation with demons is evidence of healing and an interest in moral, physical, and spiritual well-being.

The so-called libertine behaviors have also come under reconsideration, though no new information about libertine groups has been discovered. Some scholars are arguing either that such libertines never existed (that is, they were the fantasized products of Christian polemics), or that libertine practices had ritual aims that were intended not to reject the body (by flaunting its uses) but to use parts of the body to express the preservation of life (through the collection of menstrual and seminal fluids, in which life was especially present).[46] In either case, the context for stereotyping

Gnostic views as necessarily amoral, whether leading to libertine or ascetic behaviors, belongs to intra-Christian polemic, not historical description.

In this polemical context, issues of judgment are clearly at stake. As June O'Connor writes:

> Rational persons—reasoning and reasonable persons—often root their choices in very different, sometimes opposing, grounds . . . Both choices are rational but what is sufficient or satisfying to the one is insufficient or incredible for the other because of differing world views, because they are operating out of totally different pre-suppositions.[47]

Since value is understood and assigned within a framework of how one perceives things to be, differences in worldview can easily lead to misunderstanding; differing views or practices appear to be "irrational" because they are unacceptable and unconvincing.[48] It is also possible, as I argue here, that even within a shared cultural world, persons inhabiting different positions and hence standing in different relations to the particular conditions of existence in that world (such as class or gender differences) will have varying perceptions of what is reasonable, and will interpret the meaning of particular practices differently.[49]

Clement of Alexandria, Irenaeus, and Epiphanius all note that some heretics engaged in ascetic practices that were virtually indistinguishable from the practices they themselves advocated, yet they asserted that the ascetic practices of heretics could not be based on any valid moral principle; rather, they were a sham devised to lead people astray.[50] They could not understand how their opponents' worldviews—based at times on quite different concepts of the creator God and human nature—could result in practices with a moral value similar to their own.[51]

The tendency of modern scholars to reproduce these misunderstandings in their interpretations of the new primary texts may reflect a reliance on outdated scholarship, on the polemicists' perspectives, or on theological categories that argue for the uniqueness and superiority of Christianity by contrasting its ethic with those of Judaism, paganism, or heresy.[52] The view that Gnosticism is incapable of a positive ethic is contravened by the evidence, such as the ethnographic studies of Mandaeism, which have made it abundantly clear that a dualistic Gnostic cosmology is compatible with an ethic that can sustain a community over time.[53]

The publication of original texts from Nag Hammadi and elsewhere has provided an opportunity to re-evaluate this outdated position. Some recent (and not-so-recent) studies have begun to displace the patristic polemics from descriptions of Gnostic ethics.[54] Let me mention three. An important step was taken by Luise Schottroff in her 1969 study on *ApocAdam* and Valentinianism, *"Animae naturaliter salvandae."*[55] The polemicists had argued that Gnostic anthropology was completely deterministic and therefore did not allow for the exercise of free will necessary for moral choice. According to Irenaeus' description, Valentinian thought divided humanity into three classes by nature: *pneumatics, psychics,* and *choics.* Members of the first possessed the divine spirit and were destined to return to God; those of the second possessed only souls but could be saved through good deeds; while those of the third were material by nature and destined for destruction. This stereotype appears in many summary treatments of Gnosticism, which contrast the supposedly Gnostic claim to be saved by nature with the Christian doctrine of salvation by grace.[56]

Schottroff points out, however, that in fact the self (not just humanity) was tripartite. The division of the self meant that the psychic self was never lost, even to a spiritual Gnostic. The self is always both *psyche* (soul) and *pneuma* (spirit); the *psyche* represents the imperative to choose salvation (free will), the *pneuma* the indication of salvation (divine providence and necessity). Short of the final eschaton, the two stand in complementary tension with each other. The Valentinian division of humankind into three classes is combined with this tripartite view of the self without any contradiction.[57] Schottroff's results undermine the polemicists' sweeping condemnation by showing that the determinism of divine providence is only one side of the anthropological equation in Valentinian thought.

Michel Desjardins comes to similar conclusions in his study of sin in Valentinianism. While he notes that *TriTrac* does in fact divide humanity into three classes of persons—the only work ascribed to Valentinians in our possession that clearly does so—it nonetheless insists that only the Savior can be sinless. Moreover, the Valentinians uniformly defined sin as "a human act or thought not in harmony with the supreme God or Father"; they understood the cause of human sin to be ignorance of the Father, as well as the force of "an outside power hostile to God."[58] Desjardins concludes that "Valentinians were extremely concerned about acting and thinking correctly. Ethical indifference is definitely not a feature of Valentinianism."[59]

Kurt Rudolph's impressive introductory volume, *Gnosis,* extends the discussion beyond Valentinian Christianity and sets out a variety of ethical possibilities documented both by the polemicists and by new textual finds. In addition to asceticism and amoralism (libertinism), a variety of moderate views find representation. For example, Clement of Alexandria demonstrates that Isidore was capable of sophisticated ethical reasoning concerning the need to strive rationally against the forces that seek to drag the soul down. He interpreted Paul's advice in Corinthians that it is better to marry than to burn with passion "as a recommendation to 'those who burn' to endure a 'quarrelsome wife' in order through her to be free from passion." Passages from *ActsPeter12, GosThom, AuthTeach,* and *GosPhil* all give evidence of the importance of ethical striving.[60] To this list we could add the view promulgated by *OrigWorld* that deeds are in fact crucial to determining one's true nature: "It is necessary that every one enter the place from whence he came. For each one *by his deeds* and his knowledge will reveal his nature."[61] Rudolph concludes that the spiritual nature of a Gnostic does not preclude ethical effort, but rather "in these texts a high premium is placed on the exertions of the gnostic toward the just life and . . . there are also borrowings from the contemporary literature of wisdom and morality."[62] His brief survey challenges the validity of the typological stereotype.[63]

I certainly do not intend to deny that various texts grouped under the rubric of Gnosticism provide evidence for ascetic behavior—they certainly do—nor even to argue that there were no libertine Gnostics (a problematic issue in many regards, owing in part to the paucity of source material). Rather, I want to challenge the polemicists' dichotomization of Gnostic ethics as either libertine or ascetic, and their charge that Gnostic myth was incapable of generating authentic ethics. In all the texts we have examined, values are at stake and choices are encouraged. It is quite clear that belief in the divine nature of the soul or spirit does not necessarily imply that no moral effort is required on the part of the individual. For

*ApJohn,* for example, creation in the spiritual image of God is the basis for hope of salvation. Ethical teaching is focused on orienting the soul more and more toward its divine likeness to God. While *ApJohn* certainly advocates an ascetic style of life, there is nothing to suggest that the motives are pride or hatred of the world's beauty. Rather, the myth offers motives and goals similar to those widespread throughout antiquity: freedom from the passions and demonic influences, and spiritual development through study, prayer, ascetic practice, and ritual. If there is an element of "revolt" in *ApJohn,* it lies in perceiving malevolent intent behind the forces that lead to human suffering; proper ethical effort includes resistance to those forces.

Dichotomizing Gnostic ethics into asceticism or libertinism has become a superficial and stereotypical cliché, which impedes any serious treatment of the ethical implications of these texts. Setting aside the cliché is the first step toward enabling critical analysis.

## Docetic Christology

Most accounts of Gnosticism emphasize its docetic Christology, the view that Jesus only appeared to have a body but in reality never suffered the humiliation of the cross; or alternatively that Jesus truly suffered and died but is distinguished from the Savior, Christ, who never suffered or died.[64] The new *locus classicus* for this perspective is the portrait of the laughing Savior from the third-century Nag Hammadi text *ApocPeter.* Surprisingly, Peter—of all people, the rock of the orthodox Church—is the messenger of this revelation! The Savior appears to him and shows him a vision of the crucifixion:

> I saw him (Jesus) seemingly being seized by them. And I said, "What do I see, Lord, that it is you yourself whom they take, and that you are grasping me? Or who is this one, glad and laughing on the tree? And is it another one whose feet and hands they are striking?" The Savior said, "He whom you saw on the tree, glad and laughing, this is the living Jesus. But this one into whose hands and feet they drive the nails is his fleshly part, which is the substitute, being put to shame, he who came into being in his likeness. But look at him and me."[65]

The Savior goes on to explain to Peter that the one whom "they crucified is the first-born, the home of demons, and the stony vessel in which they dwell, of Elohim, of the cross, which is under the Law." The living Jesus mocks the violent and ignorant men, who mistakenly think they can harm him. Meanwhile, the Savior explains, he himself is "the intellectual Spirit filled with radiant light."[66] As Desjardins puts it: "The crucifixion releases his 'incorporeal body' (83:7–8), allowing this 'living Jesus' (82:27–30) to separate himself fully from the bodily one. The bodily Savior suffers and dies, while the living Savior is unaffected. The historical occurrence of the crucifixion is not denied, but in this work the cross has no soteriological function."[67] Surely no clearer exposition of a docetic Christology could be made—and the apostle Peter is styled as its apostolic guarantor.

In *I ApocJames,* a work that probably also dates from the third century, James learns why the Savior tolerated even this sham of a crucifixion. The Lord told James beforehand that he would allow the crucifixion in order to reprove the lower world rulers by his resurrection.[68] After the resurrection, he returns and reassures James: "Never have I suffered in any way, nor have I been distressed. And this people has done me no harm."[69] The point of the crucifixion was to expose the impotence and arrogance of the world rulers. Again, a traditionally orthodox apostle, James, is the recipient of this docetic revelation.

James and Peter appear again in the second- or third-century *ApJames,* but this time as guarantors of a different tradition. Here the Lord insists that he did suffer and that his disciples must likewise suffer and die if they wish to be saved. The Lord admonishes James and Peter: "Remember my cross and my death, and you will live!" Peter, in his usual role as stalwart but errant disciple, replies: "Lord, do not mention to us the cross and death, for they are far from you." The Savior responds by affirming his own suffering and death and urging the disciples to follow his path: "None will be saved unless they believe in my cross. But those who have believed in the cross, theirs is the kingdom of God." And later: "For your sakes I have placed myself under the curse, that you may be saved."[70] Here the Savior attempts to show the disciples that they have not yet comprehended his teaching if they continue to fear suffering and death. Like him, they must accept these as the way to overcome Satan, because that is the lot of those who oppose the wickedness of the world.

For those Christians like Irenaeus and Tertullian who believed in the resurrection of the body, death held no fear because the body would be raised again. In *ApJames,* however, fearlessness in the face of death is meant to demonstrate precisely the opposite point: that the body is not the self; only the soul will be saved. Satan cannot harm the true spiritual self by harming the body.

*ApJames* does not, however, imply that the body is necessarily evil. Rather, its condition depends entirely on the condition of the soul:

> For without the soul, the body does not sin, just as the soul is not saved without the spirit. But if the soul is saved (when it is) without evil, and the spirit is also saved, then the body becomes free from sin. For it is the spirit that raises the soul, but the body that kills it; that is, it is it which kills itself.[71]

The body is neither the source of sin nor one's true self. It can kill the soul, however, if a person mistakenly believes that the body is the true self.[72] Fear of suffering and death exposes ignorance; it exposes the fact that the disciples do not understand that they are soul and spirit, not flesh. Once they understand their true spiritual nature, they will not fear suffering or death.

*ApJames* portrays suffering and death, not as good in and of themselves, but as necessary consequences of teaching the gospel, for Satan opposes the teaching of God and seeks to destroy believers. The disciples are required to suffer in order to demonstrate their love of others by teaching the Lord's truth without fear of the consequences. Moreover, they cannot ascend to God without first bringing others along with them. The Lord is particularly concerned that they understand this point, because he himself will not be able to ascend unless they do. In what at first appears to be an odd ending to the work, James and Peter desire to send their spirits upward and even begin the ascent, but they are called back by the other disciples. As Jessica McFarland has argued, before they can ascend, they have to continue the mission the Lord began.[73] Their salvation hinges on loving and enlightening others. Here there is a definite reciprocity: on the one hand, they are to be "the cause of life in many"; on the other hand, "we would be [saved] for their sakes." The Lord is quite explicit about this point; if they hasten, they might arrive even before he himself does!: "Verily I say unto you, none of those who fear death will be saved; the kingdom belongs to those who put themselves to death. Become better than I; make yourselves like the child of the Holy Spirit!"[74]

This insistence that one's own salvation depends on the salvation of others exposes the inaccuracy of claims that so-called Gnostic views of salvation necessarily resulted in extreme individualism. The Lord tells his disciples to be earnest about the Word: "For as to the Word, its first part is faith; the second love; the third, works; for from these comes life."[75] This point is underscored by the concern for the well-being of others, evinced in other texts such as *Gos Truth,* cited above.

The charge of docetism is insufficient to convey this kind of theology: the Lord truly came in the flesh and truly suffered. So, too, his followers must suffer martyrdom in order to attain their own salvation and that of others. But at the same time, the flesh is not the true self and is not destined for salvation. Fearlessness in the face of suffering comes not because believers can expect a physical resurrection, but because they know that the destruction of the body brings life to the soul and spirit. The text appears to have been written to exhort them to preach the gospel of the kingdom, despite the obvious dangers of persecution and martyrdom.

Another work to be discussed with regard to Christology is the late second- or early third-century *LetPetPhil.* Here again Peter is the spokesperson. Initially, his exhortation to his fellow disciples follows the standard passion narrative, such as is found, for example, in the Gospel of John:

> And Peter opened his mouth, and he said to his disciples, "Did our Lord Jesus, when he was in the body, show us everything? For he came down. My brothers, listen to my voice." And he was filled with a holy spirit. He spoke thus: "Our illuminator, Jesus, came down and was crucified. And he bore a crown of thorns. And he put on a purple garment. And he was crucified on a tree and he was buried in a tomb. And he rose from the dead."[76]

But then Peter goes on to tread new ground in explaining why Jesus was crucified: "My brothers, Jesus is a stranger to this suffering. But we are the ones who suffered through the transgression of the mother. And because of this he did everything like us. For the Lord Jesus, the Son of the immeasurable glory of the Father, he is the author of our life."[77] The "transgression" refers to the foolishness of their spiritual mother, a lower divine entity who wanted to raise up aeons and acted on her own, apart from any command from the Father. The result was the creation of the lower world and mortal bodies, ruled by an ignorant and arrogant demigod. The Savior came down into the body in order to illumine the seed of the mother, now confined in mortal bodies. Jesus became incarnate, suffered, died, and rose again in order to show humanity that the mortal body was molded only to trap the immortal spirit. He proved that human beings do not belong to this mortal sphere; they should resist the false powers of this world in order to be saved. His disciples are called upon to fight against the ruler of the lower world by teaching the message of salvation. Here again, we witness the easy affirmation that the Lord truly had a physical body, truly suffered and died. Yet once more this teaching is tied to a view that rejects the body as the self.

In the intellectual milieu of late antiquity, the argument for the resurrection of the flesh was actually the stranger and more difficult position to defend. It was much easier to argue that the gods had taken on flesh and visited humans than to argue that corpses could be (or ought to be) resuscitated.[78] The second- or third-century Valentinian *Treatise on the Resurrection* argued this point with extreme clarity. Addressing a man named Rheginos, the author asks:

> How did the Lord proclaim things while he existed in flesh and after he had revealed himself as Son of God? He lived in this place where you remain, speaking about the law of nature—but I call it "Death." Now the Son of God, Rheginos, was Son of Man. He embraced them both, possessing the humanity and the divinity, so that on the one hand he might vanquish death through his being the Son of God, and that on the other through the Son of Man the restoration to the fullness might occur . . . Do not think the resurrection is an illusion. It is no illusion, but it is truth. Indeed, it is more fitting to say that the world is an illusion, rather than the resurrection which has come into being through our Lord the Savior, Jesus Christ.[79]

Yet this resurrection is not the resuscitation of the flesh but the ascent out of the flesh to the fullness of God. "We are drawn to heaven by him," the author writes, "like beams by the sun, not being restrained by anything. This is the spiritual resurrection which swallows up the soul in the same way as the flesh."[80] The body of flesh is only a temporary housing, left behind when the soul ascends to God at death. And for this teaching, the Valentinians have Paul as a support, since he had written, "Flesh and blood will never inherit the kingdom of God."[81]

The works discussed here illustrate that the early Christian controversy about the nature of Christ covered much more territory than the simple dichotomy between docetism and incarnation implies. At issue is more than the affirmation that the Savior truly had a body, suffered, and died. Not only Christology but anthropology—the fundamental issue of what it means to be a human being—was at stake. Is the true self located in the body or in the soul/spirit? Tertullian argued vociferously that the soul and the body came into being as a unity and would continue as a unity for all eternity in the resurrection. *ApJames* and *LetPetPhil* disagree: the location of the soul in the body is a temporary arrangement; only the spiritual soul will rise to life with God. Christology in these cases conforms to anthropology. Here again, the cliché that Gnostic Christology is docetic has to give way to a much more complex treatment of early Christian debates about Christology and anthropology. The differences among early Christians were hugely significant, but if we want to understand what was at stake theologically, ethically, and socially in such debates, we must abandon the clichés and replace them with critical analysis.

Although I have treated only three of the most common stereotypical characterizations of Gnosticism (radical anticosmic dualism, incapacity for true ethics, and docetism), similar reservations could be raised about the general applicability of all the other typological characteristics used to define Gnosticism.[82] The so-called Gnostic works provide evidence of a wide variety of ethical orientations, theological and anthropological views, spiritual disciplines, and ritual practices, confounding any attempt to develop a single set of typological categories that will fit everything scholars have labeled Gnosticism. In order to comprehend the complexity of early

Christianity in its formative centuries, scholars need to reject the old typologies.

The clearest recognition of these problems appears in the excellent study by Michael Williams titled *Rethinking "Gnosticism."* His goal throughout is to expose the inadequacy of several standard typological characteristics of Gnosticism. Repudiating the traditional reliance on clichés, slogans, and caricatures, he demonstrates both the inadequacy of categories such as "protest exegesis" or "parasite" to describe the full range of materials classified as Gnostic, and the distortion resulting from attempts to force the primary texts into those categories.[83] In the end, he concludes that the term "Gnosticism" is not merely inadequate but "as a typological category has increasingly proven to be unreliable as a tool for truly illuminating analysis and more often has begun to function as a laborsaving device conducive to anachronism, caricature, and eisegesis."[84] He suggests that scholarship is better off without the term and should dispense with it altogether.

His suggestion, however, is intended to reject not typological methodology but only the specific category of Gnosticism.[85] Yet without adequate alternatives, the result of Williams's study has been merely to lead scholars to put Gnosticism in quotation marks and continue to use it more or less as always. Moreover, the structure of Williams's study actually undermines the conclusion he wishes to reach. Although he fully recognizes the variety of the materials, he frames his arguments in terms of competing alternatives: either parasites or innovators; either anticosmic world rejection or sociocultural accommodation; either hatred of the body or perfection of the human; either deterministic elitism or inclusive theories of conversion. This rhetorical framework implies that an incorrect typology of the Gnostic materials can be replaced by a correct one. Nonetheless, he does show that the evidence can be interpreted to reach conclusions quite different from those of standard scholarship, and here the study offers some very intriguing insights. In the end, however, the complexity of the phenomena is ill served by this either/or dichotomy. Williams's final suggestion to remedy the stereotyping of Gnosticism exemplifies the problem. In place of "Gnosticism," he offers the category "biblical demiurgical myth":

> Biblical demiurgical myth would not be just another name for "gnosticism" because the intent of the new category would be precisely to cut free from baggage surrounding the old one. While it would be grouping most of the same myths together for study and comparison, it would not make the series of mistakes that I have tried to argue in this study have been made with the category "gnosticism." The definition of the category "biblical demiurgical" says nothing in itself about "anticosmism," and assumes nothing, and therefore it allows for the range of attitudes about the cosmos and its creator(s) that are actually attested in the works. This category would not require the assertion that some particular hermeneutic program underlay all the sources involved, but would rather allow for the diversity of approaches that we encounter. And so forth.[86]

His goal is laudable, but in the end he falls back into the old mold. First of all, the category itself privileges one mythic element over all others as the determinant characteristic. He rationalizes that selection by claiming that "this particular feature, which is in principle easy to identify, does comprise some important constellations of ideas that we know to have been catalysts of controversy in late antiquity."[87] That is, he is still taking his lead from the polemicists about which features are most important to focus on in reading these texts. I argue that it is precisely by reinscribing the polemicists' themes and discourses and privileging their perspectives that we distort the interpretation of the texts—and indeed are kept from a fuller and richer understanding of what the controversies were really about. The polemicists offer only one range of views; if we want to understand the views of their opponents, we have to take a different starting point.

Second, Williams notes that the new category would contain more or less the same set of materials as the old one. But the inadequacy of typological methodologies for coping with the variety of the materials only serves to raise the question of whether they should be grouped together at all. Thus while Williams's book does an excellent job of exposing the shortcomings of the current typology of Gnosticism and offers some fascinating alternatives for reading the data, it does little to help us move toward an alternative framework. The study of the materials continues to be governed by the traditional approach, established by the polemicists and reinscribed in scholarly study. What we need is an alternative framework and a set of methodologies appropriate to it.

Scholarship since the discovery of the Nag Hammadi collection has been engaged in a dual enterprise. On the one hand, it has continued in the framework of previous discourses, especially that of orthodoxy and heresy, reinscribing its discursive themes and focusing on origins and typology. On the other hand, study of the individual works has increasingly led scholars to question whether it will ever be possible to resolve the enormous variety of the materials into a single common origin or a single typological schema. Previous views about the origin of Gnosticism in Hellenistic contamination or Oriental syncretism have been thoroughly undermined. More recent attempts to establish Gnostic origins in either Judaism or New Testament Christianity have proved equally problematic. At the same time, every feature of existing characterizations of Gnosticism has been called into question. The categories inherited from an earlier generation of scholars, who based their work to a large degree on the testimonies of the polemicists or later Manichaean and Mandaean materials, have produced inaccurate and even distorting interpretations of the new materials. Although they are still widely used, specialists are becoming increasingly wary of them. It is time to rethink the entire framework for studying these texts.

Specialists have made attempts in this direction through the creation of subcategories and suggestions to limit or eliminate use of the term "Gnosticism," as well as through critiques of the adequacy of the typological categories. More indirectly, some have called into question the sociological presuppositions underlying the framework. What do we really know about the persons and groups who wrote and used these works? What can we say about how new religious ideas and narratives are generated? Is the model of "syncretic borrowing" adequate to understand the ways in which ancient pluralistic societies operated?

Despite substantial progress, we are only beginning to comprehend the enormous significance of the Nag Hammadi find and the impact it will have on scholarship. But whatever the outcome, it is clear that the discovery marks a turning point in the history of the study of Gnosticism. Scholars have shown where the problems lie and have taken some initial steps toward their resolution. In the final chapter of this book I take up the question, Where do we go from here?

# 8

# The End of Gnosticism?

What will happen now to the category of Gnosticism? In the end, I think the term "Gnosticism" will most likely be abandoned, at least in its present usage. Perhaps scholars will continue to use it to designate a much more delimited group of materials, such as "Sethian Gnosticism" or "Classical Gnosticism." Perhaps not. It is important not so much to eliminate the term *per se,* but to recognize and correct the ways in which reinscribing the discourses of orthodoxy and heresy distort our reading and reconstruction of ancient religion. These distortions have both confused historiography and undermined the legitimate work of theological reflection.

Having recognized the old frameworks' entanglement with anti-Catholic Protestant polemics, anti-Judaism, and colonial ideology that we have no desire to support, we can develop more adequate frameworks to address the many issues of our own postcolonial, pluralistic world—as well as to provide enriched resources for a fuller appreciation of the historical and theological wealth of Christianity, Judaism, and other ancient religions.

By perceiving how thoroughly the study of Gnosticism is tied to defining normative Christianity, we have been able to analyze where and how the academic study of Gnosticism in the twentieth century reinscribes and reproduces the ancient discourse of orthodoxy and heresy. We can also see shifts in that discourse where modern discourses of historicism and colonialism have intersected it. Such shifts fit very comfortably into the pattern that Michel Foucault has led us to expect when examining the history of discourse.[1] Rather than linear lines of causal continuity, we see substitutions, transformations, disjunctures, incompatibilities, and entanglements. Gnosticism was substituted for heresy as the object of the discourse. The functions of this object were transformed, at times still working to establish Christian identity, but now in the face of new contestations and new definitions of normativity, such as those raised by Protestant-Catholic disputes, or Orientalism and its colonial enterprises, leading to notable disjunctures and incompatibilities, for example when pre-Christian, Oriental origins conflicted with notions of Gnostic heresy as a late development. Its relation to other fields also varied, at times deeply entangled with philology and Enlightenment historiography; at other times allied with forms and statements of theology, existential philosophy, phenomenology, or comparative religions. Its enunciative modes have also shifted dramatically, bearing our theme, Gnosticism, back and forth between the forums of church and university. While this theme remained nominally the same, it became lodged in different types of discourse, where it took on different functions, participated in a variety of strategies, and moved among distinct sets of power relations. Yet the function of this discourse has remained unchanged: to represent the other. The study of Gnosticism is thus imbricated in intellectual discourses and power relations that extend far beyond any notion of disinterested objectivity and often far beyond the explicit intentions of individual scholars.[2]

The challenge before us is to propose a new framework for the study of religion in antiquity by rethinking the methodologies and theoretical foundations of historiography as they are employed in the study of Gnosticism. What I am suggesting is not so radical as some may fear or others may hope. The basic methods of historiography remain fundamental to the task at hand, but I want to deploy them toward different ends and emphases, and that will require some theoretical reassessments, especially with regard to methods of approach and sociological assumptions.

## Rethinking Methodology

The ancient discourse of orthodoxy and heresy has affected not only the goals and substance of the study of Gnosticism but its methods as well. I suggest that in the development of modern historical scholarship the concerns of ancient discourse with origins, essence, and purity were transformed into disciplinary methodologies. The search for origins was taken over by historicism; the delineation of purity and contamination became lodged in the terminology and methodologies of antisyncretism; and the determination of essence was grounded in phenomenological methods of typology or existential philosophy.[3] Genealogy, as the historical enterprise of tracing a phenomenon from its origins through its varied developments, intersected all three.[4]

I have two suggestions for disentangling historical methods from this apparatus. First, as Elisabeth Schüssler Fiorenza has argued, historians must scrutinize their goals in order to make historiography's ethical character apparent and subject to critique. Though historiography will always be involved in power relations, such relations need not operate under clandestine cover. Second, historiography can do its work better once it has been disentangled from a focus on origins, purity, and essence. None of these has a legitimate place in historical research, given that historical phenomena never have a pure origin but are always *in media res;* given that there is no purity, only mixtures; no essence, only continuity in difference.

To illustrate further, I will take up each method in turn and then discuss how it might be approached differently.

## Historical Investigation and the Search for Origins

The goal of historical methods in Gnosticism studies has often been to get at the original phenomenon itself, shorn of historical accretions and errors. Too often determining the site and impulse of this primal origin has seemed to be sufficient for describing the true nature of Gnosticism, without further need for interpretation or explanation.

Textual criticism, for example, has proceeded by analyzing the textual variants in existing manuscripts in order to produce a critical edition, whose goal is to establish "the original text" so far as possible. This goal has frequently led scholars to treat all variants (except one) as secondary corruptions of the authentic, original work. Transmission history has often been pressed into the service of textual criticism, functioning to locate and eliminate textual corruptions—whether inadvertent or intentional. The goal is to discern and remove all traces of the theological or sociological interests ("tendencies") of later traditors, with the result that copyists, editors, and interpreters are all treated as "corrupters" of the original work. In this scenario, the interests of traditors become motives for corruption, not evidence of practice. Specialists are now reconsidering these methods, especially by exploring the performative and hermeneutical aspects of textuality and transmission.[5]

Similarly, source criticism had worked to identify the origin of Gnosticism by dismantling a work into its "source" components, seen either as independent literary works or as intellectual "influences." Those component sources were aligned with normative traditions, such as Judaism or Platonism (themselves operating within the parameters of Christian identity discourse); that is, a source was identified and then said to be properly Jewish (like Genesis) or philosophical (like Plato's *Timaeus*). Scholars arranged them hierarchically, either typologically in terms of their foundational importance to the myth, or chronologically in terms of a hypothetical history of composition. (So, for example, one might claim that the Jewish sources of *ApJohn* are primary; the Platonizing elements, secondary.) Finally, they ascribed the origin of Gnosticism to the site of the most primary source materials (for example, Judaism). The last move requires a logical leap of Olympic proportions: if the most logically primary or chronologically early source materials of Gnostic works are shown to be Jewish, then the origin of Gnosticism is said to lie in Judaism. The same is true for Platonism or Iranian myth or some other authentic religious tradition. The generation of a literary work and its provenance cannot, however, be ascertained in this way for several reasons. The first is that the component sources themselves are insufficient to account for the resulting phenomenon; it is the generation of the whole that has to be accounted for. Second, literary works, let alone "intellectual influences," can "belong" to and move among heterogeneous social groups (as did Scripture and Platonic writings among Jews, Christians, and Greek philosophers), so knowing who "originally" produced a particular literary work is not a sure indication of who is using it as a "source" for a later work. Finally, the fact that the literary works of Valentinian myth or Sethian Gnosticism evince heterogeneous source materials itself blurs the lines between the normative traditions to which such sources are aligned. Using factors such as misinterpretation of Scripture, impiety or rebellion, historical crisis, or existential alienation to account for the introduction of difference into stable and well-bounded spheres is a desperate course of action. Source criticism can help determine the resources authors employed in mythmaking, but this method will not lead to the origin of Gnosticism.

## Syncretism as Impurity and Inauthenticity

Source criticism has served not only the quest for origins but also the rhetoric of purity. In the case of Gnosticism, the practice of assigning each source to its true, normative tradition has led to the conclusion that "Gnosticism has no tradition of its own, but only a borrowed one." As Rudolph puts it:

> A further peculiarity of the gnostic tradition . . . lies in the fact that it frequently draws its material from the most varied existing traditions, attaches itself to it, and at the same time sets it in a new frame by which this material takes on a new character and a completely new significance. Seen from the outside, the gnostic documents are often compositions and even compilations from the mythological or religious ideas of the most varied regions of religion and culture: from Greek, Jewish, Iranian, Christian (in Manichaeism also Indian and the Far East). To this extent Gnosis, as has already been repeatedly established, is a product of hellenistic syncretism, that is the mingling of Greek and Oriental traditions and ideas subsequent to the conquests of Alexander the Great . . . Yet the expression "Kunstmythen" for the gnostic systems is misleading and should for preference be avoided. It is not at all a case of "artificial" and fundamentally unimportant compilations, but of illustrations of existential situations of the gnostic view of the world. Since this view of the world attaches itself in the main to the older religious imagery, almost as a parasite prospers on the soil of "host religion," it can be also described as *parasitic. To this extent Gnosticism strictly speaking has no tradition of its own but only a borrowed one.* Its mythology is a tradition consciously created from alien material, which it has appropriated to match its own basic conception.[6]

Here the charge of syncretism functions to show not only the impurity of Gnostic tradition but also to evaluate it negatively: if it cannot properly be called *Kunstmythen* (artificial myth), it should at least be called "parasitic."

A rare point of universal agreement in Gnostic studies is that Gnosticism is syncretic.[7] Syncretism, it is said, is one clear factor that differentiates Christianity from Gnosticism. The essence of Christianity is

described as original and authentic, while Gnosticism is said to be derivative, artificial, and parasitic.[8] As Rudolph said above, it has no tradition of
its own but simply borrowed from others. Christianity, by contrast, is said
to be original and to have developed "naturally" out of Judaism.[9]

Yet the comparative study of religion has made it clear that all religions
are syncretic, that is to say, they are subject to processes of "amalgamation,
of blending heterogeneous beliefs and practices."[10] Syncretism is "an aspect of religious interaction over time"; it is about change, about the dynamics of religious beliefs and practices through time and across geographical and cultural space.[11] There is no question that Gnostic materials
are syncretistic in this sense, but the same can of course be said for Christianity. Since all religions are both syncretic and unique, it is redundant to
characterize any tradition in these terms.

How, then, are we to understand the claim that as a syncretic religion,
Gnosticism is derivative while Christianity is original? As discussed in
Chapter 2, the term "syncretism" not only denotes historical processes of
amalgamation but also contains implicit rhetorical evaluations of those
processes. As Peter van der Veer writes:

> The term "syncretism" refers to a politics of difference and identity
> and . . . as such the notion of power is crucial in its understanding.
> At stake is the power to identify true religion and to authorize some
> practices as "truthful" and others as "false." Syncretism is regarded
> positively by some, as promoting tolerance and negatively by others,
> as promoting the decline of the pure faith . . . Syncretism is a term
> within that discourse [of identity] which acknowledges the perme-
> ability and fluidity of social life, but is used to evaluate it.[12]

Modern discourse about Gnostic syncretism has been thoroughly negative, replicating to a large degree the polemicists' indictments of heresy.
Claims that Christianity is original while Gnosticism is derivative have
rested on a sociologically untenable distinction between originality as
pure and syncretism as mixed. Pitting Gnostic syncretism against some
pure essence of Christianity does not merely *identify* "heresy" or "Gnosticism" (both in the singular); it *produces* them as the "other" of Christianity.

Of course the phenomena meant to be covered by the terms "heresy" and "Gnosticism" already existed in some sense; that is, Valentinus, Basilides, and others did live in the past, they did write documents and hold ideas that the church fathers opposed, and so on. But they did not exist as heretics or as examples of "Gnosticism" until those categories were invented by polemicists or modern scholars to serve specific purposes in their politics of religious identity. The point is that in both ancient and modern writings about heresy and Gnosticism, antisyncretism serves as a strategic discourse that produces "heresy" or "Gnosticism" primarily to function in the identity formation, boundary-setting, authorization, and defense of an authentic Christianity.

Antisyncretism has been central to these apologetic enterprises. According to van der Veer, the term "syncretism" came into parlance during the Reformation, almost solely in the context of intra-Christian controversy.[13] It was deployed largely by Protestants as a rhetorical tool to discredit Catholicism by charging Catholics with corrupting the original truth of Christianity through the incorporation of pagan (idolatrous) elements.[14] Simultaneously, the discourse served to buttress Protestants' own claims to represent a return to pristine Christian origins.[15] Antisyncretistic discourse clearly functioned here in the defense of religious boundaries and in the construction of "authenticity" and "purity."

It is no coincidence that the term "Gnosticism" was also coined in this same period and in the same anti-Catholic context. The identification of Catholicism with Gnosticism and both of them with idolatrous heresy reinscribes the antisyncretistic discourse of the polemicists within the Reformation context. Numerous variations of antisyncretistic discourse appeared in nineteenth- and twentieth-century historiography as well, where they have exerted considerable influence.

## Phenomenology and the Determination of Essence

Typological characterizations of Gnosticism such as that of Hans Jonas have sought to determine the essence (*Wesensbestimmung*) of Gnosticism through the use of phenomenological method. In the study of religion, phenomenology drew on three coalescing streams of thought: the phenomenological movement in philosophy, comparative studies in history of religions, and existentialism. Philosophical phenomenology aimed at providing a philosophical basis for making truth statements about phenomena. In practice, this method called for the suspension of judgment (*epoche*) in order to attend to phenomena as they appeared, describing rather than explaining them, and equalizing each aspect. The goal was to focus on a phenomenon in order to determine its structural or variant and invariant features so as finally to identify the "directional shape" of the experience that generated and was generated by the phenomenon.[16] Comparative religions used typology to analyze traditional religious categories and their symbolic structures. The goal was to arrange groups of religious phenomena (such as sacrifice or asceticism) so that the essentials of the phenomena themselves could emerge and be understood without recourse to dogmatic presuppositions.[17] Impulses from existential philosophy also came into play, especially where the goal was to unveil the deep structures and meanings concealed within the life-world of religious experience. Jonas's use of phenomenological method in his development of a Gnostic typology drew on each of these. The irony, however, is that in the end Jonas came to much the same conclusions as the polemicists had offered, with the addition that Gnosticism could now be seen as a religion of alienation and revolt, with features similar to that of twentieth-century nihilism.

Phenomenological method has been criticized for its claims to purely objective and presuppositionless analysis. More important for historiography, the historical character of a phenomenon is lost when it is defined in terms of abstracted essences.[18] Phenomenology eschews the messy, fragmentary, particularistic, and relativizing character of historical methods in favor of analytic purity, in which all presuppositions are suspended and all historical contingency, all politics, all social particularities, drop away like tissue and reveal "the thing in itself." Needless to say, in practice the thing itself is a product of its own production, reproducing its producer's positionality, particularity, and contingency. It reveals some things and hides others; it serves some purposes and defies others. While phenomenology laudably intended to lead to an appreciation of religious phenomena apart from dogmatic judgments or reductionist explanations, in the case of Gnosticism, the method succeeded largely in reinscribing the polemicists' denigrations and in separating the distinctive expressions of Gnosticism from the social-historical and political contexts in which they were meaningful. Moreover, by presupposing Gnosticism to be a distinct entity subject to phenomenological analysis, it necessarily rendered Gnosticism as a product of its methodology. It was in the hands of phenomenology that Gnosticism came to be most thoroughly reified as a distinct entity in its own right.

Yet as I have argued above, the variety of phenomena classified as "Gnostic" simply will not support a single, monolithic definition, and in fact *none of the primary materials fits the standard typological definition.*[19] Of course part of the reason for this seemingly astonishing fact is that the defining characteristics themselves are distorting. But another crucial reason is that typological lists are by definition synthetic products. Such lists are culled from a wide variety of materials and therefore do not necessarily describe any of them in particular. The same is true for characterizations of "the Gnostic myth." It, too, is a synthetic product that the history of religions scholars assembled from widely disparate materials in Mandaean, Manichaean, Persian, and heresiological sources. Although it was produced to consolidate the essential elements held in common by these disparate materials, it in fact succeeded only in giving the false impression of a monolithic Gnostic myth spread across a wide geographical and culturally heterogeneous area.

Because none of the texts contains all the listed characteristics, typological phenomenology raises the question of how many elements of the ideal type any particular case has to evince in order to qualify as an example of Gnosticism.[20] Some scholars emphasize a single characteristic as determinative, such as anticosmic dualism, consubstantiality of the human with the divine, or salvation by knowledge, though a particularly popular choice has been the distinction between the true God and the creator God of Genesis.[21] Others list a set of characteristics whose combination signals a phenomenon to be Gnostic. This method has also given rise to unfortunate compromise terms like "proto-Gnosticism," "pre-Gnosticism," and "Gnostoid" to refer to phenomena that contain some, but not all (or at least not enough of) the necessary characteristics to deserve the unreserved designation. Such terms serve to illustrate how blurry this definitional method is and how imprecise its results. The synthetic character of typological definitions also works to project a false and artificial uniformity onto what are quite varied phenomena. By erasing or at least submerging the differences among Gnostic phenomena, typology hides the problem of variety rather than resolves it.

Some of these problems are inherent in the methodology of typological delimitation itself, apart from the distortions of identity politics and the multiformity of the various materials.[22] It would seem, for example, that typology functions to simplify phenomena by reducing them to their most basic characteristics; inherent in this process, however, are the dangers of oversimplification and stereotyping. Misrepresentation easily can occur when such syntheses become mere short-hand denotations or reifications bearing little resemblance to the materials from which they were supposedly derived.[23] The attempt to overcome problems of variety and lack of sociological information by "bracketing" them works not to clarify but to obscure the phenomena they are designed to describe.

Further, it is easy to appreciate the charge that the selectivity involved in typological delimitation is arbitrary and hides the operations of an unarticulated agenda.[24] Selecting particular aspects of a phenomenon as primary makes them dominant and relegates other aspects to marginality or invisibility. With *ApJohn*, for example, dualism and impious interpretation of Scripture so predominate the standard readings that its utopian theology or techniques for physical healing are slighted or missed altogether. What criteria are employed to distinguish the essential from the incidental features of a phenomenon, and who decides what they will be? Some criteria must underlie these decisions, but too often their purposes are not articulated and therefore cannot be critically scrutinized for adequacy. Many typological definitions of Gnosticism, for example, are based on an unarticulated but implicit comparison with normative constructions of Christianity and Judaism or some more vague notion of "true religion."

In the end, the most important problems arising from typological method have less to do with the improper application of the method than with its ahistoricizing, essentializing, and homogenizing effects. Trying to fine-tune application will not resolve these difficulties. This means, not that we should dispense with typologies altogether, but rather that their purposes and positionalities need to be clearly articulated and their provisionality recognized. For example, Schenke's list of Sethian characteristics has been extremely helpful in moving the analysis of these materials forward.[25] It would be misleading, however, to lose sight of the intellectual status of the resultant construction, "Sethian Gnosticism," as a typological construct.

## Rethinking History

The most intractable problems in Gnostic studies—the disputes over the origins of Gnosticism, the inadequacy of syncretism to model cultural change and interaction, and the untenability of typological characteristics—are tied to methods concerned with determining origins, purity, and essence. I am not suggesting that the disciplinary methods of historical inquiry be jettisoned—far from it. But they must be reoriented toward different ends and complemented by new forms of analysis. What I am calling for is a shift in historical-critical and literary methods away from the search for origins to the analysis of practice.[26]

Initially this rethinking means that certain inherited assumptions need to be abandoned. Chief among them are the following:

- the association between truth and chronology. The ancient polemicists and apologists held that truth is chronologically prior to error. We see this presupposition still at work in the resistance to Bauer's thesis that in some places "heresy" might have arisen earlier than "orthodoxy." It is inscribed even more consistently in battles over dating the composition of early Christian sources. Those who wish to support normative claims for the New Testament argue for the early dating of these and other "orthodox" works, while simultaneously resisting attempts to date noncanonical, especially "heretical," works early. Those who argue for relatively early dates for noncanonical or "heretical" materials understand full well what is at stake and often intend to undermine the authority of "orthodoxy" through the dating game. There was a time when merely calling a work "Gnostic" assumed a late date (mid-to-late second century at the earliest), but this assumption can no longer be sustained. It is becoming increasingly clear that the early Jesus tradition generated a variety of responses, not all of which would later become "orthodox." The history of religions school had posited a pre-Christian origin for Gnosticism, but despite this apparently radical claim, it retained the assumption that truth has a chronological dimension, demonstrated by charting phenomena from their primitive origins to their full development. But neither model is acceptable. Chronology in and of itself neither guarantees nor refutes theological truth or superiority.

- the notion that truth is pure; mixing is contamination. This assumption is thoroughly embedded in the antisyncretistic discourse of both ancient polemics and modern scholarship. Historical phenomena do not, however, admit of purity in the sense that they have no precedents, or that they are unique in ways that other phenomena are not. All religions are syncretistic, and all are unique in that no historical phenomenon is fully identical to any other. Purity and contamination are therefore not amenable to historical analysis. They belong instead to social-rhetorical claims that groups make in constructing their collective identity and setting boundaries for continuity and change that are acceptable to them.

- the assumption that truth ("orthodoxy") is characterized by unity, uniformity, and unanimity; falsehood ("heresy"), by division, multiformity, and diversity. History cannot support this assertion. "Orthodox" Christianity itself is diverse and multiform, and repeatedly wracked by division; so, too, with other religious traditions. Difference is not necessarily in itself a problem; indeed differences are constructive and constituent of reality.[27]

An alternative approach is to reconceive religious tradition and identity in terms of *continuity in difference*. This perspective assumes that there is no such thing as pure beginnings. As George Eliot puts it so eloquently: "No retrospect will take us to the true beginning; and whether our prologue be in heaven or on earth, it is but a fraction of that all-presupposing fact with which our story sets out."[28] History is not a "tableau vivant" of static essences but a drama of change and movement. The moment in the flow of events that we fix upon as "the beginning" does not reveal essence in any epistemologically privileged way; it, too, like all that follows, is always *in medias res*.

Throughout this book, I have tried to show that religions are not fixed entities with a determinate essence or decisive moment of pure origination. They are constructions that require assiduous, ongoing labor to maintain in the face of both contested power relations within, and porous, overlapping boundaries with traditions without. Relations among such traditions therefore cannot properly be conceived as stable or neat. As Virginia Burrus puts it so aptly: "Christianity and Gnosticism, and for that matter Judaism, are neighboring, indeed overlapping and repeatedly cross-fertilizing, hybrid, multifarious, ever-shifting, co-emergent discourses participating in a broader 'Hellenistic' field of cultural hybridity; thus none of them can be used to anchor or encompass definitionally (far less 'originate') the other."[29] From this perspective, it is simply inaccurate to say that Gnosticism arose from Judaism or Christianity or Hellenic philosophy—or even that Christianity arose from Judaism.[30] Rather, such religious designations or genetic claims have to be analyzed for their rhetorical ends and multifarious effects.[31]

Continuity in difference affirms that tradition and identity are not pure and fixed but constantly in processes of formation, deformation, and reformation if they are alive. Indeed, as Cornel West puts it, "Tradition is not just a given, it is fought for."[32] And tradition is never the whole story of identity; it is only a part of the mix. As Homi Bhabha writes, "In restaging the past it introduces other, incommensurable cultural temporalities into the invention of tradition. This process estranges any immediate access to an originary identity or a 'received' tradition."[33] Continuity in difference implies a process of cultural change in which breaking and joining occur simultaneously, in which "the terms of cultural engagement, whether antagonistic or affiliative, are produced performatively."[34] It eschews the identity politics of antisyncretistic rhetoric by refusing to assume, construct, or reify essentialist categories of religious identity. Hybridity, not purity, characterizes historical processes.[35] Every religious tradition contains the plural possibilities of its past and present circumstances.

Recent views assume that "boundedness, continuity, and homogeneity are not objective aspects of social life" but rather rhetorical terms that construct particular ways of talking about and understanding the identity of a religious community.[36] Social groups are constantly engaged in identity formation and boundary-setting, using the available resources to think with. To understand these processes, it is critical to shift the perspective away from understanding "religions as ready-made systems of meaning awaiting interpretation," as Ortner puts it, to the view that "people are spinning what Geertz called 'webs of meaning' all the time, with whatever cultural resources happen to be at hand." As Ortner sees it, the fundamental assumption we need to work with is that "people are always trying to make sense of their lives, always weaving fabrics of meaning, however fragile and fragmentary."[37] Viewed this way, the study of ancient cultural hybridity should focus less on identifying which materials are combined in syncretic amalgamation than on the discourses, processes, and practices by which people make sense of their lives in contexts of ancient pluralism, the governing regimes and institutions that further and constrain such practices, and the power relations that are at stake.

The task of history, then, is to analyze these processes, not to identify the "true" provenance of particular ideas, stories, and practices, nor designate who "authentically" owns them. Rather, historians have to ask who makes such claims, upon what are they based, and what purposes they serve. It is precisely these kinds of questions that are under contention, for example, in the ancient arguments over the correct interpretation of Scripture: to whom does Scripture really belong? Who can interpret it correctly?

The pertinent historical question is not whether a tradition is pure or not, or who really owns it, but what are the resources being used to think with—whether literary or nonliterary "texts," cultural codes, or discursive structures. What hermeneutical strategies are at work? What are the generative, rhetorically constructed problems being addressed and to what ends are they employed? Orienting analysts toward practice rather than origins significantly shifts the functions of historical-critical and literary methods. Textual criticism focuses on the understanding of textuality itself, including a work's own account of its production. Variants are analyzed for clues to the shifting meaning and uses of the work throughout its transmission history; so, too, such factors as translation from Greek to Coptic, variations in scribal hand, dialect, codicological construction, the grouping of specific works in particular codices, and even the jar in which they were buried. Transmission history needs to be written in two directions: for example, with Nag Hammadi, backward from the discovery of the jar toward reconstructing its increasingly hypothetical states of use and production; and forward from the rediscovery in 1945 toward its meanings and uses in contemporary contexts. Analysis of genre, structure, literary strategies, and themes would be used to identify a work's generative problematics and hermeneutical strategies.

Source criticism needs to shift from identifying precedents to analyzing the hermeneutical logic of the work. Instead of deconstructing a work into its subunits or determining the "background" of the "influences" exerted on it, the task of source criticism is to determine what resources are being used to think with and what hermeneutical strategies of intertextual reading are being employed to shape a work's meaning and rhetorical argument. Comparison with other works using shared resources, such as Philo and *ApJohn*'s readings of Plato's *Timaeus* or Genesis, would elucidate how such strategies and arguments operate.[38]

The difference between the antisyncretistic approach of source criticism and intertextuality lies in how we conceive of the practices of textual production. Genealogical approaches, aided by the notion of "syncretism," assume that authors borrow or are influenced by ideas and literary sources created by others. The original ideas and literary sources are usually ascribed some fixed and essential meaning (often figured as the intention of the original author), which is distorted by appropriation into the new context. Analysis is concerned with determining how much the new author/redactor has created and how much he or she has borrowed. Source criticism is employed to determine those parameters. Intertextuality, by contrast, focuses on the reader. It eschews notions of essence and instead insists that texts are always replete with alternative meanings because they are characterized by gaps, incongruity, and polyphony. No composition is ever an act of "pure creativity," in that all texts contain citation of earlier discourses, and because cultural codes constrain, as well as enable, literary production.[39] Intertextuality focuses on the transformation of meaning rather than the genealogy of appropriation. The issue, then, is not to determine what is creatively new or original, but to understand the literary practices, cultural codes, discursive structures, hermeneutical strategies, and rhetorical ends that constrain and make possible the production of a particular literary work.

Similarly, rhetorical criticism is not limited to identifying the literary modes of persuasion taught in the ancient school tradition, though that

would remain an important task. Rhetorical analysis instead seeks to identify a work's construction of the implied author and audience, its ends as
well as its means of persuasion, the issues under contention, and the symbolic world it assumes as well as the world it constructs. In this mode, rhetorical criticism is not one method among others but a strategic interven-
tion in historical epistemology insofar as it cautions against confusing a
work's *rhetorical construction* of its author, readers, problematics, and situation with the *actual historical* world of its author, readers, problematics,
and situation.[40] In short, literary works are not mirrored reflections of reality but interventions aimed at achieving specific effects. Such aims, of
course, are never solely those consciously intended by the author; rather,
they are shaped by the "'world' as reservoir of signs, as fields of action, as
networks of power, and as constructions of symbolic universes."[41] Rhetorical analysis helps us get at the dynamic inter-relationship between textual
inscription and the world of symbols, power relations, and action.

As readers, audiences, and contexts shift over time, so will the rhetorical effects of the work. Insofar as possible, we need to know what the
shifting intertexts are (not simply the literary resources of the work itself,
but the world as a resource of signs) and what the social-political contexts
are in order to see what work they are doing and for whom. For example,
the works contained in the Nag Hammadi codices had meanings and
functions in their compositional contexts that were different from those
they had for the Pachomian monks who collected and hid them or for the
polemicists who wrote against them, and yet again different from the
meanings and functions they serve in the hands of their twentieth-century
interpreters. This kind of analysis should help us get at those and other
meanings and functions of these works.

## Time and History

Such a historical methodology would have definite repercussions for writing the history of Christianity. We would have to abandon the two most
pervasive narrative structures for telling the story of Christian origins: the
plot of pure origin and subsequent decline and the plot of progress from
primitive state to progressive development. It would no longer be possible
to divide the phenomena into two and only two types (orthodoxy and

heresy), nor into linear trajectories of diverse forms of Christianity, nor into a set of coherent and internally consistent, but mutually exclusive and antagonistic, "varieties of Christianities" (however diverse). In each case, the coherence of the phenomenon established by these approaches is the effect of scholarly discourses, not the practices of first- to fourth-century writers and readers.

Only a few plots remain available to us, constrained as we are by our own cultural codes, and not least by our notion of time.[42] The new physics, from relativity to subatomic particle studies, is in the process of reconceptualizing the Western construction of time.[43] In quantum physics, the relationship between events is a consequence of measurement; the causal relation between two events is not perceptible, except as a gap.[44] Although I cannot claim to understand this research in any detail, it is clear that time can no longer be plotted in terms of the relation of parts to the whole, as a set of causal links, unifying past and present in a direct linear scheme. This perspective suggests that we must begin instead with the whole, but the whole is not readily apparent.[45]

Now it is far from clear that the events of history follow the laws of physics, but there would nonetheless seem to be certain conceptual similarities between science and the philosophy of history. Ricoeur, for example, speaks of "the unrepresentability of time" in narrative. In the conclusion to his massive three-volume work on time and narrative, he writes that "the confession of the limits of narrative, correlative to the confession of the mystery of time . . . gives rise to the exigence to think more and to speak differently." This confession is no warrant for obscurantism. We must maintain, he argues, "that the reaffirmation of the historical consciousness within the limits of its validity requires in turn the search, by individuals and by the communities to which they belong, for their respective narrative identities."[46]

Foucault, by contrast, argues:

The historical sense gives rise to three uses that oppose and correspond to the three Platonic modalities of history. The first is parodic, directed against reality, and opposes the theme of history as reminiscence or recognition; the second is dissociative, directed against identity, and opposes history given as continuity or representative of a tradition; the third is sacrificial, directed against truth, and opposes history as knowledge. They imply a use of history that severs its connection to memory, its metaphysical and anthropological model, and constructs a counter-memory—a transformation of history into a totally different form of time.[47]

This new form of time is discontinuous and unpatterned; it is not serious, real, or true; it provides no orientation for values, meaning, or identity; it produces no positive definition, no absolutes. It rejects the notion that meaning can be found in the return to origins, in the apocalyptic culmination of time, or in history itself (as in salvation theology). History is not about truth but about power relations of domination.

Where does this philosophical analysis leave narratives of Christian origins? It suggests that no narrative can offer an adequate representation of the past as an objective or objectified entity; that a genealogical history of Foucault's sort will display the workings of discourse—charting gaps, incongruities, discontinuities, and transformations—and therefore cease to connect events causally or attempt to show that events follow any pattern leading to inevitable outcomes. The challenge will be to understand the parts by first grappling with the unfathomable whole, and yet at the same time to see events in terms of the episodic operations of discourses and understand identity formations as the discontinuous and incongruent deployments of the strategies and themes of shifting power relations.

Yet I believe that Ricoeur is also right. The poetics of narrative will not cease to struggle against the aporetics of time; individuals and communities will continue to represent truth, meaning, and identity in narrative. But a correlative recognition of the "unrepresentability of time" means that we must "think more and speak differently." Above all, that means that the ethics of identity construction, cognizant of the power relations in such enterprises, must come to the fore.

How, then, should we speak differently? How might we represent the history of Christianity, and to what ends? For whom should this history be written? What story of truth and identity ought it to tell?

In answering these questions, I can offer only partial perspectives of some of the principles such a task would assume. The analysis I propose here aims to get at practice rather than at origins and essence. It offers no larger connected totality but rather a set of episodes no longer linked in any causal-linear frame of origins and development. The results of this historiographical method would be to demonstrate where and how the "textual" resources, cultural codes, literary themes, hermeneutical strategies, social-political situations, and religious interests of various rhetorical acts of Christian literary production, theological reflection, ritual and ethical practices, and social construction simultaneously form multiple overlapping continuities, disjunctures, contradictions, and discontinuities. Such historiographical enterprises will result in more than one true and authentic narrative, but not in a narrative of Christian triumph or a naturalization of the development of orthodoxy, since they would chart the decisive acts that construct "orthodoxy" through rhetorical-political acts of erasure, harmonization, and fiat within the complex of Christian practices in the Mediterranean world. They would note throughout what was at stake and for whom. These twenty-first-century historical practices would without doubt result in more than one possible, legitimate narrative of Christianity, based as they would be not only in the different perspectives of scholars and the communities to which they are accountable, but also in different ethical orientations. Discussions of Christian identity, theology, spirituality, and practice would constructively and critically engage this enriched and complexified set of historical portraits.

This book by no means offers a complete analysis of the twentieth-century study of Gnosticism. Its aim was more limited—to locate some of the incongruities in the construction of Gnosticism in order to aid in "thinking hard and speaking differently" about religious identity formation. I have suggested that to think hard and speak differently require revising our notions of tradition and history, reshaping discourse, categories, and methods, and above all, rethinking the ethically informed goals of historical analysis.

Note on Methodology

Bibliography

Notes

Index

# Note on Methodology

Taking up the question of how to define Gnosticism has been a part of my own effort to make sense of the frameworks, methods, goals, and uses of historical study and interpretation of texts. My perspectives about writing history have been informed by a set of larger questions being debated in the academy concerning the polyvalence of symbols, the multiformity of religious traditions, cultural hybridity, language and representation, the ontological and epistemological bases for historiography, Orientalism, race, gender, and postcolonial politics. Work in feminism, rhetorical criticism, sociology, anthropology, philosophy of history, new historicism, postmodern philosophy, and postcolonialism has led me to reshape the project in significant ways.[1]

On the surface, this project appears to be structured as a history of ideas, but it attempts to move beyond the limitations of that enterprise.[2] The book is framed, not in terms of a description of previous historical practice in the study of Gnosticism, but in terms of an analysis and critique of discourse, in particular the discourse of orthodoxy and heresy. The notion of discourse at work here is primarily influenced by Foucault, for whom the analysis of discourse focuses not on grammatical, logical, or psychological links among groups of verbal performances, but on links among statements. Statements include a principle of differentiation (for example, between orthodoxy and heresy); prescribe the position of subjects who speak (for example, as apostolic defender of the faith or as deviant innovator); articulate an associated field (not the real context or historical situation of a verbal performance, but, for example, the co-existence of philosophical truth or religious piety with orthodoxy); and define the status and possibilities for using and reusing elements of a strategy (such as claiming that a statement is eternal revelation from God; institutionalizing such claims in canon and creed, doctrines of apostolic succession, and ecclesiastical authority).[3]

The discourse of orthodoxy and heresy produces and organizes the practices of normative Christian identity formation and the institutions in which they operate, such that certain ways of speaking—in terms of the concept of Gnosticism, its origin and development in relation to true Christianity, its essential characteristics, and so forth—differentiate and construct literary remains as "evidence of Gnosticism" so as to constitute a mode of knowledge about religious truth and falsehood. This discourse both enables and constrains how claims, about the way the world is, about proper social relations among persons and groups, and about appropriate ethical values and orientations, can be made and contested. The discourse of orthodoxy and heresy, like all discourses, contains within it gaps, incongruities, discontinuities, and disjunctions that allow for transformations, substitutions, and entanglements with other fields and discursive formations, notably Enlightenment philosophy, historicism, and Orientalism.

I have found it helpful to read Foucault's notion of discourse in terms of the sociological framework offered by Pierre Bourdieu. Bourdieu's work helps me better understand the dynamics of discursive formations *as practices* within the operations of social construction and the power relations they establish and constrain.[4] His notion of *habitus* is crucial here:

> The conditionings associated with a particular class of conditions of existence produce *habitus,* systems of durable, transposable dispositions, structured structures predisposed to function as structuring structures, that is, as principles which generate and organize practices and representations that can be objectively adapted to their outcomes without presupposing a conscious aiming at ends or an express mastery of the operations necessary in order to attain them. Objectively "regulated" and "regular" without being in any way the product of obedience to rules, they can be collectively orchestrated without being the product of the organizing action of a conductor.[5]

Discourse analysis, it seems to me, provides a method to understand the processes of the regulated practices of *habitus* in operation. Bourdieu's work is more useful than Foucault's in understanding the practical aims and effects of discursive formations in the material and social world. Bourdieu emphasizes not only the regularity of practice but also its improvisational character and rhetorical logic.

Moreover, Bourdieu's social theory allows for a framework that rejects both essentializing and functionalist approaches to the study of religion. Although I do talk about the work that Gnostic myth does, my framework is not functionalism but Bourdieu's theory of practice. This perspective avoids essentialism in that religious expressions such as myth are understood to be socially constructed; it avoids a purely functionalist approach in that the construction of myth is understood within the dynamics of Bourdieu's concept of *habitus*. Practice is always about power relations, insofar as practices both produce and reproduce a social group's understanding of the way things are. That understanding rationalizes certain social relations and power dynamics, while simultaneously establishing the framework for contesting them. Human practices are always directed toward some purpose; they are always involved in the processes of meaning-making; and they always inscribe, reinscribe, or contest certain relations of power.

The practices of meaning-making are always involved in constructing, deconstructing, and reconstructing the structures of *habitus*, in reinscribing and contesting the power relations of the divisions of the social order. Yet consciousness of what one is doing is always limited by the constraints of *habitus*, by one's acceptance of the way things are, inscribed already on the human body itself through social inculcation. This approach allows us to affirm (with essentialists) that religion has a basis in social and material reality, a reality that is by no means entirely arbitrary. It also allows us to affirm (with functionalists) that religious practices are directed toward and achieve certain ends, at once deliberate (insofar as authors have particulars goals of persuading particular audiences toward particular ends) and unconscious (insofar as they necessarily reproduce the structures of the *habitus* and the discourses of the division of the social order; in this sense, the rhetorical argument always exceeds the intention of the authors and readers). It further allows us to affirm the intellectual, ethical, and spiritual value of practice as a fundamental activity of human meaning-making and belonging. In no case, however, does this approach allow us to condense religion into a transcendent or materialist essence, nor to dismiss it as simply a social or psychological function.[6]

In order to analyze the discourse of orthodoxy and heresy, we can conceptualize religion in terms of *field*, a site of struggle with its own goals, strategies, and institutions, as well as its own ideological-theoretical frameworks in which certain kinds of practices are rationalized and contested. Struggles within the religious field in question can then be analyzed to determine the discourses with which the field operates, the practices it generates, as well as whose interests and what ends it serves.[7] This approach is helpful in gaining a more general comprehension of the dynamics of orthodoxy and heresy. As Bourdieu notes, "Practical taxonomies, which are transformed, misrecognizable forms of the real divisions of the social order, contribute to the production of that order by producing objectively orchestrated practices adjusted to those divisions."[8] Thus the taxonomies of orthodoxy and heresy contribute to producing the divisions of the social order of which they are a product in such a way as to establish that (arbitrary) order as the natural order of things (in Bourdieu's terms as *doxa*).[9] When this naturalization succeeds, the social order appears to be self-evident, necessary, and authoritative precisely because it is collectively affirmed as such.

Orthodoxy and heresy or heterodoxy, however, imply "awareness and recognition of the possibility of different or antagonistic beliefs."[10] Heterodoxy becomes possible, Bourdieu writes, when "the social world loses its character as a natural phenomenon" owing to some crisis, such as "culture contact," changes in material conditions, or political-economic crises; it is then that "the question of the natural or conventional character (*phusei* or *nomo*) of social facts can be raised."[11] Questioning the established order is, however, never complete because the contest between orthodoxy and heresy rests to some degree on a shared field of opinion. Rather, the struggle is over the boundaries of *doxa* itself. As Bourdieu puts it:

> The dominated classes have an interest in pushing back the limits of *doxa* and exposing the arbitrariness of the taken for granted; the

dominant classes have an interest in defending the integrity of *doxa*
or, short of this, of establishing in its place the necessarily imperfect
substitute, orthodoxy . . . But the manifest censorship imposed by
orthodox discourse, the official way of speaking and thinking the
world, conceals another, more radical censorship: the overt opposition between "right" opinion and "left" or "wrong" opinion, which
delimits the universe of possible discourse, be it legitimate or illegitimate, euphemistic or blasphemous, masks in its turn the fundamental opposition between the universe of things that can be stated, and
hence thought, and the universe of that which is taken for granted.[12]

In practice this means that the limits of any critique of *doxa* are established precisely by the fact that, in the struggle over the boundaries of orthodoxy, all parties to the struggle necessarily unconsciously or subcon-
sciously accept a great deal of the *doxa* of their shared society—not only
the rules of the game, that is, what kinds of arguments or evidence are
considered to be valid or persuasive, but even more the underlying structuring structures that make claims to knowledge of the truth possible at
all.[13]

Bourdieu's model is extremely useful, not just for analyzing the operations of the discourse of orthodoxy and heresy within early Christianity,
but also for identifying the strategies Christians employed in struggles
with non-Christians. Moreover, it works well to describe the goals of my
own analysis of Gnosticism in twentieth-century historiography. I am actually doing what I am critiquing: writing the origins and history of
Gnosticism in order to "subvert the game." Bourdieu talks about this kind
of struggle with regard to the competition between established and avant-
garde designers in the field of fashion:

To counter the subversion strategies of the newcomers, the possess-
ors of legitimacy, that's to say those who are in the dominant position, will always utter the vague and pompous discourse of the inef-
fable, of what "goes without saying." Like the dominant groups in
the field of relations between the classes, they have conservative, defensive strategies, which can remain silent, tacit, because these people only have to be what they are in order to be *comme il faut*. By

contrast, the left-bank couturiers have strategies that aim to overthrow the very principles of the game—but always in the name of
the game, the spirit of the game. Their strategies of returning to the
sources consist in turning against the dominant figures the very principles in the name of which they justify their domination . . . But the
precondition for entry to the field is recognition of the values at
stake and therefore recognition of the limits not to be exceeded on
pain of being excluded from the game. It follows that the internal
struggle can only lead to partial revolutions that can destroy the hierarchy but not the game itself. Someone who wants to achieve a revolution in the cinema or in painting says, "That is not *real* cinema" or
"That is not *real* painting." He pronounces anathemas, but in the
name of a purer, more authentic definition of the principles in whose
name the dominant dominate.[14]

Or again, with regard to the sociology of art:

Specific revolutions, which overthrow the power relations within a
field, are only possible in so far as those who import new dispositions
and want to impose new positions find, for example, support outside
the field, in the new audiences whose demands they both express and
produce.[15]

So too, one way to conceptualize this study is to see it as an attempt to
subvert the game of orthodoxy and heresy as it is played out in the academic field of religious studies. Twentieth-century debates over the question of how to define Gnosticism are largely played out within a field
whose goal and stakes are very much tied to the politics of Christian identity formation, as well as to the academic practices of hiring, tenure, promotion, and prestige. Those who have much invested in particular normative definitions seek to keep alive the self-evident nature of Gnosticism
as a reified entity so that it can continue to play its role as the heretical
"other." As the work of scholars such as Walter Bauer and Helmut Koester
shows, to expose the constructed character of Gnosticism is to effect a
"revolution" in the field by putting in doubt the identity of normative
Christianity. The legitimacy of any alternative claim depends on its being

accepted by new audiences whose interests lie precisely in subverting the game that has dismissed their demands for a hearing as "heresy." Yet any "revolution" will necessarily be partial precisely because the critique is pronounced "in the name of a purer, more authentic definition of the principles in whose name the dominant dominate."

In short, the enterprises of academic analysis are thoroughly involved in politics, whether acknowledged or not. Insofar as academics and religious adherents alike claim the right to say how the world is, enterprises designed to defend those claims are as much involved in politics as are those designed to contest them. As Bourdieu puts it: "The theory of knowledge is a dimension of political theory because the specifically symbolic power to impose the principles of the construction of reality—in particular, social reality—is a major dimension of political power."[16] It is in this sense that writing history requires engaging in the politics of current regimes and power relations of knowledge.

Although the analysis in this book has historiographical and political dimensions, my purpose is preeminently ethical. In this regard I have learned a great deal from the work of Elisabeth Schüssler Fiorenza on the ethics of historiography.[17] She argues that all interpretation has an ethical dimension: "Scholarship, current and past, is always produced by and for people with certain experiences, values, and goals. Hence one must investigate the implicit interests and unarticulated goals of scholarship, its degree of conscious responsibility, and its accountability."[18] An ethics of interpretation "must foster an ethos of critical reflexivity, democratic debate, intellectual, multilingual, and multidisciplinary competence. It takes as its goal publicly accountable scholarship and the responsible production and communication of such scholarship."[19] The goal, in short, is not to replace scientific objectivity as the criterion of valid scholarship, but to relativize[20] it appropriately in order to insist on the ethical dimension of the pursuit of truth.

Such an approach does not deny the reality of the phenomena but only insists that ethical, self-reflexive critique ought to be a necessary part of all historical writing. There are many workable ways of construing reality (that is, of acting consistently with existing material and social conditions), but not all would be equally desirable ethically. Although comprehending historical reconstructions as relative (as socially constructed) does undermine claims to possess a single, objective truth, it does not undermine the capacity for making (multiple) truth claims or for establishing standards of normativity. The effect is rather to shift the criteria for the adequacy of truth claims away from objectivity to ethics. Ethics will not eschew impartiality in investigation and the disciplined use of historical methods, but will require them.

The task at hand is to enable an ethics of critical-reflexive practice in historiography and theology. My objective has been, not to replace "orthodoxy" with "heresy" as a new normative foundation, but to further critical reflexivity with regard to the discourses and methods of historiographical scholarship. Insofar as religious tradition is understood as fixed and given, we can only accept or reject it. But insofar as it is understood as under constant construction and reformation, there is room for human agency and thus human responsibility. This is true even in ideally impartial historical reconstruction. As Bourdieu points out, the objectification of the past is itself part and parcel of our relationship to it. In writing history, we construct not just the past but our own ethical, social, and political relationship to it.[21] Our own ethical practice is at stake in that we unwittingly may be reproducing elements we consciously abhor—such as Christian anti-Judaism or colonialist and racist relations of power. I say "unwittingly" because the notions of *habitus* and *doxa* fully imply the limits of consciousness and intentionality. It is precisely because of such limits that we must not think it is always "safe" to internalize and appropriate religious traditions; rather, we must explore critically their past and potential implications in violence as well as liberation, in injustice as well as justice. Critical practice necessarily involves accountability; it involves asking to whom one is accountable. Whom do historical reconstructions and theological beliefs and practice serve? Whom do they exclude or harm?

The goal is not to destroy tradition but to open up space for alternative or marginalized voices to be heard within it. A fuller historical portrait of religious piety can enrich the funds of religious tradition, providing more complex theological resources to attend to the complex issues of our own day. One's own faith is not diminished by hearing other voices; it may even be strengthened and enriched.

Historical study will not be able to provide alternative horizons and visions for human imagination or theological construction, but it can provide an increasingly sound basis for reflection by charting as accurately as possible, not just "the facts" of the processes of identity formation, but also the historically and socially constructed discourses that produce knowledge, so that the ethical implications of those discourses may be critically considered. Critical historiography can help to overcome ignorance about the ways in which religious traditions and their discourses have been constructed and have functioned in promoting human well-being or in furthering violence and injustice. It can provide resources for theological and ethical reflection within communities of faith so that they may engage in constructive critique and reformation of their own traditions, practices, and discourses.

From our position of hindsight, it is possible to see that the academic study of Gnosticism has participated in colonialist and pseudoscientific, evolutionary discourses of race and culture that have come under considerable criticism in the late twentieth century. Ours is a postcolonial and postmodern world, struggling with the complex legacies of the increasingly pluralistic and multicultural globe we inhabit. It is essential that we gain a critical grasp on these discourses in order to disentangle them from our own work. Yet we do so with respect and appreciation for the contributions of scholars whose work constitutes our own past, knowing that our own enterprises will effect only a partial revolution, and no doubt will be subject to the critical hindsight of those who follow.[22]

# Bibliography

Abelson, Raziel. "Definition." In *The Encyclopedia of Philosophy,* vol. 2, pp. 314–324. Ed. Paul Edwards. New York: Macmillan Publishing, 1967.

Aland, Barbara, ed. *Gnosis. Festschrift für Hans Jonas.* Göttingen: Vandenhoeck and Ruprecht, 1978.

———. "Was ist Gnosis? Wie wurde sie überwundern? Versuch einer Kurzdefinition." In *Religionstheorie und Politische Theologie,* vol. 2: *Gnosis und Politik,* pp. 54–65. Ed. Jacob Taubes. Munich: Wilhelm Fink Verlag, 1984.

Allen, Graham. *Intertextuality.* London: Routledge, 2000.

Asad, Talal. *Genealogies of Religion: Discipline and Reasons of Power in Christianity and Islam.* Baltimore, Md.: Johns Hopkins University Press, 1993.

Aveni, Anthony F. *Empires of Time: Calendars, Clocks, and Cultures.* New York: Kodansha International, 1995.

Bakhtin, M. M. *The Dialogic Imagination: Four Essays.* Austin: University of Texas, 1981.

Barnard, Leslie William. Trans. with Introduction and notes. *St. Justin Martyr: The First and Second Apologies.* Ancient Christian Writers, no. 56. New York: Paulist Press, 1997.

Barns, J. W. B., G. M. Browne, and J. C. Shelton. *Greek and Coptic Papyri from the Cartonnage of the Covers.* NHS XVI. Leiden: E. J. Brill, 1981.

Barth, Fredrik. "The Analysis of Culture in Complex Societies." *Ethnos* 54 (1989), 120–142.

———. *Cosmologies in the Making: A Generative Approach to Cultural Variation in Inner New Guinea.* Cambridge, England: Cambridge University Press, 1987.

———. "Enduring and Emerging Issues in the Analysis of Ethnicity." In *The Anthropology of Ethnicity: Beyond "Ethnic Groups and Boundaries,"* pp. 11–

32. Ed. Hans Vermeulen and Cora Govers. The Hague: Het Spinhuis, 1994.

———. "Problems in Conceptualizing Cultural Pluralism, with Illustrations from Sohar, Oman." In *The Prospects for Plural Societies, 1982 Proceedings of the American Ethnological Society,* pp. 77–87. Ed. Stuart Plattner and David Maybury-Lewis. Washington, D.C.: The American Ethnological Society, 1984.

Barthes, Roland. *S/Z.* New York: Hill and Wang, 1974.

Bauer, Walter. *Orthodoxy and Heresy in Earliest Christianity,* 2nd ed. Philadelphia, Penn.: Fortress Press, 1971.

Benko, Stephen. "The Libertine Gnostic Sect of the Phibionites according to Epiphanius." *VC* (1967), 103–119.

———. *Pagan Rome and the Early Christians.* Bloomington: Indiana University Press, 1984.

Berkhofer, Robert F., Jr. *Beyond the Great Story. History as Text and Discourse.* Cambridge, Mass.: Belknap Press of Harvard University Press, 1995.

Bhabha, Homi K. *The Location of Culture.* London: Routledge, 1994.

Bianchi, Ugo, ed. *Le Origini dello Gnosticismo. Colloquio di Messina 13–18 Aprile 1966.* SHR XII. Leiden: E. J. Brill, 1967.

Bidney, David. "Myth, Symbolism, and Truth." In *Myth: A Symposium,* pp. 3–24. Ed. Thomas A. Sebeok. Bloomington: Indiana University Press, 1994.

Bloom, Harold. *The Flight to Lucifer: A Gnostic Fantasy.* New York: Farrar, Straus, Giroux, 1979.

Böhlig, Alexander. "Die Adamsapokalypse aus Codex V von Nag Hammadi als Zeugnis jüdisch-iranischer Gnosis." *Oriens Christianus* 48 (1964), 44–49.

———. "Der jüdische und jüdenchristliche Hintergrund in gnostischen Texte von Nag Hammadi." In *Le Origini dello Gnosticismo. Colloquio di Messina 13–18 Aprile 1966,* pp. 109–140. Ed. Ugo Bianchi. SHR XII. Leiden: E. J. Brill, 1967.

Borg, Marcus. "A Temperate Case for a Non-Eschatological Jesus." *Forum* 2/3 (1986), 81–102.

Bourdieu, Pierre. *The Logic of Practice.* Stanford, Calif.: Stanford University Press, 1990.

———. *Outline of a Theory of Practice.* Trans. Richard Nice. Cambridge Studies in Social Anthropology 16. Cambridge, England: Cambridge University Press, 1977.

———. *Sociology in Question.* Trans. Richard Nice. London: Sage Publications, 1993.

Bousset, Wilhelm. "Gnosis, Gnostiker." In *Real-Encyclopädie der klassischen Altertumswissenschaft* VII.2, pp. 1503–1546. Ed. A. Pauly, G. Wissowa. Reprinted in *Religionsgeschichtliche Studien. Aufsätze zur Religionsgeschichte des Hellenistischen Zeitalters,* pp. 44–96. Ed. Anthonie F. Verheule. Leiden: E. J. Brill, 1979.

————. *Hauptprobleme der Gnosis.* Neudruck der 1. Auflage von 1907. Göttingen: Vandenhoeck and Ruprecht, 1973.

————. *Jesu Predigt in ihrem Gegensatz zum Judentum: Ein religions- geschichtlicher Vergleich.* Göttingen: Vandenhoek and Ruprecht, 1892.

————. *Kyrios Christos: A History of the Belief in Christ from the Beginnings of Christianity to Irenaeus.* Trans. John E. Steely. Nashville, Tenn.: Abingdon Press, 1970.

————. "Die Religion der Mandäer." *Theologische Rundshau* 20 (1917), 185–205.

————. *Die Religion des Judentums in späthellenistischen Zeitalter,* 3rd ed. Ed. H. Gressman. Tübingen: Mohr, 1966.

Boyarin, Daniel. *Dying for God: Martyrdom and the Making of Christianity and Judaism.* Stanford, Calif.: Stanford University Press, 1999.

————. "The Gospel of the *Memra:* Jewish Binitarianism and Prologue to John." *HTR* 94/3 (2001), 243–284.

————. *Intertextuality and the Reading of Midrash.* Bloomington: Indiana University Press, 1990.

Brandt, Wilhelm. *Die Mandäer: ihre Religion und ihre Geschichte.* Amsterdam: Johannes Muller, 1915.

————. *Die mandäische Religion. Eine Erforschung der Religion der Mandäer in theologischer, religioser, philosophischer, und kultureller Hinsicht dargestellt.* Leipzig, 1889; reprint Amsterdam: Philo Press, 1973.

————. *Mandäische Schriften.* Göttingen: Vandenhoeck and Ruprecht, 1893.

Brooks, Cleanth. "Walter Percy and Modern Gnosticism." In *The Art of Walker Percy,* pp. 260–279. Ed. P. R. Broughton. Baton Rouge: Louisiana State Press, 1979.

Brumlik, Micha. *Die Gnostiker. Der Traum von der Selbsterlösung des Menschen.* Frankfurt am Main: Eichborn, 1992.

Buckley, Jorunn Jacobsen. "Evidence for Women Priests in Mandaeism." *Journal of Near Eastern Studies* 59 (2000), 93–106.

————. "Libertines or Not: Fruit, Bread, Semen and Other Body Fluids in Gnosticism." *JECS* 2.1 (1994), 15–31.

————. *The Mandaeans: Ancient Texts and Modern People.* Oxford: Oxford University Press, 2002.

————. "The Salvation of the Spirit Ruha in Mandaean Religion." In *Female Fault and Fulfilment in Gnosticism,* pp. 20–38. Chapel Hill: University of North Carolina Press, 1986.

——. "With the Mandaeans in Iran." *Religious Studies News* (September 1996), 8.

Buell, Denise Kimber. *Making Christians: Clement of Alexandria and the Rhetoric of Legitimacy.* Princeton, N.J.: Princeton University Press, 1999.

——. "Race and Universalism in Early Christianity." *JECS* 10.4 (2002), 429–468.

——. "Rethinking the Relevance of Race for Early Christian Self-Definition." *HTR* 94.4 (2001), 449–476.

——. *"Why This New Race?" Ethnic Reasoning in Early Christianity* (forthcoming).

Bultmann, Rudolf. "Die Bedeutung der neuerschlossenen mandäischen und manichäischen Quellen für das Verständnis der Johannesevangeliums." *ZNW* 24 (1925), 100–146.

——. "Christianity as a Religion of East and West." In *Essays: Philosophical and Theological,* pp. 209–233. London: SCM Press, 1955.

——. *The Gospel of John: A Commentary.* Trans. G. R. Beasley-Murray et al. Philadelphia, Penn.: Westminster Press, 1971.

——. "Johanneische Schriften und Gnosis." *Orientalistische Literaturzeitung* 43 (1940), 150–175.

——. "Points of Contact and Conflict." In *Essays: Philosophical and Theological,* pp. 133–150. London: SCM Press, 1955.

——. *Primitive Christianity in Its Contemporary Setting.* Trans. R. H. Fuller. London: The New English Library Limited, 1956.

——. "Die religionsgeschichtliche Hintergrund des Prologs zum Johannes Evangelium," vol. 2. In *Eucharistarion. Studien zur Religion und Literatur des Alten und Neuen Testaments. Hermann Gunkel zum 60. Geburtstag,* pp. 3–26. Ed. Hans Schmidt. Göttingen: Vandenhoek and Ruprecht, 1923.

Cameron, Ron. "The Gospel of Thomas and Christian Origins." In *The Future of Early Christianity: Essays in Honor of Helmut Koester,* pp. 381–392. Ed. Birger Pearson with A. Thomas Kraabel, George W. E. Nickelsburg, and Norman R. Petersen. Minneapolis, Minn.: Fortress Press, 1991.

Cameron, Ron, and Arthur Dewey. *The Cologne Mani Codex (P. Colon. Inv. Nr. 4700): Concerning the Origin of His Body.* Missoula, Mont.: Scholars Press, 1979.

Casey, R. P. "The Study of Gnosticism." *JTS* 36 (1935), 45–60.

Chadwick, Henry. *The Early Church.* New York: Viking Penguin Inc., 1967.

——. Intro. and trans. *Origen: Contra Celsum.* Cambridge, England: Cambridge University Press, 1980.

Chakrabarty, Dipesh. *Provincializing Europe: Postcolonial Thought and Historical*

*Difference.* Princeton Studies in Culture/Power/History. Princeton: Princeton University Press, 2000.

Cohen, Shaye J. D. *The Beginnings of Jewishness: Boundaries, Varieties, Uncertainties.* Berkeley: University of California Press, 1999.

———. *From the Maccabees to the Mishnah.* Philadelphia: Westminster Press, 1987.

Colpe, Carsten. "Gnosis. I. Religionsgeschichtlich." Col. 1648–1652 in *Die Religion in Geschichte und Gegenwart. Handwörterbuch für Theologie und Religionswissenschaft.* 3rd ed. Tübingen: J. C. B. Mohr, 1958.

———. "Die gnostische Gestalt des Erlöst Erlösers." *Der Islam* 32 (1956/57), 194–214.

———. *Die religionsgeschichtliche Schule. Darstellung und Kritik ihres Bildes vom gnostischen Erlösermythus.* Forschungen zur Religion und Literatur des Alten und Neuen Testamentes N. F. 60. Göttingen: Vandenhoeck and Ruprecht, 1961.

Conze, Edward. "Buddhism and Gnosticism." In *Le Origini dello Gnosticismo. Colloquio di Messina 13–18 Aprile 1966,* pp. 651–667. Ed. Ugo Bianchi. SHR XII. Leiden: E. J. Brill, 1967.

Cooper, James Fenimore. *The Last of the Mohicans.* Oxford: Oxford University Press, 1998.

Countryman, L. William. "Tertullian and the Regula Fidei." *Second Century* 2.4 (1982), 208–227.

Coxe, A. Cleveland. *The Ante-Nicene Fathers: Translations of the Writings of the Fathers Down to A.D. 325,* vol. 3: *Tertullian;* vol. 5: *Hippolytus, Cyprian, Cius, Novation, Appendix.* Grand Rapids, Mich.: Wm. B. Eerdmans, reprint 1978.

Crossan, John Dominic. *Four Other Gospels: Shadows on the Contours of Canon.* Minneapolis, Minn.: Winston Press, 1985.

Cumont, Franz. *Oriental Religions in Roman Paganism.* New York: Dover Publications, 1956.

Davids, Adelbert. "Irrtum und Häresie: I Clement—Ignatius von Antioch—Justinus." *Kairos* 15 (1973), 165–187.

Davies, Stevan L. *The Gospel of Thomas and Christian Wisdom.* New York: Seabury Press, 1983.

Dawson, David. *Allegorical Readers and Cultural Revision in Ancient Alexandria.* Berkeley: University of California Press, 1992.

Deismann, Adolf. *Light from the Ancient Near East.* New York: Harper and Brothers, 1922.

Denzey, Nicola Frances. "Under a Pitiless Sky: Conversion, Cosmology and the

Rhetoric of 'Enslavement to Fate' in Second-Century Christian Sources."
Ph.D. diss. Princeton University, 1998.

Desjardins, Michel. "Bauer and Beyond: On Recent Scholarly Discussions of
*hairesis* in the Early Christian Era." *Second Century* 8.2 (1991), 65–82.

———. *Sin in Valentinianism.* Society of Biblical Literature Dissertation Series
108. Atlanta, Ga.: Scholars Press, 1990.

Détienne, Marcel. *The Creation of Mythology.* Chicago: University of Chicago
Press, 1986.

Dillon, John M. *The Middle Platonists: A Study of Platonism 80 b.c. to a.d. 220.*
London: Duckworth, 1977.

———. "'Orthodoxy' and 'Eclecticism': Middle Platonists and Neo-Pythagore-
ans." In *The Question of "Eclecticism": Studies in Later Greek Philosophy,*
pp. 103–125. Ed. J. M. Dillon and A. A. Long. Hellenistic Culture and Society 3. Berkeley: University of California Press, 1988.

Drower, E. S. *The Canonical Prayerbook of the Mandaeans.* Leiden: E. J. Brill,
1959.

———. *The Haran Gawaita and the Baptism of Hibil-Ziwa.* Studi e Testi 176.
Vatican City: Biblioteca Apostolica Vaticana, 1953.

———. *The Mandaeans of Iraq and Iran.* Leiden: E. J. Brill, 1962.

Dunderberg, Ismo. "John and Thomas in Conflict?" In *The Nag Hammadi
Library after Fifty Years: Proceedings of the 1995 Society of Biblical Literature
Commemoration,* pp. 361–380. Ed. John D. Turner and Anne McGuire.
NHMS 44. Leiden: E. J. Brill, 1997.

Durkheim, Emile. *The Elementary Forms of Religious Life.* New York: The Free
Press, 1965.

Edgar, Andrew, and Peter Sedgwick, eds. *Key Concepts in Cultural Theory.*
London: Routledge, 1999.

Ehrman, Bart D. *The Orthodox Corruption of Scripture: The Effect of Early
Christological Controversies on the Text of the New Testament.* Oxford:
Oxford University Press, 1993.

Eliot, George. *Daniel Deronda.* Edinburgh: W. Blackwood, 1876.

Eltester, W., ed. *Christentum und Gnosis.* BZNW 47. Berlin: Verlag Alfred
Töpelmann, 1969.

Fallon, Francis T. *The Enthronement of Sabaoth: Jewish Elements in Gnostic Creation Myths.* NHS 10. Leiden: E. J. Brill, 1978.

Feldman, Burton, and Robert D. Richardson, eds. *The Rise of Modern Mythology: 1680–1860.* Bloomington: Indiana University Press, 1972.

Feldman, Louis H. *Jew and Gentile in the Ancient World: Attitudes and Interac-*

*tions from Alexander to Justinian.* Princeton, N.J.: Princeton University Press, 1993.

Filoramo, Giovanni. *A History of Gnosticism.* Oxford: Basil Blackwell, 1990.

Fossum, Jarl. "Gen. 1,26 and 2,7 in Judaism, Samaritanism, and Gnosticism." *Journal for the Study of Judaism* 26 (1985), 202–239.

———. "The Origin of the Gnostic Concept of the Demiurge." *Ephermerides Theologicae Lovanienses* 61 (1985), 142–152.

Foucault, Michel. *The Archaeology of Knowledge and the Discourse on Language.* Trans. A. M. Sheridan Smith. New York: Pantheon Books, 1972.

———. "Nietzsche, Genealogy, History." In *Language, Counter-Memory, Practice,* pp. 139–164. Ed. Donald F. Bouchard. Ithaca, N.Y.: Cornell University Press, 1977.

Fox, Robin Lane. *Pagans and Christians.* New York: Alfred A. Knopf, 1987.

Frankfurter, David. *Religion in Roman Egypt: Assimilation and Resistance.* Princeton, N.J.: Princeton University Press, 1998.

Freud, Sigmund. *The Future of an Illusion.* Garden City, N.Y.: Anchor Books, Doubleday and Co., 1964.

Frizzell, Lawrence E. "'Spoils from Egypt': Between Jews and Gnostics." In *Hellenization Revisited: Shaping a Christian Response within the Greco-Roman World,* pp. 139–164. Ed. Wendy Helleman. Lanham, Md.: University Press of America, Inc., 1994.

Funk, Wolf-Peter. "The Linguistic Aspect of Classifying the Nag Hammadi Codices." In *Les Textes de Nag Hammadi et le Problème de leur Classification. Actes du colloque tenu á Québec du 15 au 19 septembre 1993,* pp. 107–147. Ed. Louis Painchaud and Anne Pasquier. BCNH.SÉ 3. Quebec: Les Presses de l'Université Laval, 1995.

Geertz, Clifford. *The Interpretation of Cultures: Selected Essays.* New York: Basic Books, 1973.

———. *Local Knowledge: Further Essays in Interpretive Anthropology.* New York: Basic Books, 1983.

———. "The World in Pieces: Culture and Politics at the End of the Century." *Focaal* 32 (1998), 91–117.

Gero, Stephen. "With Walter Bauer on the Tigris: Encratite Orthodoxy and Libertine Heresy in Syro-Mesopotamian Christianity." In *Nag Hammadi, Gnosticism, and Early Christianity,* pp. 287–307. Ed. Charles W. Hedrick and Robert Hodgson, Jr. Peabody, Mass.: Hendrickson, 1986.

Goehring, James E. *Ascetics, Society, and the Desert: Studies in Early Egyptian Monasticism.* SAC. Harrisburg, Penn.: Trinity Press International, 1999.

————. "Libertine or Liberated: Women in the So-Called Libertine Gnostic Communities." In *Images of the Feminine in Gnosticism*, pp. 329–344. Ed. Karen L. King. SAC. Philadelphia, Penn.: Fortress Press, 1988.

Grant, Robert M. *Gnosticism and Early Christianity.* New York: Columbia University Press, 1959.

Green, Henry. "Gnosis and Gnosticism: A Study in Methodology." *Numen* 24 (1977), 95–134.

Greenslade, S. L., trans. and ed. *Early Latin Theology: Selections from Tertullian, Cyprian, Ambrose and Jerome.* The Library of Christian Classics. Philadelphia, Penn.: Westminster Press, 1956.

Gressman, Hugo. "Das religionsgeschichtliche Problem des Ursprungs der hellenistischen Erlösungsreligion." *Zeitschrift für Kirchengeschichte* 40 (1922), 178–191.

Guerra, Anthony J. "Polemical Christianity: Tertullian's Search for Certitude." *Second Century* 8.2 (1991), 109–123.

Gunkel, Hermann. *Zum religionsgeschichtlichen Verständnis des Neuen Testaments,* 2nd ed. Göttingen: Vandenhoek and Ruprecht, 1910.

Haardt, Robert. "Bemerkungen zu den Methoden der Ursprungsbestimmung von Gnosis." In *Le Origini dello Gnosticismo. Colloquio di Messina 13–18 Aprile 1966,* pp. 161–189. Ed. Ugo Bianchi. SHR XII. Leiden: E. J. Brill, 1967.

————. "Zur Methodologie der Gnosis Forschung." In *Gnosis und Neues Testament. Studien aus Religionswissenschaft und Theologie,* pp. 183–202. Ed. Karl-Wolfgang Tröger. Gerd Mohn: Gütersloher Verlagshaus, 1973.

Haenchen, Ernst. "Gab es eine vorchristliche Gnosis?" *Zeitschrift für Theologie und Kirche* 49 (1952), 316–349.

Hall, David D., ed. *Lived Religion in America: Toward a History of Practice.* Princeton, N.J.: Princeton University Press, 1997.

Hamilton, Paul. *Historicism.* London: Routledge, 1996.

Handler, Richard, and Jocelyn Linnekin. "Tradition, Genuine or Spurious." *Journal of American Folklore* 97 (1984), 273–290.

Harnack, Adolf von. *History of Dogma.* 4 vols. Trans. from 3rd German ed. New York: Dover Publications, 1961.

————. *Marcion: The Gospel of the Alien God.* Eng. trans. J. E. Steely and L. D. Bierma. Durham, N.C.: The Labyrinth Press, 1990.

————. *The Mission and Expansion of Christianity in the First Three Centuries.* Trans. James Moffatt. Gloucester, Mass.: Peter Smith, 1972.

————. *The Rise of Christian Theology and of Church Dogma.* Eng. trans. Neill Buchanan. Reprint New York: Russell and Russell, 1958.

———. *What Is Christianity?* New York: Harper Torchbooks, 1957.

Harrington, Daniel. "The Reception of W. Bauer's Orthodoxy and Heresy in Earliest Christianity during the Last Decade." *HTR* 73 (1980), 289–298.

Hedrick, Charles W., and Paul A. Mirecki, *Gospel of the Savior: A New Ancient Gospel.* CCL. Santa Rosa, Calif.: Polebridge Press, 1999.

Helleman, Wendy E. "Tertullian on Athens and Jerusalem" and "Epilogue." In *Hellenization Revisited: Shaping a Christian Response within the Greco-Roman World,* pp. 361–382 and 429–511. Ed. Wendy Helleman. Lanham, Md.: University Press of America, Inc., 1994.

Henaut, Barry W. "Alexandria or Athens as the Essence of Hellenization: A Historian Responds to a Philosopher." In *Hellenization Revisited: Shaping a Christian Response within the Greco-Roman World,* pp. 99–106. Ed. Wendy Helleman. Lanham, Md.: University Press of America, Inc., 1994.

Heron, A. I. C. "The Interpretation of I Clement in Walter Bauer's 'Recht-gläubigkeit und Ketzerei im ältesten Christentum.'" *Ekklesiastikos Pharos* 55 (1973), 517–545.

Horsley, Richard A. *Archaeology: History and Society in Galilee. The Social Context of Jesus and the Rabbis.* Valley Forge, Penn.: Trinity Press, 1996.

Hughes, Richard T., ed. *The Primitive Church in the Modern World.* Urbana and Chicago: University of Illinois Press, 1995.

Hultgren, Arland J. *The Rise of Normative Christianity.* Minneapolis, Minn.: Fortress Press, 1994.

Johnson Hodge, Caroline E. "'If Sons, Then Heirs': A Study of Kinship and Ethnicity in Paul's Letters." Ph.D. diss., Brown University, 2002.

Jonas, Hans. "Delimitation of the Gnostic Phenomenon—Typological and Historical." In *Le Origini dello Gnosticismo. Colloquio di Messina 13–18 Aprile 1966,* pp. 90–108. Ed. Ugo Bianchi. SHR XII. Leiden: E. J. Brill, 1967.

———. "Evangelium Veritatis and the Valentinian Speculation." In *Studies Patristica VI. Papers Presented at the Third International Conference on Patristic Studies Held at Christ Church, Oxford, 1959,* pp. 96–111. Ed. F. L. Cross. TU 81. Berlin: Akademie-Verlag, 1962.

———. *Gnosis und spätantiker Geist. I. Die mythologische Gnosis.* 3rd ed. Göttingen: Vandenhoek and Ruprecht, 1964.

———. *The Gnostic Religion: The Message of the Alien God and the Beginnings of Christianity,* 2nd ed. Boston, Mass.: Beacon Press, 1958.

———. "Myth and Mysticism." In *Philosophical Essays: From Ancient Creed to Technological Man,* pp. 291–304. Englewood Cliffs, N.J.: Prentice Hall, 1974.

———. "Response to G. Quispel's 'Gnosticism and the New Testament.'" In

*The Bible in Modern Scholarship,* pp. 279–293. Ed. J. Philip Hyatt. Nashville, Tenn.: Abingdon Press, 1965.

Kasser, Rodolphe. "Textes gnostiques: Remarques à propos des éditions récent du Livre secret de Jean et des Apocalypses de Paul, Jacques et Adam." *Muséon* 78 (1965), 71–98.

King, Karen L. "Approaching the Variants of the *Apocryphon of John.*" In *The Nag Hammadi Library after Fifty Years: Proceedings of the Society of Biblical Literature Commemoration, November 17–22, 1995,* pp. 105–137. Ed. John D. Turner and Anne McGuire. NHMS XLIV. Leiden: E. J. Brill, 1997.

———. "The Body and Society in Philo and the *Apocryphon of John.*" In *The School of Moses: Studies in Philo and Hellenistic Religion in Memory of Horst R. Moehring,* pp. 82–97. Ed. John Peter Kenney. BJS 304. Studia Philonica Monographs 1. Atlanta, Ga.: Scholars Press, 1995.

———. *The Gospel of Mary.* Santa Rosa, Calif.: Polebridge Press, 2003.

———. "The Gospel of Mary Magdalene." In *Searching the Scriptures,* vol. 2: *A Feminist Commentary,* pp. 601–634. Ed. Elisabeth Schüssler Fiorenza. New York: Crossroads Press, 1994.

———. "Is There Such a Thing as Gnosticism?" Paper for the SBL/AAR Annual Meetings, Washington, D.C., November 20–23, 1993.

———. "Mackinations on Myth and Origins." In *Reimagining Christian Origins: A Colloquium Honoring Burton L. Mack,* pp. 157–172. Ed. Elizabeth A. Castelli and Hal Taussig. Valley Forge, Penn.: Trinity Press International, 1996.

———. "The Origins of Gnosticism and the Identity of Christianity." Paper presented to the section "Nag Hammadi and Gnosticism," International Society of Biblical Literature Meeting, Helsinki and Lahti, Finland, July 18–21, 1999.

———. "The Politics of Syncretism and the Problem of Defining Gnosticism." *Retrofitting Syncretism.* Ed. William Cassidy. Special volume of *Historical Reflections/Réflexions Historiques* 27.3 (2001), 461–479.

———. "The Rationale of Gnostic Ethics." Paper for the Fifth International Congress of Coptic Studies, August 11–16, 1992, Catholic University of America, Washington, D.C. Revised version delivered at the SBL/AAR Annual Meetings, San Francisco, November 21–23, 1992.

———. *Revelation of the Unknowable God with Text, Translation and Notes to NHC IX,3 Allogenes.* CCL. Santa Rosa, Calif.: Polebridge Press, 1995.

———. "Translating History: Reframing Gnosticism in Postmodernity." In *Tradition und Translation. Zum Problem der interkulturellen Übersetzbarkeit religiöser Phänomene. Festschrift für Carsten Colpe zum 65. Geburtstag,* pp. 264–277. Ed. Christoph Elsas, Renate Haffke, Hans-Michael Haußig, Andreas Löw, Gesine Palmer, Bert Sommer, and Marco S. Torini. Berlin: Walter de Gruyter, 1994.

Klimkeit, Hans-Joachim. *Gnosis on the Silk Road: Gnostic Parables, Hymns and Prayers from Central Asia*. San Francisco, Calif.: Harper and Row, 1993.

Kloppenborg, John S., Marvin W. Meyer, Stephen J. Patterson, and Michael G. Steinhauser. *Q-Thomas Reader*. Sonoma, Calif.: Polebridge Press, 1990.

Koenen, Ludwig, and Cornelia Römer. *Der Kölner Mani-Kodex. Über das werden seines Leibes*. Opladen: Westdeutscher Verlag, 1988.

Koester, Helmut. *Ancient Christian Gospels: Their History and Development*. Philadelphia, Penn.: Trinity Press International, 1992.

———. "The History-of-Religions School, Gnosis, and Gospel of John." *Studia Theologica* 40 (1986), 115–136.

———. "La Tradition apostolique et les Origines de Gnosticisme." *Revue de Théologie et de Philosophie* 119 (1987), 1–16.

Koschorke, Klaus. "Patristische Materialen zur Spätgeschichte der valentinianischen Gnosis." In *Gnosis and Gnosticism: Papers Read at the Eighth International Conference on Patristic Studies (Oxford, September 3rd–8th, 1979)*, pp. 120–139. Ed. Martin Krause. NHS 17. Leiden: E. J. Brill, 1981.

Kraeling, C. H. "The Origin and Antiquity of the Mandaeans." *American Oriental Society Journal* 49 (1929), 195–218.

Krause, Martin. "The Christianization of Gnostic Texts." In *The New Testament and Gnosis: Essays in honour of Robert McLachlan Wilson*, pp. 187–194. Ed. A. H. B. Logan and A. J. M. Wedderburn. Edinburgh: T. and T. Clark, 1983.

Kümmel, Werner Georg. *The New Testament: The History of the Investigation of Its Problems*. Trans. S. McLean Gilmour and Howard C. Kee. Nashville, Tenn., and New York: Abingdon Press, 1972.

Lake, Kirsopp. *The Apostolic Fathers*. 2 vols. Loeb Classical Library. Cambridge, Mass.: Harvard University Press, 1977.

Layton, Bentley. *The Gnostic Scriptures: A New Translation with Annotations and Introductions*. Garden City, N.Y.: Doubleday and Company, 1987.

———. "Prolegomena to the Study of Ancient Gnosticism." In *The Social World of the First Christians: Essays in Honor of Wayne A. Meeks*, pp. 334–350. Ed. L. Michael White and O. Larry Yarbrough. Minneapolis, Minn.: Fortress Press, 1995.

———. "The Recovery of Gnosticism: The Philologist's Task in the Investigation of Nag Hammadi." *Second Century* 1.2 (1981), 85–99.

————, ed. *Nag Hammadi Codex II, 2–7 Together with III,2\*, Brit. Lib. Or.4926(1), and P.Oxy. 1, 654, 655.* 2 vols. NHS XX and XXI. Leiden: E. J. Brill, 1989.

————, ed. *The Rediscovery of Gnosticism: Proceedings of the International Conference on Gnosticism at Yale, New Haven, Connecticut, March 28–31, 1978,* vol. 1: *The School of Valentinus;* vol. 2: *Sethian Gnosticism.* SHR XLI. Leiden: E. J. Brill, 1981.

Lazreg, Marnia. "Decolonizing Feminism." In *Feminism and "Race,"* pp. 281–293. Ed. Kum-Kum Bhavnani. Oxford: Oxford University Press, 2000.

Le Boulluec, Alain. *Le Notion d'hérésie dans la littérature grecque II<sup>e</sup>–III<sup>e</sup> siècles.* Paris: Études augustiniennes, 1985.

Lebreton, Jules, and Jacques Zeiller. *Heresy and Orthodoxy: The Early Challenges to Christian Orthodoxy in the First Half of the Third Century, from the Gnostic Crisis to the Pagan Opposition.* New York: Collier Books, 1962 (reprint from 1946).

Lessa, William A., and Evon Z. Vogt. *Reader in Comparative Religion: An Anthropological Approach,* 3rd ed. New York: Harper and Row, 1972.

Lévi-Strauss, Claude. *Mythologiques II: Du Miel aux cendres.* Paris: Libraire Plon, 1966.

————. "The Structural Study of Myth." In *Myth: A Symposium,* pp. 81–106. Ed. Thomas A. Sebeok. Bloomington: Indiana University Press, 1994.

Lidzbarski, Mark. "Alter und Heimat der mandäischen Religion." *ZNW* 27 (1928), 321–327.

————. *Ginza: Der Schatz oder das Grosse Buch der Mandäer.* Göttingen: Vandenhoeck and Ruprecht, 1925.

————. *Das Johannesbuch der Mandäer.* 2 vols. Giessen, 1905; reprint Berlin: Walter de Gruyter, 1966.

————. "Mandäische Fragen." *ZNW* 26 (1927), 70–75.

————. *Mandäische Liturgien.* Abhandlung der Kirchengeschichtliche Geschichte der Wisssenschaft zu Göttingen, philologische-historische Klasse N. F. XVII 1. Berlin: Weidmannsche Buchhandlung, 1920.

————. "Die Münzen der Characene mit mandäischen Legende." *Zeitschrift für Numismatik* 33 (1922), 83–96.

Lietzmann, Hans. "Ein Beitrag zur Mandäerfrage." In *Sitzungsberichte der Preussischen Akademie der Wissenschaften, philo. hist. Klasse* 1930, pp. 596–608; reprint in *TU* 67, 124–140.

Lieu, Samuel N. C. *Manichaeism in the Later Roman Empire and Medieval China.* Tübingen: J. C. B. Mohr, 1992.

Lipsius, Richard A. *Die Quellen der ältesten Ketzergeschichte.* Leipzig: J. A. Barth, 1875.

Logan, Alastair H. B. *Gnostic Truth and Christian Heresy: A Study in the History of Gnosticism.* Peabody, Mass.: Hendrickson Publishers, 1996.

Löhr, W. A. "Gnostic Determinism Reconsidered." *VC* 46 (1992), 381–390.

Loisy, Alfred. *The Gospel and the Church.* Trans. Christopher Home. Lives of Jesus Series. Philadelphia, Penn.: Fortress Press, 1976.

Lorde, Audre. "Age, Race, Class, and Sex: Women Redefining Difference." In *Sister Outsider,* pp. 114–123. Freedom, Calif.: The Crossing Press, 1984.

Lupieri, Edmondo F. *The Mandaeans: The Last Gnostics.* Grand Rapids, Mich.: Eerdmans, 2001.

Luttikhuizen, Gerard P. "Intertextual References in Readers' Responses to the Apocryphon of John." In *Intertextuality in Biblical Writings: Essays in Honour of Bas van Iersel,* pp. 117–126. Ed. S. Draisma. Kampen: J. H. Kok, 1989.

———. "The Thought Pattern of Gnostic Mythologizers and Their Use of Biblical Traditions." *The Nag Hammadi Library after Fifty Years,* pp. 89–101. Ed. John D. Turner and Anne McGuire. NHMS XLIV. Leiden: E. J. Brill, 1997.

———. "Traces of Aristotelian Thought in *The Apocryphon of John.*" In *For the Children, Perfect Instruction: Essays in Honor of Hans-Martin Schenke on the Occasion of the Berliner Arbeitskreis für koptisch-gnostische Schriften's Thirtieth Year,* pp. 181–202. Ed. Hans-Gebhard Bethge, Stephen Emmel, Karen L. King, and Imke Schletterer. NHMS. Leiden: E. J. Brill, 2002.

MacMullen, Ramsay. *Paganism in the Roman Empire.* New Haven, Conn.: Yale University Press, 1981.

MacRae, George W. "The Coptic Gnostic Apocalypse of Adam." *Heythrop Journal* 6 (1965), 27–35.

———. "The Jewish Background of the Gnostic Sophia Myth." *NovTest* 12 (1970), 86–101.

———. *Studies in the New Testament and Gnosticism.* Good News Studies 26. Wilmington, Del.: Michael Glazier, Inc., 1987.

———. "Why the Church Rejected Gnosticism." In *Studies in the New Testament and Gnosticism,* pp. 251–262. Good News Studies 26. Wilmington, Del.: Michael Glazier, Inc., 1987.

Maçuch, Rudolf. "Alter und Heimat des Mandäismus nach neuerschlossenen Quellen." *Theologische Literaturzeitung* 82 (1957), 410–418.

———. "Gnostische Ethik und die Anfänge der Mandäer." In *Christentum am Roten Meer,* vol. 2, pp. 254–274. Ed. Franz Altheim and Ruth Stiehl. Berlin: Walter de Gruyter, 1973.

———. *Handbook of Classical and Modern Mandaic.* Berlin: Walter de Gruyter, 1965.

———. "The Origins of the Mandaeans and Their Script." *Journal of Semitic Studies* 16 (1971), 174–192.

Magne, Jean. *From Christianity to Gnosis and from Gnosis to Christianity: An Itinerary through the Texts to and from the Tree of Paradise.* BJS 286. Atlanta, Ga.: Scholars Press, 1993.

Maier, Johann. "Jüdische Faktoren bei der Entstehung der Gnosis?" In *Altes Testament—Früjudentum—Gnosis. Neue Studien zu 'Gnosis und Bibel,'* pp. 239–258. Ed. Karl-Wolfgang Tröger. Berlin: Evangelische Verlagsanstalt, 1980.

Malinowski, Bronislaw. *Magic, Science and Religion.* Garden City, N.Y.: Doubleday Anchor Books, 1954.

Markschies, Christoph. *Valentinus Gnosticus? Untersuchungen zur valentinianischen Gnosis mit einem Kommentar zu den Fragmenten Valentins.* Tübingen: J. C. B. Mohr (Paul Siebeck), 1992.

Markus, Robert A. *The End of Ancient Christianity.* Cambridge, England: Cambridge University Press, 1990.

Masuzawa, Tomoko. *In Search of Dreamtime: The Quest for the Origin of Religion.* Chicago, Ill.: University of Chicago Press, 1993.

McCue, J. F. "Orthodoxy and Heresy: Walter Bauer and the Valentinians." *VC* 33 (1979), 118–130.

McDonald, Lee M. *The Formation of the Christian Biblical Canon.* Rev. and expanded ed. Peabody, Mass.: Hendrickson Publishers, 1995.

McGuire, Anne. "Kurt Rudolph, *Gnosis: The Nature and History of Gnosticism.*" Book review in *Second Century* 5 (1985), 47–49.

———. "Valentinus and the 'Gnostikê Hairesis': An Investigation of Valentinus's Position in the History of Gnosticism." Ph.D. diss. Yale University, 1983.

———. "Valentinus and the *gnostikê hairesis:* Irenaeus, *Haer.* I.xi.1 and the Evidence of Nag Hammadi." In *Papers of the IXth International Conference on Patristic Studies, Oxford University, 1983,* pp. 247–252. Studia Patristica 18. Ed. Elizabeth A. Livingstone. Kalamazoo, Mich.: Cistercian Press, 1985.

Mead, G. *The Gnostic John the Baptizer: Selection from the Mandaean John-Book.* London: J. M. Watkins, 1924.

Ménard, Jacques. *L'Évangile de vérité.* NHS 2. Leiden: E. J. Brill, 1972.

Miller, Robert J. *The Apocalyptic Jesus: A Debate.* Santa Rosa, Calif.: Polebridge Press, 2001.

Moffatt, James. "Walter Bauer, *Orthodoxy and Heresy in Earliest Christianity.*" Book review in *Expository Times* 45 (1933/34), 475–476.

Mosse, David. "The Politics of Religious Synthesis: Roman Catholicism and

Hindu Village Society in Tamil Nadu, India." In *Syncretism/Anti-Syncretism: The Politics of Religious Synthesis,* pp. 85–107. Ed. Charles Stewart and Rosalind Shaw. New York: Routledge, 1994.

Nagy, Gregory. *Homeric Questions.* Austin: University of Texas Press, 1996.

———. *Poetry as Performance: Homer and Beyond.* Cambridge, England: Cambridge University Press, 1996.

Nock, Arthur Darby. *Conversion: The Old and the New in Religion from Alexander the Great to Augustine of Hippo.* Reprint of 1933 edition by Brown Classics in Judaica. Lanham, Md.: University Press of America, 1985.

Nöldeke, Theodore. *Mandäische Grammatik.* Halle: Buchhandlung des Waisenhauses, 1875.

Norris, Frederick. "Ignatius, Polycarp, and I Clement: Walter Bauer Reconsidered." *VC* 30 (1976), 23–44.

North, John. "The Development of Religious Pluralism." In *The Jews among Pagans and Christians in the Roman Empire,* pp. 174–193. Ed. Judith Lieu, John North, and Tessa Rajak. London: Routledge, 1992.

O'Connor, June. "On Doing Religious Ethics." *Journal of Religious Ethics* 7.1 (1979), 81–96.

Olender, Maurice. *The Languages of Paradise: Race, Religion, and Philology in the Nineteenth Century.* Cambridge, Mass.: Harvard University Press, 1992.

Orsi, Robert. "Everyday Miracles: The Study of Lived Religion." In *Lived Religion in America: Toward a History of Practice,* pp. 3–21. Ed. David D. Hall. Princeton, N.J.: Princeton University Press, 1997.

Ortner, Sherry B. "Introduction." *Representations* 59 (1997), 1–13.

Otto, Rudolph. *The Idea of the Holy: An Inquiry into the Non-Rational Factor in the Idea of the Divine and Its Relation to the Rational,* 2nd ed. Trans. John W. Harvey. London: Oxford University Press, 1970.

Oxtoby, Willard. "Religionswissenschaft Revisited." In *Religions in Antiquity,* pp. 590–608. Ed. Jacob Neusner. Leiden: E. J. Brill, 1968.

Pagels, Elaine. "Exegesis and Exposition of the Genesis Creation Accounts in Selected Texts from Nag Hammadi." In *Nag Hammadi, Gnosticism, and Early Christianity,* pp. 257–285. Ed. Charles W. Hedrick and Robert Hodgson, Jr. Peabody, Mass.: Hendrickson, 1986.

———. *The Gnostic Paul: Gnostic Exegesis of the Pauline Letters.* Philadelphia, Penn.: Trinity Press, 1975.

Painchaud, Louis. "Le projet d'édition de la bibliothèque copte de Nag Hammadi à l'Université Laval." *Studies in Religion/Sciences Religieuses* 27 (1998), 467–480.

Painchaud, Louis, and Anne Pasquier, eds. *Les Textes de Nag Hammadi et le*

*Problème de leur Classification. Actes du colloque tenu á Québec du 15 au 19 septembre 1993.* BCNH.SÉ 3. Quebec: Les Presses de l'Université Laval, 1995.

Pallis, S. A. *A Mandaean Bibliography, 1560–1930.* London: V. Pio, 1933; reprint, Amsterdam: Philo, 1974.

Parker, David C. *The Living Text of the Gospels.* Cambridge, England: Cambridge University Press, 1997.

Pearson, Birger. *Gnosticism, Judaism, and Egyptian Christianity.* SAC. Minneapolis, Minn.: Fortress Press, 1990.

———. "Is Gnosticism a Religion?" In *The Notion of "Religion" in Comparative Research: Selected Proceedings of the XVI Congress of the International Association for the History of Religions, Rome, 3–8 September 1990,* pp. 105–114. Ed. Ugo Bianchi. Storia delle Religione 8. Rome: L'Erma di Bretschneider, 1994.

———. "Jewish Sources in Gnostic Literature." In *Jewish Writings of the Second Temple Period: Apocrypha, Pseudepigrapha, Qumran Sectarian Writings, Philo, Josephus,* pp. 443–481. Ed. Michael E. Stone. Assen: Von Gorcum; Philadelphia, Penn.: Fortress Press, 1984.

———. "The Problem of Jewish Gnostic Literature." In *Nag Hammadi, Gnosticism and Early Christianity,* pp. 15–35. Ed. C. W. Hedrick and R. Hodgson, Jr. Peabody, Mass.: Hendrickson, 1986.

———. "Use, Authority and Exegesis of Mikra in Gnostic Literature." In *Mikra. Text, Translations, Reading and Interpretation of the Hebrew Bible in Ancient Judaism and Early Christianity,* pp. 635–652. Compendia Rerum Iudaicarum ad Novum Testamentum I. Ed. Martin Jan Mulder. Assen: Van Gorcum; Philadelphia, Penn.: Fortress Press, 1988.

———, ed. *Nag Hammadi Codex VII.* NHMS XXX. Leiden: E. J. Brill, 1996.

———, ed. *Nag Hammadi Codicex IX and X.* NHS XV. Leiden: E. J. Brill, 1981.

Perkins, Pheme. *The Gnostic Dialogue: The Early Church and the Crisis of Gnosticism.* Studies in Contemporary Biblical and Theological Problems. New York: Paulist Press, 1980.

———. *Gnosticism and the New Testament.* Minneapolis, Minn.: Fortress Press, 1993.

———. "Irenaeus and the Gnostics: Rhetoric and Composition in *Adversus haereses* Book One." *VC* 30 (1976), 193–200.

Petermann, H. *Thesaurus sive Liber Magnus, vulgo "Liber Adami" appelatus, opus Mandaeorum summi ponderis.* 2 vols. Berlin-Leipzig, 1867.

Pétrement, Simone. *A Separate God: The Christian Origins of Gnosticism.* San Francisco, Calif.: Harper and Row, 1990.

Plotinus. *Enneads.* Trans. Arthur Hilary Armstrong. Loeb Classical Library. 7
    vols. Cambridge, Mass.: Harvard University Press, 1966–1988.
Poirier, Paul-Hubert. "The Writings Ascribed to Thomas and the Thomas Tra-
    dition." In *The Nag Hammdi Library after Fifty Years: Proceedings of the
    1995 Society of Biblical Literature Commemoration,* pp. 295–307. Ed. John
    D. Turner and Anne McGuire. NHMS LXIV. Leiden: E. J. Brill, 1997.
Pokorny, Petr. "Der soziale Hintergrund der Gnosis." In *Gnosis und Neues Testa-
    ment. Studien aus Religionswissenschaft und Theologie,* pp. 77–87. Ed. Karl-
    Wolfgang Tröger. Gerd Mohn: Gütersloher Verlagshaus, 1973.
Porphyry. *Life of Plotinus.* In Plotinus, *Enneads,* vol. 1. Trans. Arthur Hilary
    Armstrong. Loeb Classical Library. Cambridge, Mass.: Harvard University
    Press, 1966.
Price, S. R. F. *Rituals and Power: The Roman Imperial Cult in Asia Minor.* Cam-
    bridge, England: Cambridge University Press, 1984.
Quispel, Gilles. "Gnosticism and the New Testament." In *The Bible in Modern
    Scholarship,* pp. 252–271. Ed. J. Philip Hyatt. Nashville, Tenn.: Abingdon
    Press, 1965.
———. "Der gnostische Anthropos und die jüdische Tradition." *Eranos
    Jahrbuch* 22 (1954), 195–234.
———. "Judaism, Judaic Christianity and Gnosis." In *The New Testament and
    Gnosis: Essays in Honour of Robert McLachlan Wilson,* pp. 47–68. Ed.
    A. H. B. Logan and A. J. M. Wedderburn. Edinburgh: T and T Clark,
    1983.
———. "The Origins of the Gnostic Demiurge." In *Gnostic Studies,* vol. 1,
    pp. 213–220. Istanbul: Nederlands Historisch-Archaeologisch Instituut in
    het Nabije Oosten, 1974.
Reitzenstein, Richard. "Gedanken zur Entwicklung der Erlöserglaubens."
    *Historische Zeitschrift* 126 (1922), 1–57.
———. *Die Göttin Psyche in der hellenistischen und frühchristlichen Literatur.*
    Sitzungberichte der Heidelberger Akademie der Wissenschaften, 1917.
———. *The Hellenistic Mystery Religions.* Pittsburgh, Penn.: Pickwick Press,
    1978.
———. "Iranischer Erlösungsglaube." *ZNW* 20 (1921), 1–23.
———. *Das mandäische Buch des Herrn der Grösse und die Evangelien-
    überlieferung.* Heidelberg: C. Winter, 1919.
———. *Poimandres. Studien zur griechisch-ägyptischen und frühchristlichen
    Literatur.* Leipzig: B. G. Teubner, 1904.
Reitzenstein, Richard, and Hans Schaeder. *Studien zum Antiken Synkretismus aus
    Iran und Griechenland.* Leipzig: B. G. Teubner, 1926.

Richardson, Cyril C. *Early Christian Fathers.* New York: Collier Books (Macmillan Publishing), 1970.

Ricoeur, Paul. *Time and Narrative.* 3 vols. Trans. Kathleen Blamey and David Pellauer. Chicago: University of Chicago Press, 1984–1985.

Riley, Gregory J. *Resurrection Reconsidered: Thomas and John in Controversy.* Minneapolis, Minn.: Fortress Press, 1995.

Robinson, James M. "From Cliff to Cairo: The Story of the Discoverers and Middlemen of the Nag Hammadi Codices." In *Colloque international sur les Textes de Nag Hammadi (Québec, 22–25 août 1978),* pp. 21–58. Ed. Bernard Barc. BCNH.SÉ 1. Quebec and Louvain: Les Presses de l'Université Laval and Éditions Peeter, 1981.

———. "The Coptic Gnostic Library Today." *New Testament Studies* 14 (1968), 365–401.

———. "Jesus from Easter to Valentinus (or to the Apostle's Creed)." *JBL* 101 (1982), 5–37.

———. "Nag Hammadi: The First Fifty Years." In *The Nag Hammadi Library after Fifty Years: Proceedings of the 1995 Society of Biblical Literature Commemoration,* pp. 3–33. Ed. John D. Turner and Anne McGuire. Leiden: E. J. Brill, 1997.

———. *The Nag Hammadi Codices: A General Introduction to the Nature and Significance of the Coptic Gnostic Library from Nag Hammadi.* Claremont, Calif.: Institute for Antiquity and Christianity, 1977.

Robinson, James M., and Helmut Koester. *Trajectories through Early Christianity.* Philadelphia, Penn.: Fortress Press, 1971.

Robinson, James M., and Richard Smith, eds. *The Nag Hammadi Library in English.* 3rd ed. San Francisco, Calif.: Harper and Row, 1988.

Robinson, T. A. *The Bauer Thesis Examined: The Geography of Heresy in the Early Christian Church.* Studies in the Bible and Early Christianity 11. Lewiston, N.Y.: Mellen Press, 1988.

Roukema, Riemer. *Gnosis and Faith in Early Christianity: An Introduction to Gnosticism.* Trans. John Bowden. Harrisburg, Penn.: Trinity Press International, 1999.

Rousseau, Jean-Jacques. *A Discourse on Inequality.* Trans. Maurice Cranston of the 1755 ed. London: Penguin, 1984.

Rowe, William V. "Adolf von Harnack and the Concept of Hellenization." In *Hellenization Revisited: Shaping a Christian Response within the Greco-Roman World,* pp. 69–98. Ed. Wendy Helleman. Lanham, Md.: University Press of America, Inc., 1994.

Rudolph, Kurt. *Gnosis: The Nature and History of Gnosticism.* Trans. R. McL. Wilson. San Francisco, Calif.: Harper and Row, 1983.

————. "Gnosticism." In *Early Christianity: Origins and Evolution to AD 600. In Honour of W. H. C. Frend*, pp. 186–197. Ed. Ian Hazlett. London: SPCK, 1991.

————. *Die Mandäer.* 2 vols. Forschungen zur Religion und Literatur des Alten und Neuen Testaments 74, 75. Göttingen: Vandenhoeck and Ruprecht, 1960–1961.

————. "Die mandäische Literatur. Bemerkungen zum Stand ihrer Textausgaben." In *Gnosis und spätantike Religionsgeschichte. Gesammelte Aufsätze*, pp. 339–362. Leiden: E. J. Brill, 1996.

————. "Das Problem einer Soziologie und 'socialen Verortung' der Gnosis." *Kairos* 39.1 (1977), 35–44.

————. "Problems of a History of the Development of the Mandaean Religion." *History of Religions* 8 (1969), 210–235.

————. "Quellenprobleme zum Ursprung und Alter der Mandäer." In *Gnosis und spätantike Religionsgeschichte. Gesammelte Aufsätze*, pp. 403–432. Leiden: E. J. Brill, 1996.

————. "Randerscheinungen des Judentums und das Problem der Entstehung des Gnostizismus." *Kairos* 9 (1967), 105–122.

Said, Edward. *Orientalism.* New York: Random House, 1978; reprint Vintage Books, 1979.

Schenke, Hans-Martin. "The Book of Thomas (NHC II.7): A Revision of a Pseudepigraphical Epistle of Jacob the Contender." In *The New Testament and Gnosis: Essays in Honor of Robert McL. Wilson*, pp. 213–228. Ed. A. H. B. Logan and A. J. M. Wedderburn. Edinburgh: T. and T. Clark, 1983.

————. "Nag Hammadi Studien I: Das literarische Problem des Apocryphon Johannis." *Zeitschrift für Religions-und Geistesgeschichte* 14 (1962), 57–63.

————. "The Phenomenon and Significance of Gnostic Sethianism." In *The Rediscovery of Gnosticism: Proceedings of the International Conference on Gnosticism at Yale, New Haven, Connecticut, March 28–31, 1978*, vol. 2, pp. 588–616. SHR XLI. Leiden: E. J. Brill, 1981.

————. "The Problem of Gnosis." *Second Century* 3.2 (1983), 73–87.

————. Review of *Koptisch-gnostische Apokalypsen aus Codex V von Nag Hammadi im koptischen Museum zu Alt-Kairo* by Alexander Böhlig and Pahor Labib. In *Orientalistische Literaturzeitung* 61 (1966), 23–34.

————. "Das sethianische System nach Nag-Hammadi-Handschriften." In *Studia Coptica*, pp. 165–174. Ed. Peter Nagel. Berlin: Akademie Verlag, 1974.

————. *Das Thomas-Buch: Nag-Hammadi-Codex II,7.* TU 138. Berlin: Akademie Verlag, 1989.

————. "Was ist Gnosis? Neue Aspekte der alten Fragen nach dem Ursprung und dem Wesen der Gnosis." In *Gnosis. Vorträge der Veranstaltungsfolge des Steirischen Herbstes und der Österreichischen URANIA für Steiermark vom Oktober und November 1993,* pp. 180–203. Ed. Johannes B. Bauer and Hannes D. Galter. Grazer Theologische Studien 16. Graz: RM-Druck-& Verlag, 1994.

———. "The Work of the *Berliner Arbeitskreis* Past, Present, and Future." In *The Nag Hammdi Library after Fifty Years: Proceedings of the 1995 Society of Biblical Literature Commemoration,* pp. 62–71. Ed. John D. Turner and Anne McGuire. NHMS XLIV. Leiden: E. J. Brill, 1997.

Schmidt, Carl, ed., and Violet MacDermot, trans. *The Books of Jeu and the Untitled Text in the Bruce Codex.* NHS XIII. Leiden: E. J. Brill, 1978.

———. *Pistis Sophia.* NHS IX. Leiden: E. J. Brill, 1978.

Schmitt, Richard. "Phenomenology." In *The Encyclopedia of Philosophy,* vol. 6, pp. 135–151. Ed. Paul Edwards. New York: Macmillan and Free Press; London: Collier Macmillan, 1967.

Schoedel, William R. "Gnostic Monism and the Gospel of Truth." In *The Rediscovery of Gnosticism: Proceedings of the International Conference on Gnosticism at Yale, New Haven, Connecticut, March 28–31, 1978,* vol. 1: *The School of Valentinus,* pp. 379–390. Ed. Bentley Layton. SHR XLI. Leiden: E. J. Brill, 1981.

Scholem, Gershom. "Jaldabaoth Reconsidered." In *Mélanges d'Histoire des Religions offert à Henri-Charles Puech,* pp. 405–421. Paris: Presses Universitaires de France, 1974.

Scholer, David M. *Nag Hammadi Bibliography 1948–1969.* NHS 1. Leiden: E. J. Brill, 1971.

———. *Nag Hammadi Bibliography 1970–1994.* NHMS 32. Leiden: E. J. Brill, 1997.

Scholten, Clemens. "Probleme der Gnosisforschung: alte Frage—neue Zugänge." *Internationale Katholische Zeitschrift/Communio* 26 (1997), 481–501.

Schottroff, Luise. "*Animae naturaliter salvandae:* Zum Problem der himmlischen Herkunft der Gnostikers." In *Christentum und Gnosis,* pp. 65–97. Ed. Walther Eltester. BZNW 37. Berlin: Alfred Töpelmann, 1969.

Schüssler Fiorenza, Elisabeth. *Rhetoric and Ethic: The Politics of Biblical Studies.* Minneapolis, Minn.: Fortress Press, 1999.

———. "The Rhetoricity of Historical Knowledge: Pauline Discourse and Its Contextualizations." In *Religious Propaganda of Missionary Competitions in the New Testament World,* pp. 443–469. Ed. Lukas Bormann et al. New York: E. J. Brill, 1994.

————. *Sharing Her Word: Feminist Biblical Interpretation in Context.* Boston, Mass.: Beacon Press, 1998.

Schweitzer, Albert. *The Mystery of the Kingdom of God: The Secret of Jesus' Messiahship and Passion.* Trans. Walter Lowrie. New York: Macmillan, 1954.

Scott, Joan W. "'Experience.'" In *Feminists Theorize the Political,* pp. 22–40. Ed. Judith Butler and Joan W. Scott. Routledge: New York, 1992.

Segal, Alan. *Two Powers in Heaven: Early Rabbinic Reports about Christianity and Gnosticism.* Leiden: E. J. Brill, 1977.

Segal, Robert A., ed. *The Allure of Gnosticism: The Gnostic Experience in Jungian Psychology and Contemporary Culture.* Chicago and LaSalle, Ill.: Open Court, 1995.

————, ed. *The Gnostic Jung.* Princeton, N.J.: Princeton University Press, 1992.

Sevrin, J.-M. *Le dossier baptismal séthien: Études sur la sacramentaire gnostique.* BCNH.SÉ 2. Quebec: Les Presses de l'Université Laval, 1986.

Shaw, Rosalind, and Charles Stewart. "Introduction: Problematizing Syncretism." In *Syncretism/Anti-Syncretism: The Politics of Religious Synthesis,* pp. 1–26. Ed. Charles Stewart and Rosalind Shaw. London: Routledge, 1994.

Sider, Robert D. "Approaches to Tertullian: A Study of Recent Scholarship." *Second Century* 2.4 (1982), 228–260.

Simon, Marcel. "The religionsgeschichtliche Schule, Fifty Years Later." *Religious Studies* 11 (1975), 135–144.

Slusser, Michael. "Docetism: A Historical Definition." *Second Century* 1.3 (1981), 163–172.

Smith, Jonathan Z. "Differential Equations: On Constructing the 'Other.'" Thirteenth Annual University Lecture in Religion. Arizona State University, Department of Religious Studies, March, 5, 1992.

————. *Drudgery Divine: On the Comparison of Early Christianities and the Religions of Late Antiquity.* Jordan Lectures in Comparative Religion, XIV. School of Oriental and African Studies, University of London. Chicago: University of Chicago Press, 1990.

————. "Fences and Neighbors: Some Contours of Early Judaism." In *Imagining Religion: From Babylon to Jonestown,* pp. 1–18. Chicago: University of Chicago Press, 1982.

————. *Map Is Not Territory.* Chicago: University of Chicago Press, 1978.

————. "Religion, Religions, Religious." In *Critical Terms for Religious Studies,* pp. 269–284. Ed. Mark C. Taylor. Chicago: University of Chicago Press, 1998.

Smith, Morton. "The History of the Term Gnostikos." In *The Rediscovery of Gnosticism: Proceedings of the International Conference on Gnosticism at Yale, New Haven, Connecticut, March 28–31, 1978,* vol. 2: *Sethian Gnosticism,* pp. 796–807. Ed. Bentley Layton. SHR LXI. Leiden: E. J. Brill, 1981.

Smith, Richard. "Afterword: The Modern Relevance of Gnosticism." In *The Nag Hammadi Codices in English,* 3rd ed., pp. 532–549. Ed. James M. Robinson and Richard Smith. San Francisco, Calif.: Harper and Row, 1988.

———. "The Revival of Ancient Gnosis." *The Allure of Gnosticism: The Gnostic Experience in Jungian Psychology and Contemporary Culture,* pp. 204–223. Ed. Robert A. Segal. Chicago and LaSalle, Ill.: Open Court, 1995.

Standaert, Benoit. "'Evangelium Veritatis' et 'veritatis evangelium': Le question du titre et les témoins patristiques." *VC* 30 (1976), 243–275.

Strecker, Georg. "The Reception of the Book." In Walter Bauer, *Orthodoxy and Heresy in Earliest Christianity,* 2nd ed., Appendix 2, pp. 286–316. Philadelphia, Penn.: Fortress Press, 1971.

Stroumsa, Gedaliahu A. G. *Another Seed: Studies in Gnostic Mythology.* NHS XXIV. Leiden: E. J. Brill, 1984.

Tardieu, Michel. "Le Congrès de Yale sur le Gnosticisme (28–31 mars 1978)." *Revue des Études Augustiniennes* 24 (1978), 188–209.

Tardieu, Michel, and J.-D. Dubois. *Introduction à la literature gnostique.* Paris: Editions du Cerf, 1986.

Taylor, Joan E. "The Phenomenon of Early Jewish-Christianity: Reality or Scholarly Invention?" *VC* 44 (199), 313–334.

Tertullian, *Against the Valentinians.* In *The Ante-Nicene Fathers,* pp. 503–520. Ed. A. Cleveland Coxe. Grand Rapids, Mich.: Eerdmans, 1978.

Thomas, Brook. *The New Historicism and Other Old-Fashioned Topics.* Princeton, N.J.: Princeton University Press, 1991.

Thomassen, Einar. "Notes pour la délimitation d'un corpus Valentinien à Nag Hammadi." In *Les Textes de Nag Hammadi et le Problème de leur Classification. Actes du colloque tenu á Québec du 15 au 19 septembre 1993,* pp. 243–259. Ed. Louis Painchaud and Anne Pasquier. BCNH.SÉ 3. Quebec: Les Presses de l'Université Laval, 1995.

Thompson, E. P. "Time, Work-Discipline, and Industrial Capitalism." *Past and Present* 38 (1990), 56–97.

Tiessen, Terrance. "Gnosticism as Heresy: The Response of Irenaeus." In *Hellenization Revisited: Shaping a Christian Response within the Greco-Roman World,* pp. 339–360. Ed. Wendy Helleman. Lanham, Md.: University Press of America, Inc., 1994.

Till, Walther, and Hans-Martin Schenke. *Die gnostischen Schriften des koptischen Papyrus Berolinensis 8502.* TU 602. Berlin: Akademie Verlag, 1972.

Trinh T. Minh-ha. *Woman, Native, Other: Writing Postcoloniality and Feminism.* Bloomington and Indianapolis: Indiana University Press, 1989.

Tröger, Karl-Wolfgang. "The Attitude of the Gnostic Religion towards Judaism as Viewed in a Variety of Perspectives." In *Colloque international sur les textes de Nag Hammadi (Québec, 22–25 août 1978),* pp. 86–92. Ed. Bernard Barc. BCNH.SÉ 1. Louvain, Belgium: Éditions Peeters, 1981.

———. "Gnosis und Judentum." In *Altes Testament-Früjudentum-Gnosis. Neue Studien zu 'Gnosis und Bibel,'* pp. 155–168. Ed. Karl-Wolfgang Tröger. Berlin: Evangelische Verlagsanstalt, 1980.

Trombley, Frank R. *Hellenic Religion and Christianization c. 370–529.* Religions in the Graeco-Roman World 115/1–2. Leiden: E. J. Brill, 1993.

Turner, H. E. W. *The Pattern of Christian Truth: A Study in the Relations between Orthodoxy and Heresy in the Early Church.* Bampton Lectures. London: A. R. Mowbray, 1954.

Turner, John D. *The Book of Thomas the Contender.* SBL Dissertation Series 23. Missoula, Mont.: Scholars Press, 1975.

———. "Sethian Gnosticism: A Literary History." In *Nag Hammadi, Gnosticism, and Early Christianity,* pp. 55–86. Ed. Charles W. Hedrick and Robert Hodgson, Jr. Peabody, Mass.: Hendricksen, 1986.

———. "Typologies of the Sethian Gnostic Treatises from Nag Hammadi." In *Les Textes de Nag Hammadi et le Problème de leur Classification. Actes du colloque tenu á Québec du 15 au 19 septembre 1993,* pp. 169–217. Ed. Louis Painchaud and Anne Pasquier. BCNH.SÉ 3. Quebec: Les Presses de l'Université Laval, 1995.

Turner, John D., and Ruth Majercik, eds. *Gnosticism and Later Platonism: Themes, Figures, and Texts.* SBL Symposium Series 12. Atlanta, Ga.: SBL, 2000.

Turner, Victor. "Myth and Symbol." In *International Encyclopedia of the Social Sciences,* vol. 10, pp. 576–582. Ed. David L. Sills. New York: Macmillan Company and the Free Press, 1968.

———. *The Ritual Process: Structure and Anti-Structure.* Ithaca, N.Y.: Cornell University Press, 1969.

Unger, Dominic J. With revisions by John J. Dillon. *St. Irenaeus of Lyons: Against the Heresies.* Ancient Christian Writers 55. New York: Paulist Press, 1992.

Usener, Hermann. "I Abhandlungen. Mythologie." *Archiv für Religionswissenschaft* 7 (1904), 6–32.

Vallée, Gérard. "Theological and Non-Theological Motives in Irenaeus' Refutation of the Gnostics." *Jewish and Christian Self-Definition,* vol. 1: *The Shaping of Christianity in the Second and Third Centuries.* Philadelphia: Fortress Press, 1980.

Van der Leeuw, Gerardus. *Religion in Essence and Manifestation.* Trans. J. E. Turner. New York: Harper and Row, 1963.

Van der Veer, Peter. "Syncretism, Multiculturalism and the Discourse of Tolerance." In *Syncretism/Anti-Syncretism: The Politics of Religious Synthesis,* pp. 196–211. Ed. Charles Stewart and Rosalind Shaw. London: Routledge, 1994.

van Unnik, Willem Cornelis. "Gnosis und Judentum." In *Gnosis. Festschrift für Hans Jonas,* pp. 65–86. Ed. Barbara Aland. Göttingen: Vandenhoeck and Ruprecht, 1978.

———. "The 'Gospel of Truth' and the New Testament." In *The Jung Codex: A Newly Recovered Gnostic Papyrus,* pp. 79–129. Ed. Frank L. Cross. London: A. R. Mowbray, 1955.

———. *Newly Discovered Gnostic Writings: A Preliminary Survey of the Nag Hammadi Find.* Studies in Biblical Theology 30. Naperville, Ill.: Alec R. Allenson Inc., 1960.

Veeser, H. Aram, ed. *The New Historicism.* New York: Routledge, 1989.

———, ed. *The New Historicism Reader.* New York: Routledge, 1994.

Voegelin, Eric. *Science, Politics and Gnosticism.* Washington, D.C.: Regnery Gateway, 1968.

Von Staden, Heinrich. "Hairesis and Heresy: The Case of the *hairesis iatrikai.*" In *Jewish and Christian Self-Definition.* Volume 3: *Self-Definition in the Greco-Roman World,* pp. 76–100. Ed. Ben F. Meyer and E. P. Sanders. Philadelphia: Fortress Press, 1982.

Waldstein, Michael. "Hans Jonas' Contruct 'Gnosticism': Analysis and Critique." *Journal of Early Christian Studies* 8.3 (2002), 341–372.

Wallis, Richard T., and Jay Bregman, eds. *Neoplatonism and Gnosticism.* Studies in Neoplatonism: Ancient and Modern 6. Albany: SUNY Press, 1992.

Waszink, J. H. "Tertullian's Principles and Methods of Exegesis." In *Early Christian Literature and the Classical Intellectual Tradition in Honorem Robert M. Grant,* pp. 17–31. Ed. William R. Schoedel and Robert L. Wilken. Théologie historique 54. Paris: Éditions Beauchesne, 1979.

Webster, Daniel. *Webster's New Collegiate Dictionary.* Springfield, Mass.: G. and C. Merriam Company, 1980.

Weiss, Johannes. *Jesus' Proclamation of the Kingdom of God.* Trans. from German

1st ed., 1892. With Introduction by R. H. Heirs and D. L. Holland. "Lives of Jesus" series. Philadelphia, Penn.: Fortress Press, 1971.

Weltin, E. G. *Athens and Jerusalem: An Interpretive Essay on Christianity and Classical Culture.* AAR Studies in Religion 49. Atlanta, Ga.: Scholars Press, 1987.

White, Hayden. *The Content of the Form: Narrative Discourse and Historical Representation.* Baltimore, Md.: Johns Hopkins University Press, 1987.

———. *Metahistory: The Historical Imagination in Nineteenth-Century Europe.* Baltimore, Md.: Johns Hopkins University Press, 1973.

———. "The Real, the True, the Figurative in the Human Sciences." *Profession* (1992), 15–17.

———. *Tropics of Discourse: Essays in Cultural Criticism.* Baltimore, Md.: Johns Hopkins University Press, 1978.

White, L. Michael. "Adolf Harnack and the 'Expansion' of Early Christianity: A Reappraisal of Social History." *Second Century* 5.2 (1985/86), 97–127.

Wilken, Robert L. *The Myth of Christian Beginnings: History's Impact on Belief.* Garden City, N.Y.: Doubleday and Co., 1971.

Williams, Michael A. *The Immovable Race: A Gnostic Designation and the Theme of Stability in Late Antiquity.* NHS XXIX. Leiden: E. J. Brill, 1985.

———. "The Nag Hammadi Library as 'Collection(s).'" In *Les Textes de Nag Hammadi et le Problème de leur Classification. Actes du colloque tenu á Québec du 15 au 19 septembre 1993,* pp. 3–50. Ed. Louis Painchaud and Anne Pasquier. Bibliothèque copte de Nag Hammadi Section "Études" 3. Quebec: Les Presses de l'Université Laval, 1995.

———. "Psyche's Voice: Gnostic Perceptions of Body and Soul." Manuscript of paper distributed for the Nag Hammadi and Gnosticism section/Platonism and Neoplatonism group joint session, AAR/SBL National Meetings, Kansas City, Mo., November 24, 1991.

———. *Rethinking "Gnosticism": An Argument for Dismantling a Dubious Category.* Princeton, N.J.: Princeton University Press, 1996.

Williams, Rowan. "Does It Make Sense to Speak of Pre-Nicene Orthodoxy?" In *The Making of Orthodoxy: Essays in Honor of Henry Chadwick,* pp. 1–23. Ed. R. Williams. Cambridge, England: Cambridge University Press, 1989.

Wilson, Robert McL. "From Gnosis to Gnosticism." In *Mélanges d'Histoire des Religions offert à Henri-Charles Puech,* pp. 423–436. Paris: Presses Universitaires de France, 1974.

———. "Gnosis and Gnosticism: The Messina Definition." In *Agathē elpis.*

*Studi Storico-Religiosi in Onore di Ugo Bianchi*, pp. 539–551. Ed. Guilia
Sfameni Gasparro. Rome: "L'Erma" di Bretschneider, 1994.

——. *Gnosis and the New Testament.* Philadelphia, Penn.: Fortress Press, 1968.

——. "Gnostic Origins Again." *VC* 11 (1957), 93–110.

——. "Jewish 'Gnosis' and Gnostic Origins: A Survey." *Hebrew Union College
Annual* 45 (1974), 179–189.

——. "Slippery Words, II: Gnosis, Gnostic, Gnosticism." *Expository Times* 89
(1978), 296–301.

——. "Valentinianism and the Gospel of Truth." In *The Rediscovery of
Gnosticism: Proceedings of the International Conference on Gnosticism at Yale,
New Haven, Connecticut, March 28–31, 1978*, vol. 1: *The School of Valen-
tinus*, pp. 133–141. Ed. Bentley Layton. SHR XLI. Leiden: E. J. Brill, 1981.

Wimbush, Vincent. *Renunciation towards Social Engineering (An Apologia for the
Study of Asceticism in Greco-Roman Antiquity).* Occasional Papers of the In-
stitute for Antiquity and Christianity 8. Claremont, Calif.: Claremont
Graduate School, 1986.

Wink, Walter. *Cracking the Gnostic Code: The Powers in Gnosticism.* SBL Mono-
graph Series 46. Atlanta, Ga.: Scholars Press, 1993.

Wintermute, O. "A Study of Gnostic Exegesis of the Old Testament." In *The
Use of the Old Testament in the New and Other Essays: Studies in Honor of
William Franklin Stinespring*, pp. 241–270. Ed. James Efird. Durham,
N.C.: Duke University Press, 1972.

Wisse, Frederik. "The Nag Hammadi Library and the Heresiologists." *VC* 25
(1971), 205–223.

——. "The 'Opponents' in the New Testament in Light of the Nag
Hammadi Writings." In *Colloque International sur les Textes de Nag
Hammadi (Quèbec, 22–25 août 1978)*, pp. 99–120. Ed. Bernard Barc.
BCNH.SÉ 1. Quebec: Les Presses de l'Université Laval; Louvain: Éditions
Peeters, 1981.

——. "Stalking Those Elusive Sethians." In *The Rediscovery of Gnosticism:
Proceedings of the International Conference on Gnosticism at Yale, New
Haven, Connecticut, March 28–31, 1978*, vol. 2: *Sethian Gnosticism*, pp. 563–
576. Ed. Bentley Layton SHR XLI. Leiden: E. J. Brill, 1981.

——. "The Use of Early Christian Literature as Evidence for Inner Diversity
and Conflict." In *Nag Hammadi, Gnosticism, and Early Christianity*,
pp. 177–190. Ed. Charles W. Hedrick and Robert Hodgon, Jr. Peabody,
Mass.: Hendrickson Publishers, 1986.

Yamauchi, Edwin. *Gnostic Ethics and Mandaean Origins.* Harvard Theological
Studies 24. Cambridge, Mass.: Harvard University Press, 1970.

———. *Pre-Christian Gnosticism*. Grand Rapids, Mich.: Eerdmans, 1973.

Yoder, John Howard. "Primitivism in the Radical Reformation: Strengths and Weaknesses." In *The Primitive Church in the Modern World*, pp. 74–97. Ed. Richard T. Hughes. Urbana and Chicago: University of Illinois Press, 1995.

Young, Robert J. C. *Colonial Desire: Hybridity in Theory, Culture and Race*. London: Routledge, 1995.

———. *White Mythologies: History Writing and the West*. London: Routledge, 1990.

Zukav, Gary. *The Dancing Wu Li Masters: An Overview of the New Physics*. New York: William Morrow and Co., 1979.

# Notes

## Introduction

1. See, for example, Williams, *Rethinking Gnosticism.*

2. "Jaldabaoth Reconsidered," in *Mélanges d'Histoire des Religions offert à Henri-Charles Puech* (Paris: Presses Universitaires de France, 1974), 405.

3. See M. Smith, "The History of the Term Gnostikos," 806–807.

4. Although it is not accurate to say that normative interests are equally the concern of every scholar—the work of Hans-Martin Schenke and Bentley Layton on defining Sethian or Classical Gnosticism are excellent counterexamples, among others—it is fair to say that attempts to define Gnosticism are pervaded by such interests. Thus the study of Gnosticism has been almost unavoidably entangled with various apologetic enterprises.

5. See, for example, Asad, *Genealogies of Religion.*

## 1. Why Is Gnosticism So Hard to Define?

An earlier draft of a portion of this chapter was read at the International SBL Meetings in Helsinki and Lahti, Finland, in 1999.

1. See Chadwick, *The Early Church,* 32–41. For further general discussion of Gnosticism and contemporary culture, see Filoramo, "Gnosis and Modern Culture" (in *A History of Gnosticism,* xiii–xviii); R. Smith, "Afterword: The Modern Relevance of Gnosticism"; Perkins, "Epilogue: Gnosis and the Modern Spirit" (*The Gnostic Dialogue,* 205–217); and Segal, *The Allure of Gnosticism.*

2. See Conze, "Buddhism and Gnosticism"; Kenneth O'Neill, "Parallels to Gnosticism in Pure Land Buddhism" (in Segal, *The Allure of Gnosticism,* 190–198); Hans Jonas, "Epilogue: Gnosticism, Existentialism, and Nihilism" (in *The Gnostic Religion,* 320–340); Voeglin, *Science, Politics and Gnosticism.*

3. See a selection of Jung's works in Segal, ed., *The Gnostic Jung.*

4. Brooks, "Walter Percy and Modern Gnosticism." See the discussion in Perkins, *The Gnostic Dialogue,* 207–211.

5. See Buckley, "With the Mandaeans in Iran" and *The Mandaeans;* Lupieri, *The Mandaeans,* 3–5.

6. See R. Smith, "The Revival of Ancient Gnosis," and the magazine *Gnosis.*

7. See the summary discussion of Wilson, "Slippery Words."

8. Michael Williams, for example, has suggested "biblical demiurgical" (*Rethinking Gnosticism,* 265). While Williams discusses at length several significant ways in which the category is problematic, he does not address the question of why and how it became so problematic, and why people continue to use it even when the problems are widely recognized.

9. I thank Karen Torjesen for this perceptive question.

10. See Layton, "Prolegomena," 348–349.

11. The other phenomena identified by contemporary church historians as ancient heresies are treated differently from these two in that scholars regard them as rather less fundamental errors. Casey, for example, suggests that it is important to distinguish between those kinds of heresy that "would have altered the texture but not the structure of Christian thought" (such as Sabellianism, Donatism, or Arianism) from those that "would have meant a complete change in the edifice" (among which he includes Marcionism, Valentinianism, and Manichaeanism). See Casey, "The Study of Gnosticism," 58.

12. Personal correspondence, March 7, 2002.

13. Jonathan Z. Smith, *Map Is Not Territory,* 151, n. 12.

14. See Rudolph, "Das Problem einer Soziologie."

15. For an excellent summary of the available information, see Layton, *The Gnostic Scriptures,* especially the essays entitled "Historical Introduction" at the beginning of each section.

16. For example, the condemnation of Valentinus, Basilides, Isidore, and the Simonians (*TestTruth* 56.2–5; 57.6–8; 58.2–3); the possible ascription of the *GosTruth* to Valentinus (see Irenaeus, *AgHer* 3.11.9; van Unnik "The 'Gospel of Truth' and the New Testament," 90–97); or dates and names from the cartonnage (papyrus used to stiffen the leather covers), which seem to indicate a connection of at least some of the Nag Hammadi codices (I, Vi, VII, and XI) to the local Pachomian monastery (see Barns et al., *Greek and Coptic Papyri,* 11; Goehring, *Ascetics, Society and the Desert,* 173–179).

17. V. Turner, "Myth and Symbol," 577.

18. Turner stresses that myth offers a state of liminality that can be "regarded as a time and place of withdrawal from normal modes of social action," so that "it

can be seen as potentially a period of scrutinization of the central values and axioms of the culture in which it occurs." V. Turner, *The Ritual Process,* 167.

19. V. Turner notes, for example, that "by making the low high and the high low, they (rituals of status reversal) reaffirm the hierarchical principle. By making the low mimic (often to the point of caricature) the behavior of the high, and by restraining the initiatives of the proud, they underline the reasonableness of everyday culturally predictable behavior between the various estates of society" (*The Ritual Process,* 176). This suggestion leads us to ask how appropriate it is to assume that the "reversals" in *ApJohn's* myth (for example, of the relative status of gods and humans) should be seen as impiety rather than as an affirmation of society's values accompanied by a certain social critique of power relations (that is, "restraining the initiatives of the proud").

20. For a brief discussion of the philosophical issues involved in definition, see Abelson, "Definition," 314–324; on essentialism, 314–317.

21. See Abelson, "Definition," 316.

22. Ibid., 318.

23. Layton, "Prolegomena," 340–341. In Layton's words: "'Gnosticism' thus means an inductive category based on these data alone" (343).

24. See Abelson, "Definition," 321.

25. See, for example, Layton's grouping of primary sources in *The Gnostic Scriptures* into "Classic Gnostic Scripture" (Sethianism), "Valentinus" and "The School of Valentinus," "The School of St. Thomas," and "Other Early Currents" (including Basilides and the Hermetic Corpus).

26. Abelson, "Definition," 322. Abelson lists the rules of thumb generally employed in definition:

> 1) A definition should give the essence or nature of the thing defined, rather than its accidental properties.
> 2) A definition should give the genus and differentia of the thing defined.
> 3) One should not define by synonyms.
> 4) A definition should be concise.
> 5) One should not define by metaphors.
> 6) One should not define by negative terms or by correlative terms (e.g., one should not define north as opposite of south, or parent as a person with one or more children). (Abelson, "Definition," 322)

See Abelson's critique of these "rules of thumb," 322–323.

27. Provisionality points to the quality of a definition as never entirely capable of representing a phenomenon in absolute (let alone objective) terms. Every definition assumes, reproduces, and is constituted by a position from which it is

addressed. Even objectivity assumes such a positionality in the way it posits the relation of subject and object. See Bourdieu, *The Logic of Practice,* 30–41.

28. *Kyrios Christos,* 22.

29. In Bousset's words, the professionals are "those whose calling it is" (*Kyrios Christos,* 22); see the critique of Schüssler Fiorenza, who notes that scholarly fraternities "are not just scholarly investigative communities but also authoritative communities. They possess the power to ostracize or to embrace, to foster or to restrict membership, to recognize and to define what 'true scholarship' entails" (*Rhetoric and Ethic,* 22). Although Schüssler Fiorenza is here referring to the Society of Biblical Literature, her comment applies more broadly to the profession of academic Biblical studies, which admits students, grants degrees, defines academic positions, and controls hiring, promotion, and tenure.

30. Again following Abelson, "Definition," 322.

31. Here I am thinking in dialogue with Bourdieu. He wrote: "objectivist discourse tends to constitute the model constructed to account for practices as a power really capable of determining them" (see *The Logic of Practice,* 36–37).

32. See, for example, Chadwick, *The Early Church,* 41–45; Lebreton and Zeiller, *Heresy and Orthodoxy,* chap. 2, "The Catholic Reaction."

33. Needless to say, given the ongoing controversy over who is able to say what normative Christianity is and what its content and forms are, the structures of heretical discourse are present in many places where actual consideration of Gnosticism is not an issue. Yet an analysis of the discourse of defining Gnosticism nonetheless exposes structures common to all discussions of heresy in Christianity, as will be shown in Chapter 2.

## 2. Gnosticism as Heresy

The epigraph to this chapter is from Trinh, *Woman Native, Other,* 61, my emphasis.

1. Although Justin Martyr's book against heresy is lost, scholars are in general agreement that Justin was pivotal in the development of heresiological discourse (see Le Boulluec, *La notion d'hérésie,* 35–36). There are other persons of note as well, but these are the foremost figures in setting the agenda for the shape of the discourse of Christian heresiology. For an excellent introductory discussion of these persons and their primary works, see Rudolph, *Gnosis,* 10–25. The polemicists preserved theological and mythic materials, including a collection of excerpts from the writings of the Valentinian Theodotus, Justin's *Baruch,* and a portion of a text with literary connections to the Sethian *ApJohn;* exegetical materials, such as Ptolemy's fascinating *EpFlora,* which details a Valentinian approach

to Biblical exegesis; and cultic materials, like the Naassene Hymn. Le Boulluec points out the relationship between the genre of the treatise against heresy and the doxographical work of ancient authors, such as Diogenes Laertius (*La notion d'hérésie*, 40).

2. Le Boulluec, *La notion d'hérésie*, 15–16, also notes the similarities of the discursive themes and strategies employed by Justin Martyr in his refutation of heresy, his treatise against Trypho the Jew, and his two apologies.

3. Le Boulluec has already given us a splendid study of the Christian discourse on heresy for the early period. See *La notion d'hérésie*.

4. See ibid., 18–19.

5. Le Boulluec suggests that the strategies developed in conflict with Jews and Greeks were "imitated and transposed" to deal with the troubles provoked by internal differences (*La notion d'hérésie*, 16).

6. See, for example, Dawson, *Allegorical Readers*. It should be noted that the precise contours of Scripture had not yet been set (see McDonald, *The Formation of the Christian Biblical Canon*).

7. In discussing the Alexandrian medical literature, Heinrich von Staden notes that "the paucity of testimonia concerning the content of the Alexandrian *hairesis* literature unfortunately leaves us only vaguely informed about what qualifies a group for the label *hairesis* or what qualifies an individual for membership in a *hairesis*. But the evidence suggests that a group with fairly coherent and distinctive theories, with an acknowledged founder (*hairesi-arches*), and with publicly identifiable leaders who articulate (a) their rejection of rival theories through theoretically founded polemics, as well as (b) their own systematic alternatives, would qualify as a *hairesis*. Unanimity on *all* doctrinal questions is not a requirement . . . and neither a single geographical centre nor any institutional organization is necessarily implied by this use of *hairesis*" ("Hairesis and Heresy," 79–80). Alain Le Boulluec has brilliantly demonstrated that the Christian concept of heresy developed from ancient notions and genres. Ancient writers employed the term, and so they described the variety of ancient philosophical teachings in terms of *haireseis* (pl.). They used an essentially biographical genre to portray the succession of the philosophers, offering doxographical information, including anecdotes and apophthegms, to describe their teachings (see *La notion d'hérésie*, 40–41).

8. Le Boulluec, *La notion d'hérésie*, 37. See also von Staden, "Hairesis and Heresy," 81.

9. As J. Z. Smith puts it: "Meaning is made possible by difference. Yet thought seeks to bring together what thought necessarily takes apart by means of a dynamic process of disassemblage and reassemblage which results in an object

no longer natural but rather social, no longer factual but rather intellectual. Relations are discovered and reconstituted through projects of differentiation" ("Differential Equations," 14). I add the notion of politics to Smith's statement in order to include consideration of the power dynamics of social relations more generally.

10. From Trinh, *Woman, Native, Other,* 61. Other postcolonial theorists have noted the ambiguity of such identity projects; see Bhabha, *The Location of Culture,* 1–18.

11. J. Z. Smith, "Differential Equations," 13, 14.

12. If not by that name, by appeal to the Christ figure as Lord, Savior, or Revealer.

13. Cited in J. Z. Smith, "Differential Equations," 3.

14. See Chadwick, *The Early Church,* 41–45.

15. Contra Helleman ("Epilogue," 451); see also R. Williams, "Does It Make Sense to Speak of Pre-Nicene Orthodoxy?" In discussing the work of Walter Bauer, Le Boulluec suggests avoiding the terms "orthodoxy" and "heresy" and speaking instead of "heresiological representation" because "this is the means of avoiding reviving the illusion of an irreducible priority of orthodoxy" (*La notion d'hérésie,* 19). But then he goes on to say: "This is not to deny that the forms susceptible of furnishing the basis of an orthodoxy existed quite fully in Christianity. The proposal is simply to grasp a reckoning of the great variety of pretensions to orthodoxy and of searching in the heresiological texts for the means of affirming one of them to the exclusion of all others" (*La notion d'hérésie,* 20). He seems to be suggesting, with some ambivalence, that one needs to keep open the possibility that those forms of Christianity labeled as "heretical" might also be drawing upon early forms for their development; that is, that orthodoxy may not uniquely be able to claim an originality that other types of Christianity could not also claim.

16. Even in writings in which the polemicists attempt to report the views of their opponents accurately, those views have been absorbed into alternative frameworks that may shift (distort) their meaning. This is true of any act of appropriation to a new context. My aim here is not to malign the polemicists but to note that their practices limit what we can hope to learn about the views of those they opposed.

17. Hippolytus (*Ref* VI, 37) says, for example, that the Marcosians disagreed with Irenaeus' description of their practices.

18. Many examples of this problem can be found by comparing the work of the polemicists with the new discoveries. For example, the polemicists attacked their opponents as elitist determinists because the opponents purportedly said

that the basis for salvation lies in the spiritual nature of humanity. From the polemicists' perspective, this position undermines the doctrine of divine grace in the face of human sin. But texts such as *ApJohn* do not deny the need to turn away from sin and seek the power of the spirit in order to gain salvation; indeed, the teaching about humanity's spiritual nature is aimed to offer hope, not excuse immorality.

19. See Lipsius, *Die Quellen,* 191–225; M. Smith, "The History of the Term Gnostikos"; McGuire, *Valentinus and the "Gnostike Haeresis,"* and "Valentinus and the *gnostikê haeresis*"; Layton, *The Gnostic Scriptures,* 5–214, and especially "Prolegomena."

20. Reported by Eusebius, *EcclHist* V, 7; see *AgHer* II, Preface. Compare I Tim. 6:20. Irenaeus' work is more commonly known as *Against the Heresies.*

21. See, for example, *GosTruth.*

22. See especially the discussion of Koester, *Ancient Christian Gospels,* 31–48, esp. 32, and "La Tradition apostolique." Davids concludes that Ignatius considered everyone who did not follow the bishop to be a heretic (a term Ignatius did not use) by that fact alone (see "Irrtum und Häresie," 187); contrast *GosMary* (see King, *The Gospel of Mary*).

23. *PresHer* 17–19 (trans. Greenslade, *Early Latin Theology,* 42–43).

24. See, for example, the approach of the Valentinian Justin in his *EpFlora* (trans. in Layton, *Gnostic Scriptures,* 308–315).

25. *PresHer* 17 (trans. Greenslade, *Early Latin Theology,* 42).

26. See MacDonald, *The Formation of the Christian Biblical Canon.*

27. Tertullian, *PresHer* 3 (trans. Greenslade, *Early Latin Theology,* 32). Tertullian's remark is a bit sarcastic in that he argues that they cannot really be the wisest, since "if heresy could pervert them, they cannot be counted wise or faithful or experienced." Yet it would seem that others to whom Tertullian writes considered them wise.

28. See *PresHer* 13; Counryman, "Tertullian and the Regula Fidei"; Tiessen, "Gnosticism as Heresy."

29. *PresHer* 14 (trans. Greenslade, *Early Latin Theology,* 40).

30. See the discussion of Le Boulluec, *La notion d'hérésie,* esp. 21–112; Perkins, "Irenaeus and the Gnostics"; Standaert, "'Evangelium Veritatis.'"

31. *AgHer,* Preface 2 (trans. Unger, *St. Irenaeus of Lyons,* 22). This is a standard approach in ancient rhetoric; see Perkins, "Irenaeus and the Gnostics," 195. See also *AgHer* I, 31, 3, where Irenaeus writes: "Indeed, the very manifestation of their doctrine is a victory against them" (trans. Unger, *St. Irenaeus of Lyons,* 103).

32. See Perkins, "Irenaeus and the Gnostics"; Vallée, "Theological and Non-Theological Motives in Irenaeus' Refutation of the Gnostics."

33. See *AgHer* I, 9–11, 22; Clement of Alexandria, *Strom* 7.108.1–2.

34. M. Williams, *Rethinking "Gnosticism,"* 34–35, provides a table listing the groups categorized as heresies by Irenaeus, Hippolytus, Pseudo-Tertullian, and Epiphanius.

35. For more on the notion that heresy belongs to the Devil and implies moving away from an originally pure tradition, see Davids, "Irrtum und Häresie."

36. So, too, Epiphanius' list of heresies was extended to eighty groups(!) in order to associate these heretics allegorically with the eighty concubines in the Song of Songs 6:8 (see M. Williams, *Rethinking "Gnosticism,"* 40).

37. In making this argument, Irenaeus incorporated a genealogy from Justin Martyr's lost work against all the heresies, or at least a later version of it. In *Apol* 26, Justin Martyr refers to a treatise he composed "against all heresies which have arisen" (trans. Barnard, *St. Justin Martyr,* 41). He supplies an ordering of heretics from Simon Magus similar to that of Irenaeus, *AgHer.* For further discussion, see Wisse, "The Nag Hammadi Library," 213–215 (who notes that this suggestion was first made by R. A. Lipsius in 1965); Perkins, "Irenaeus and the Gnostics," 197–198; Desjardins, "Bauer and Beyond," 78–79. In *Le notion d'hérésie,* 40–41, Le Boulluec discusses the development of the Christian genealogy of heresy out of Hellenistic treatises on the succession of the philosophers.

38. See Buell, *Making Christians,* 50–106. This is an important and sophisticated study on the use of metaphors of procreation, genealogy, and kinship to naturalize certain relations and to fight against opponents.

39. See the discussion of philosophical *haireseis* in Le Boulluec, *Le notion d'hérésie,* 40–41. Irenaeus talks about the heretics as having the same "mothers and fathers and ancestors" (*AgHer* I, 31, 3). For tree and fruit, see *AgHer* I, 22, 2. In *AgHer* I, 30, 15, Irenaeus states that the Valentinian school was "generated like the Lernaean serpent, a wild beast with many heads" (trans. Unger, *St. Irenaeus of Lyons,* 102).

40. See Wisse, "The Nag Hammadi Library," esp. 208–209.

41. As Le Boulluec makes clear (*Le notion d'hérésie,* 45–47), in ancient terminology, *haireseis* indicated a certain doctrinal coherence or tendency, but it did not necessarily imply an organization or a distinct group (such as a school).

42. The tactic most decisive for contemporary discussions of difference was linking uniformity of belief with group cohesion. Difference by definition implied social divisiveness. We encounter this discursive operation again in modern scholarship whenever differences in theological views are used to imply the existence of distinct social groups. That is to say, too often the recognition of early Christian multiformity has led scholars to posit "communities in conflict." The mere fact of theological difference is not, however, sufficient to posit a conflict

relationship (see, for example, Riley's contention that the communities of John and Thomas were in conflict [*Resurrection Reconsidered*] and the rejoinder of Dunderberg, "John and Thomas in Conflict?"). After all, we know that most groups are able to maintain a range of ideological differences without division; the very existence of such differences should not lead us to assume a sociological break.

43. See Irenaeus, *AgHer* II, 14, 2–6; Tertullian, *PresHer* 8, 5; and also Hippolytus, *Ref* I, intro. 11. These charges, too, were flying in all directions; Lieu (*Manichaeism*, 41–42), for example, says that Paul's epistles were considered by some to be heretical because of their adherence to Greek doctrines.

44. Shaw and Stewart, "Introduction," 7, 14.

45. Ibid., 1.

46. The ambivalence of this argument was felt rather deeply by Clement of Alexandria, who argued that a proper use of philosophy would indeed uphold the true faith. See the elegant discussion of Le Boulluec, *La notion d'hérésie*, vol. 2, chap. 4.

47. So, too, Hippolytus, *Ref* I, Preface 8–9, argued that the heresies derived from Greek philosophy, the mystery cults, or astrology.

48. *PresHer* 40. Quote from *PresHer* 7 (Greenslade, *Early Latin Theology*, 35, slightly modified).

49. No doubt Tertullian is relying here on the tradition from the Acts of the Apostles that Paul taught in Athens. Critical-historical scholars agree that it was the author of the Acts, not Paul, who wrote the speech in chapter 17:22–31.

50. *PresHer* 7 (Greenslade, *Early Latin Theology*, 36).

51. See, for example, Waszink, "Tertullian's Principles and Methods of Exegesis"; Helleman, "Tertullian on Athens and Jerusalem"; Guerra, "Polemical Christianity," 113–114.

52. See *PresHer* 13, 20–21, 32.

53. *PresHer* 20, 31, 35 (Greenslade, *Early Latin Theology*, 43–44, 52, 56).

54. Ibid., 34 (Greenslade, *Early Latin Theology*, 55–56).

55. As, for example, the plot of Eusebius' *Ecclesiastical History*.

56. A major issue was precisely where to locate the original revelation: in Christ's death and resurrection (Paul), in the baptism of Jesus (Gospel of Mark), in the incarnation (Irenaeus), in the pre-existent Logos (Gospel of John), in creation (*GosThom*); in the kerygma, in the gospel narrative, in prophetic speech or post-resurrection appearances, in the apostolic teaching, in the rule of faith, in creed, in canon, and so on.

57. Although constant, this theme could be strategically figured in a variety of ways, for example, in claiming that the divine is the creative source of everything

that exists, or the model for everything that came into being, or merely the locus of power and immortality.

58. Geertz, "The World in Pieces," 109.

59. See Asad, *Genealogies of Religion.*

60. One thinks, for example, of the militant Christian Identity Movement, or the ways in which U.S. law and society reflect the heritage of Protestantism.

61. If we want to understand how any particular group or self-identity is produced, we have to ask whether and how various social constructions (such as political roles, economic conditions, social status, ethnicity, spheres of activity, division of space and time, or ritual activity) intersect in forming, defining, and bounding the religious self. See, for example, Barth's notions of complex, pluralistic societies (*Cosmologies in the Making;* "The Analysis of Culture in Complex Societies"; "Enduring and Emerging Issues in the Analysis of Ethnicity"; "Problems in Conceptualizing Cultural Pluralism").

62. See Buell, *Making Christians;* "Race and Universalism in Early Christianity"; and "Rethinking the Relevance of Race."

63. See Harnack's treatment of the origins and development of the designation "third race," in *Mission and Expansion of Christianity,* 240–278. In my terms, Harnack's chapter treats the development of normative Christian identity discourse; see also Buell, "Rethinking the Relevance of Race."

64. Both gender and class, however, had to be ideologically Christianized, for example, by using gender metaphors to characterize ascetic behavior (females becoming male) or calling believers "slaves of Christ." Nonetheless, Christian understandings of gender and class remained fairly stable and indistinguishable from those of others around them.

65. For more on Jewish constructions of identity, see J. Z. Smith, "Fences and Neighbors"; and Cohen, *The Beginnings of Jewishness.* Historians of Judaism in antiquity constantly stress the varied character of the Judaisms at that time, but often to little avail. For a recent discussion that criticizes essentializations and presents an alternative, see Horsley, *Archaeology, History and Society in Galilee,* esp. 63–64, 139–140, 182.

66. See Boyarin, *Dying for God,* 1–21. As Boyarin perceptively points out, "The social and cultural processes by which Christian orthodoxy constituted itself as such over-against the so-called heresies are structurally very similar to the processes through which Jewish orthodoxy (rabbinic Judaism) constituted itself and its authority over-against early Christianity." As an example, he notes that "the very distinctness of Judaism has been articulated by Jews as precisely its distance from a 'syncretistic' Christianity whose defining feature is that it is somehow a composite of Judaism and Hellenism" (p. 11).

67. See Rom 9–11; Galatians; Hodge, "'If Sons, Then Heirs.'"

68. See Matt 5:17–20.

69. For more on the problematic designation "Jewish-Christianity," see Taylor, "The Phenomenon of Jewish-Christianity," especially 319–320, where she notes that in third-century Egypt, Origen of Alexandria refers to people who attend the synagogue on Saturday and the Church on Sunday (*Homily on Leviticus* 5.8); in Syria, Ephrem notes Christians who shared the Passover supper with Jews (*Hymn* 19); and in the fourth century, John Chrysostom wrote eight homilies to discourage Christians from celebrating the Jewish festivals.

70. I want to thank Daniel Boyarin for his extraordinarily helpful comments on an earlier version of this manuscript. Our conversation emphasized how fascinating for the issues of identity formation is the claim that "the covenant if both theirs and ours."

71. *EpBarn* 6.6–8 (trans. Lake, *The Apostolic Fathers* I, 351, my emphasis), 14.1 (ibid., 391).

72. *Didache* 8.1 (trans. Lake, *The Apostolic Fathers* I, 321).

73. In contrast to the author of *EpBarn,* Justin did not think that following the law was wrong in itself. He conceded that those who followed Jewish practices, such as circumcision and Sabbath observance, could still be saved, but only if they accepted Christ and did not teach Gentiles that such practices were necessary for salvation (see *DialTrypho* 47; and also the nuanced discussion of Buell in "Rethinking the Relevance of Race").

74. See *DialTrypho* 137.

75. Other apologists, such as Athenagoras, would also emphasize the superior character of the Christian way of life. Apparently this kind of argument had some effect, for people like the famous physician Galen praised Christians for their moral restraint and courage (see Benko, *Pagan Rome and the Early Christians,* 140–142).

76. See L. Feldman, *Jew and Gentile in the Ancient World.*

77. Taylor, "The Phenomenon of Early Jewish-Christianity," 318, 319.

78. In his *EpPhil* 3 and 8.2 (cited by Taylor, "The Phenomenon of Early Jewish-Christianity," 318).

79. *EpBarn* 3.3; *EpBarn* 10.9 (trans. Lake, *The Apostolic Fathers* I, 377).

80. *EpBarn* 5.1 (trans. Lake, *The Apostolic Fathers* I, 355).

81. For further discussion of Sethian Gnosticism, see below 156–158.

82. Cited in Epiphanius, *Against Heresies* 33.3.1–33.7.10.

83. Or in the case of *EpBarn,* how they were said to read them. In this case, of course, where *EpBarn* caricatures Jewish Scriptural interpretations, beliefs, and practices, negating Judaism meant first constructing the Judaism *EpBarn* negated

as part of the strategy of hiding the processes of appropriation. Moreover, it is not always clear that Christians had more than superficial knowledge of Jewish beliefs, practices, and interpretations. That knowledge varied considerably, from almost total ignorance to considerable familiarity. Among educated Christians, there was a much higher degree of familiarity with works available in Greek (such as the Septuagint, Philo, and Josephus) than with Hebrew works.

84. Gal 2.11–14; Irenaeus, *AgHer* III, 12, 6. Irenaeus defends the apostles against this charge by recourse to his own formulation of apostolic tradition and authority.

85. *TestTruth* 29,9–15 (trans. Giverson and Pearson, in Robinson, *Nag Hammadi Library,* 449–550). See also *ApocPeter,* 79,22–30.

86. See Fox, *Pagans and Christians,* 30–31. Fox argues for a local approach to studying "paganism" (see *Pagans and Christians,* 33). Yet while there were significant variations locally, there was also a good deal of overlap and acculturation (see, for example, MacMullen, *Paganism,* 112–130). Scholars of ancient religion have frequently used the term "syncretism" to describe the religious interactions of cultural groups around the Mediterranean in this period (from Alexander through the Roman imperial period). This pattern fits well into Christian antisyncretistic discourse, insofar as it may allow these varied traditions to be treated more easily as a whole, and also because the pejorative use of the term "syncretism" is unproblematic for Christian self-definition in relation to paganism. The phenomenon of religious interaction in the ancient Mediterranean has been studied without Christian antisyncretistic discourse (see, for example, Price, *Rituals and Power*).

87. See the discussion of Harnack, *Mission and Expansion,* 266–278; and now the brilliant study of Buell, "Rethinking the Relevance of Race." Aristides may have referred to four groups.

88. Harnack, *Mission and Expansion,* 250.

89. Arthur Darby Nock expressed this point clearly in relationship to the problem of conversion: "Genuine conversion to paganism will appear in our inquiry only when Christianity had become so powerful that its rival was, so to speak, made an entity by opposition and contrast" (*Conversion,* 15). See now Frankfurter, *Religion in Roman Egypt.*

90. An excellent study is Weltin, *Athens and Jerusalem.*

91. Or as Weltin puts it: "Even though young Christianity's converts after 150 were predominantly 'Greek,' the new religion was quite choosy in its encounter with contemporary pagan values and attitudes: it elected in the long run to adopt some, to compromise with some, and to reject some" (*Athens and Jerusalem,* 1).

92. See the summary of Helleman, "Epilogue," 469.

93. The *preparatio evangelica* motif could also be expressed in political terms; note, for example, Origen: "In the days of Jesus, righteousness arose and fullness of peace, beginning with his birth. God prepared the nations for his teaching, by causing the Roman emperor to rule over all the world; there was no longer to be a plurality of kingdoms, else would the nations have been strangers to one another, and so the apostles would have found it harder to carry out the task laid on them by Jesus, when he said, 'Go and teach all nations'" (*Contra Celsum* II, 30, trans. Chadwick).

94. See, for example, Otto, *The Idea of the Holy.*

95. For an interesting comparative example from among the Nag Hammadi literature, see *Eugnostos* III, 70.2–71.1; *SophJesChr* III, 92.6–93.8.

96. *A Plea* 7 (trans. Richardson, *Early Christian Fathers,* 306–307).

97. See Harnack, *Mission and Expansion,* 255–256.

98. Helleman, "Epilogue," 471. See also Origen, *Homily on Leviticus* 7:6; Augustine, *De doctrina christiana* II, 40, 60; Frizzell, "Spoils from Egypt."

99. See, for example, Markus's discussion of the transformation of Christianity in the fourth to sixth centuries, in which new distinctions had to be made between "genuine survivals of the old religion—which would need extirpation—and secularized or de-sacralised practices surviving as remnants cut off from their original religious roots—which could be tolerated" (*The End of Ancient Christianity,* 2). Trombley, *Hellenic Religion and Christianization,* takes up similar issues with a broader range of material, treating this transformation as a process of "Christianization." As Markus notes, determining what is culture (and therefore could be appropriated or tolerated) and what is religion (and therefore has to be excluded) is a problem that continues, and is especially prominent for missionary enterprises. For a contemporary example, see Mosse, "The Politics of Religious Synthesis."

100. See, for example, MacRae, "Why the Church Rejected Gnosticism." MacRae offers three primary reasons: libertine behavior, rejection of the continuity between God the creator and salvation history, and docetic Christology.

101. Wilson, for example, recognized quite clearly that part of the problem of defining Gnosticism, and especially of determining its relationship to the New Testament, lies in the anachronistic association of Gnosticism and related terms with heresy. Yet he limited the anachronism to the first and early second centuries and otherwise accepts the normative historical portrait of Gnosticism as a Christian heresy (see "Slippery Words," 299–300). It is precisely the degree to which normative categories are ever adequate for a historical reconstruction of the phenomena (in contrast to normative theological discussion) that requires examination.

### 3. Adolf von Harnack

1. Citations here are from the English translation (*The History of Dogma*) made from the third German edition of 1893. Harnack, *History of Dogma* I, 226, 230.

2. Note that Harnack's medical metaphor, "acute," naturalizes the diagnosis of heresy as a disease. Later, scholars describe Gnosticism as a parasite.

3. *PresHer* 7 (trans. Greenslade, *Early Latin Theology,* 35).

4. Harnack, *History of Dogma,* I, 48, n. 1.

5. Ibid.

6. Harnack, *What Is Christianity?*, 200.

7. It is important here to realize the crucial distinction between "background" and "situatedness." The former term allows the possibility that a phenomenon can remain *essentially* untouched by its historical conditions; background is only the scenery against which the main objects are set in relief. "Situatedness" implies a theoretical position denying the possibility of separating a phenomenon from its historical conditions.

8. Harnack, *What Is Christianity?*, 8.

9. Ibid., 51. For further discussion of the kingdom, see ibid., 62. He finds the second idea so crucial that he claims the whole of Jesus' message can be reduced to it (see ibid., 63, 68). Harnack elaborates what he means by the "higher righteousness" in four points in ibid., 71–73.

10. Harnack, *What Is Christianity?*, 55–56.

11. See Weiss, *Jesus' Proclamation of the Kingdom of God;* and Schweitzer, *The Mystery of the Kingdom of God.*

12. Harnack, *What Is Christianity?*, 54, 56.

13. One of Bultmann's sharpest criticisms of Harnack was the ease with which he dispensed with eschatology as a central feature of Jesus' teaching (see his introduction to *What Is Christianity?*, x–xii). But Harnack's point is now yet again raised by scholars from the Jesus Seminar, among others, who have been arguing that historical analysis indicates that the apocalyptic eschatology in the canonical Gospels is a secondary layer of the historical Jesus tradition, that is, that Jesus did not himself teach the imminent end of the world and the future coming of the kingdom. So this issue is still a point of lively debate. See Borg, "A Temperate Case for a Non-Eschatological Jesus"; Miller, *The Apocalyptic Jesus.*

14. Harnack, *What Is Christianity?*, 191. An adequate evaluation of Harnack's writing would involve coming to terms with the significant inadequacies of his historical understanding of Judaism and the repugnance of his anti-Jewish rhetoric. Historicizing Harnack's work would further include an analysis of the atti-

tudes toward Jews and Judaism in Germany at the turn of the century and his relationship to the conditions of the time. One sees such attitudes in his predecessors; Ernst Renan, for example, wrote: "The thought of Jesus stemmed from a high conception of divinity, which, owing nothing to Judaism, was in its entirety a creation of his great soul . . . Fundamentally there was nothing Jewish about Jesus" (from the notebooks of Renan; cited in Olender, *The Languages of Paradise*, 69).

It should also be noted that Harnack's complete severance of the essence of Christianity from Judaism did not go without criticism, even in his own day. No less a figure than the great Catholic modernist Alfred Loisy took Harnack to task quite severely in *L'Evangile et l'eglise* (1904). He noted, for example, that "the essential distinction between religions lies in their differences, but it is not solely of their differences that they are constituted. It is, therefore, in the highest degree arbitrary to decide that Christianity in its essence must be all that the gospel has not borrowed of Judaism, as if all that the gospel has retained of the Jewish tradition must be necessarily of secondary value" (*The Gospel and the Church*, 10). He goes on to criticize the very suggestion that an "essence of Christianity" can be separated from the tradition: "Whatever we think, theologically, of tradition, whether we trust it or regard it with suspicion, we know Christ only by the tradition, across the tradition, and in the tradition of the primitive Christians. This is as much as to say that Christ is inseparable from His work, and that the attempt to define the essence of Christianity according to the pure gospel of Jesus, apart from tradition, cannot succeed" (*The Gospel and the Church*, 13). He does not reject the idea that Christianity has an essence, but insists that it can only be found in the tradition itself: "the principal features of primitive Christianity are recognizable throughout their development" (18). Or again: "The essence of Christianity is constituted by the general features of this figure, the elements of this life and their characteristic properties; and this essence is unchangeable, like that of a living being, which remains the same while it lives, and to the extent to which it lives. The historian will find that the essence of Christianity has been more or less preserved in the different Christian communions: he will not expect this essence to have been absolutely and definitely realized at any point of past centuries; he will believe that it has been realized more or less perfectly from the beginning, and that it will continue to be realized thus more and more, so long as Christianity shall endure" (18–19). The basic issue here is where the essence of Christianity is located: in the distinctive teaching of Jesus (Harnack) or in the tradition of the Church (Loisy).

Although Loisy defends a Jewish Jesus and the inseparability of Jesus and his teaching from Judaism, it cannot be said that his view of Judaism was more adequate or more acceptable than that of Harnack. Like Harnack, he caricatured Judaism as "nationalistic" and "particularistic," and he saw the fulfillment of Judaism in Christianity (see 10–11). An adequate discussion of Judaism, and hence of the relation to Christianity, is not to be found in these works. For discussion of the relationship of Christianity to history, see *What Is Christianity?*, xiii, 13–14, 54, 124, 129–130, 149, 187, 191.

15. Harnack takes up this topic in response to critics, who he says claim: "The Gospel . . . is a great and sublime thing and it has certainly been a saving power in history, but it is indissolubly connected with an antiquated view of the world and history; and, therefore, although it be painful to say so, and we have nothing better to put in its place, it has lost its validity and can have no further significance for us." To this Harnack responds: "I have tried to show what the essential elements in the Gospel are, and these elements are 'timeless.' Not only are they so; but the [one] to whom the Gospel addresses itself is also 'timeless,' that is to say, it is the [one] who, in spite of all progress and development, never changes in his inmost constitution and in his fundamental relations with the external world. Since that is so, this Gospel remains in force, then, for us too" (*What Is Christianity?*, 149). Here the stability of "human nature" makes possible a continued significance, indeed the same significance, to the Gospel across two millennia from antiquity to the twenty-first century.

One must, however, read this "timeless man" with a hermeneutic of suspicion. No doubt Harnack intended the term to be used inclusively, but contemporary feminist, womanist, and postcolonial scholarship has made it clear that the construction of "universal man" is far from inclusive, not only in terms of gender, but also in terms of sexuality, race, and class.

16. On "Late Judaism," see Harnack, *History of Dogma*, I, 48, n. 1; quote is from Harnack, *What Is Christianity?*, 200.

17. For an insightful consideration of how the Christian and Enlightenment ideal of universalism is used to denigrate Jewish "particularism," see Denise Buell, "Race and Universalism."

18. See Henaut, "Alexandria or Athens," 101, for an analysis of Harnack's view. Henaut goes on to note that this perspective of Judaism as particularistic is "insupportable historically." See also Rowe, "Harnack and the Concept of Hellenization," 73–75; Buell, "Race and Universalism in Early Christianity."

19. Harnack, *What Is Christianity?*, 199–200.

20. In an illuminating summary, Wilken describes Harnack's position as follows: "What Christianity *becomes* does not shed any light on what Christianity *is*. What it *is* is defined by what it was at the beginning" (*The Myth of Christian Beginnings*, 146).

21. Harnack, *What Is Christianity?*, 199, 193.

22. Quote is from Harnack, *History of Dogma*, I, 17; see also ibid., 14–15.

23. Harnack, *What Is Christianity?*, 202.

24. Ibid., 200–201.

25. Rowe, "Harnack and the Concept of Hellenization," 76–77.

26. See Harnack, *What Is Christianity?*, 206.

27. Harnack, *History of Dogma*, I, 253.

28. See ibid., 257–264.

29. Harnack's discussion of Marcion is fascinating in this respect, since he notes that while Marcion excluded the Old Testament from his canon, it was nonetheless an essential source of his theology of the alien God. In short, the primary issue was not acceptance or rejection of the Old Testament but how it was to be interpreted. The Old Testament was necessary for the development of Marcion's theology of two gods, for he held that the Old Testament *accurately* teaches the character of the world creator.

30. See Harnack, *History of Dogma*, I, 238, 240–241.

31. Ibid., I, 230.

32. Ibid., I, 247.

33. See, for example, Pearson, *Gnosticism, Judaism, and Egyptian Christianity*, 51; Williams, *Rethinking Gnosticism*, 54–79; Origen, *On First Principles* IV.2.1.

34. See Harnack, *History of Dogma*, I, 250.

35. Ibid., I, 228–229.

36. Harnack, *What Is Christianity?*, 207–208.

37. Harnack, *History of Dogma*, I, 227–228. The positive contributions are listed in ibid., 254–257.

38. See Harnack, *Marcion: The Gospel of the Alien God*, 123–124, 134.

39. Harnack, *What Is Christianity?* 199.

40. Such a goal was motivated in part by the need to find a Christianity suited to his own day that satisfied certain criteria, both theological and political. It had to address the legitimate criticism of nineteenth-century Biblical scholarship that there was a great deal of myth in the Bible, even the New Testament, that was unacceptable to Enlightenment reason. And it had to satisfy the political realities of the institutional separation of Protestantism from Catholicism. In locating the essence of Christianity in a religion of enthusiasm centered in the Gospel before the foundations of institutionalized religion, Harnack went far toward meeting these requirements.

41. See Rowe, "Harnack and the Concept of Hellenization," 85–88. Because of this criticism, Rowe sees in Harnack a prophetic voice of "authentic" Christianity (see 87–88).

42. At the end of his discussion of Christianity as a syncretistic religion in *Mission and Expansion,* Harnack summarizes his position: "But the reasons for the triumph of Christianity in that age are no guarantee for the permanence of that triumph throughout the history of mankind. Such a triumph rather depends upon the simple elements of the religion, on the preaching of the living God as the Father of men, and on the representation of Jesus Christ. For that very reason it depends also on the capacity of Christianity to strip off repeatedly such a collective syncretism and unite itself to fresh coefficients. The Reformation made a beginning in this direction" (318).

43. Ultimately, of course, Harnack locates the essence of Christianity beyond any particular historical manifestation. See, for example, *What Is Christianity?,* 149, 190–191.

44. See, for example, Rousseau, *A Discourse on Inequality;* or James Fenimore Cooper, *The Last of the Mohicans.*

45. As Bultmann also noted (in his introduction to *What Is Christianity?,* xii–xiii).

46. Aspects of this issue are explored in Hughes, *The Primitive Church;* see especially Yoder, "Primitivism in the Radical Reformation." Yoder writes that "there was no one in the sixteenth century who did not *in some way* claim first-century validation" (75), but he also notes that what people appealed to from the first century could vary widely (for example, the church of Acts, the Pauline Gospel, or Petrine succession). See also Wilken, *The Myth of Christian Beginnings.*

47. Scholars now generally refer to this stage of "Late Judaism" in the history of Judaism as "Early Judaism"; see the discussion of Cohen, *From the Maccabees to Mishnah,* 18–20.

## 4. The History of Religions School

1. Harnack vigorously opposed this approach. In the *History of Dogma,* he had already repudiated the view that the Oriental elements in Hellenistic syncretism exerted any decisive influence on Christianity (see I, 229–230). Harnack's later argument was that early Christians did not need a myth of a dying and rising god to understand the resurrection, because Jesus in fact really did die and his disciples did not doubt that reality because of their postresurrection visions. Similarly, he argued that Paul was a Jewish thinker, and that any use of language from the mystery religions was merely secondary, superficial, and carried a different meaning. The real core of Paul's theology, as with the author of the Gospel of John, was his own experience. In this way Harnack gestured toward the historical Jesus and the *experience* of the first Christians as the sources of early Chris-

tian theology, not Oriental mysticism or Hellenistic mystery piety. (See *Die Entstehung der christlichen Theologie und des kirchlichen Dogmas* [1927]; trans. *The Rise of Christian Theology*.) Harnack may have opposed the Oriental approach because he shared many of the assumptions about the character of East and West current in the colonialist ideology of his day, which rhetorically identified the Orient with myth and "crass superstition" (see *History of Dogma* I, 229–233). Hence he could not affirm that Christianity had been influenced to any significant degree by such Oriental influence until the latest stages of Hellenization. Even in his treatment of syncretism, he insisted that the Oriental elements were dominated by the Greek spirit.

2. Such men as Hermann Usener and Albrecht Dieterich had picked up the methods of folklore research and applied them to the study of religion (especially Christianity) in late antiquity (see Kümmel, *History,* 245–247). By 1907 the classical philologist Paul Wendland could conclude: "Christianity . . . was influenced in many respects by streams of popular thought and ephemeral literature produced in that time" (*Die hellenistische-römische Kultur,* 50; cited from Kümmel, *History,* 247).

3. See Said's classic study *Orientalism.*

4. See, for example, the monumental work of Gunkel, *Zum religionsgeschichtliche Verständnis.*

5. I use the term "field" here in Bourdieu's sense: "an area, a playing field, a field of objective relations among individuals or institutions competing for the same stakes" (*Sociology in Question,* 133; see also pp. 72–77, 132–148; and *The Logic of Practice,* 56–58, 66–68).

6. Mazusawa, *In Search of Dreamtime,* 21.

7. For the typological classification of religions, see J. Z. Smith, "Religion, Religions, Religious."

8. J. Z. Smith, "Religion, Religions, Religious," 277.

9. See Chakrabarty, *Provincializing Europe,* 22–23; Hamilton, *Historicism.*

10. J. Z. Smith, "Religion, Religions, Religious," 272.

11. See the discussion of Mazusawa, *In Search of Dreamtime,* 58–60, 67. Müller focused on the study of individual words, connecting the history of language directly to the history of religion (see the discussion of Olender, *The Languages of Paradise,* 83–84).

12. See Deismann, *Light,* 392, 250, 251, 396, 407, 408; Reitzenstein, "Iranischer Erlösungsglaube," 1–2.

13. Olender, *The Languages of Paradise,* 17.

14. Ibid., 37, 4–5.

15. Pictet, cited in ibid., 102.

16. See ibid., 103.

17. Compare, for example, the views of Ernest Renan (see Olender, *The Languages of Paradise*, 79).

18. Said, *Orientalism*, 1; for an excellent summary of recent critiques of Said, see Young, *Colonial Desire*, 158–166.

19. Said, *Orientalism*, 42. In some authors, one sees the express connection with European colonialism in the notion that Aryans were destined to conquer the world (see Olender, *The Languages of Paradise*, 95–96). In other scholars, the notion of Aryan superiority offered a complementary justification that European civilization and religion should be spread in order to "improve the other races." These notions were, of course, also disputed in various ways.

20. A particularly profound example is Max Müller. Few scholars contributed more than he to a sympathetic knowledge of Oriental language and religion. Yet he, too, acknowledged the essential superiority of Christianity: "The Science of Religion will for the first time assign to Christianity its right place among the religions of the world; it will show for the first time what was meant by the fullness of time; it will restore to the whole history of the world, in its unconscious progress towards Christianity, its true and sacred character" (cited in Olender, *The Languages of Paradise*, 91–92).

21. See Cumont, *Oriental Religions;* Rudolph, *Gnosis,* 30–52.

22. See Olender, *The Languages of Paradise*, 19.

23. See, for example, Fontenelle, who writes: "In the first centuries of the world, and among the nations who had never heard of or who had not preserved the traditions of the family of Seth, ignorance and barbarism must have existed to a degree which we are now hardly able to imagine. Consider the Kafirs, the Laplanders, or the Iroquois; but even this must be done with caution, since these peoples are already ancient and must have come to a degree of knowledge and manners that the earliest men did not have. The more ignorant one is and the less experience one has, the more miracles one will see. The first men saw plenty of them, and naturally, as the fathers told their children what they had seen and what they had done, there were nothing but prodigies in the tales of those times" ("The Origins of Fables," in Feldman and Richardson, *The Rise of Modern Mythology,* 11).

24. Tyler writes in *Primitive Culture* (1873): "One great element of religion, that moral element which among the higher nations forms its most vital part, is indeed little represented in the religion of the lower races. It is not that these races have no moral sense or no moral standard, for both are strongly marked among them, if not in formal precept, at least in that traditional consensus of society which we call public opinion, according to which certain actions are held to be

good or bad, right or wrong. It is that the conjunction of ethics and Animistic philosophy, so intimate and powerful in the higher culture, seems scarcely to have begun in the lower" (in Lessa and Vogt, *Reader*, 11). Fontenelle writes: "But if one eventually rids himself of the customary way of seeing things, it is impossible not to be appalled at seeing the entire ancient literature of a people nothing but a pile of chimeras, dreams and absurdities" ("The Origins of Fables," in Feldman and Richardson, *The Rise of Modern Mythology*, 10). Fontenelle also claims: "Although we are incomparably more enlightened than those whose crude mentality in-vented the fables in all good faith, we easily recover the same outlook that made these fables so agreeable to them. They glutted themselves on them because they believed them, and we indulge ourselves in them with just as much pleasure but without believing in them; and nothing could better prove that imagination and reason rarely have any dealing with one another, and that things concerning which reason is fully disabused lose nothing of their appeal to the imagination" ("On the Origin of Fables," in Feldman and Richardson, *The Rise of Modern My-thology*, 17). Referring to F. Max Müller's oft-quoted phrase that mythology is "a disease of language," Lessa and Vogt write: "The impulse to religious thought and language arises in the first instance from sensuous experience—from the influ-ence of external nature on man. Nature contains surprise, terror, marvels, mira-cles. This vast domain of the unknown and infinite, rather than the known and the finite, is what provided the sensation from which religions are derived. Fire, for example, would create such an impression on the mind of man. So could the sun and rivers and the wind, to name but a few phenomena. Religions only came into being, however, when the forces of nature were transformed by man from abstract forces into personal agents, that is, spirits. This came about through a 'disease of language.' Language influences the way in which people classify newly learned things. Natural phenomena came to be compared to human acts, and ex-pressions originally used for human acts came to be applied to natural objects. A thunder bolt was called Something that tears up the soil or spreads fire, the wind Something that sighs or whistles, a river Something that flows, and so on. After this had been done, spirits had to be invented to account for the acts attributed to them by their names and so arose pantheons of gods. The myth-making process then took hold and carried matters still further by endowing each god with a bi-ography. Thus religion is really a fabric of errors. The supernatural world was composed of beings created out of nothing" (*Reader*, 8–9). But see now Masuzawa, "Accidental Mythology: Max Müller in and out of His Workshop" (chapter 3 of *In Search of Dreamtime*).

25. For example, Johann Gottfried Herder (1744–1803) wrote: "The mythol-ogy of the Greeks flowed from the fables of various countries; and these consisted

either of the popular faith, the traditional accounts that the different generations preserved of their ancestors, or the first attempts of reflecting minds to explain the wonders of the earth and give a consistency to society" ("Reflections on the Philosophy of the History of Mankind," in Feldman and Richardson, *The Rise of Modern Mythology,* 233–234). Herder, of course, believed that however laudable, their endeavors were of course ultimately mistaken. See also Malinowski: Myth "is the historical statement of one of those events which once for all vouch for the truth of magic . . . Myth, it may be added at once, can attach itself to any form of social power or social claim . . . [and] the function of myth is not to explain but to vouch for, not to satisfy curiosity but to give confidence in power, not to spin out yarns but to establish the flowing freely from present-day occurrences frequently similar validity of myth . . . The pragmatic function of myth [is] in enforcing belief" (*Magic, Science, and Religion,* 84).

26. See the critique of Renan by Ignaz Goldziher, discussed by Olender, *The Languages of Paradise,* 115–135.

27. Some of these materials, such as the Mandaean texts and some of the Manichaean materials, of course had never been "lost." To say they were "discovered" takes the perspective of the European scholars who had previously not known about them. The Egyptian texts, by contrast, were recovered only in recent times from burial sites, and had truly disappeared from anyone's awareness.

28. Text and English translation of *The Bruce Codex* may be found in Schmidt and Macdermot, *The Books of Jeu and the Untitled Text in the Bruce Codex;* text and English translation of *Pistis Sophia,* in Schmidt and Macdermot, *Pistis Sophia.*

29. See Till and Schenke, *Die gnostische Schriften,* 1–3. This work contains an edited transcription of the Coptic text and a German translation.

30. See Klimkeit, *Gnosis on the Silk Road,* xvii–xx; for a summary discussion of Manichaeism, see Rudolph, *Gnosis,* 326–342; for the Mani-Codex, see Ludwig Koenen and Carl Römer, *Der Kölner Mani-Kodex* (Opladen, 1988), and Ron Cameron and Arthur Dewey, *The Cologne Mani Codex.*

31. For further general discussion of the Mandaeans, see Rudolph, *Gnosis,* 343–366; Lupieri, *The Mandaeans.* Jorunn J. Buckley reports that recent wars and the current political situation in Iran and Iraq have made life more difficult for the Mandaeans in these areas and have led to some limited Mandaean emigration to the West, including to the United States (New York, Detroit, and San Diego), Sweden, and Australia (see "With the Mandaeans in Iran"; *The Mandaeans).*

32. See Lupieri, *The Mandaeans,* 61–125. The Mandaeans may be the only ancient group who truly call themselves "Gnostic," but as Lupieri notes, while the self-designation of the Mandaeans as *mandaiia* could be directly related to the

term for "knowledge" and hence correspond to the Greek term "Gnostic" derived from *gnosis* ("knowledge"), it is likely, he suggests, that it refers rather to "those who use the *mandi/a*" (the sacred area in which Mandaean ceremonies are performed); or alternatively, it may refer to those who believe in Manda-d-Hiia, the supreme divinity of the Mandaeans (see Lupieri, *The Mandaeans,* 7–8). The Mandaeans are known by a variety of other names as well: the Muslims called them Sabians (see the *Qu'ran,* surahs 2, 5, and 22); the Syrian Christian Theodore bar Konai, Dostaie; they themselves, either *Nasoraiyi* ("observants"), a designation that the Jesuits mistranslated as "Christians of St. John" (in Arabic, an-Nasara; this last name stuck until the nineteenth century, when Orientalists and officials from Western Europe began to study the group more closely). See Kraeling, "The Origin and Antiquity of the Mandaeans," 195–196; Lupieri, *The Mandaeans,* 61–125. See also Rudolph, *Gnosis,* 343.

33. See Colpe, *Die religionsgeschichtliche Schule,* 32. For more on the early history of Mandaean studies, see Pallis, *A Mandaic Bibliography.*

34. For example, Nöldeke, *Mandäische Grammatik* (1875); Petermann, *Thesaurus, s. Liber Magnus* (1867). A bibliography of published Mandaean sources is given by Lupieri, *The Mandaeans,* 54–60.

35. Lidzbarski, *Das Johannesbuch der Mandäer* (in 1924, G. Mead published a translation of portions of this work in English: *The Gnostic John the Baptizer*); Lidzbarski, *Mandäische Liturgien.* (Lady Drower later published a more extensive collection of these texts in *The Canonical Prayerbook of the Mandaeans.*) See also *Ginza: Der Schatz.* Of particular interest for ritual practice are Drower's *Canonical Prayerbook* and her personal account, *The Mandaeans of Iraq and Iran.* For a bibliography of her publications, see Yamauchi, *Gnostic Ethics,* 95–96.

36. Kümmel, *The New Testament,* 69.

37. In his later work, *Die Mandäer,* he still maintained this position, though he stressed more fully the Gnostic character of Mandaeanism: ". . . vielleicht in der polytheistischen Vorstellungen der Mandäer die Reste einer Gnosis enthalten seien, die vom Christentum noch gar nichts wusste, weder christlich noch antichristliche war, und auch nicht jüdisch, sondern anti-jüdisch, heidnisch" (20). Rudolph writes that basing studies on the Right Ginza is the correct approach even today, when more source material is available, because "this most comprehensive work of the Mandaean literature also contains the most important tractates about Mandaean teaching and mythology, including the old hymnic poetry" ("Problems," 211). Brandt subsequently published selections of the Right Ginza in 1893 in *Mandäische Schriften.*

38. See *Die Mandäer,* 23.

39. See Brandt, *Die mandäische Religion;* Lidzbarski, "Alter und Heimat der

mandäischen Religion" and "Mandäische Fragen"; Maçuch, "Anfänge der Mandäer" and "Gnostische Ethik."

40. See Bousset, *Die Religion des Judentums* (1903), *Hauptprobleme der Gnosis* (1907), and *Kyrios Christos* (1913); Reitzenstein, *Poimandres* (1904), *Die hellenistischen Mysterienreligionen* (1910), *Die Göttin Psyche* (1917), *Das mandäische Buch des Herrn der Grösse und die Evangelienüberlieferung* (1919), and, with Hans Schaeder, *Studien zum Antiken Synkretismus aus Iran und Griechenland* (1926); as well as works by Bultmann referred to below.

41. See Reitzenstein, *The Hellenistic Mystery Religions,* 380.

42. Reitzenstein argued, for example, that Paul borrowed the terms *pneuma* and *gnôsis* from "predominantly Hellenistic language" (*Hellenistic Mystery Religions,* 73), and often used these terms in the technical, Oriental sense (ibid., 381). The concept of *gnôsis,* said Reitzenstein, "may have penetrated late Judaism from the Mandaean religion" and from Judaism into the thought of Paul (ibid., 421). In the early churches' discussion of whether Christ on earth had a soul, the point at issue, said Reitzenstein, was clearly the opposition of *pneuma* to *psychê* stemming from pre-Pauline Hellenistic usage, where the terms *pneuma* and *psyche* formed direct oppositions: "where the *psyche* is, the *pneuma* can no longer be, and where the *pneuma* is, the *psyche* can no longer be" (ibid., 72). To be filled with *pneuma* by displacing *psyche* is to become divine. This deification was achieved through *gnôsis.* Although Reitzenstein acknowledged that the Christian discussion revolves around the Greek conception of *psyche* and the Greek view that God must be free of *pathê,* he nonetheless said that "one must not pay too little attention to the idea of *pneuma* and its source. It is only the introduction of this term by Gnosticism that makes the debate at all intelligible: if Christ is God, he has *pneuma* in place of *psychê;* but if he were man he must have a *psychê,* for the *pneumatikos,* the being with *pneuma,* is no longer human, but divine!" (see ibid., 414–415). He concluded: "It is true that the arguments are brought out of the arsenal of Greek philosophy, but the reminiscence of the basic perspective of the mystery religion is only faint; Gnosticism is overcome, but the legacy that is brought out of the Orient, the concept of the *pneumatikos,* continues to exert an influence, as it does on the Greek church even down to modern times" (ibid., 415).

43. Cited in Colpe, *Die religionsgeschichtliche Schule,* 38. Concerning the soul, he writes: "Wherever both religions [Manichaeism and Mandaeanism] are further concerned with 'Erlösungsreligionen,' the teaching of the soul is the center or at least the part, in them both or in both of the underlying forms of Iranian piety, which must have most affected other religions" ("Iranischer Erlösungsglaube," 2–3).

44. See *Das mandäische Buch,* 53.

45. Contrast with the work of Buckley on Ruha, whom she considers to be the female figuration of the soul in Mandaean thought (*The Mandaeans,* 40–48).

46. Reitzenstein himself was not conversant with the ancient languages of these works and relied throughout on published and unpublished translations by Müller, Andreas, and Lidzbarski (see "Iranischer Erlösungsglaube," 7 and 3, n. 1).

47. "The basis of Manichaeism is the Iranian Volksreligion . . . The same is also true, with the few qualifications I have added, for the Mandaean religion" (see "Iranischer Erlösungsglaube," 2). He arrives at this conclusion by comparing one of the Manichaean Turfan fragments with the Mandaean *Book of the Dead* from the *Left Ginza:* the latter, he says, matches point for point with the former. But moreover, "since this agrees with the picture and words of the Zarathustra fragments, it shows at the same time that both are based on an older Iranian text" ("Iranischer Erlösungsglaube," 7).

48. Ibid., 7–9.

49. This point is supported, he says, by Lidzbarski, who argues for a West Semitic origin on the basis of the evidence of veneration of the Jordan and baptism in the Jordan in the preface of the Mandaean *Book of John* (see ibid., 3).

50. It may be that Harnack and Reitzenstein are not in serious disagreement about the nature of religion, since for both true religion arises out of feeling (enthusiasm), while systematic thinking (whether philosophy or theology) is secondary. But they deploy this idea differently. For Reitzenstein, it means that Iranian feeling (a primary religious force) can influence philosophy (a derivative intellectual product), while for Harnack philosophy, which produced the first Christian theologians (the Gnostics), can be only secondary to the true religious enthusiasm.

51. Reitzenstein, *Hellenistic Mystery Religions,* 368. For example, he argues that the term *logos* (or *logos* and *nous*) as used in the *Poimandres* XII.13 only appears to have borrowed its concepts from philosophy. It is only the word, and not the idea, that has been borrowed. The concept is that of *noema* and its usage is Oriental (419). Similarly, he writes, "where the word *pneuma* is itself accepted into the *philosophical* terminology, it once again undergoes a partial devaluation, in the sense of the Stoic designation for the material of the soul, and in *Corpus Hermeticum* X. 13 . . . [where] the *pneuma* becomes the shell, the *enduma tês psychês,* and the latter becomes the *enduma tou vou.* This is reminiscent of Platonic teachings, but it is unlikely that it first arose in that school; the entire perspective is only the inversion, necessary in philosophy, of the Gnostic doctrine according to which the *psychê* is the *enduma tou pneumatos*" (*Hellenistic Mystery Religions,* 419–420; see also 387).

302 Notes to Pages 86–90

52. Reitzenstein, *Hellenistic Mystery Religions,* 390.

53. For example, the light theology in Judaism: "Once again, in my opinion, the usage [of τό τῆς γνωσεώς φῶς] is shown to be non-Jewish. The light theology itself, at least in its later fully stated form, appears first to have entered into Judaism from the Iranian sphere" (Reitzenstein, *Hellenistic Mystery Religions,* 373). And the doctrine of the soul in philosophy: "Philosophy does not exert any significance [on the teachings on the soul], but rather (shows) an Oriental usage" (ibid., 396).

54. Reitzenstein, *Hellenistic Mystery Religions,* 421.

55. Reitzenstein, "Iranischer Erlösungsglaube," 3.

56. See ibid.

57. See ibid., 17.

58. A point Reitzenstein considers beyond dispute (see ibid., 18, 19–20).

59. Ibid., 20–21.

60. Lidzbarski, *Ginza* 27:19–30:26 and 45:20–54:20; see Reitzenstein, *Das mandäische Buch,* 41–58; and "Iranischer Erlösungsglaube," 3–4. Hugo Gressman laid this view to rest in short order merely by pointing out that even if dependence between Q and the *Ginza* could be shown, the chronology of the texts would seem to indicate dependence in the opposite direction from Q to the *Ginza* (see Gressman, "Das religionsgeschichtliche Problem," 157 ff. 167–70). Reitzenstein had pointed to a second piece of evidence, claiming that "the liturgy of the dead of the second book of the *Left Ginza* is copied in a ritual of the Valentinians" (4), but again even if it were possible to demonstrate parallels between Mandaean and Valentinian literature, that fact would not begin to satisfy requirements for evidence of a pre-Christian Gnosticism.

61. Reitzenstein, "Iranischer Erlösungsglaube," 21.

62. In presenting the details of his analysis, Bousset was much indebted to the work of Lidzbarski and other philologists; much of the material in his study was known to him only in translation because he was not familiar with the original languages of many of the Oriental texts (see Bousset's expression of gratitude for the philological work of Brandt and Lidzbarski in "Die Religion der Mandäer," 185–187). He also relied on their theories about Mandaean origins, although he sought to refine them (see, for example, his article "Die Religion der Mandäer"), and on Reitzenstein's work on the pre-Christian Oriental (Iranian) origin of the Greek and Jewish mysteries, the Hellenistic teaching about the salvation of the soul, and the Gnostic myth of the redeemed redeemer.

63. See Bousset, *Die Religion des Judentums,* 267. At the time Bousset's work appeared, Richard Reitzenstein's *Poimandres* was in press. Reitzenstein had been working on the same problem, although he had started with the Hermetic mate-

rial, and concluded that the place to look was the "Hellenistic myth of the God *Anthropos*" (*Poimandres,* 81). He turned from there to Iranian religion.

64. In addition to the polemicists' writings, he considered the Mandaean writings translated by Brandt, the *Pistis Sophia* and the *Books of Jeû* (trans. from the Coptic by Carl Schmidt in 1905), and Manichaean writings, including the Turfan fragments newly published by F. W. K. Müller in 1904.

65. Bousset, *Hauptprobleme,* 219.

66. See ibid., 219. See also Colpe, *Die religionsgeschichtliche Schule,* 24.

67. Bousset, *Hauptprobleme,* 220, 350.

68. This quotation is the subtitle of the book.

69. In Bousset, *Kyrios Christos,* 7.

70. See Bousset's conclusion to his first chapter, "The Picture of Jesus of Nazareth," which addresses Jesus in the New Testament Gospels (*Kyrios Christos,* 116–117).

71. See ibid., 117–118.

72. Ibid., 415, 418, 419.

73. See ibid., 35 ff.

74. See ibid., 56, 48–52.

75. Ibid., 54, 57.

76. He tips his hat to "orthodoxy" when he regards "Hellenistic piety" as "outside the Old Testament and the genuinely Christian milieu" (*Kyrios Christos,* 223). See also 198, where he distinguishes a "foreign" element as that "which does not stem from the world of the Old Testament and of the gospel."

77. He writes, "In conclusion, we do not at all need, with the assumption of that process of 'hellenizing' or orientalizing of Christianity, to go back into Palestinian primitive Christianity or the gospel of Jesus" (*Kyrios Christos,* 18).

78. Bousset is very clear on the point that the primitive church believed Jesus to be the Messiah (see *Kyrios Christos,* 31).

79. Bousset, *Jesu Predigt,* 69 (cited in Kümmel, *History,* 232). He also wrote, "In late Judaism there is no really living power, no creative spirit. The characteristic feature of Judaism merely elevated itself to a mood of purely transcendental, world-denying resignation, a mood for which life has lost its meaning, intimately bound up with a legalistic striving after holiness . . . It is further clear from this that for Jesus, who was aware of the nearness of God as the basis of his whole life, that breathless longing, that pathological homesickness for the beyond that we meet especially in the later Jewish apocalypses was something utterly foreign" (cited from Kümmel, 230–231).

80. See Bousset, *Kyrios Christos,* 21.

81. Ibid., 15. Note, too, the class implications of this statement, which, fol-

lowing German folklore studies, tends to locate natural (true) feelings (like piety) among the "Folk," that is, among those untouched by the alienating forces of civilization and systematic thought.

82. Bousset, *Kyrios Christos*, 13–14.

83. See his marvelous description of early Christian communal life in ibid., 351–353. Here one senses something of his reasoning about why people might have joined this "odd cult."

84. Bousset, *Kyrios Christos*, 402, 403, 21, 12.

85. See ibid., 15, 21, 153–210. So sure is Bousset that this point about the Gospel of John has already been established by history of religions research that he claims: "This no longer needs detailed proof," merely a reference to Reitzenstein's *Hellenistische Mysterienreligionen* (see *Kyrios Christos*, 231).

86. See Bousset, *Kyrios Christos*, 245–254. Bultmann also required a mere ten pages in *Primitive Christianity* for this same task (see *Primitive Christianity*, 162–171).

87. Citing Plotinus, *Ennead* II, 9.9 (Bousset, *Kyrios Christos*, 249).

88. *Kyrios Christos*, 249.

89. Ibid., 15–16.

90. "In Gnosticism a decidedly dualistic-pessimistic and for this reason specifically un-Hellenic mental tendency, which also stands in strict opposition to the Old Testament and Judaism, has been attached to Christianity" (Bousset, *Kyrios Christos*, 280).

91. Ibid., 267.

92. Ibid., 281. See also ibid., 275–279.

93. Bousset himself did not consider Jesus to have been influenced by the forces of either Hellenization or Orientalization. He criticized Drews and B. W. Smith for dissolving "the person and the gospel of Jesus" in "pushing the process of Hellenization and Orientalization back into the Palestinian primitive community" (*Kyrios Christos*, 20).

94. Ibid., 280; see also the extended discussion, 254–271.

95. Pagels, in her study of Gnostic interpretation of Paul, agrees in large part, writing: "Some of what has been described as 'gnostic terminology' in the Pauline letters may be explained more plausibly instead as Pauline (and deutero-Pauline) terminology in the *gnostic* writings" (*The Gnostic Paul*, 164). By contrast, contemporary interpretations of Paul have been "to some extent distorted" by reading Paul in terms of the second-century debates, whether as hyperorthodox or hypergnostic. Pagels suggests that understanding these debates and moving beyond them may provide fresh readings of Paul's own text (see *The Gnostic Paul*, 164).

96. See Bousset, *Kyrios Christos,* 280. According to Bousset, one of the distinguishing characteristics of Gnosticism is that it has abandoned history for myth (see ibid., 267). Bousset does not, however, entirely dismiss the religious impact of myth; if I understand him correctly, it would seem that he is implying that the "historical" element here is the experience of the believer enlivened in ritual, not the "referential" content of the narrative "myth."

97. Bousset, *Kyrios Christos,* 267.

98. See ibid., 451. Bousset writes: "The fact that the Christianity of the first half of the second century does not refer directly to Paul, and in fact passes over him in silence, becomes understandable when one sees that the 'hellenizing' of Christianity in the apologists with their optimistically rational total outlook is something wholly different from its amalgamation with oriental syncretistic mysticism with its dualism and pessimism as it is found in Paul (John) and in Gnosticism. What then emerges at the end of the second century as the culmination of the development is neither the one nor the other. We can call it the ecclesiastically tempered Paulinism, the Paulinism that has been divested of all Gnostic dangers and tendencies. It is, if we wish to choose our *termini* following a famous example [Harnack], the gradual orientalizing and re-forming of Christianity into syncretism as over against the acute orientalizing in Paul and in Gnosticism. And thus also is the *altissimum silentium* about Paul in the first half of the second century A.D. to be understood" (ibid., 21).

99. Ibid., 446. See the evaluation of Pauline theology by Pagels, *The Gnostic Paul.*

100. Bousset, *Kyrios Christos,* 451.

101. Ibid.

102. On the one hand, he does not actually use normative, evaluative terminology like "heresy" to characterize Gnosticism. Indeed, he says that "the lines of connection with Paulinism are not completely broken off. The basic form of religion remained similar . . . And even in Paul the historical redemption was already on the way to developing into a myth" (*Kyrios Christos,* 281). On the other hand, he does describe it negatively, telling us that "Gnosticism shows the dangers with which one side of the Pauline piety threatens the further development of the Christ piety" (ibid., 281). In short, for Bousset Gnosticism is a threat to Christ piety. For additional examples, see *Kyrios Christos,* 67, 194, 236.

103. Bousset, *Kyrios Christos,* 231. For an example, see 233.

104. Bultmann, "Die religionsgeschichtliche Hintergrund," 13.

105. Ibid., 19 ff., 21–22, 30, 32. Bultmann had a solid appreciation for the complexity of the material with which he was dealing. Although he was clearly willing to follow Bousset and Reitzenstein in their search through the wider literature of

the ancient world in order to establish the history of religions background of the New Testament passages—even to the point of asserting that "the question of the origin of this speculation can in this case not be determined by reason of question of literary priority" ("Die religionsgeschichtliche Hintergrund," 27), thereby opening the door for chronological difficulties—he still seems conscious of the enormous difficulty of this task. His conclusion, therefore, went no further than his data had allowed, and he was willing to admit its speculative nature: "It may be clearly said that a *Vorlage* was used for vs. 1–13. The *Vorlage*'s contents and train of thought are comparable to those in Jewish Wisdom speculation. Perhaps it may also probably be said that the view set forth in the Johannine prologue belongs to the wider context of West Asian speculation concerning the revelatory deity, who is embodied in her messenger on earth." But rather than stop here with his modest conclusion, Bultmann goes on to speculate on the origin and content of the "wider context of West Asian speculation," relying primarily on the work of Reitzenstein.

106. Bultmann, "Die religionsgeschichtliche Hintergrund," 34.

107. Ibid., 33, 35.

108. In a later article, he also drew on Philo and Paul (esp. I Cor 2:6 ff. and Phil 2:2 ff.); see Bultmann, "Die Bedeutung," 141.

109. Bultmann, "Die Bedeutung," 104.

110. See ibid., 139, 140–141.

111. Ibid., 142. By "us" he presumably meant contemporary Christians.

112. Bultmann, "Die Bedeutung," 144. This comparison of John and Gnosticism is undertaken in more detail in his 1940 study "Johanneische Schriften und Gnosis." Bultmann also held that the Johannine Christianity represented an older type of Palestinian Christianity than did the Synoptics, that the activity and message of Jesus was more closely connected to the Gnostic baptizing movement than the Synoptic tradition allowed (see "Die Bedeutung," 144).

113. For further discussion, see Koester, "The History-of-Religions School, Gnosis, and the Gospel of John."

114. See the summary of Bultmann, *The Gospel of John*, 8–9.

115. See Bultmann, *Primitive Christianity*, 162–171.

116. Ibid., 162. See also Bultmann, "Christianity as a Religion of East and West."

117. Bultmann, *Primitive Christianity*, 177–178. Bultmann claims that his terminology and conception of syncretism were taken from Hermann Gunkel, *Zum religonsgeschichtlichen Verständnis des Neuen Testaments,* 2nd ed., 1910.

118. Bultmann, *Primitive Christianity*, 179.

119. Bultmann, "Points of Contact and Conflict," 133.

120. Christianity and Gnosticism both conceive of "man's situation in the world as a bondage to the hostile cosmic powers, as a fate brought upon him by the fall of the archetypal man . . . Both systems agree that empirical man is not what he ought to be. He is deprived of authentic life, true existence" (Bultmann, *Primitive Christianity,* 191). Gnosticism and Christianity further agree that humanity cannot free itself; redemption must come from the divine world. Both Paul and the Gospel of John "restate" Jesus' redemptive activity in terms of the Gnostic redeemer myth (see ibid., 196–199). In doing so, Christianity and Gnosticism agree in "placing the eschatological event in the present" (ibid., 200).

121. See Bultmann, *Primitive Christianity,* 191–192. Bultmann actually claims that fate is operative in Christianity as well, but he manages to define it in such a way as to elide the two into sin: "man's guilt has become his fate" (*Primitive Christianity,* 192). See now the insightful critique of the understanding of fate by Nicola Denzey, "Under a Pitiless Sky."

122. "There is therefore no ultimate cosmological dualism [in Christianity] such as we find in the Gnostics. This is proved by the way in which, for those who have been freed by Christ, the world recovers its character as creation, although even now it is not their home" (Bultmann, *Primitive Christianity,* 193). Or again, he writes that the idea of God's transcendence in Christianity "is not conceived ontologically as in Gnosticism. The gulf between God and man is not metaphysical" (ibid., 194; see also 201–202).

123. Ibid., 208, 179, 202, 184.

124. I emphasize that Bultmann does this overtly, because it can be argued that the value of "Gnosticism" has always been determined relative to the theological norms presupposed. Recognizing this procedure as the proper one, however, makes it possible for theological discussion and critique to claim a valid place in the discussion.

125. Rudolph, *Gnosis,* 276–277. Note that "heresy" is in quotes (presumably to mark its normative character), but that "deadly germ" and "official Christian Church" do not require quotes.

126. This view continues to be reproduced in the frequent classification of Gnosticism as an esoteric or mystical religion.

127. For a particularly notable example, see Bultmann, *Primitive Christianity,* 163–164.

## 5. Gnosticism Reconsidered

1. The second volume was scheduled to appear in two parts. Publication of the first part of the second volume was delayed until 1954, owing to the Nazi rise

to power in Germany and Jonas's emigration. The final part of volume two was never completed.

2. Jonas, *Gnosis* I, 81.

3. Bauer, *Orthodoxy and Heresy,* xxii.

4. Ibid., xxiii–xxiv.

5. Ibid., xxiv.

6. Ibid.

7. Ibid., 16–17.

8. Ibid., 53, 58.

9. See ibid., 61–94, 100–101.

10. For criticism, see H. E. W. Turner, *The Pattern of Christian Truth,* 39–94; Heron, "The Interpretation of I Clement in Walter Bauer"; McCue, "Orthodoxy and Heresy"; Strecker, "The Reception of the Book"; Harrington, "The Reception of W. Bauer"; Davids, "Irrtum und Häresie"; Moffatt, "Walter Bauer"; Norris, "Ignatius, Polycarp, and I Clement"; Gero, "With Walter Bauer on the Tigris"; T. A. Robinson, *The Bauer Thesis Examined;* and Hultgren, *The Rise of Normative Christianity,* 9–13. One sees his influence, for example, in the work of Robinson and Koester, *Trajectories;* and Robinson, "Jesus from Easter to Valentinus," 6–7.

11. See Haardt, "Zur Methodologie der Gnosisforschung"; Green, "Gnosis and Gnosticism."

12. See Jonas, *Gnosis,* I, 42–49.

13. See Bousset, "Gnosis, Gnostiker," 1510 (52–53); and Jonas, *Gnosis* I, 47. On the next page (48), Jonas offers a bit of scathing irony aimed at Bousset and others who seem unable to credit the Gnostics with any originality of their own: "From the utilitarian concord of ideal conditions, they (Gnostics) built the symbolism of their own self-construction. They did not falsify the ideas that were beguiled into their worldview through their alchemy, but they did falsify the ideas by extracting from them a meaning which they did not originally possess. In that process they may have broken up Hellenism and Iranian religion, as Bousset presents it; indeed these may even have been broken up of their own accord. But the opposite is unthinkable: that Gnosticism arose and people became Gnostics because both of these and others had mixed in their minds. Here no original impulse is forthcoming without violence."

14. See *Gnosis* I, 9–11. Jonas concluded that the essential unity of Gnosticism, that is, the depth of its underlying existence (*Dasein*), is not put in question by showing that the outer layer initially resulted from the generation, appropriation, and attachment of various elements. What is needed above all, he argued, is to reconstruct that unity hermeneutically out of the typical motifs and combinations evident in the world.

15. See Jonas's response to G. Quispel's essay "Gnosticism and the New Testament," in "Response to G. Quispel," esp. 279, 286.

16. Jonas, "Response to G. Quispel," 286.

17. Ibid.

18. Jonas, *The Gnostic Religion*, 48; see also 48–99.

19. Jonas, *Gnosis*, I, 49.

20. Ibid., 10.

21. See ibid., 77, 78.

22. For a discussion of the influence of Spengler and Heidegger on Jonas's thought, see Waldstein, "Hans Jonas' Construct 'Gnosticism.'"

23. See Jonas's discussion of Schaeder in ibid., 50–58.

24. See, for example, Jonas, *The Gnostic Religion*, 48–49.

25. Jonas, *Gnosis*, I, 50.

26. See ibid., 51, where he characterizes the conceptual antithesis between "Orientalischen" and Harnack's "hellenischen" as "griechische Philosophie," on the one hand, in contrast to "orientalische Mythologie und Mysterienfrömmigkeit," on the other.

27. Ibid., 74.

28. Ibid., 75, 76.

29. Ibid., 79.

30. Ibid., 58–73.

31. In my reading, Jonas would certainly have opposed attempts to locate the historical origin of Gnosticism more precisely because he considered the breadth of the area across which it arose simultaneously and the materials it drew on to be so vast. That is, to locate one time, one place, one cause (like the destruction of the Temple) would be insufficient, both for the origination of Gnosticism and for explaining its wide appeal.

32. See, for example, Harnack, *History of Dogma*, I, 257–264; Bousset, *Kyrios Christos*, 45–54.

33. See also Jonas, *Gnosis* I, 94–140; and *The Gnostic Religion*, 48–97; Colpe, *Die religionsgeschichtliche Schule*, 186–187.

34. See Jonas, "Delimitation," 92, 91, 99. Jonas also offered a summary of the elements of gnosis in *The Gnostic Religion*, 42–47, with "morality" added.

35. Jonas, *The Gnostic Religion*, 32, 31.

36. All the material in this section comes from Jonas, "Delimitation," 92, 93 (my emphasis).

37. Ibid., 94–95; see also 93.

38. Ibid., 97–98. These points arose from consideration of divine transcendence, lower powers, man, and salvation (see ibid., 95–99).

39. Ibid., 92; see also 98.

40. Ibid., 94, 93.

41. See the "Proposal" in Bianchi, *Le Origini dello Gnosticismo*, xxviii–xxix.

42. Jonas, "Delimitation," 96. See also M. Williams's suggestion that "biblical demiurgical" should be the primary, if not the sole, typological characteristic used to categorize these texts (*Rethinking "Gnosticism,"* 265–266).

43. Jonas, *The Gnostic Religion*, 46.

44. Ibid., 144. Of sexuality, Jonas writes, "Marcion here voices a genuine and typical *gnostic* argument, whose fullest elaboration we shall meet in Mani; that the reproductive scheme is an ingenious archontic device for the indefinite retention of souls in the world. Thus Marcion's asceticism, unlike that of the Essenes or later of Christian monasticism, was not conceived to further the sanctification of human existence, but was essentially negative in conception and part of the gnostic revolt against the cosmos" (145).

45. Ibid., 270–271.

46. Ibid., 144.

47. Jonas, "Delimitation," 100.

48. Ibid., 100, 97, 99. The extent of the Gnostic revolution is best apprehended, argued Jonas, by comparison with the classical mind. For an extended treatment of cosmology and ethics, see Jonas, *The Gnostic Religion*, 239–289.

49. Jonas, "Response to G. Quispel," 287.

50. Ibid., 288.

51. Jonas, "Delimitation," 100–102; *The Gnostic Religion*, 100.

52. Jonas, *The Gnostic Religion*, 100, 101.

53. See Detienne, *The Creation of Mythology*, 6–7; Durkheim, *The Elementary Forms of Religious Life*, 470, 477; Masuzawa, "Society versus Difference: Durkheim's Shadowboxing" (chapter 2 of *In Search of Dreamtime*).

54. For example, see Freud, *The Future of an Illusion*, 70–77; Masuzawa's essay "History on a Mystic Writing Pad: Freud Refounds Time" (chapter 4 of *In Search of Dreamtime*).

55. See Lévi-Strauss, "The Structural Study of Myth," 106, 105. See also Bidney's treatment of Cassirer in "Myth, Symbolism, and Truth," 15; V. Turner, "Myth and Symbol," 576; Lévi-Strauss, *Mythologiques* II, 407.

56. For the treatment of the distinction between myth and philosophy in ancient Greek thought, see Detienne, *The Creation of Mythology*, 63–102.

57. See Jonas, "Delimitation," 101.

58. For Jonas, myth gives a true if objectified representation of the interior state and is the "valid anticipation" or "actualization" of mysticism (see "Myth and Mysticism," 304).

59. Jonas, "Delimitation," 103.

60. Jonas, *The Gnostic Religion,* 101.

61. Jonas, "Delimitation," 100.

62. Jonas, *The Gnostic Religion,* 3–27. A version of this section was discussed in King, "Translating History."

63. See Jonas, *The Gnostic Religion,* 18.

64. Ibid., 4–6, 11.

65. Ibid., 12–14.

66. Ibid., 5–6.

67. Ibid., 18.

68. Ibid., 17, 6, 21.

69. Ibid., 21, 22.

70. Ibid., 22–23.

71. Ibid., 25, 26–27.

72. Ibid., 33.

73. Ibid., 24.

74. Jonas, *Gnosis* I, 63–64.

75. For a critique of "experience" in historical analysis, see Joan Scott, "'Experience.'" Her primary point is that experience itself is not a given, but is culturally constructed. She offers an alternative: "It is not individuals who have experience, but subjects who are constituted through experience. Experience in this definition then becomes not the origin of our explanation, not the authoritative (because seen or felt) evidence that grounds what is known, but rather that which we seek to explain, that about which knowledge is produced. To think about experience in this way is to historicize it as well as to historicize the identities it produces" (25–26). So, too, here it is that social experience of the world needs to be explained.

76. See Jonas, *Gnosis* I, 64, 66.

77. Jonas, "Delimitation," 103.

78. Jonas, *Gnosis* I, 81.

79. Ibid.

80. Ibid., 81–82.

81. Ibid., 80.

82. Ibid., 51: "Unbefriedigung über das atomistisch Vereinzelnde der vorangegangenen Forschung und der gefühlte Mangel einer einigenden Sinnganzheit, den sie hinterließ."

83. Jonas, "Delimitation," 101, 106, 102, 103, 105, 96, 97.

84. Jonas, *The Gnostic Religion,* 327–328.

85. Ibid., 272, 277.

86. Ibid., 247–248. See also his essay "Gnosticism, Existentialism, Nihilism," in ibid., 320–340.

87. Lietzmann, "Ein Beitrag zur Mandäerfrage," 139–140.

88. For example, Rudolph has argued that "the Mandaean baptism ceremony is not in any sense an imitation of the Christian Syrian, and especially the Nestorian baptism" (*Die Mandäer*, 10; "Quellenprobleme," 430).

89. See, for example, Lidzbarski, "Die Münzen der Characene." Edmondo F. Lupieri has noted that in 1652, Ignatius d'Jesus was the first European to suggest that the Mandaeans originated in a first-century baptizing sect associated with John the Baptist in Palestine/Judaea ("On the History of Early Contacts between Mandaeans and Europeans," delivered at "The Mandaeans: A Conference at Harvard University, 13–15 June, 1999").

90. See the objections of Lietzmann to an early dating, "Ein Beitrag zur Mandäerfrage." Concerning their status in Islam, see Rudolph, *Die Mändaer*, 5. Regarding Theodore bar Konai, see Kraeling, "The Origin and Antiquity," 202 and 203; and Rudolph, *Die Mändaer*, 3. See also Lidzbarski, "Mandäische Fragen," 74–75.

91. Rudolph, for example, argues that "an analysis of the style and the themes in these early Mandaean traditions and a comparison between them and various Johannine texts have shown that they were related to early Palestinian and Syrian Christian traditions," but he does not use that position to argue for Mandaean influence on the Gospel of John (*Die Mandäer*, 4). An exception among these specialists is Yamauchi, *Pre-Christian Gnosticism*.

92. See Maçuch, "The Origins of the Mandaeans and Their Script"; see also Rudolph, *Die Mandäer* I, 30, and "Quellenprobleme," esp. 428–430. Further research on this topic was reviewed by Yamauchi, "Mandean Incantation Texts," a paper delivered at "The Mandaeans: A Conference at Harvard University, 13–15 June, 1999."

93. See Rudolph, "Die mandäische Literatur."

94. Drower, *Haran Gawaita*, 3–4.

95. This thesis is clarified by noting the following points:

   1. Harran is in northwest Mesopotamia; the Median Hills in northwest Iran.

   2. There were five Parthian kings named Ardban: I. 216–191 B.C.E.; II. ca. 128–124 B.C.E.; III. 12 B.C.E.–ca. 38 C.E.; IV. 80–81 C.E.; and V. ca. 213–227 C.E. Maçuch has argued for Artabanus III, since that most clearly supports his overall thesis that the Mandaeans left Palestine before the destruction of the Temple and were in Mesopotamia by the third century.

3. Jerusalem is portrayed elsewhere in the *Haran Gawaita* and also in the *Ginza* as being under the control of the Seven (that is, the demonic planetary powers).

4. The term "Nasorean" is a Syro-Palestinian name attested in the pre-Christian period.

5. The *Haran Gawaita* (5–9) and the *Right Ginza* narrate that this migration was due to persecution by the Jews in Jerusalem.

96. See the discussion of Rudolph in *Gnosis*, 343–366; Lupieri, *The Mandaeans*, 127–165; Maçuch, *Handbook of Classical and Modern Mandai* (Berlin, 1965), p. LVI, and Yamauchi, *Gnostic Ethics*, 4–8. Yamauchi argues: "If one accepts the dates given in the colophons, one can obtain a date in the second half of the third century AD for the writing of at least part of the *Canonical Prayerbook*" (*Ethics*, 5). He cites Drower and Maçuch for support.

97. For more on Mandaean women priests, see Buckley, "Evidence for Women Priests in Mandaeism." See also "The Use of Colophons and Scribal Postscripts in Envisioning Mandaean History," a paper delivered at "The Mandaeans: A Conference at Harvard University, 13–15 June, 1999"; and Lupieri, *The Mandaeans,* 127–165.

98. And well they might, in fact, disappear under the pressures of contemporary politics and Western apathy. Buckley is offering us an alternative: the opportunity to come to know and appreciate Mandaean religion and culture in their own right. Only recently a conference on "The Mandaeans" was held at Harvard University, June 13–15, 1999, bringing together a number of scholars studying Mandaean materials, as well as a large group of Mandaean lay persons and priests from diaspora communities in Europe, North America, and Australia. For the first time, Mandaean baptisms were held on the North American continent. At the same time, it became all too apparent that the continued existence of Mandaean language and religion is uncertain. An enormous and timely effort will be needed if the heritage of this tradition is to be preserved at all.

99. Colpe, *Die religionsgeschichtliche Schule,* 69.

100. See ibid., 92.

101. In Colpe's terms, *manuhmed* is the Manichaean *salvator salvandus* (see ibid., 95).

102. *Zeitschrift der Deutschen Morganländischen Gesellschaft* (1956), 11–12; cited in Colpe, *Die religionsgeschichtliche Schule,* 95.

103. See Colpe, *Die religionsgeschichtliche Schule,* 97.

104. See Colpe, "Die gnostische Gestalt des Erlöst Erlösers"; and *Die religionsgeschichtliche Schule,* 171–174.

105. See Colpe, *Die religionsgeschichtliche Schule,* 174–176, 186.

106. Ibid., 188.

107. Ibid., 189–191.

108. See ibid., 140–170.

109. See ibid., 144–145. Colpe agreed that not even the argument that the Gayomart tradition is essentially derived from Zurvanism would change this conclusion. Zurvanism presented a monistic solution to the prevalent Zoroastrian dualism, and during the Sasanian period this solution came to be regarded as heretical. It resolved the dualism of Ormuzd and Hariman by ascribing the origin of both to one higher divine father, the Infinite (see ibid., 144). It has been demonstrated that Mani relied heavily on Zurvan tradition. But, says Colpe, it is apparent that he could not take over the Gayomart of Zurvanism as his Urmensch: "he placed him with the name Gehmurd only as the protoplast, while the real Urmensch was designated Ohrmazd" (ibid., 147).

110. See ibid., 149. As examples of the Son of Man in "late Judaism," Reitzenstein pointed to Daniel 7:4, Ezra 13, and the Ethiopian Book of Enoch. To these, we may add the figure of Wisdom; see Bultmann, "Die religiongeschichtliche Hintergrund," 23 ff.

111. Colpe, *Die religionsgeschichtliche Schule,* 150.

112. Ibid., 152.

113. Ibid., 191.

114. Ibid., 203.

115. Ibid., 203–204.

116. Ibid., 8.

117. Ibid., 200.

118. See Eltester, *Christentum und Gnosis.*

119. The practice of writing a genealogy of Gnosis (defined by one or two general characteristics) and then condemning it in terms quite reminiscent of heresy seems still to be alive and well; see, for example, Brumlik, *Die Gnostiker.*

## 6. After Nag Hammadi I

1. The precise circumstances of finds made by non-archaeologists usually remain completely obscure. We owe our excellent information about the Nag Hammadi find to the persevering investigations of J. M. Robinson (see "From Cliff to Cairo," *The Nag Hammadi Codices,* and the Introduction to *The Nag Hammadi Library in English*).

2. The find included twelve codices and one tractate. There were fifty-two tractates, but some of the codices contain different versions of the same work—for example, there are three versions of *ApJohn*—so that the number of distinct

works totals forty-six. For discussion of the Pachomian connection, see Goehring, *Ascetics, Society and the Desert,* 214–216.

3. See, for example, Aland, "Was ist Gnosis?"; Haardt, "Bemerkungen zu den Methoden"; Haenchen, "Gab es eine vorchristliche Gnosis?"; Scholten, "Probleme der Gnosisforschung"; Schenke, "Was ist Gnosis?"

4. This issue was brought home for me at a conference exploring the relationship between women's lives and goddess traditions. Scholars considering the ancient Mediterranean world painstakingly gathered shreds and fragments, and from them had to tell a story. Scholars working with living cultures, such as that of contemporary India, by contrast, were overwhelmed with the sheer volume and complexity of the available data. Yet scholars with less evidence were less hesitant to draw conclusions and produce comprehensive narrative frameworks. It seems that silence offers an enticingly uncontested space in which to pour the imagination, while cacophony leads to quieter but perhaps more insightful reflection. Or perhaps it is that the invisibility of social complexity makes general theorizing appear more plausible since one is less often contradicted by the facts.

5. See Schenke, "The Work of the *Berliner Arbeitskreis.*"

6. See Robinson, "Nag Hammadi: The First Fifty Years." A facsimile edition and a full edition of the texts have appeared in the series "Nag Hammadi Studies," published by E. J. Brill, Leiden.

7. These works appear in the series "Bibliothèque Copte de Nag Hammadi," published jointly by Les presses de l'Université Laval, Québec, and Éditions Peeters, Louvain and Paris; see Painchaud, "Le project d'édition."

8. Everyone interested in Nag Hammadi studies and Gnosticism is gratefully indebted to Scholer for this work: *Nag Hammadi Bibliography 1948–1969, Nag Hammadi Bibliography 1970–1994,* and annual updates of "Bibliographica Gnostica" in the journal *Novum Testamentum.*

9. For an excellent review and assessment of this work, see Perkins, *Gnosticism and the New Testament.*

10. We may now add the recently published *GosSavior* to this list (see Hedrick and Mirecki, *The Gospel of the Savior*).

11. See, for example, the discussions of Wisse, "The Nag Hammadi Library and the Heresiologists."

12. More than eighty pages of bibliography have been collected by Scholer for the period 1948–1994 on the polemicists alone.

13. Robinson, *Trajectories,* 62, 69.

14. Koester, *Trajectories,* 115–116. He goes on to suggest one central criterion: "whether and in which way that which has happened historically, i.e., in the

earthly Jesus of Nazareth, is present in each given case as the criterion—not necessarily as the content—of Christian proclamation and theology" (117).

15. Ibid., 116–117.

16. See especially *Ennead* II.9; Porphyry, *Life of Plotinus*, 16. For further discussion, see King, *Revelation of the Unknowable God*, 47–50.

17. The conference convened as the Sixth International Conference of the International Society for Neoplatonic Studies at the University of Oklahoma in March 1984. The papers of the conference have appeared in Wallis and Bregman, ed., *Neoplatonism and Gnosticism*. In addition, the "Gnosticism and Later Platonism" seminar convened at the national meetings of the Society of Biblical Literature. The collected papers have appeared in J. Turner and Majercik, *Gnosticism and Later Platonism*.

18. With hesitation, Michel Desjardins adds both *I* and *II ApocJames* and *LetPeterPhil* to the initial list of seven (*Sin in Valentinianism*, 5–7). Koschorke also sees some basic Valentinian influence in *I ApocJames* and *TestTruth* ("Patristische Materialen," 122). Tardieu would add *ApJames* and *TestTruth* ("Le Congrès de Yale," 192).

19. Some scholars have ascribed *GosTruth* to Valentinus on the basis of the testimony of Irenaeus and comparison with the undoubted fragments of Valentinus' writing (see the arguments of van Unnik, "The 'Gospel of Truth' and the New Testament"; Wilson, "Valentinianism and the Gospel of Truth," 133–141; Markschies, *Valentinus Gnostikus?*).

20. For example, van Unnik takes the former position (see "The 'Gospel of Truth' and the New Testament"); Jonas, the latter (see "Evangelium Veritatis and the Valentinian Speculation"). Thomassen suggests a third possibility for consideration: that *GosTruth* was originally a non-Valentinian text that was appropriated and presumably written by Valentinians (see "Notes pour l'delimitation," 251–253).

21. Einar Thomassen suggests the following degree of probability for works he considers to be of Valentinian provenance:

1. Certain or at least highly probable: *TriTrac, GosPhil, I ApocJames, InterKnow,* and *ValExp.*
2. Probable: *GosTruth* and *TreatRes.*
3. Possible: *AuthTeach* and *ExSoul.*
4. Valentinian rewriting of non-Valentinian works: *PrayerPaul* and *Eugnostos.*

(See Thomassen, "Notes pour la délimitation d'un Corpus Valentinien," esp. 258).

22. See his conclusion, *Valentinus Gnostikos?*, 402–407.

23. See Schenke, "Das Sethianische System," esp. 166–167, and "The Phenomenon and Significance of Gnostic Sethianism." Much of the following discussion is drawn from King, *Revelation of the Unknowable God,* 34–40.

24. See Schenke, "The Phenomenon of Gnostic Sethianism," esp. 593–597 and 602–607.

25. See ibid., 588–589.

26. John Turner, for example, argues for inclusion of *Trimorphic Protennoia* and *Hypsiphrone;* see *The Nag Hammadi Library in English,* ed. Robinson and Smith, 511–512, 501–502. Some argue for inclusion of *On the Origin of the World* on the basis of a possible literary relationship to *HypArch,* and for *Melchizedek* on the basis of its reference to "children of Seth" (*Melchizedek,* 5.20). See Schenke, "The Phenomenon and Significance of Gnostic Sethianism," 588–589.

27. See Wisse, "Stalking Those Elusive Sethians"; and M. Williams's discussion of sectarianism in *The Immovable Race,* 186–209. See also J. Turner, "Sethian Gnosticism: A Literary History," 56; and "Typologies of the Sethian Gnostic Treatises."

28. For example, he posits a shift away from Christianity toward Platonizing versions of the Sethian myth; my work on the manuscript variants of *ApJohn,* by contrast, shows increasing rather than decreasing conformity to other Christian works, such as the Gospel of John.

29. Noted by Thomassen, "Notes pour la délimitation," 243–244.

30. See Sevrin, *Le dossier baptismal séthien;* Logan, *Gnostic Truth and Christian Heresy,* 11 (see also xix, 34, and note 44, p. 61). In particular, Logan points to the foundational importance of Irenaeus' description of the Barbeloites in Irenaeus, *AgHer* I, 29, which Schenke had noted but not given the same foundational importance.

31. See especially the excellent article of Poirier, "The Writings ascribed to Thomas."

32. The first two have taken on especial importance. The international conference on "The Rediscovery of Gnosticism," convened by Bentley Layton at Yale University in March 1978, reflected the importance of these two categories of Gnostic literature by focusing the two main seminars on Valentinian Gnosticism and Sethian Gnosticism (see the papers collected in Layton, *The Rediscovery of Gnosticism*).

33. *AgHer* I, 11, 1 (trans. Unger and Dillon, *St. Irenaeus,* 51); Layton, "Prolegomena," 343; Markschies, *Valentinus Gnosticus?,* 405.

34. She makes this argument in some depth regarding *ApJohn* (see *A Separate God,* 387–419), but concludes that it is generally valid regarding Sethianism (485).

35. *Against the Valentinians*, 39 (trans. Cleveland Coxe in *Ante-Nicene Fathers* III, 520).

36. The papers are collected in Painchaud and Pasquier, *Les Textes du Nag Hammadi*.

37. See especially Funk, "The Linguistic Aspect of Classifying"; M. Williams, "The Nag Hammadi Library as 'Collections.'"

38. Painchaud and Pasquier, *Les Textes du Nag Hammadi*, x.

39. A good example is *ApJohn*. Some regard the work as only secondarily Christianized, and therefore not truly Christian; yet others would say that its basic content is truly Christian; all consider it Christian in its present form.

40. Yes, scholars have even established and argued over what is authentic pagan philosophy (see Dillon, "'Orthodoxy' and 'Eclecticism'"; see also his notion of "the Platonic underground" in *The Middle Platonists*).

41. For a summary of the history of this discussion before Layton, see Logan, *Gnostic Truth and Christian Heresy*, 1–13. See also M. Tardieu and J.-D. Dubois, *Introduction à la littérature gnostique I*, 21–29, for a discussion of primary sources.

42. Casey, "The Study of Gnosticism," 55.

43. See Casey, "The Study of Gnosticism," 48 and n. 3, and 54–55.

44. Ibid., 55, 58, 60, 59.

45. See M. Smith, "History of the Term Gnostikos," 806; see also 805 for discussion of the polemical usage of the term by Irenaeus. Smith had little confidence that his advice would be followed. The term is too economically and psychologically appealing. With a severely dry wit, he concludes: "'Gnosticism' is salable, therefore it will continue to be produced. Indeed, our lack of information about true, ancient gnosticism will probably prove a great advantage to manufacturers of the modern, synthetic substitute. They need no longer be distracted by consideration of ancient data, since those prove to be mostly unreliable. Now they can turn without restraint to the important question, the philosophic definition of the concept. As gnostics themselves, they can follow the gnostic saviour, escape from the lower world of historical facts, and ascend to the pleroma of perfect words that emanate forever from the primaeval void" (806–807).

46. Layton, "Prolegomena," 335.

47. Ibid., 334, 340–341, 343. The absence of this self-designation within the surviving literature attributed to them is not significant according to Layton because of the pseudepigraphic and mythic nature of the texts themselves; in short, the texts claim to be by ancient culture heroes or divine revealers, not by members of the Gnostic school themselves. "In such compositions, there is no context in which a second-century school name such as Gnostikos might naturally occur" (344).

48. M. Williams, *Rethinking Gnosticism*, 265. For further discussion of William's suggestion with regard to the problem of typology, see below, 214–216.

49. See Robinson's summary in "The Coptic Gnostic Library Today," 372–380.

50. *Le origini dello Gnosticismo*, xxvi–xxvii.

51. See the comments of Wilson, "Gnosis and Gnosticism: The Messina Definition," and his earlier article, "From Gnosis to Gnosticism."

52. *Le origini dello Gnosticismo*, xxviii.

53. See, for example, Wilson, *Gnosis and the New Testament*.

54. As George MacRae put it, with his usual candor and insight, what mattered most to scholars was "the issue of *the originality of early Christian theology and language* . . . It is over this issue ultimately that the scholarly stand-off was established" (*Studies,* 168, my emphasis). For a more extended argument of this thesis, see King, "The Politics of Syncretism"; "Mackinations on Myth and Origins."

55. See Koester, "Conclusion: The Scope and Intention of Trajectories," in Robinson and Koester, *Trajectories,* esp. 277–279.

56. See Magne, *From Christianity to Gnosis.*

57. Each category of course has a variety of possibilities and more specific determinants, such as Jewish-Christian (Christian), apocalyptic (Judaism), Iranian (Oriental), Platonizing (Greek philosophy), and so on.

58. For a summary of research on the Jewish origin of Gnosticism, see Logan, *Gnostic Truth and Christian Heresy,* xvi–xvii, and n. 15. An earlier perspective is offered by Bousset, "Die Religion der Mandäer," 190, 201. See also Maier, "Jüdische Faktoren"; Tröger, "The Attitude of Gnostic Religion" and "Gnosis und Judentum"; van Unnik, "Gnosis und Judentum"; Wilson, "Jewish 'Gnosis' and Gnostic Origins."

59. Friedländer, *Der vorchristliche jüdische Gnosticismus.* My discussion is based on the work of Pearson, "Friedländer Revisited," in *Gnosticism, Judaism, and Egyptian Christianity.*

60. Cohen notes: "The Ignatian use of the verb [*ioudaïzein*] has been taken to refer to Jewish life in general, but the context suggests that the slighting of the Lord's Day (Sunday) in favor of the Sabbath is the specific issue at hand" (*The Beginnings of Jewishness,* 187). He is no doubt on the right track, but my point here is less the meaning of "living according to Judaism" than the fact that "erroneous" behavior is linked to a misunderstanding of "the divine prophets."

61. *EpMag* 8.1–2 (cited in Lake, *Apostolic Fathers,* 205).

62. *EpSmyr,* 5.1–2 (cited in Lake, *Apostolic Fathers,* 257).

63. Cohen has carefully examined the Christian use of the Greek term *ioudaïzein,* and he concludes: "In Christian Greek *ioudaïzein* almost always has

its cultural meaning: (a) to adopt the customs and manners of the Jews. But within this definitional framework Christians invested the word with new meanings, new overtones, and a new specificity not previously attested. The specifically Christian meanings, in the order of their first attestation, are: (b) to be Jewish or to become Jewish; (c) to interpret the Old Testament 'literally'; (d) to deny the divinity of Christ. In addition, in one passage *ioudaïzein* combines the 'cultural' meaning with the political: (e) to give support to the Jews by adopting their customs and manners. Of course, there are also several passages in which the exact meaning of the word is not clear, and in any number of passages *ioudaïzein* is used with several meanings simultaneously, but all in all I think this fivefold distinction is useful" (*The Beginnings of Jewishness*, 186). Cohen's list gives us a good start toward understanding more specifically the content of the Christian construction of Judaism, but only (c) seems concerned with the issue I have raised: interpretation of Scripture. My point here is that Christian polemicists argued that all these "errors" of "Judaizing" arose as a result of the rejection of Jesus as the divine Christ, an error that they tied directly to the misunderstanding of the true meaning of Scripture.

64. On the question of heresy or "Gnosticizing," ancient and modern discourses about the relationship between Christianity and Judaism are not identical, however close their similarities. Although some modern scholars share certain assumptions and methods with the ancient Christian polemicists, shown, for example, in the attempts to establish a linear genealogy and a common origin for Gnosticism or the use of a thoroughly antisyncretistic discourse, modern scholars are faced with a greater variety of evidence (including not only the literature of the ancient polemicists, Jewish, Christian, and Greek, but also recent literary finds of Manichaean, Mandaean, and Coptic Gnostic literature), a more complex social-historical map of the Eastern Mediterranean world, and a modernist historiographical methodology. They also assume a more ambiguous relationship between Christianity and Judaism. They tend, for example, to regard nascent Christianity as one variety of ancient Judaism. Rather than understand Christianity to have superseded Judaism, modern scholars see these as essentially independent religions. Historical critics acknowledge the legitimacy of Jewish interpretation of Hebrew Scripture, albeit in tension with reading the Old Testament as Christian Scripture and prophecy. Modern scholars are, nonetheless, also heirs to a long history of Christian anti-Judaism. All this vastly complicates the understanding of the relationship of Gnosticism to Christianity.

65. See the discussion of Layton, *The Gnostic Scriptures*, 21.

66. See Bousset, *Kyrios Christos*, 16–17. For a summary of the position on Jewish origins, see Perkins, *Gnosticism and the New Testament*, 39–42; see also

Pearson, "The Development of Gnostic Self-Definition," (in *Gnosticism, Judaism and Egyptian Christianity,* 126–130); J. M. Robinson, *Trajectories,* 66–67, 266.

67. See Quispel, "Der gnostische Anthropos and die jüdische Tradition." See also MacRae, "The Jewish Background of the Gnostic Sophia Myth"; Böhlig, "Der jüdische und jüdenchristliche Hintergrund"; Stroumsa, *Another Seed;* Fallon, *The Enthronement of Sabaoth;* and Pearson, especially "Jewish Sources," "Use, Authority, and Exegesis of Mikra in Gnostic Literature," "The Problem of Jewish Gnostic Literature," and the essays collected in *Gnosticism.*

68. See, for example, the recent work of Luttikhuizen, "The Thought Pattern" and "Traces of Aristotelian Thought."

69. See, for example, Wisse, "The Nag Hammadi Library and the Heresiologists," 222–223.

70. See Böhlig, "Die Adamsapokalypse"; MacRae, "The Coptic Gnostic Apocalypse of Adam."

71. See, for example, Kasser, "Textes gnostiques" and Schenke's review *Koptisch-gnostische Apokalypsen aus Codex V.* The point is summarized by Douglas Parrot in Robinson and Smith, ed., *The Nag Hammadi Library in English,* 278.

72. Even Pearson concedes that "such Jewish influence as can be found in it belongs to its prehistory, i.e., the earlier formulations of the Sethian system which is reflected in it" (in Robinson and Smith, *Nag Hammadi Library,* 446).

73. See Layton, *Gnostic Scriptures,* 21.

74. See Schenke, "Nag Hammadi Studien I"; "The Book of Thomas: A Revision of a Pseudepigraphical Epistle of Jacob the Contender"; and *Das Thomas-Buch.* King has argued that the framework of *ApJohn,* which presents the work as a revelation from Christ to John, is essential to the work as it is now titled (see "Approaching the Variants of the *Apocryphon of John*"). Pagels has argued that the reference to "the great apostle" at the beginning of *HypArch* is not a superficial Christianization, but that the work draws broadly on Pauline interpretation of Genesis for its own presentation (see "Genesis Creation Accounts from Nag Hammadi," esp. 265–285). John Turner places *BookThomas* within the Syrian Christian Thomas tradition (see *The Book of Thomas the Contender,* 233–237). See also the summary of Perkins, *Gnosticism and the New Testament,* 26–27; Krause, "The Christianization of Gnostic Texts."

75. In *Nag Hammadi Codices IX and X,* 101–120.

76. Pearson, *Gnosticism, Judaism, and Egyptian Christianity,* 39–51.

77. *Gnosticism, Judaism, and Egyptian Christianity,* 50.

78. In a set of similar moves, Pearson takes up the Sethian corpus, dividing it into non-Christian and non-Jewish literature, and secondarily Christianized literature (See "The Development of Gnostic Self-Definition" in *Gnosticism, Judaism,*

*and Egyptian Christianity,* 124–135). From these he abstracts Schenke's typological list of distinctively Sethian traits and traces them all back to speculations on Jewish literature. These again are interpreted in terms of alienation and revolt of Jews from their own traditions. In this case, Pearson concluded that "the essential feature of Gnosticism in its earliest history is its revolutionary attitude toward Judaism and Jewish traditions" (ibid., 134). The Christian elements he treats as secondary; the importance of Platonizing elements he also attributes to "intellectuals . . . able to incorporate ideas and traditions from the syncretistic milieu of the Hellenized Levant," apparently at a later stage in the history of Sethianism (ibid., 133). This method produces its conclusion: removing all non-Jewish materials as secondary leaves only Jewish remains.

Using this same method, Pearson also located Jewish tradition and worship patterns in the Hermetic *Poimandres;* in this case, however, he did not attribute the origins of Hermeticism to Judaism, but regarded Hermeticism as a syncretizing product of Roman Egypt (see "Jewish Elements in *Corpus Hermeticum I (Poimandres),*" in *Gnosticism, Judaism, and Egyptian Christianity,* 147).

79. For example, *Allogenes, Marsanes,* and *Zostr. StelesSeth* forms a special case, since the name of Seth is from Genesis, though the text otherwise shows little knowledge of Judaism. Another special case is *Eugnostos.* Although this work represents a type of ancient philosophical speculation, it has been secondarily converted into a dialogue between Jesus Christ and his disciples (twelve men and seven women), titled *SophJesChr.* These works have generally been considered to be "late" and thus not useful for locating the *origin* of Gnosticism. See also Wisse, "The Nag Hammadi Library and the Heresiologists," 222–223.

80. See Turner, "A Literary History."

81. English translation: *A Separate God: The Christian Origins of Gnosticism* (1990), 4, 12.

82. This methodology appears clearly in her own summary of procedure (Pétrement, *A Separate God,* 26).

83. See, for example, her arguments concerning *ApJohn* (Pétrement, *A Separate God,* 387–419).

84. Logan, *Gnostic Truth and Christian Heresy,* 34, 37–39, xviii, 42. For a summary of his reconstruction of the contents of this myth, see ibid., 42.

85. See ibid., xix.

86. The issue is evident, for example, in his discussion of *Allogenes* and *GosEgypt,* cases where he argues explicitly that "the apparent lack of Christian features does not make the work necessarily non-Christian: the basic mythological and ritual structure I have argued derive from Christianity, and Porphyry's testimony suggests that a work, like *Allogenes* (and *The Three Steles of Seth?*), was the

product of Christian Gnostic groups" (Logan, *Gnostic Truth and Christian Heresy*, 53).

87. See Grant, *Gnosticism and Early Christianity*, 27–38, esp. 35 and 37. He arrives at this conclusion by comparing Gnosticism to a dubious and itself problematic analysis of the defeat of Plains Indians in nineteenth-century America: "When their warfare failed, their traditional culture 'became inadequate and disorganized.' Under these circumstances, 'the usual symptoms of social maladjustment appeared: preoccupation with the problem situation, questioning of custom, social unrest, increased nonconformity, breakdown of social controls, social disorganization, and personality maladjustment.' The same difficulties are to be found among most Gnostics" (*Gnosticism and Early Christianity*, 34–35).

88. Grant, *Gnosticism and Early Christianity*, 118. The inclusion of Gentiles also accounted for the non-Jewish elements.

89. See MacRae, *Studies*, 172–174. Note here the partial reinscription of Jonas's position.

90. See, for example, MacRae, "The Jewish Background of the Gnostic Sophia Myth."

91. See also the summary of Rudolph, *Gnosis*, 277–282, and "Randerscheinungen"; Pokorny, "Der soziale Hintergrund."

92. Pearson points to the "six dimensions of what constitutes 'a religion'" suggested by Ninian Smart: "doctrinal, mythic, ethical, ritual, experiential, and social" (*Gnosticism, Judaism, and Egyptian Christianity*, 8, n. 27; see also "Is Gnosticism a Religion?"). He then applies each of them to Gnosticism (see pages 7–9 for a description of these "dimensions" following a typological model). The presence of all these dimensions, however, shows not that Gnosticism is an independent religious tradition, but only that Gnostic texts and materials do belong to the sphere of religion. Otherwise we would have to proclaim, for example, that Pauline Christianity is a separate religion, since it, too, shows all these dimensions. Although these dimensions are *necessary* to show the existence of a religious tradition, they are not *sufficient* to establish a set of materials as constituting a separate religion in its own right. As to the origin of Gnosticism in Judaism, he traces this thesis back to the 1898 work of Friedländer, *Der vorchristliche jüdische Gnosticismus* (see Pearson, "Friedländer Revisited," in *Gnosticism, Judaism, and Egyptian Christianity*, 10–28). See also ibid., 125, on the relation to Christianity.

93. Ibid., 130.

94. Pearson, *Gnosticism, Judaism, and Egyptian Christianity*, 51 (my emphasis). See also 134: "The essential feature of Gnosticism in its earliest history is its revolutionary attitude toward Judaism and Jewish traditions."

95. Ibid., 51. Of course, Harnack had already explored the importance of her-

meneutics in considerable depth in relation to Marcion. Harnack's fundamental insight was the importance of Biblical hermeneutics, combined with a "resentment" toward Judaism, for the generation of Marcion's theology (Harnack, *Marcion,* 15). Although his Christian critics saw only Marcion's rejection of the Old Testament as canon, the fact is, Harnack argued, that the fundamental framework for Marcion's thought was tied to the Old Testament (Harnack, *Marcion,* 23; see especially 25–63). The Old Testament was the source of his teaching about the nature of the creator God, and hence the basis for positing the existence of an alien God. The portrayal of God in the Old Testament was problematic for Marcion precisely because, rather than employing allegory, retelling, or some other midrashic technique to diminish the impact of these problems, as so many other Jewish and Christian exegetes were doing, he read the Scriptures as *literally true.* Marcion appears radical simply because he accepts the problematic portraits of God as a limited, jealous, and arbitrary deity as literal description. As M. Williams points out (*Rethinking Gnosticism,* 54–79), certain passages were widely recognized as problematic ("scriptural chestnuts"), but in correcting the facile and largely negative caricature of Gnostic interpretation as "protest exegesis," Williams downplays the denunciatory results of such exegesis. Certainly there were recognized problems with the portrayal of God in the Hebrew Scriptures, but how did denunciation of those portrayals lead not to simple rejection but to the generation of an entirely new mythology?

96. See, for example, Quispel, "The Origins of the Gnostic Demiurge"; Fossum, "Gen. 1,26 and 2,7," and "The Origin of the Gnostic Concept of the Demiurge."

97. Perkins, *Gnosticism and the New Testament,* 187–188.

98. The same could be said for the so-called *mînîm* discussed below. There is no evidence from Rabbinic polemic that these "heretics" actually saw the world-creator as the God of Genesis and styled him as evil and ignorant. It is a long step from "two powers in heaven" (an idea Daniel Boyarin has suggested may have been aimed at the likes of Philo's *logos*) to the Yaldabaoth of *ApJohn.* See "The Gospel of the Memra."

99. Although ascetic practice was not foreign to various types of Judaism in this period (one has only to think of Qumran or the Theraputae praised by Philo), in no case are sexuality and reproduction regarded as antithetical to righteousness before God *as such.* That, of course, might precisely make Jews the target of accusations of impurity by ascetic-tending Gnostics, but it makes it highly unlikely that the *source* of such criticism of Jewish belief and practice would come from within Judaism.

100. Segal, *Two Powers in Heaven,* 255.

101. He states this point quite directly (see Quispel, "Judaism, Judaic Chris-

tianity and Gnosis," 59), and reaffirms it in "The Origins of the Gnostic Demiurge": "Such expressions of *Selbsthass* are possible, because there are historical parallels for them" (213).

102. Quispel, "Judaism, Judaic Christianity and Gnosis," 60.

103. These remarks were framed in his response to an earlier essay by Quispel ("Gnosticism and the New Testament"), and indeed the essays I just quoted (n. 101) may very well have been framed in part as a response to Jonas.

104. Jonas found these embedded in Quispel's essay "Gnosticism and the New Testament." Jonas, "Response to G. Quispel," 289.

105. See ibid., 288–289.

106. Jonas writes (sardonically): "Was that reaction perhaps begotten, incubated and brought forth in the midst of Judaism itself—by Jews? Who would say that this is impossible? We have learned that almost nothing is impossible in human psychology, not even anti-Semitism among Jews. And what an exciting nay soul-shaking spectacle that would be: the greatest iconoclasm before modernity erupting in Judaism—Jews themselves turning against their holiest, tearing it down, trampling it into the dust, reveling in its utter humiliation, proclaiming the complete devaluation of all traditional values—Nietzsche, Sartre, Saint Genet rolled into one: how fascinating, how modern. Of all the many genealogies of Gnosticism tried out so far, this would surely be the most interesting. But before we surrender to the lure of mere possibility, we ask for evidence" ("Response to G. Quispel," 289–290).

107. He writes with what must be a certain irony: "In the spirit of generosity after the holocaust, our (the Jews') credit for creativity has been vastly extended; and Jewish vanity, which of course is not lacking, might be pleased to welcome into the record even the disreputable, which in the present climate (with all the alienation going around) enjoys its own paradoxical prestige" (ibid., 291).

108. In his rejoinder to Jonas's response, Quispel points to one example of Jewish Gnostics, the Magharians, "who taught a highest God and an inferior creator of the world." Although the evidence about this group dates from the fourteenth century, Quispel argues that it should be dated to pre-Christian times ("The Origins of the Gnostic Demiurge," 215). See also Jonas, "Response to G. Quispel," 292.

109. Jonas, "Response to G. Quispel," 293.

110. Filoramo apparently misunderstands Jonas here. Although he himself takes Jonas's position—without attributing it to Jonas (*A History of Gnosticism,* 144, 146)—he reads Jonas's response to Quispel as an argument for the Jewish origins of Gnosticism! (see *A History of Gnosticism,* 234, n. 14).

111. In "Nag Hammadi and the New Testament" (first published in Aland, *Gnosis. Festschrift für Hans Jonas,* 144–157; reprint in MacRae, *Studies,* 173).

112. See Pétrement, *A Separate God,* 15. For example, in treating *Allogenes* (NHC XI,2), a primary example of non-Christian, philosophical Gnosticism, she writes: "It is silence that teaches about God. (But silence is nothing other than the meaning of the cross.)" See *A Separate God,* 433. *Allogenes,* however, offers no evidence for such a conclusion.

113. See Pétrement, *A Separate God,* 493–494, n. 69. She also suggests that later forms of non-Christian Gnosticism, such as Manicheism, Mandaeism, or the *Corpus Hermeticum,* could have arisen out of Christian Gnosticism (25–26).

114. Pétrement, *A Separate God,* 9, 10–11.

115. See ibid., 9–10. Note that she anachronistically defines Christianity in canonical terms.

116. Ibid., 22, 23, 24. Later Pétrement insists that such a vision of another world is necessary for human moral orientation: "Nietzsche was wrong simply to regard the Christian attitude as entirely negative and blameworthy. It is good, as he puts it, to want 'to remain faithful to the earth.' But looked at from another angle, not to want to judge things from the point of view of a *value,* a *good* that is above all things, that is foreign, like the God of the Gnostics, that is finally *absolute,* apart, is in the end to justify all injustice, all lies, and all evil from the moment they begin to exist" (ibid., 23). We see here what she no doubt considers to be the ethical core of Christianity.

117. See ibid., 10–11, 15. From my summary of Pétrement's work, one might think that she saw Gnosticism as an authentic variety of Christianity. That conclusion would not be quite accurate, for she still considered Gnosticism to be a secondary and "excessive" (heretical) development of Christianity, however much it relied on impulses fundamental to original Christianity.

118. Jonas, "Response to G. Quispel," 293.

119. Burrus, private communication, January 23, 2002.

120. For example, the fundamental difference between scholars like Pearson and Pétrement lies less in their analysis of the evidence than in their definitions of Christianity. Both worked out of the same evidence with very similar methods and presuppositions, yet they came to very different conclusions. We could suggest that where one begins is crucial. Pearson, for example, focused primarily on the Sethian material, while Pétrement began with the Church fathers and the Valentinian sources. Logan can start with the Sethian materials and end up supporting Pétrement's theory of Gnostic origins in Christianity because he reads the Sethian material quite differently from Pearson and has a different understanding of the essential character of Gnosticism. But much more fundamentally, the crux is that while Pétrement discerns authentically Christian elements in Gnostic thought, especially in the need for human liberation from the world through a revelation not of this world, Pearson cannot see anything authentically Christian

here because the Gnostic denial that the world was created by the true God looms so large for him. Such a perspective is, in his opinion, so essentially non-Christian that it must be attributed to a different religious attitude altogether—and one for which he has no appreciation. It is ironic that although Pétrement relies more directly than Pearson on the Christian polemicists, Pearson's theological evaluation of Gnosticism is closer to them than is Pétrement's. My point is that their positions are fundamentally opposed because they understand Christianity in essentially different ways, even though they share a common methodological approach and a similar understanding of Gnosticism.

121. Jonas, *The Gnostic Religion,* 326.

122. See Schenke, "The Problem of Gnosis," 79; Colpe, "Gnosis, I. Religionsgeschichtlich," 1651.

## 7. After Nag Hammadi II

1. I raised these issues in "The Rationale of Gnostic Ethics" (1992) and "Is There Such a Thing as Gnosticism?" (1993), both papers read at the Society of Biblical Literature meetings (cited in the bibliography of M. Williams, *Rethinking Gnosticism*). This chapter is based largely on these papers. See also King, "The Body and Society in Philo and the *Apocryphon of John.*"

2. In his widely read history of early Christianity, Henry Chadwick describes Gnosticism in terms of the Gnostic redeemer myth, a Gnostic ethic of asceticism or libertinism, a docetic Christology, devaluation of the Old Testament, and "a rigidly deterministic scheme" in which "redemption was from destiny, not from the consequences of responsible action, and was granted to a pre-determined elect in whom alone was the divine spark" (Chadwick, *The Early Church,* 35–38). "The details of the myths of the various sects were widely divergent," he states, "but the basic pattern can be seen to be constant" (ibid., 36).

3. The proposal of the Messina Congress recognized the problem with dualism and so tried to define it and distinguish among different types: "Dualism is a genus with several species" (Bianchi, *Origini dello Gnosticismo,* xxviii). The genus involves a dichotomy: "i.e. the drastic separation, or opposition between the principles which—be they co-eternal or not—underlie the *existence* of what, in one way, or another, is found in the world" (ibid). The species were defined by the *value* they attributed to the created world: Gnosticism is anticosmic and regards the world as evil; Zoroastrian dualism regards the world favorably; Greek philosophy sees the constitution of the world as a dialectic of two irreducible and complementary principles (ibid., xxviii–xxix). The Messina definition tries to distinguish these species solely on the basis of evaluations of the goodness of creation. This use of a Christian theological category as the prime distinguishing element

shows up the context in which the categories were formed and their continuing interest, but it is not very useful for the actual task of description because the three options are actually structurally very similar and difficult to differentiate in practice.

4. See Schoedel, "Gnostic Monism and the Gospel of Truth."

5. See *Gos Truth* 17.5–9.

6. This view is expressed by saying that He "encircles all spaces while there is none that encircles Him" (*Gos Truth* 22.25–27, following the translation of George MacRae in Robinson and Smith, *The Nag Hammadi Library in English*, 45). Schoedel notes that this view is "a theme of fundamental importance in the doctrine of God in the early church" and is found in "writings of both the Greek and Latin fathers." He suggests that the concept can be traced back as far as the pre-Socratics but appears most clearly in Philo (see "Gnostic Monism and the Gospel of Truth," 380–381). Layton suggests that "the cosmological model of GTr [*Gos Truth*] is provided by Stoic pantheistic monism and by astronomy" (*The Gnostic Scriptures*, 250).

7. See *Gos Truth* 18.10–26. Quote is from *Gos Truth* 32.31–33.32 (trans. George MacRae, in Robinson and Smith, *The Nag Hammadi Library in English*, 46–47).

8. See Pearson, "Gnosticism as Platonism," in *Gnosticism, Judaism, and Egyptian Christianity*, 148–164. In keeping with his thesis about the Jewish origins of Gnosticism, Pearson sees this text as an example of "a definite tendency to move away from the radical dualism of early Gnosticism in the direction of a more monistic and procosmic understanding of reality. In my opinion this tendency is directly attributable to the influence of Platonic philosophy, and can be accounted for by positing a considerable degree of discussion between Gnostics and Platonists in schools such as that of Plotinus in Rome" (162). There is, however, no evidence within the text that it developed from "radical dualism."

9. *Marsanes* 5.24–26; 7.5–6 (trans. Pearson, *Nag Hammadi Codices IX and X*, 265, 269).

10. See King, *Revelation of the Unknowable God*, especially 16–20. At only one point in the work is there even a hint about the existence of the world: at 51.30–32, we are told that Autogenes is "the savior who corrects the sins deriving from nature." It is difficult to know precisely what is meant by this statement since the connection of "nature" with the material world is not made explicit. The term "nature" (φύσις) refers at least once to "incorporeal natures" (*Allogenes* 57.17–18) and hence does not necessarily refer to material existence.

11. See *Allogenes* 61.32–66.38; and notes in King, *Revelation of the Unknowable God*, 154–176.

12. See King, *Revelation of the Unknowable God*, 12–16.

13. See *Allogenes* 52.25–28.

14. *BookThomas* 139.25–140.5, 18–37 (trans. J. Turner, in *Nag Hammadi Codex II,2–7*, ed. Layton, 185, 187, 189).

15. Ibid., 145.8–16 (in *Nag Hammadi Codex II, 2–7*, 205).

16. The text is very androcentric, as is shown especially by its condemnation of those "who love intimacy with womankind and polluted intercourse with them!" (*BookThomas*, 144.9–10). Assuming that the discourse is heterosexual, this condemnation would seem not to include women among those whom the text addresses.

17. *GosThom* 29 (trans. Lambdin, in *Nag Hammadi Codex II,2–7*, ed. Layton, 67). See also sayings 56, 87.

18. See, for example, sayings 4, 11, 16, 22, 23, 49, 75, 106.

19. Saying 110 (trans. Lambdin, in *Nag Hammadi Codex II,2–7*, ed. Layton, 93).

20. Such dietary restrictions need not necessarily refer to Jewish purity regulations. Irenaeus, for examples, described some vegetarian groups (see *AgHer* I, 28, 1). See also *GosThom*, sayings 6, 14, 27, 89, and 104.

21. See saying 104. Jesus concludes: "When the bridegroom leaves the bridal chamber, then let them fast and pray." Although this admonition is often interpreted to refer to the death of Jesus (cp. Mark 2.19–20 and par.), *GosThom* provides no support for this suggestion. Instead, it is followed by the saying: "He who knows the father and the mother will be called the son of a harlot." However unclear that saying is, it certainly suggests that an interpretation other than passion prediction is appropriate for saying 104.

22. See sayings 45, 47, 63, 65, 76, 95.

23. Trans. Lambdin, in *Nag Hammadi Codex II,2–7*, ed. Layton, 93, with modification.

24. See Crossan, *Four Other Gospels*, 32–33.

25. *GosThom* 3b (trans. Lambdin, in *Nag Hammadi Codex II,2–7*, ed. Layton, 55, with modification).

26. See *GosThom* 3; compare Deut. 30:11–16.

27. *GosThom* 24 (trans. Lambdin, in *Nag Hammadi Codex II,2–7*, ed. Layton, 65, with modification). See also saying 30.

28. See sayings 28, 77, 82, 108, among others. Modern scholars often compare Jesus with Jewish Wisdom (see especially Davies, *The Gospel of Thomas and Christian Wisdom*, 81–99); see also Borg, "A Temperate Case."

29. *GosThom* 50 (trans. Lambdin, in *Nag Hammadi Codex II,2–7*, ed. Layton, 73).

30. See, for example, Patterson, in Kloppenborg et al., *Q-Thomas Reader*, 96–97.

31. Trans. Lambdin, in *Nag Hammadi Codex II,2–7*, ed. Layton, 73.

32. Patterson, in *Q-Thomas Reader,* 119.

33. Another text that is generally taken to fit the standard description of Gnosticism, *HypArch,* makes it clear that the creation of the world and the body was part of the true God's plan to save the spiritual element of humanity (see, for example, *HypArch* 87.20–23; 88.10–11; 88.33–89.3).

34. Jonas, *The Gnostic Religion,* 253.

35. Rudolph, *Gnosis,* 60.

36. Filoramo, *The History of Gnosticism,* 55.

37. Precisely because of this kind of eisegesis, it has taken us a long time to see that the list of demons in the longer version of *ApJohn* is proof, not of Gnostic demonization of the body, but of belief that exorcism is effective in healing the body.

38. This is especially true when works like *GosThom* or *GosMary* are read as mere allusions to a fully developed Gnostic salvation myth. No doubt they *could* be read that way—their presence in codices containing *ApJohn* indicates that they *were* read that way, at least in the fourth and fifth centuries. We would lose a very important piece of information about the history of the meaning of these Gospels if we were to deny the validity of reading them gnostically; but we would similarly lose very important meanings if we were to reduce their meaning solely to the fourth- and fifth-century readings. Moreover, the appropriation of a text like *GosThom* for diverse hermeneutical projects points less toward the "one, true meaning" of *GosThom* than toward the plural hermeneutic strategies of ancient intertextuality.

39. Jonas, *The Gnostic Religion,* 4, 6; Rudolph, *Gnosis,* 253; Filoramo, *A History of Gnosticism,* chap. 11, esp. 188, 245, n. 88. This perspective is criticized by M. Williams, *Rethinking "Gnosticism,"* 139–140, who refers to my earlier paper "The Rationale of Gnostic Ethics" (293, n. 6).

40. Jonas, for example, cites Irenaeus, *AgHer* I, 6, 2–3, to establish his argument (see *The Gnostic Religion,* 270–271).

41. Irenaeus, *AgHer* I, 6.

42. See, for example, Irenaeus, *AgHer* I, 6, 24–25; Clement of Alexandria, *Strom* V, 1; V, 3, 3.

43. Clement of Alexandria, for example, writes that the Marcionites were led to abstention "not from a moral principle, but from hostility to their maker and unwillingness to use his creation" (*Strom* III, 4, 25). Jonas follows Clement's conclusion, writing: "Thus Marcion's asceticism, unlike that of the Essenes or later of Christian monasticism, was not conceived to further the sanctification of human existence, but was essentially negative in conception and part of the gnostic revolt against the cosmos" (*The Gnostic Religion,* 145). See also Irenaeus, *AgHer* I, 6.

44. *AgHer* I, 28, 1 (trans. Unger and Dillon, *St. Irenaeus of Lyon,* 93).

45. Unger, in Unger and Dillon, *St. Irenaeus of Lyon,* 254.

46. The idea that libertines were creations of the polemicists was most recently argued by M. Williams, "Psyche's Voice" and *Rethinking "Gnosticism,"* 163–188. See Benko, "The Libertine Gnostic Sect of the Phibionites"; Goehring, "Libertine or Liberated"; Buckley, "Libertines or Not."

47. O'Connor, "On Doing Religious Ethics," 91.

48. O'Connor writes: "Since reason in ethics often takes the form of a person giving *reasons* to justify certain actions, the reasons articulated become subject to scrutiny by others. Reasons found to be unacceptable are often labeled 'unreasonable' or 'irrational' when what is really meant (and therefore should be stated) is that the reasons cited are unacceptable because unconvincing" (ibid., 90).

49. See the discussion of Bourdieu, *Outline of a Theory of Practice,* 82–83.

50. See also Epiphanius, *Panarion* 40,1,4; Irenaeus, *AgHer* I, 24, 2.

51. It has, however, become increasingly clear from comparative study that similar types of ascetic behavior can be associated with a wide variety of motivations and rationales (see Wimbush, *Renunciation towards Social Engineering*). The task of the historian of religion is to discover what those motivations and rationales were, as well as to describe the behaviors themselves where there is sufficient information to do so.

52. Often Gnosticism is aligned with paganism (see Ménard, *L'Évangile de vérité,* 167).

53. See, for example, Drower, *The Mandaeans.*

54. Rudolph notes that this point had already been made in 1881 by Koffmane (*Gnosis,* 382, n. 38). See also Löhr, "Gnostic Determinism Reconsidered."

55. Schottroff concludes unequivocally that "the Valentinian texts, which explicitly teach salvation by nature, understand that the one who is saved is not ensured of salvation because of (possessing) some heavenly essence; rather, they use such designations of essence in order to describe the certainty of salvation . . . The misinterpretation of Gnosticism as having a theology of salvation based on the possession of a certain essence stems from the biased polemic of the church fathers and from gnostic anti-Christian polemics such as Irenaeus, *AgHer* 6,2–4, which use the essentialist presentation (as a foil) in order to prove the character of salvation as grace" ("*Animae naturaliter salvandae*," 97).

56. A good recent example is found in an introduction to Gnosticism by the Dutch scholar Riemer Roukema. He states that "the generalization that gnostic knowledge was reserved for an elite is not true. Gnostics were ready to share their special gnosis with others or saw this as their task. Nor did they always think that they alone had a share in redemption. The secret Book of John appears to offer the prospect that all souls will be redeemed apart from those of the apostates. Gnostic Christians did not segregate themselves by definition. They did not ini-

tially always have a separate organization but also formed part of the 'catholic' communities. Initially the dividing line between 'gnostic' and 'catholic' Christianity was not always a sharp one" (*Gnosis and Faith*, 168). But he continues: "It is possible that a number of gnostics did not intend to stand out by their special insight and thus cause offence to catholic Christians and their leaders. Nevertheless, this is the effect that their rise had. The objection to the Gnostics thus related on the one hand to the content of their speculative development of Christian faith, and on the other hand to the attitude that they radiated, as if they knew better. Perhaps Gnostic knowledge was not always meant to be elitist, but that is how it came over" (ibid., 169). He then goes on to contrast Gnostics with the Church: "Over against these Gnostics stood the church, which at that time was called 'apostolic' and 'catholic.' 'Catholic' means 'universal' and was initially used to denote the world-wide church and thus to distinguish it from a local church. However, this term also has another meaning. 'Catholic' as a name for the Christian church also means that salvation is available for all believers and not simply for a particular group which has been initiated into a special gnosis . . . There is room in this church for both the simple and those with knowledge, preferably without anyone referring to a supposed sense of superior insight" (ibid., 169–170). Thus while he begins by treating Gnostics as Christians, and illustrating the nonexclusive character of at least some Gnostics, the rhetoric shifts back to drawing a sharp line between elitist Gnostics and tolerant catholic Christians. Somehow this loses sight of the fact that the apostolic and catholic Church also possessed an internal hierarchy (and one that excluded women). Regarding outsiders, the Church claimed to possess an exclusive revelation of truth—that only those who had a special (baptismal) initiation could expect salvation, while everyone else would go to hell. In contrast, as Roukema himself notes, *ApJohn* insists that all except apostates will be saved.

57. Schottroff, *"Animae naturaliter salvandae,"* 83–86, 90–93, 94.

58. See Desjardins, *Sin in Valentinianism*, 115, 118–119, 116.

59. Ibid., 118. Indeed, he concludes, "Our study has shown that the Valentinian understanding of sin is fundamentally Christian in nature, and that it emerges naturally out of Pauline speculations about sin. Moreover, we have seen how Valentinian ethics in general reflect the gospel injunctions in the NT, notably those in Matthew's Sermon on the Mount" (131).

60. Rudolph, *Gnosis*, 258–259, 261–264.

61. *OrigWorld*, 127.14–17 (my emphasis).

62. Rudolph, *Gnosis*, 261. He also maintains that "from (the new texts) it is clear that the 'pneuma-nature' of the gnostic can on the one hand be understood also as the grace of God, while on the other hand salvation is not automatically assured, but must be accompanied by a corresponding way of life which matches

the acquired condition of one 'redeemed'" (117). He also states: "A life governed by gnostic principles is required of every true gnostic; this is not a matter of indifference to his salvation" (261).

63. M. Williams's similar survey across a wide range of material (*Rethinking "Gnosticism,"* 140–162) yielded a similar result, often based on the same materials. Williams concluded: "We can see that the term 'asceticism' by itself hardly captures the spectrum of attitudes and practices represented among these sources. There was clearly not only room for but encouragement of marriage and procreation in some of these circles. And where sexual procreation was renounced, this did not necessarily mean the renunciation of marriage and family" (160–161).

64. See Slusser, "Docetism."

65. *ApocPet* 81.4–24 (trans. James Brashler and Roger Bullard, in Robinson, *The Nag Hammadi Library in English,* 377).

66. Ibid., 82.21–26, 83.8–10 (in *The Nag Hammadi Library in English,* 377).

67. In Pearson, *Nag Hammadi Codex VII,* 205.

68. *I ApocJames* 30.1–6.

69. Ibid., 31.18–22 (trans. Douglas Parrott, in Robinson and Smith, *The Nag Hammadi Library in English,* 265).

70. *ApJames* 5.33–6.1, 6.1–6, 13.23–25 (trans. Douglas Parrott, in Robinson and Smith, *The Nag Hammadi Library in English,* 32).

71. Ibid., 11.38–12.9 ( in *The Nag Hammadi Library in English,* 35).

72. Compare *GosMary* 3.7–8: "He (the Savior) said, 'This is why you get si[c]k and die: because [you love] what de[c]ei[ve]s [you],'" that is, the body (my translation).

73. The following thesis about the meaning of this passage comes from a seminar paper by Jessica McFarland, "'As We Would Be Saved for Their Sakes': The Structure of Salvation in the *Apocryphon of James*" (January 2000).

74. *ApJames* 10.30–32, 16.1–2, 7.10–16, 6.14–20 (in *The Nag Hammadi Library in English,* 34, 37, 32).

75. Ibid., 8.10–15 (in *The Nag Hammadi Library in English,* 33).

76. *LetPetPhil* 139.9–21 (trans. Frederik Wisse, in Robinson and Smith, *The Nag Hammadi Library in English,* 436).

77. Ibid., 139.21–28 (in *The Nag Hammadi Library in English,* 436).

78. See the discussion of Riley, *Resurrection Reconsidered,* 7–68.

79. *TreatRes* 44.13–33; 48.10–19 (trans. Malcolm Peel, in Robinson and Smith, *The Nag Hammadi Library in English,* 54, 56).

80. Ibid., 45.36–46.2, in *The Nag Hammadi Library in English,* 55.

81. I Cor 15.

82. For further discussion of some other characteristics, see M. Williams, *Rethinking "Gnosticism."*

83. He concludes, "Perhaps some of the above clichés individually are more appropriate in the case of this or that source, but they do not at all capture something essential or characteristic about the collection of 'gnostic' sources" (*Rethinking "Gnosticism,"* 264). Concerning "protest exegesis" and attitudes toward the body, see ibid., 264.

84. Ibid., 51.

85. Ibid.

86. Ibid., 265.

87. Ibid., 266.

## 8. The End of Gnosticism?

1. See especially *The Archaeology of Knowledge.*

2. See recent work in cultural and ideological criticism, for example, Schüssler Fiorenza, *Rhetoric and Ethics;* Young, *Colonial Desire;* Olender, *The Languages of Paradise;* and Chakrabarty, *Provincializing Europe.*

3. See Hamilton, *Historicism;* Young, *White Mythologies;* and Chakrabarty, *Provincializing Europe.*

4. What this means is that these modern disciplinary enterprises can easily do essentializing, hegemonic work to accomplish whatever ends they are set. They can be used to liberate people from unjust constraints, or they can be used to solidify certain kinds of power relations. Such methodologies are neither good nor bad in themselves—their results will be determined as good or bad depending on who is judging—but in and of themselves, they belong to essentializing and hegemonic enterprises, however ambiguous, incomplete, or fractured such enterprises may operate in practice.

5. See Nagy, *Homeric Questions* and *Poetry as Performance;* Parker, *The Living Text of the Gospels;* Ehrman, *The Orthodox Corruption of Scripture.*

6. Rudolph, *Gnosis,* 54–55. My emphasis.

7. The following paragraphs are taken with modification from King, "The Politics of Syncretism," 462–466.

8. See Jonas, "Delimitation," 100–101; Pearson, *Gnosticism, Judaism, and Egyptian Christianity,* 8–9; Rudolph, *Gnosis,* 54–55.

9. See, for example, Casey, "The Study of Gnosticism," 59–60.

10. Van der Veer, "Syncretism," 208. As G. van der Leeuw already observed in 1938 following Wach (see *Religion in Essence and Manifestation,* II, 609). As Rosalind Shaw and Charles Stewart put it: "Simply identifying a ritual or tradition as 'syncretic' tells us very little and gets us practically nowhere, since all religions have composite origins and are continually reconstructed through ongoing pro-

cesses of synthesis and erasure" ("Introduction," 7). Or as Peter van der Veer puts it, syncretism "can be seen as such a broad process that indeed every religion is syncretistic, since it constantly draws upon heterogeneous elements to the extent that it is often impossible for historians to unravel what comes from where" ("Syncretism," 208).

11. Van der Veer, "Syncretism," 208.

12. Ibid., 196, 209.

13. See the discussion of van der Veer, "Syncretism," 196–197. Syncretism also appears as a call for tolerance, for example, in the work of Erasmus and the Deists (see ibid.), but its dominant usage in this period is pejorative.

14. See J. Z. Smith, *Drudgery Divine*, 22, 34–35. He provides an excellent summary of the Protestant position by focusing on the eighteenth-century work of the American Joseph Priestly: "Priestly held that . . . philosophical or platonizing Christians, in the early Christian centuries . . . adopted . . . religious ideas taken from contemporary Greek thought—of either 'Oriental' or 'Platonic' derivation—which . . . corrupted . . . the purity of primitive Christianity . . . so as to result in either Christian idolatry (i.e., 'Papism' embarrassing to post-Reformation Christians as well as 'Jews and Mahommedans') or philosophical absurdities which made Christianity seem ridiculous in the eyes of 'unbelievers' and critics of the 'Left'" (ibid., 11–12).

15. For further discussion of the meanings and uses of "primitivism," see Hughes, *The Primitive Church in the Modern World*.

16. See Schmitt, "Phenomenology."

17. See, for example, van der Leeuw, *Religion in Its Manifestation and Essence*.

18. See the critique of Oxtoby, "Religionswissenschaft Revisited."

19. For an early expression of this problem, see Wisse, "The Nag Hammadi Library and the Heresiologists."

20. See Jonas, "Delimitation," 103.

21. Ibid., 96; Pétrement, *A Separate God*, 9–10. Both see this characteristic as determinative. See also M. Williams, *Rethinking "Gnosticism,"* 265–266.

22. Here I depart from M. Williams's analysis of typology. He understood the basic problem to be finding characteristics that were "more truly typological" (*Rethinking "Gnosticism,"* 51).

23. This difficulty is exemplified in the excellent introduction to Gnosticism by Rudolph, *Gnosis*. As the title indicates, the work is divided into two main parts: a typological definition of the essential nature of Gnosticism, and an account of its historical manifestations. The first part of the book sets out the coherence of the material; the second part, its diversity. In organizing his book in this manner, Rudolph is reproducing the intellectual shape of the field in a

tightly argued, analytic form. In a review of the book, Anne McGuire succinctly summed up the relevant issues. I quote them here because, as she notes,
Rudolph's book is important not only in its own right as an introduction to
Gnosis/Gnosticism but also as a summary reproduction of the current state of the
field. McGuire writes: "Rudolph's adoption of the list of elements from the
Messina colloquium, like his decision to 'set aside historical, chronological, and
sociological problems,' creates both hermeneutical and historical problems, as it
creates the impression that 'Gnosis,' or any religious phenomenon, can be separated from its particular, concrete forms and social contexts. By connecting only
parts of the text to the 'constituent elements' of Gnosis, Rudolph ignores their
more important relation to the literary and socio-historical contexts from which
they emerged. At the same time, the attempt to illustrate the common features of
all varieties of Gnosis, even with repeated reference to its 'manifold diversity,'
leads to grand generalizations in which one element, found perhaps in one or two
texts, suddenly becomes characteristic of 'Gnosis' as a whole. Almost invariably,
this method obscures the historical particularity and distinctiveness of the texts,
figures, and communities that constitute the phenomenon" (McGuire, "Kurt
Rudolph, *Gnosis*," 48).

24. As Jonas has rightly noted, the methodology of typological determination
is circular ("Delimitation," 90). See also Morton Smith's more acerbic description
of the circularity of defining Gnosticism, in "The History of the Term Gnostikos," 798.

25. See Schenke, "Das sethianische System" and "The Phenomenon and
Significance."

26. Such an analysis needs to be grounded in a sociology of practice, such as
Pierre Bourdieu offers.

27. See Audre Lorde, "Age, Race, Class, and Sex"; Lazreg, "Decolonizing
Feminism."

28. Eliot, *Daniel Deronda*, 1.

29. Personal correspondence, January 28, 2002.

30. To say that Christianity did not originate from Judaism does not deny
their intimate relationship; it asks us to rethink the contours of that relationship
in terms other than the interaction of separate, well-bounded spheres. The approach does, however, undercut supersessionist definitions of Christian origins
and history.

31. Bourdieu notes that "common sense" is a function of the operations of
*habitus;* it is the "'lived' experience of the social world, that is, apprehension of
the world as self-evident, 'taken for granted.' This is because it excludes the question of the conditions of possibility of this experience, namely the coincidence of

the objective structures and the internalized structures which provides the illusion of immediate understanding, characteristics of practical experience of the familiar universe, and which at the same time excludes from that experience any inquiry as to its own conditions of possibility" (*The Logic of Practice*, 25–26). What I am suggesting here is precisely inquiring into the conditions that made these religious designations and posited genetic relationships a possibility.

32. Presentation at a panel on "Political Liberalism: Religion and Public Reason." Harvard Divinity School, Cambridge, Mass., May 3, 1995.

33. Bhabha, *The Location of Culture*, 2.

34. Ibid.

35. Recently, cultural difference has begun to be discussed in terms of cultural hybridity, since the old terminology of "syncretism" largely implies an essentialist mode. This terminology may, in the end, be more useful than trying to reform the old term "syncretism." What I share with these discussions is the notion of the impossibility of essentialism in matters of culture. There are, however, limits to celebrating hybridity without qualification (see Young, *Colonial Desire*).

36. From Richard Handler, cited in van der Veer, "Syncretism," 208–209.

37. Ortner, "Introduction," 9.

38. At this level of analysis, comparison would not be used to establish genealogies of borrowing or influence—though when direct literary relationships can be established, they would be useful in the subsequent and differentiated task of constructing historical and rhetorical relations.

39. Here I draw on Boyarin, *Intertextuality*, 12; see also Barthes, *S/Z*; Bakhtin, *The Dialogical Imagination*; Allen, *Intertextuality*.

40. See especially Schüssler Fiorenza, *Rhetoric and Ethic*, 105–128.

41. Ibid., 125. Schüssler Fiorenza argues that "practices of understanding 'the world'—such as speaking, writing, reading, or reasoning—are never outside of language or outside of time and history; that is, they are never transcendentally located outside of 'the world.' Hence this approach focuses on the ambiguity and instability of grammatically gendered language and text, and works with a theory of language that does not assume linguistic determinism. Rather it understands language as a convention or tool that enables writers and readers to negotiate linguistic tensions and inscribed ambiguities and thereby to create meaning in specific contexts and sociopolitical locations" (Schüssler Fiorenza, *Sharing Her Word*, 95–96).

42. For the notion of time as a cultural construct, see Aveni, *Empires of Time*; and Thompson, "Time, Work-Discipline, and Industrial Capitalism."

43. See, for example, Zukav, *The Dancing Wu Li Masters*. He characterizes the two most fundamental differences between Newtonian physics and quantum me-

chanics. The first has to do with perception; the second, with the capacity to predict events: "Quantum theory not only is closely bound to philosophy, but also—and this is becoming increasingly apparent—to theories of perception . . . Bohr's principle of complementarity also addresses the underlying relation of physics to consciousness. The experimenter's choice of experiment determines which mutually exclusive aspect of the same phenomenon (wave or particle) will manifest itself. Likewise, Heisenberg's uncertainty principle demonstrates that we cannot observe a phenomenon without changing it. The physical properties which we observe in the 'external' world are enmeshed in our own perceptions not only psychologically, but ontologically as well. The second most fundamental difference between Newtonian physics and quantum theory is that Newtonian physics predicts events and quantum mechanics predicts the probability of events. According to quantum mechanics, the only determinable relation between events is statistical—that is, a matter of probability" (322–323).

44. Zukav writes: "We commonly say, for example, that we detect an electron at point A and then at point B, but strictly speaking, this is incorrect. According to quantum mechanics, there was no electron which traveled from point A to point B. There are only the measurements that we made at point A and at point B" (*The Dancing Wu Li Masters*, 322).

45. Zukav writes: "According to Bohm, 'We must turn physics around. Instead of starting with parts and showing how they work together (the Cartesian order) we start with the whole.' Bohm's theory is compatible with Bell's theorem. Bell's theorem implies that the apparently 'separate parts' of the universe could be intimately connected at a deep and fundamental level. Bohm asserts that the most fundamental level is an *unbroken wholeness* which is, in his words, 'that-which-is.' There is an order which is enfolded into the very process of the universe, but that enfolded order may not be readily apparent" (*The Dancing Wu Li Masters*, 323).

46. Ricoeur, *Time and Narrative*, III, 274.

47. Foucault, "Nietzsche, Genealogy, History," 160.


## Note on Methodology

1. Although my own work is not based in new historicist theory, I do share many of the assumptions of the so-called New Historicism: "1) that every expressive act is embedded in a network of material practices; 2) that every act of unmasking, critique, and opposition uses the tools it condemns and risks falling prey to the practice it exposes; 3) that literary and non-literary 'texts' circulate inseparably; 4) that no discourse, imaginative or archival, gives access to unchang-

ing truths or expresses unalterable human nature; and 5) that a critical method and a language adequate to describe culture under capitalism participate in the economy they describe" (Veeser, *The New Historicism Reader*, 2; see also Veeser, *The New Historicism;* Thomas, *The New Historicism*).

2. See Foucault, *The Archaeology of Knowledge*, 3–30.

3. See ibid., 115–116.

4. Bourdieu would, I believe, have welcomed this approach given his generally favorable view of Foucault's work, except that he precisely criticizes Foucault for his essentializing refusal to "look outside 'the field of discourse' for the explanatory principle of each of the discourses in the field." Bourdieu sees his own work as a crucial corrective (see Bourdieu, "Principles for a Sociology," esp. 178–179).

5. Bourdieu, *The Logic of Practice*, 53.

6. The limits of the sociology of religion are now beautifully critiqued by Chakrabarty: "The second assumption running through modern European political thought and the social sciences is that the human is ontologically singular, that gods and spirits are in the end 'social facts,' that the social somehow exists prior to them. I try, on the other hand, to think without the assumption of even a logical priority of the social. One empirically knows of no society in which humans have existed without gods and spirits accompanying them. Although the God of monotheism may have taken a few knocks—if not actually 'died'—in the nineteenth-century European story of 'the disenchantment of the world,' the gods and other agents inhabiting practices of so-called 'superstition' have never died anywhere. I take gods and spirits to be existentially coeval with the human, and think from the assumption that the question of being human involves the question of being with gods and spirits. Being human means, as Ramachandra Gandhi puts it, discovering, 'the possibility of calling upon God [or gods] without being under an obligation to first establish his [or their] reality.' And this is one reason why I deliberately do not reproduce any sociology of religion in my analysis" (*Provincializing Europe*, 16). In the face of this critique, we need to distinguish between the social analysis of religion as a field and ontological statements about the existence of God (gods) or spirits. We can analyze the construction and operations of the field of religion in a particular historical context without the need to generalize ontologically. Indeed, Chakrabarty suggests that the practice of historicization is made possible by the fact that the worlds in which the gods exist are never really lost (ibid, 112).

7. See, for example, Bourdieu, *The Logic of Practice*, 95.

8. Bourdieu, *Outline of a Theory of Practice*, 163.

9. See ibid., 164–168.

10. Ibid., 164.

11. Ibid., 169.

12. Ibid., 169–170.

13. While Bourdieu figures this struggle in terms of the dominant and the dominated classes, in early Christianity what we see is precisely the struggle to *become* the dominant group. To suggest that those on the side of what became "orthodoxy" were already the dominant group would be to reinscribe the assumption that orthodoxy is prior to heresy; but that issue is itself one element at stake in early Christian struggles.

14. Bourdieu, "Haute Couture and Haute Culture," in *Sociology in Question*, 134. So, for example, in critiquing the currently dominant typology of Gnosticism, Williams calls for "typological categories that are both clearer and more truly typological than the old" (*Rethinking Gnosticism*, 51).

15. Bourdieu, "But Who Created the 'Creators'?" in *Sociology in Question*, 143.

16. Bourdieu, *Outline of a Theory of Practice*, 165.

17. In thirteen theses, Schüssler Fiorenza offers a comprehensive proposal for an ethics of interpretation (see *Rhetoric and Ethic*, 193–198).

18. Schüssler Fiorenza, *Rhetoric and Ethic*, 197; see also "The Rhetoricity of Historical Knowledge"; *Sharing Her Word*.

19. Schüssler Fiorenza, *Rhetoric and Ethic*, 198.

20. Here Schüssler Fiorenza uses the language of "relativism" in a way that satisfies the feminist critique of relativizing practices of "liberal political pluralism that overlooks the inequities of power relationships in producing knowledge" (see the discussion of Berkhofer, *Beyond the Great Story*, 209–214; quote from p. 210).

21. See Bourdieu, *The Logic of Practice*, chaps. 1 and 2, esp. 33–35.

22. As Robert Young notes: "There is an historical stemma between the cultural concepts of our day and those of the past from which we tend to assume that we have distanced ourselves. We restate and rehearse them covertly in the language and the concepts we use . . . How does that affect our own contemporary revisions of that imagined past? The interval that we assert between ourselves and the past may be much less than we assume. We may be more bound up with its categories than we like to think. Culture and race developed together, imbricated within each other: their discontinuous forms of repetition suggest, as Foucault puts it, 'how we have been trapped in our own history.' The nightmare of the ideologies and categories of racism continue to repeat upon the living" (*Colonial Desire*, 27, 28). As with race and colonialism, so also with the ideologies and categories of difference inscribed in the discourses of ancient Christian identity formation and their twentieth-century variations. Every time we engage the ideology of orthodoxy and heresy, we reinscribe some part of those discourses.

# Index

*Act of Peter,* 80
*Acts of Peter and the Twelve Apostles,* 207
*Acts of Thomas,* 162
*Allogenes,* 153, 157, 160, 164, 193–194, 322nn79,86, 326n112
Antisyncretism, 33–35, 48, 49, 51, 52, 68, 72, 73, 220, 224, 229, 230, 232, 288n86, 320n64. *See also* Syncretism
*Apocalypse of Adam,* 157, 164, 172, 177, 183, 206
*I Apocalypse of James,* 154, 209, 316nn18,21
*II Apocalypse of James,* 154, 316n18
*Apocalypse of Peter,* 53, 208
*Apocryphon of James,* 151, 153, 154, 163, 209–211, 316n18
*Apocryphon of John,* 10–11, 27, 28–29, 45, 46, 80, 137, 157, 160, 172, 178, 179, 180, 199–200, 204, 208, 221, 227, 232, 279n19, 280n1, 283n18, 314n2, 317nn28,34, 318n39, 321n74, 322n83, 330nn37,38, 331n56
*Asclepius,* 162
Athenagoras, 49–50, 287n75
*Authoritative Teaching,* 207, 316n21

Basiledes, 63
Bauer, Walter, 110–115, 148, 152, 173, 228, 244, 282n15
*Book of Thomas,* 162, 178, 194–196, 321n74
*Book of Zoroaster,* 158
*Books of Jeu,* 80, 303n64
Bousset, Wilhelm, 16–17, 84, 90–100, 101, 108, 119, 137–138, 141, 176, 302n62, 305nn96,105, 308n13
Bultmann, Rudolf, 84, 93, 100–107, 137, 138, 139, 143, 290n13, 304n86, 305n105

Categorizing Gnostic texts, 15, 153–165
Clement of Alexandria, 20, 165, 203, 205, 207, 285n46, 330n43
Codex Askewianus (Askew Codex), 80–81
Codex Berolinensis (Berlin Codex), 10, 80–81, 151
Codex Brucianus (Bruce Codex), 80–81, 157
Colpe, Carsten, 141–147, 148, 176, 189

Deismann, Adolf, 74–75
Demythologizing, 11–12, 13, 100, 128, 148
*Dialogue of the Savior,* 151, 153, 163
*Didache (Teaching of the Twelve Apostles),* 41–42
*Discourse on the Eighth and Ninth,* 162
Docetism, 8, 62, 98, 192, 208–213, 289n100
Drower, Lady, 82–83, 139, 140
Dualism, 62, 97, 123–124, 170, 192–201, 204, 213, 227, 307n122, 314n109, 327n3, 328n8

Epiphanius, 20, 157, 205, 284n36
*Epistle of Barnabas,* 41, 42, 44, 47, 287n83
*Epistle to Flora,* 45, 280n1
Ethics, Gnostic, 8, 52, 63, 105–106, 123–124, 135, 160, 191, 192–193, 196, 200, 201–208, 210–211, 213, 326n116, 331n51, 333n63
*Eugnostos the Blessed,* 156, 163, 316n21, 322n79
Eusebius of Caesarea, 113, 285n55
*Exegesis on the Soul,* 316n21

Gnosticism: relation to Christianity, 2–4, 7, 17, 18, 55, 61–67, 89–90, 92–93, 97–100, 104–109, 110–115, 133–134, 151, 164, 166, 171–175, 179–181, 182, 216, 218, 230; definitions of, 4, 5, 7–8, 52, 62–63, 97–99, 119–132, 169–170, 191; processes of defining, 5–19, 165–169; coinage of, 7; Jewish origin of, 7, 174, 175–187, 216,

Gnosticism *(continued)*
    230, 336n30; Oriental origin of, 71, 78, 84, 95,
    99, 118, 174, 175, 176; anti-Jewish animus of,
    125–126, 181–185, 186–187; sub-categories of,
    154–165, 168–169
Gnostic redeemer myth (Gnostic salvation
    myth), 84–85, 100, 101–103, 104, 109, 121–122,
    137–138, 141–143, 146, 147, 148, 170, 191, 196,
    198–199, 226, 307n120, 327n2
Gnostics, social groups of, 9, 26, 216
*Gospel of the Egyptians*, 157, 322n86
Gospel of John, 72, 83, 85, 88, 89, 96, 97, 100–
    104, 133, 138, 155, 172, 173, 187, 211, 285n56,
    294n1, 304n85, 306nn105,112, 307n120,
    312n91, 317n28
Gospel of Luke, 45
Gospel of Mark, 285n56
*Gospel of Mary*, 44, 80, 151, 163, 172, 283n22,
    330n38
Gospel of Matthew, 41, 46, 89, 332n59
*Gospel of Philip*, 154, 161, 207, 316n21
*Gospel of the Savior*, 163, 315n10
*Gospel of Thomas*, 1, 151, 152, 153, 163, 172, 196–
    199, 285n56, 329n21, 330n38
*Gospel of Truth*, 1, 44, 154–155, 156, 160–161, 164,
    192–193, 211, 278n16, 316nn19,20,21, 328n6

Harnack, Adolf von, 11, 12, 55–70, 71, 75, 76, 86,
    93, 95, 96, 108, 118, 286n63, 290n14,
    292nn15,20, 293n40, 294nn42,1, 301n50,
    305n98, 309n26, 323n95
Hellenization, 55–56, 58–61, 65–66, 67, 68, 118,
    130–131, 175, 176, 295n1, 304n93
Heracleon, 112
Heresy / heretics, 2, 3, 7, 22, 23–38, 53, 68, 72,
    107, 168, 171, 172–173, 174, 177, 179, 186, 200,
    205, 219, 223–224, 278n11, 281n7, 283n22,
    284nn34,35,36,37,39,41, 289n101, 290n2,
    305n102, 307n125, 314n119, 324n98, 326n117.
    *See also* Orthodoxy and heresy
Hermeticism, 4, 84, 91, 118, 162, 279n25,
    302n63, 322n78, 326n113
Hippolytus, 20, 34, 203, 282n17, 285n47
*Hypostasis of the Archons*, 45, 157, 317n26, 321n74,
    330n33
*Hypsiphrone*, 157, 317n26

Ignatius of Antioch, 44, 175, 283n22, 319n60
*Interpretation of Knowledge*, 154, 316n21
Iranian religion, 7

Irenaeus, 3, 7, 20, 31–32, 33, 34, 37, 47, 69, 99–
    100, 106, 112, 155, 157, 162, 165, 203, 205, 206,
    210, 278n16, 282n17, 283n31, 284nn37,39,
    285n56, 288n84, 316n19, 317n28, 318n45,
    329n20, 331n55

Jewish Christianity, 7, 175, 287n69, 319n63
Jonas, Hans, 11–12, 74, 110, 115–137, 143, 144,
    146, 148, 185–186, 188, 189, 224–225, 330n43,
    336n24˙
Judaism: in relation to Christianity, 38, 40–47,
    56, 58–59, 63, 64, 68, 69, 85, 90, 91–92, 94–
    95, 96, 111, 148, 171, 175–176, 177–178, 205,
    221, 223, 230, 286n66, 287n83, 290n14,
    292nn17,18, 303n79, 319n63, 320n64; in rela-
    tion to Mandaeism, 87, 145, 300n42; in rela-
    tion to Gnosticism, 125. *See also* Gnosticism,
    Jewish origin of; Jewish Christianity
Justin Martyr, 20, 21, 28–29, 42–43, 69, 280n1,
    281n2, 284n37, 287n73

*Letter of Peter to Philip*, 154, 211–212, 316n18
Lidzbarski, Mark, 82, 84, 86, 87, 103, 138, 139,
    301n46, 302n62

Maçuch, Rudolf, 84, 138, 139–140, 312n95
Mandaeism, 4, 5, 72, 82–84, 85–86, 87, 88, 89,
    90, 101, 102, 103, 118, 137, 138–141, 145, 146,
    162, 165, 171, 172, 205–206, 216, 226,
    298n31,32, 299n37, 300n43, 301nn45,47,49,
    302nn60,62, 303n64, 312nn88,89,91,95,
    313n98, 320n64, 326n113
Manichaeism, 4, 72, 81, 85–86, 90, 101, 102, 113,
    116, 118, 141, 145, 146, 158, 162, 171, 216, 226,
    278n11, 300n43, 301n47, 310n44, 313n101,
    314n109, 320n64, 326n113
Marcion, 34, 45, 46, 66, 112, 113, 116, 118, 134,
    187, 202, 203, 278n11, 293n29, 310n44,
    323n95, 330n43
*Marsanes*, 157, 160, 193, 322n79
*Melchizedek*, 157, 158, 317n26
Myth, theories of, 78–79, 126–128, 131, 278n18,
    279n19, 296nn23,24, 297n25, 305n96,
    310nn56,58

Nag Hammadi manuscripts (and texts), 10, 150–
    153, 176, 186, 188, 200, 203, 204, 206, 208–
    209, 216, 233; discovery of, 1, 6, 113, 149, 176,
    217, 231, 314nn1,2
Nominalist definitions, 14–15

*On the Origin of the World,* 157, 207, 317n26

Orientalism, 3, 7, 72, 74, 76–78, 86–87, 95–96, 108, 130–132, 136, 219

Origen of Alexandria, 20, 287n69, 289n93

Origin and genealogy, 11–12, 14, 31–32, 37, 52, 72, 73, 79, 88, 90–92, 106, 115–117, 148, 150, 171, 179, 180, 182, 220–221, 232, 236, 320n64

Orthodoxy, 22, 25, 31, 36, 38, 67, 100, 104, 108, 148, 180, 203, 208, 236. *See also* Orthodoxy and heresy

Orthodoxy and heresy, 2, 3, 7, 17, 37, 54, 110–115, 148, 152–153, 175, 228, 229, 233–234, 282n15, 340n12; discourse of, 3, 4, 19, 21, 24, 37, 43, 53, 70, 73, 135, 136, 148, 150, 176, 179, 190, 216, 218–220, 239–247, 280nn33,1, 284n42, 286n66, 320n64, 340n21

Pachomian monastery / monks, 163, 233, 278n16, 315n2

Paganism, in relation to Christianity, 38, 48–52, 68

Paul, 40, 45, 47, 71, 72, 84, 85, 88, 89, 96, 97, 99–100, 114, 133, 160, 172, 173–174, 187, 202, 207, 213, 285nn43,49,56, 294n1, 300n42, 304n95, 305nn98,102, 307n120, 321n74, 332n59

*Pistis Sophia,* 80, 303n64

Plotinus, 165, 304n87

Pragmatic-contextualist definitions, 15–16

*Prayer of Thanksgiving,* 162

*Prayer of the Apostle Paul,* 154, 156, 316n21

Reitzenstein, Richard, 75, 84–90, 100, 101–102, 103, 119, 137–138, 139, 141–144, 301nn46,50, 302nn62,63, 305n105, 314n110

*Republic* (Plato), 163

"Salvation by nature," 8, 62–63, 97–98, 105, 124, 136, 191, 194, 196, 200, 202, 206, 283n18, 331n55

*Sentences of Sextus,* 163

Sethian Gnosticism, 4, 45, 156–162, 163, 164, 172, 179–180, 193–194, 204, 218, 221, 227,

277n4, 279n25, 317nn28,32,34, 321nn72,78, 326n119

Simon Magus, 31, 63–64, 146, 183, 185, 278n16, 284n37

Son of Man motif, 84, 87–89, 90–92, 93, 94–95, 96, 102, 144–145, 173, 212, 314n110

*Sophia of Jesus Christ,* 80, 163, 322n79

Syncretism, 3, 11, 33, 49, 51, 63, 64, 77–78, 79, 90, 96, 104–106, 117, 119, 128, 129, 130, 132–133, 134, 136, 153, 169, 182, 189, 191, 200, 216, 222–224, 228, 229, 230, 286n66, 288n86, 294nn42,1, 305nn98,117, 322n78, 334n10, 335n13, 337n35. *See also* Antisyncretism; Hellenization

Tertullian, 3, 20, 27–28, 29, 33, 34–36, 37, 55, 56, 66, 67, 69, 105, 106, 112, 114, 162, 165, 173, 203, 210, 283n17, 285n49

*Testimony of Truth,* 47, 53, 154, 178, 183, 203, 278n16, 316n18

Thomas Christianity, 162, 163, 164, 279n25, 321n74

*Thought of Norea,* 157, 177

*Three Steles of Seth,* 157, 322nn79,86

*Thunder Perfect Mind,* 158

*Treatise on the Resurrection,* 154, 212–213, 316n21

*Trimorphic Protennoia,* 157, 158, 317n26

*Tripartite Tractate,* 154, 155–156, 206, 316n21

Typology, 11, 12–14, 73–74, 75, 77, 79, 115, 119–129, 148, 150, 191–216, 220, 225–228, 310n42, 335nn22,23, 336n24, 340n13

*Untitled Text,* 80

*Valentinian Exposition, A,* 154, 316n21

Valentinus / Valentinianism / Valentinians, 34, 45, 53, 63, 91, 99, 116, 118, 154–156, 158, 159–162, 163, 164, 172, 178, 180, 192, 202, 206–207, 212, 213, 221, 224, 278nn11,16, 279n25, 280n1, 283n24, 302n60, 316nn19,20,21, 317n32, 326n119, 331n55, 332n59

*Zostrianos,* 157, 322n79